Poems in Their Place

Poems in Their Place
The Intertextuality and Order
of Poetic Collections

Edited by Neil Fraistat

The University of North Carolina Press
Chapel Hill and London

For Stuart Curran

and Joe Wittreich

© 1986 The University of North Carolina Press

All rights reserved

Manufactured in the United States of America

Library of Congress Cataloging-in-Publication Data
Poems in their place.
    Includes index.
    1. English poetry—History and criticism. 2. American poetry—History and criticism. 3. Poetry—Editing.
I. Fraistat, Neil, 1952–   II. Title: Intertextuality and order of poetic collections.
PR403.P64   1986   821'.009   85-28926
ISBN 0-8078-1695-7

Excerpts from *The Collected Poems of Sylvia Plath,* edited by Ted Hughes and published by Faber and Faber, copyright Ted Hughes, 1960, 1965, 1971, 1981, are reproduced by permission of Olwyn Hughes.

Excerpts from *The Collected Poems of Sylvia Plath,* edited by Ted Hughes, copyright 1960, 1965, 1971, 1981 by the Estate of Sylvia Plath, are reproduced by permission of Harper & Row, Publishers, Inc.

Excerpts from *Sphere: The Form of a Motion* by A. R. Ammons, copyright 1974 by A. R. Ammons, are reproduced by permission of W. W. Norton and Company, Inc.

Contents

Acknowledgments / vii

Introduction: The Place of the Book and the Book as Place / 3
 Neil Fraistat

Some Issues for Study of Integrated Collections / 18
 Earl Miner

The Theory and Practice of Poetic Arrangement
from Vergil to Ovid / 44
 William S. Anderson

Sequences, Systems, Models: Sidney and the Secularization
of Sonnets / 66
 S. K. Heninger, Jr.

Jonson, Marvell, and Miscellaneity? / 95
 Annabel Patterson

The Arrangement and Order of John Donne's Poems / 119
 John T. Shawcross

"Strange Text!": "Paradise Regain'd . . .
To which is added *Samson Agonistes*" / 164
 Joseph Anthony Wittreich, Jr.

"Images Reflect from Art to Art": Alexander Pope's Collected *Works*
of 1717 / 195
 Vincent Carretta

Multum in Parvo: Wordsworth's *Poems, in Two Volumes*
of 1807 / 234
 Stuart Curran

The Book of Byron and the Book of a World / 254
  Jerome J. McGann

The Arrangement of Browning's *Dramatic Lyrics* (1842) / 273
  George Bornstein

Whitman's *Leaves* and the American "Lyric-Epic" / 289
  James E. Miller, Jr.

The Two *Ariels:* The (Re)Making of the Sylvia Plath Canon / 308
  Marjorie Perloff

Index / 335

Notes on the Contributors / 343

Acknowledgments

Many people have helped me to shape this collection and bring it to its final form. I would like especially to thank Iris Tillman Hill for her editorial acumen and constant encouragement. I am indebted as well to all of the contributors for their care and their counsel, and in particular to Marjorie Perloff, John Shawcross, George Bornstein, and Tim Heninger for various acts of kindness. For his discerning reading of the entire manuscript, I am grateful yet again to Robert Gleckner. My friend and colleague Ted Leinwand read over the introductory essay with characteristic rigor and sensitivity. And my wife Rose Ann has, once more, cheerfully given of her time to help in every stage of the production of this book, from its conception to its final proofreading. Finally, I can scarcely express all that the continual generosity and vast learning of Joe Wittreich and Stuart Curran have meant to me personally and to the evolution of this book. I dedicate *Poems in Their Place* to them with much admiration, affection, and gratitude.

N. F.
6 September 1985

Poems in Their Place

Neil Fraistat
Introduction
The Place of the Book and
the Book as Place

I t is a simple fact of our reading experience that poems take place, in the words of Albert Thibaudet, "as a function of the Book." That is to say that the book—with all of its informing contexts—is the meeting ground for poet and reader, the "situation" in which its constituent texts occur. As such, the book is constantly conditioning the reader's responses, activating various sets of what semioticians call "interpretive codes." And yet, as Thibaudet shrewdly goes on to observe, "there are few things to which a man of books gives less thought than the Book."[1] The essays of this collection are designed specifically to foster such thought—and to make clear that its implications extend from the fields of textual scholarship and literary history to those of hermeneutics and literary theory.

To read poems in their place, then, is to make the poetry book itself—as both idea and material fact—an object of interpretation. A fundamental assumption of such an approach is that the decisions poets make about the presentation of their works play a meaningful role in the poetic process and, hence, ought to figure in the reading process. Studied within the context of their original volumes, poems reveal a fuller textuality, which is to say, an *inter*textuality.

Perhaps no single word adequately conveys the special qualities of the poetic collection as an organized book: the contextuality provided for each poem by the larger frame within which it is placed, the intertextuality among poems so placed, and the resultant texture of resonance and meanings. I have recently proposed, however, that the word "contexture" be used for such a purpose because of its utility in suggesting all three of these qualities without being restricted to any one.[2] A contexture might thus be seen as the "poem" that is the book itself. By raising such questions as the significance of selection and arrangement within particular books, we are led not only to consider the integrity of these larger "poems" but also to pose new questions about poets' notions of order within their canons and the types of connections they make among their individual poems.

Reading poems in their place is, moreover, a means of rehistoricizing texts, returning them to a book that itself has a particular place in its own culture and society. Books as wholes might then be viewed in terms of several converging contexts: as indices of poets' conceptions about their audience and representations of how they would like to present themselves to that audience; as entries into ongoing cultural, literary, or social debates—that is, as ideological statements; and as products of contemporary conventions regarding the ordering, publishing, and reading of poetic volumes. In illuminating these contexts, as several of the following essays demonstrate, material details of the book such as its format, typography, and illustrations can prove significant.[3]

Relatively little thought has previously been given to the methods, theory, and appropriate terrain for what could be called "contextural poetics." Such a poetics, it seems to me, would study a wide range of forms, including paired poems, sonnet and other types of sequences, poetic works published in parts (for example, *The Seasons, Don Juan, The Cantos*), individual collections—as well as clusters of poems within them, and the shape of a poet's canon.[4] Accordingly, in addition to the kinds of approaches already suggested, contextural poetics might consider concepts of structure and theories of perception in order to discuss how the mind distinguishes between poetic parts and wholes, as well as to understand how the position of poems within a particular book affects the reading process. Since the facts about any given contexture include what is *not* in the book but might have been, contextural poetics would also account for a poet's decisions to exclude works on hand or to hold them for other collections. It would, in short, be sensitive to the numerous ways that the context of the book affects interpretation and to the special theoretical problems that arise when the book becomes central to the interpretive process. And, finally, contextural poetics would develop its own literary history, tracing the evolution of various types of poetic collections and practices for assembling them, citing important historical models, and establishing—where possible—lines of influence. The brief sketch that follows will help raise several relevant issues and, in so doing, provide a general backdrop for the collection of essays as a whole.

To a great extent, the physical configuration of the first Western volumes of poetry—Hellenistic book-rolls—dictated the manner in which poems could be read and conditioned the way they were arranged, establishing a set of expectations for both the reader and the poet that is still largely in force today, long after the advent of the codex.[5] The reader's enforced sequential progress through a book-roll encouraged Alexandrian poets to create meaningful juxtapositions, contrasts, and continuities among the poems. Any such effects would be especially heightened once the reader had reached the conclusion of the book and began to rewind the roll. For as he or she rerolled the parchment, the reader's original diachronic understanding of the poems was augmented by a synchronic perception of the book as a whole. "Return," explains John Van Sickle, "would enhance awareness of sequentiality, of the similarities and contrasts among the segments, beginnings, ends, in short of what makes the contents of the roll an articulated ensemble—a book."[6]

Callimachus, who is probably the first Western poet to advise the reader about the shape of his canon, also seems the first to use sophisticated techniques to unify his individual books.[7] In both *Iambs* and *Aetia* (that is, "legendary origins"), he chooses poems to serve as prologue and epilogue to a larger collection that itself displays other structural symmetries as well as thematic and imagistic resonances among the poems.[8] Nor is Callimachus the sole Alexandrian author to attend to the selection and arrangement of his poems. *Soros,* an anonymous early book of epigrams, suggests through its title that its diverse poems, like winnowed grain, have been sorted and organized, with all of the chaff removed. Even *The Garland* of Meleager, a selection of poems written by others, shows signs of sophisticated arrangement.[9] In fact, by the time of the Augustans, in "light of what was 'normal' in the making and use of books," poets could have presumed that good readers would as a matter of course respond "to sequential variation, enjoy the play of contrast in return of theme, admire a felicitous change, sense the import of positioning—proximities, and deferrals, beginnings, articulations, ends."[10]

It has long been known that Augustan poets such as Horace, Virgil, Propertius, Tibellus, and Ovid were concerned with the structure of their books. Yet while most Augustan books tend to be more homogeneous in meter, subject, and tone than those of the Alexandrians, Horace in the *Odes* (books 1–3) appears just as interested as Callimachus in achieving coherence primarily through artful arrangement rather than through uniform selection.[11] In *Odes,* Horace utilizes many Alexandrian organizational strategies, including structural framing and symmetries, as well as the development of thematic progressions and verbal echoes among the poems. Centuries before Petrarch and Dante, Horace—and his predecessor Catullus—had shown how a recognizable narrative of love could emerge from a collection of discrete lyrics arranged in temporal sequence.[12]

Dante's *La vita nuova* is, nonetheless, a new kind of poetic aggregate: the first fictive work blending prose with poetry to provide not only a connective narrative fabric between the poems but also a critical and "autobiographical" commentary upon them.[13] Although a great deal has been written about the influence of *La vita nuova* on the *Canzoniere*,[14] the contextural strategies of Dante and Petrarch diverge in important ways. There is a considerable difference, after all, between Dante's grouping of thirty-one short poems with connective prose and Petrarch's arrangement of 366 lyrics into a meaningful whole. Moreover, *La vita nuova* is a work Dante designed once, early in his career, and never subsequently rearranged, whereas the *Canzoniere* continually evolved: Petrarch reorganized it some nine separate times—adding poems, deleting others, and revising the order of the contents. Whereas Dante considered *La vita nuova* to be a finished work—a stable contexture—Petrarch conceived of the *Canzoniere* as an elastic form: one allowing him to shape and re-shape all of the shorter poems he wished to acknowledge publicly within an overarching, if continually refocused, vision.[15] Ultimately, then, although Petrarch bequeathed to later sonneteers a limited and easily exhausted set of conventions, he also left behind a strikingly flexible structural model in which—through a series of generically mixed short poems written on various subjects and at different times—a poet could maintain shifting, even contradictory, perspectives and, above all, an openness before experience.

The Petrarchan paradigm had implications for succeeding poetic collections whether or not they were designed as sonnet cycles. In a definitive way, it showed how a collection of diverse poems might itself aspire toward the complexity and variety of a long poem. There are probably few who would agree with Poe that in *Paradise Lost,* "What we term a long poem is in effect, merely a succession of brief ones, . . ." yet we all might acknowledge that at times the dividing line between a long poem and a poetic aggregate can be thin indeed.[16] Like optical illusions, such highly integrated "collections" as *La vita nuova* or *The Shepheardes Calender* may be seen alternatively as long poems, whereas the individual sections of loosely unified "long poems" such as Hart Crane's *The Bridge* or James Thomson's *The Seasons* may seem to be integral poems within a larger collection.[17]

Perhaps the strongest formal unity is achieved in a contexture when the poems are organized so that each "follows" logically or temporally from the other: presenting a narrative, advancing an argument, or appearing in some pattern of serial arrangement (for example, calendrical, liturgical, numerological). In such arrangements an identifiably integrated, progressive structure is generated throughout the collection. Nor need narrative within a book depend upon the radical of plot, as both Earl Miner and Annabel Patterson demonstrate elsewhere in this volume. Purposeful thematic iteration among the poems is in itself enough to establish an overall narrative pattern, what Miner calls "plotless narrative." Indeed, Miner, in the essay that follows, provides a seminal discussion of the structural dynamics by which collections are integrated, offering a theoretical basis both for discriminating between collections and long poems and for articulating varying degrees of integration within collections. We might, therefore, more profitably turn here to another set of variables governing the integrity of collections: those introduced by the act of reading and the process of interpretation. For, if the author's own structural strategies, as well as received tradition, play a large role in conditioning our perception of the unity characterizing a poetic book, other significant circumstances may vary not only from reader to reader but also between readings.

As Stanley Fish might remind us, the "facts" of a text never speak for themselves, we speak for them. The reader construing a book of poems, no less than the poet constructing it, engages in a process of selection and arrangement. Moreover, the methodological problems involved in reading a single poem are necessarily compounded in the reading of a collection, since special demands are placed by the poetry book as a unit on the reader's memory, interest, attention, and mental capacity.[18] In especially large collections, as William Wordsworth recognized, one poem may even stand "in the way of the other" so that poems "must either be read a few at once, or the Book must remain some time by one before a judgement can be made of the quantity of thought and feeling and imagery it contains . . . and what variety of moods and mind it can either impart or is suited to. . . ."[19] Wordsworth nonetheless expected his reader to respond to the significance of order in his books, going so far as to claim in the preface to his first collected edition, *Poems* (1815), that "for him who reads with reflection, the arrangement [of *Poems*] will serve as a commentary unostentatiously directing his attention to my purposes, both particular and general" (p. xv).[20] Although it is true that not many poets are as self-conscious about their contextural practices as Wordsworth and that readers cannot always be depended upon to read every poem in a book, it is also true that most poets count on those who read "with reflection" to recognize the significance (or insignificance) of order in their volumes.

Our past experience as readers of poetry, of particular poets, and of poetic volumes all affect what gestaltists call our "set to perceive" and what semioticians term our "horizon of expectations." We are not likely, therefore, to begin most books of poems expecting to find the kind of formal unity we normally seek in a long poem. After all, we know that poets are under no constraints to unify their collections, nor do they as a rule provide linear sequence or plot in their books. In fact, because the individual poems in a contexture are rarely written to fill a specific place in the whole, the continuities between them are more likely to be associative than causal—and the discontinuities may sometimes be sharp.

As readers, we gather data about the cohesiveness of a volume not only from explicit prefatory material or cues such as titles and epigraphs but from our growing awareness of the formal and thematic repetitions, contrasts, and progressions among the poems. Thus, our perception of unity in a book depends upon the process Barbara Herrnstein Smith has labeled "retrospective patterning." That is, in the movement from poem to poem, "connections and similarities are illuminated, and the reader perceives that seemingly gratuitous or random events, details, and juxtapositions have been selected in accord with certain principles."[21] The ending of each poem, therefore, is apt to serve analogously to what Fish would call a "perceptual closure," a moment in which inferences about the overall structure of the book can be reevaluated and adjusted. Like the opening poem, which generates our initial expectations, the concluding poem will have special significance in our understanding of the whole, because (as Smith says about the ending of a poem) "it is only at that point that the total pattern—the structural principles which we have been testing—is revealed."[22] Because reading is a process of patterning, to read an individual poem in isolation or outside of its original volume is not only to lose the large retroactive sweep of the book as a whole—with its attendant dynamics and significance—but also to risk losing the meanings within the poem itself that are foregrounded or activated by the context of the book.

Regardless of whether we proceed consecutively from beginning to end—presumably the order chosen by the poet—or out of sequence, on completing a book we are likely to have noted the import of positioning and the relationships among the poems (tonalities, common genre, themes, imagery). In books without plot or linear sequence, we may even have hypothesized some principles of formal unity to be tested and confirmed by subsequent readings. However, as Fish duly notes, once "the criterion of formal unity is dictated . . . it in turn dictates the setting up of a procedure designed to discover and validate it." In other words, our assumptions as readers and critics have a tendency to be self-fulfilling: we "discover" whatever unity we have presupposed, since "only ingenuity limits the ability of the critic to impose unity of either a cognitive or purely formal kind on his materials."[23] Moreover, even ingenious accounts of the patterns within or the "unity" of a volume may falter before the discovery that the poems were placed at random or selected and arranged by someone other than the poet. Hermeneutic wheels will turn nevertheless. We can at least help prevent them from spinning in place by elaborating some principles by which they might reasonably be guided.

Perhaps it should be stipulated first that, because the arrangement of poems inevitably affects the reading process, contextural critics ought to prefer over other arrangements an authorially sanctioned ordering—whether that ordering is the product of the poet alone or the result of a collaborative effort (for example, with co-author, editor, literary advisor) that is ultimately approved by the poet.[24] When an author reorganizes a book in subsequent editions, we might view each edition as maintaining an integrity that is not completely superseded by later orderings. One might fruitfully discuss, for instance, the *Lyrical Ballads* of 1798 even though Wordsworth changed the contents and ordering in both 1800 and 1802. Indeed, *Lyrical Ballads* is an example of how each edition of a book may not only reward separate interpretation, but may also provide the keys for more fully understanding the others.[25]

When the author's intentions concerning the ordering of his books cannot be positively determined, we ought to prefer the organization of the original printed volumes unless discredited by manuscript or other evidence, since these are presumably printed from texts the poet prepared for the press or taken directly from manuscripts and might therefore best reflect the poet's wishes. In such cases, as Annabel Patterson argues in a subsequent essay, the discovery of significant order can itself be powerful—if circular—evidence of the author's intentions. Conversely, books printed posthumously whose arrangements are not based on reliable evidence and books for which the author is known to have played no role whatsoever have far less contextural value, even though they too, of course, might be interpreted—and may demonstrate principles of significant order of one kind or another.

Having recognized in principle the right of poets to determine the shape of their books, we ought not allow them further to dictate the *meaning* of this shape. That is, interpretations of a book should not be limited to the author's conscious intentions (though these surely must be taken into account)—since there are a wealth of unconscious connections and fortuitous circumstances that contribute to the meaning of a contexture, just as they do to an individual text. Here, the gestaltist Law of Prägnanz might best be invoked: the "richest organization compatible with the data is to be preferred."[26] Consequently, poets who remark that there is no real significance to the arrangement of their books are performing an act of interpretation; subsequent interpreters might well prove them right or illuminate connections previously gone unnoticed. Poets, on the other hand, who alter the organization of their books, change the meaning of the contexture.

A poetic contexture is thus liable to present a mass of complex data, both tempting and defying the reader to articulate its structure. Indeed, an *agon* of sorts might be said to take place between readers working to assert their own patterns and coherences on previously organized materials and poets attempting to constrain reader response via the book by means unavailable in a single poem. When seen in this light, Wordsworth's use of arrangement to direct the reader "to my purposes, both particular and general," may seem anxious and overbearing. Yet if the poetry book might therefore be viewed as a potential hermeneutic straitjacket, fashioned to restrict the reader's movements, it might also be seen as a form through which poets can supplant or destabilize the meaning of one poem by that of others, freeing the reader to pursue any number of interpretive paths. And the cost of this freedom is the troublesome recognition that our articulation of any pattern in a book will inevitably be at the expense of other, perhaps equally conceivable, schemes. For, as Iser observes, "The moment we try to impose a consistent pattern on the text, discrepancies are bound to arise."[27] So, before we begin mapping the intricate angles of intersection among the poems in a book, we should be careful, in the words of one critic, not to sacrifice "texture for architecture."[28] We must even reckon with the possibility that a poet has deliberately avoided neat patterns of any kind while assembling a book. It is clear, for instance, that there are verbal and conceptual links among the poems in Herbert's *The Temple* that add to the larger unifying pressure of the book's metaphoric title. Nonetheless, Rosalie Colie points out shrewdly that the volume as a whole "resists schemes to organize it into a consistent structure." Colie argues that all attempts to do so—and there have been many—not only risk distorting the poems but invariably miss Herbert's reason for avoiding a rigidly articulated structure: "in good Protestant form, [Herbert] planned to call upon a reader's ever-revived capacity to contribute to his own revelation."[29]

In a similar way, Robert Gleckner hypothesizes that William Blake is attempting an "anti-book" in *Poetical Sketches* by militantly avoiding cycle or sequence in arrangement and by refusing to give the book as a whole strong closure, though the poems throughout are related thematically and imagistically. Blake's purpose in such an arrangement, according to Gleckner, is to deter "casual perusal and 'normal' reader expectation," thereby forcing the reader to comprehend imaginatively the "allusive intertextuality" of the whole.[30] In other words, by rejecting any overall sequential patterns, Blake insists that his volume be understood as a synchronic structure, whose unity is perceivable only to the reader approaching it on what he calls elsewhere the "fiery wings of Contemplation."

Dissatisfied with past readers' attempts to force rigid structure on resistant material, both Colie and Gleckner might themselves be accused of finessing structural problems in *The Temple* and *Poetical Sketches* by providing such cogent rationales for the absence of consistent patterns. Although their accounts seem conformable to the "facts" of the book as well as the vision of each poet, neither Colie nor Gleckner is completely free of the kind of ingenuity that Fish identifies. Nor, for that matter, is any critic. Yet, if by forswearing silence a critic is bound to "falsify" somewhat the complexities of a text or collection, then Colie and Gleckner at least demonstrate that, when a critic treats data responsibly and imaginatively, the process of delimiting need not be merely limiting.

As readers we tend to bestow unity of a sort on a volume even when no formal principles are apparent. For we are wont to synthesize the subjects, themes, tonalities, and genres of a contexture into the preoccupations and perspectives of a "speaker" (present or implied) who is responsible for them all.[31] This speaker's voice is "revealed" to us in the verbal and imagistic echoes among the poems, as well as in their individual rhetorical, metrical, and grammatical structures. In effect, as we read a volume by a single poet, part of what might be called the "centrifugal energy" of each poem will be directed toward fashioning and reflecting an image of that poet. On at least one level, then, the poetic collection can present itself as autobiographical narrative. Poets can thus literally "publicize" themselves in their books, attempting to shape a public identity through the process of selection and arrangement. Autobiographical narratives so constructed by poets, however, may be deformed or, even, entirely re-formed by editors who alter the selection and arrangement of a volume. One stunning example of such an alteration is offered below by Marjorie Perloff, who shows how Ted Hughes significantly reshaped *Ariel* from the version planned by Sylvia Plath before her death—creating, in the process, a strategically transformed portrait of Plath.

Poets as diverse as Milton, Pope, Byron, Whitman, and Yeats were all adept at fashioning miscellaneous collections into autobiographical narratives that served as acts of self-advertisement and, more important, self-creation.[32] For instance, William Riley Parker observes that Milton published his first collection, *The Poems of Mr. John Milton* in 1645, "when he had felt dirtied by the unexpected notoriety of his divorce tracts, and worried about his public image." Parker then goes on to ask rhetorically, "Was it only coincidence that in 1673, when he was chafing at the latest attacks upon his reputation, he decided to bring out a second edition of his minor verse?"[33] Elsewhere I have considered what these two volumes can tell us about Milton's sense of himself as poet and the way he wished to be perceived by his contemporaries.[34] Suffice it to say here that, ever the master of his craft, Milton fashioned these miscellaneous books into profound explorations of the appropriate roles for poetry and the poet, while at the same time seizing the opportunity they afforded him to become his own creator—to invent, publicize, and defend his own identity as poet-prophet.

One hardly needs reminding that selection and arrangement translate into ideology as well as personality. But it is worth noting with James E. Miller, Jr., that a poet such as Walt Whitman in *Leaves of Grass* can so conflate personality with ideology that the act of creating a public personality in a collection becomes inextricably connected to that of representing—and, in so doing, recreating—the cultural and social values of a nation. Furthermore, as the example of Whitman again demonstrates, the poetic book as a collective form is in itself adaptable to ideological uses. If for Renaissance sonneteers the poetic collection could provide an embodiment of Augustinian aesthetics—reflecting the multeity in unity of God's own creation, it could also provide for a Yankee poet writing several hundred years later the poetic equivalent of the democratic body politic—a group of equal, diverse, but ultimately united *Leaves of Grass*.[35]

Perhaps the title Petrarch himself chose for the *Canzoniere*—*Rerum vulgarium fragmenta* (*Fragments of vernacular poetry*)—most fully illuminates the special nature of the poetic collection. For if the radical incompleteness of any one short poem as an act of vision renders it essentially a "fragment," Petrarch implies that such fragments can be gathered and assimilated into the multiplicity comprising the collection as a whole. Robert Durling, observing that Petrarch may have been the first to use the term "fragment" to describe a work of art, perceives the *Canzoniere* as reflecting the "provisional, even threatened nature of the integration of experience possible for natural man."[36] As the grave consequences of that provisionality have come home to the poets of the nineteenth and twentieth centuries, the poetic book, with its open-ended, heterogeneous collection of "fragments," has become an essential vehicle for exploring the conditions of a world that seems itself increasingly fragmented.

Most of us, nonetheless, read, teach, and interpret poems as they are presented in anthologies or in posthumous editions arranged chronologically. Such habits exist for understandable reasons of convenience and have been fostered by the long-prevailing tendency of New Criticism to treat each poem in self-contained isolation. But the thirteen essays of *Poems in Their Place* urge us to consider instead how the context within which a poem is placed and read inevitably affects our understanding of the text.

It would, perhaps, be anomalous to present such a collection without some comment upon its own organization and integrity. As a group arranged by rough chronology, these essays begin to outline a literary history for contextual poetics, even as they offer readings of particular books or explore associated issues. Because it raises theoretical questions pertinent to the others, Earl Miner's cross-cultural study of the integrated collection as "plotless narrative" has been placed first. It should be noted, moreover, that although several poets and collections are discussed here in detail, no attempt at comprehensiveness has been made. For instance, the arrangements of such poets as Herbert, Dickinson, Yeats, and Auden all deserve lengthier treatment than could be provided, but, at least, they are already receiving substantial attention from critics. The fact is that most prominent poets since Petrarch—and many before—have given thought to the organization of their volumes. It would be impossible within a single book to give fair treatment to them all. Further, because this book focuses primarily on collections organized by their authors, several related topics have been forgone or only touched upon, including psalters, songbooks, anthologies, miscellanies, the Bible as collection, and Medieval manuscript collections. Each of these would provide fertile ground for future study.

Whereas any book of essays on the scale of *Poems in Their Place* necessarily reflects a series of difficult choices and compromises, it is to be hoped that the collection presented here will generate enough excitement to draw others into the project it advances. Indeed, though at the heart of this collection are such issues as order, arrangement, and intertextuality, the book as a whole is intended to demonstrate the rich plurality of concerns and strategies these issues can engender. Hence the essays range, for example, from S. K. Heninger's investigation of the sonnet sequence as an evolving generic system, to John Shawcross's textual critique of order and arrangement in Donne's canon, to Jerome McGann's discussion of the intertextual dynamics among the separate volumes comprising *Don Juan,* as well as the historical circumstances by which those dynamics are conditioned. Yet, however varied, these essays not only share many points of contact but also work toward a common goal. Collectively, they argue for the importance of studying the poetry book as an interpretive object, help develop a theory of such study, and provide a generous set of models for a related practical criticism. For it is only by better understanding the book as place that we will ever fully appreciate the appropriate place of the book in the editing, reading, and teaching of poetry.

NOTES

1. These comments by Thibaudet are cited by Jonathan Culler in *Structuralist Poetics: Structuralism, Linguistics, and the Study of Literature* (Ithaca, N.Y.: Cornell University Press, 1975), p. 131.

2. Common in seventeenth-century usage but now rare, "contexture" denotes an "interwoven structure," according to the Oxford English Dictionary, which also lists a specifically literary application: "the construction or composition of a writing as consisting of connected and coherent members." See also Neil Fraistat, *The Poem and the Book: Interpreting Collections of Romantic Poetry* (Chapel Hill: University of North Carolina Press, 1985), p. 4. Parts of this introductory essay have already appeared in chapter 1 of *The Poem and the Book*.

3. See, for instance, the essays below by Vincent Carretta and Jerome J. McGann.

4. Although my own definition of contexture is expressed in terms of forms arranged by the author, the concerns of contextual poetics might be widened fruitfully to include miscellanies, anthologies, and other types of collections characterized by corporate authorship or editorial arrangement. A contextural critic might study, for example, an editor such as George Bannatyne, who, working no doubt with the *Greek Anthology* and Meleager's *Garland* as models, was probably the first in Britain to organize an anthology generically and one of the first to attempt to unify an anthology through careful arrangement. From such studies, we might go on to develop a set of distinctions between characteristic authorial and editorial strategies for organizing collections. For an interesting discussion of corporate authorship in Japanese collections, see Earl Miner's essay below. For the importance of genre as a means of organization in Donne's canon, see John Shawcross's essay below.

5. The Alexandrians were certainly not the first Western poets to arrange groups of their own poems, however. Although our evidence is sketchy, Sappho, Mimnermos, and Theognis—among others—may all have done so before the rise of the poetry book in Alexandria. See, for example, H. J. Rose, *A Handbook of Greek Literature: From Homer to the Age of Lucian,* 4th ed. rev. (London: Methuen, 1954), pp. 83, 85-88, 97, and passim.

6. John Van Sickle, "The Book-Roll and Some Conventions of the Poetic Book," *Arethusa* 13 (1980): 6. I have found Van Sickle's entire discussion of the book-roll enlightening, pp. 5-42. For additional observations on the effect of the book-roll on the reading process, see William S. Anderson's essay below.

7. See Matthew S. Santirocco, "Horace's *Odes* and The Ancient Poetry Book," *Arethusa* 13 (1980): 46-47.

8. Santirocco notes about *Iambs* that "on material grounds, two groups of stichic poems (1–4, 8–13) surround a group of epodes. On thematic grounds, 7–11 are all placed together since all offer aetiologies, whereas 11 and 12 are set side by side to juxtapose their forms, an epitaph and genethliacon" ("Horace's *Odes*," p. 46).

9. Indeed, the idea of a garland is in itself suggestive of artful arrangement and, of course, appears frequently in volumes in the Renaissance and after. Although it is tempting to add Theocritus (the first seven *Idylls*) and Herodas (*Mimiamboi*) to the list of Hellenistic poets who organized their books, it is uncertain just how responsible either poet is for the arrangement of his poems.

10. Van Sickle, "The Book-Roll," p. 6.

11. For the arrangement of the Augustan book in general, see William S. Anderson's essay below. The connections between Horace's *Odes* and the formally and thematically heterogeneous poems in Alexandrian books are elaborated in J. V. Cody, *Horace and Callimachean Aesthetics, Collection Latomus 147* (Bruxelles: Latomus, 1976). For the general influence of Callimachus on the Augustans, see W. V. Clausen, "Callimachus and Latin Poetry," *GRBS* 5 (1964): 181–96. Van Sickle mentions the influence of the Alexandrian poets on Virgil's *Eclogues*, "The Book-Roll," p. 3. In *Petrarch's Lyric Poems* (Cambridge, Mass.: Harvard University Press, 1978), Robert Durling notes that Horace's *Odes* and Virgil's *Eclogues*, as well as the elegies of Propertius and Ovid, are classical models for Petrarch's *Canzoniere* (p. 10).

12. The Catullan corpus begins with a sequence of poems (2–11) designed to trace the progression and final dissolution of a love affair. See Santirocco, "Horace's *Odes*," p. 49. We cannot be sure, however, that Catullus arranged his corpus as we now know it.

13. Needless to say, *La vita nuova* is not the first work to combine prose and poetry. This practice, for instance, was not uncommon in Latin didactic texts. Although the *vidas* and *razos* often found in manuscript collections of Provençal poets have been cited as vernacular precedents for the prose explanations in *La vita nuova*, Sarah Sturm-Maddox distinguishes between these earlier examples and Dante's innovation by noting that the former were not provided by the poet himself. See her "Transformations of Courtly Love Poetry: *Vita Nuova* and *Canzoniere*," in *The Expansion and Transformation of Courtly Literature*, ed. Nathaniel B. Smith and Joseph T. Snow (Athens, Ga.: University of Georgia Press, 1980), p. 129. In one of the earliest English sequences, *The Hekatompathia or Passionate Centurie of Love* (1582), Thomas Watson may well be following Dante by including his own commentary in the headnote to each poem. S. K. Heninger, Jr., suggests, moreover, that Watson is probably influenced by the Continental vogue of annotating sonnets, two prominent examples of which are Bembo's commentary on Petrarch and that of Muret and Belleau on Ronsard's *Amours*. See Heninger's edition of Watson's book (Gainesville, Fla.: Scholar's Facsimile and Reprints, 1964), p. ix. The impact on English collections of this Continental vogue and of Dante's own critical prose in *La vita nuova* has not, to my knowledge, been sufficiently ex-

plored. George Gascoigne, for example, seems to draw from both traditions in *The Adventures of Master F. J.*, where he uses a fictitious editor "G. T." to provide the critical and "biographical" commentary linking a sequence of love poems written by the equally fictitious "F. J." It is interesting to note as well Michael McCanles's assertion that E. K.'s commentary in *The Shepheardes Calender* ought to be regarded as part of the larger fiction of the book. See "*The Shepheardes Calender* as Document and Monument," *Studies in English Literature* 22 (1982): 5–19.

14. See, for instance, Sturm-Maddox, "Transformations of Courtly Love Poetry," pp. 128–32, and S. K. Heninger's essay below.

15. For the evolving and open form of the *Canzoniere,* see E. H. Wilkins, *The Making of the "Canzoniere," and Other Petrarchan Studies* (Rome: Edizioni di Storia e litteratura, 1951), pp. 145–89.

16. *The Complete Works of Edgar Allan Poe,* ed. James A. Harrison (1902; rpt. New York: AMS Press, 1965), 14:195–96.

17. The distinction between collections and long poems blurs further in what M. L. Rosenthal and Sally M. Gall have identified as the "modern sequence": a form that is at once integrated aggregate and long poem, whose unity depends not on plot or theme but on "lyrical structure" (that is, a dynamic "progress of tonalities and affects"). Grouped under the rubric of "modern sequence"—which Rosenthal and Gall claim as the major genre in modern English poetry—are such diverse works as Emily Dickinson's hand-threaded fascicles, Pound's *Cantos,* Eliot's *Waste Land,* and Lowell's *Life Studies.* See *The Modern Poetic Sequence: The Genius of Modern Poetry* (Oxford: Oxford University Press, 1983). The scope of this recent study demonstrates the extent to which (and virtuosity with which) modern poets practice sophisticated contextural strategies.

18. These are all elements Wolfgang Iser describes as determining the "degree to which the retaining mind will implement the perspective connections inherent in the text." See *The Act of Reading: A Theory of Aesthetic Response* (Baltimore: Johns Hopkins University Press, 1978), p. 118. Fish, of course, would deny that any such connections inhere in the "text."

19. *The Letters of William and Dorothy Wordsworth: Part 2, The Middle Years, 1806–1820,* ed. Ernest de Selincourt, Mary Moorman, and Alan G. Hill, 2d ed. rev. (Oxford: Clarendon Press, 1969), 1:95.

20. See Stuart Curran's essay below for the shape of the sonnet sequences in Wordsworth's 1807 *Poems, in Two Volumes.*

21. Barbara Herrnstein Smith, *Poetic Closure: A Study of How Poems End* (Chicago: University of Chicago Press, 1968), p. 119.

22. Ibid., p. 13.

23. Stanley Fish, *Is There A Text in this Class?: The Authority of Interpretive Communities* (Cambridge, Mass.: Harvard University Press, 1980), p. 105.

24. Editors, of course, have often helped poets organize their books (sometimes even demanding significant order)—and perhaps never more so than currently. Peter Davison, a prominent poetry editor at the *Atlantic Monthly Press,* stated in an interview published 8 August 1984 in *The New York Times:* "I don't do very much line-by-line,

word-by-word editing of poetry books. . . . But I often make detailed suggestions about how to arrange a collection for publication. Depending on how you arrange poems, they can have a different effect for people who read the book from beginning to end. Not many people read that way, but I would like a book to have some progression." Davison's desire for "progression" in a book suggests that the effect of editors upon the shape of poetry books merits more attention than it has previously received.

25. See, for instance, chapter 3 of Fraistat, *The Poem and the Book*, where *Lyrical Ballads* (1798) is discussed at length.

26. See Culler, *Structuralist Poetics*, p. 174. Yet, even here, it might be argued that *we* decide what will count as data.

27. Wolfgang Iser, "The Reading Process," in *Reader-Response Criticism From Formalism to Post-Structuralism*, ed. Jane Tompkins (Baltimore: Johns Hopkins University Press, 1980), p. 64.

28. Santirocco, "Horace's *Odes*," p. 43.

29. Rosalie Colie, *The Resources of Kind: Genre Theory in the Renaissance* (Berkeley: University of California Press, 1973), p. 52.

30. Robert Gleckner, *Blake's Prelude: "Poetical Sketches"* (Baltimore: Johns Hopkins University Press, 1982), p. 153.

31. Sonnet sequences especially depend upon the persona as a unifying and organizing agent. Not only do the poems of a sequence manifest the speaker's mind and voice, but they are also generally arranged to simulate the chronology of his experience. Michael Drayton gives particular attention to the persona of his *Idea* sequence (1594): his revisions for the second edition (1599) in effect alter the persona from a conventional Petrarchan lover to a playful rationalist. See F. Y. St. Clair, "Drayton's First Revision of His Sonnets," *Studies in Philology* 36 (1939): 49–50.

32. For Pope's fashioning of a public image through his collections, see below, Carretta, "'Images Reflect from Art to Art.'" See McGann's essay, below, for Byron's efforts in this vein. Perhaps Yeats, of all poets, best shows how one can not only fashion and project an identity through his individual books, but actually remodel and sophisticate this persona by revising the shape of his canon. For the shaping of Yeats's canon, see, for example, Hugh Kenner, "The Sacred Book of the Arts," in *Gnomon: Essays in Contemporary Literature* (New York: Oblensky, 1951), pp. 9–29.

33. William Riley Parker, *Milton: A Biography* (Oxford: Clarendon Press, 1968), 1:631.

34. See Fraistat, *The Poem and the Book*, pp. 17-20. See also the essays by Joseph Anthony Wittreich, Jr., and Annabel Patterson, below.

35. See the essays below by S. K. Heninger and James E. Miller, Jr., for the ideological uses of the poetic collection by Renaissance poets and by Walt Whitman, respectively.

36. Durling, *Petrarch's Lyric Poems*, p. 26.

Earl Miner
Some Issues for Study of Integrated Collections

In recent years there has been a growing interest in integrated collections. Individuals studying this or that writer have made much the same discovery—that a given collection is integrated. In the fine glow of the experience, each of us has tended to be ignorant that colleagues in literatures of other times and places are making similar discoveries. Until most recently, there has been little comparative study, and until investigation advances fully in range, criteria, and theory, we shall not make clear what it is we are studying. Being optimistic of spirit and no younger in age, I shall approach some problems as opportunities in disguise. The fact that my syntax is declarative and that I reach certain solutions should not be taken to imply that my answers are necessarily correct. I think they are, but that is another matter.

It can only be assumed that collecting derives from the human urges to have, to have conveniently, and to preserve. And that the desire for convenience and sense explains why collections are not higgledy-piggledy storehouses but, in many cases, tidied and organized arrangements, whose orderings add a new sense, a new meaning. And because these acts are so natural to us, it is also natural to ignore the significance of what we are doing. Moreover, when it occurs to us that we have discovered something of importance concealed in the obvious, we are apt to think—wrongly—that what we have discovered is either unique or always found in collections. A little reflection shows that collections of whatever kind can be found in English literature from pretty much its beginnings to the present, but it is wrong to presume that all those collections are orderly or that, if they are ordered, they are fully integrated.

It is likewise a mistake to assume that collections are a possession solely of English literature. Greek works seemed to need to await the Alexandrians before collection began in earnest, but the earliest extant poetic classic in China, the *Shih Ching* (ca. B.C. 450), is a collection. And the first of the royal anthologies in Japan, the *Kokinshū* (ca. A.D. 905–20), is an integrated collection.[1] It is a yet greater error to presume that there are only a couple of ways of integrating or ordering collections. One reason why the subject is so fresh in this and other Western countries today is that we are accustomed to thinking of collections as being ordered along the chronological lines of textbooks or *The Oxford Book* of this or that verse. We are surprised when we find that that principle is by no means invariable and that in fact there is far greater interest in other orderings.

The motives of those who study the ordering and integrating of collections also vary widely. The discovery that the book-roll used in Roman times was of a set length can turn out to have important implications. (One forgets that the codex was not devised in Rome until late times.) Some people interested in collections share with many recent critics a dissolving spirit. They are inclined to break down the privileged status of "the literary work of art," to erase the lines between author and critic (or compiler-reader), poem and collection, etc. Others are motivated to the contrary by a desire to establish integrities in danger of being unnoticed, forgot, lost. Because of the multiplicity involved on all counts, we may profitably use some less familiar examples, some deliberately different in provenance, to establish some criteria for canons of integrated collections.

It is easy to forget that in a book that did so much else, Louis L. Martz had an eighth chapter, the second on George Herbert and the last of the book: "George Herbert: The Unity of *The Temple*." The "unity" involves "a structure built upon the art of mental communion."[2] Further study of *The Temple* as a unified collection has involved refinement or redirection of Martz's argument without doing very much more than honor his insight or debate lesser issues. These typically involve the function of a single poem; a certain small critical literature has grown over the issue whether "The Church Militant" printed at the end is part of a "structure" inclusive of the whole, joining "The Church-Porch" and "The Church" in making up *The Temple*. (On the one hand, the last poem in "The Church"—"Love" [III]—is followed by a finis and a gloria; whereas on the other, "The Church Militant" is followed by "L'Envoy," which in turn is followed, first by a blessing and last by a finis.) One will believe what one believes about such details. It is more important to consider the elements that prove "the Unity of *The Temple*." Martz's chapter stresses certain meditational practices and a eucharistic emphasis. If this is not meditational poetry, it would be difficult to know where to find it, and a sequence provided from "The Altar" to the Holy Communion celebrated in "Love" (III) must surely involve the eucharist. But just which meditative conditions are invoked is a reasonable ground for speculation. And without denying the sacramental emphasis, it is possible to consider the emphasis of the majority of poems, and the fluctuations of the whole to employ the means made familiar from emblem-book sequences on the vicissitudes of the soul and the *sic vita* tradition encouraged by the emblem books.[3]

Dryden is the other seventeenth-century English poet whose integrated collections have interested me most. It is now approximately two decades since the dignity of print was given to development of the thesis that *Fables* is an integrated collection, and the argument has been developed subsequently.[4] If anyone has disagreed, the dissatisfaction seems not to have been published. *Fables* poses a special example in its length and constituents. It is about twice as long as *Paradise Lost,* and unlike Herbert's *Temple* it is not made up of poems of one or two kinds—Herbert's discursive frame poem(s) and lyrics for "The Church." Dryden uses mostly translations (from Ovid, Chaucer, Boccaccio, and Homer) with four poems original with him,. two being verse addresses and two lyrics that he had written earlier ("Alexander's Feast" and "A Monument to a Fair Maiden Lady"). In other words, to integrate such various materials required stronger measures than those used by Herbert; Dryden put Boccaccio into poetry, for example.

We shall return to *Fables* shortly, but it is my belief that it was not Dryden's first ordered collection. In 1685 there appeared *Sylvae: or, Second Part of Poetical Miscellanies.* The year before, a predecessor, *Miscellany Poems,* had appeared, and *Examen Poeticum,* labeled the "Third Part," appeared in 1693. To my view, neither the first nor the third are integrated collections. *Sylvae* begins with a dozen poems by Dryden. Actually, the first (the second part of *Absalom and Achitophel*) was more by Tate than by him. There follow two selections from the *Aeneid,* five from Lucretius, one from Theocritus, and three from Horace, all by Dryden. There then follow dozens of poems by others, often by anonymous authors, sometimes translations, poems by Jonson and Marvell (including two Mower poems, "Musicks Empire" and "The Garden"). One need only suggest the nature of the integration perceived.[5] The third poem is "The Speech by Venus to Vulcan" (*Aeneid,* 8), in which she uses her charms to persuade him to make a shield for Aeneas. The following first extract from *De Rerum Natura* is the hymn to Venus that begins the first book. The ensuing four selections combine to give a view of human life, a selective, reduced, and integrated version of Lucretius' poem. There is no need to argue the matter in detail here.[6] There is, however, one matter that must be raised. Very little is known about the responsibility for arranging poems in Dryden's miscellanies. (The title pages say "Publish'd by Mr. Dryden.") The letters Dryden exchanged with his publisher, Jacob Tonson, are silent on this matter. It therefore cannot be proved that Dryden arranged *Sylvae* or disproved that Tonson did. Or even that some third person was responsible. My presumption is that Dryden was responsible, and the evidence lies in the selections and ordering of the excerpts from Lucretius, which were certainly of Dryden's making.

There is no need to discuss fully the order of *Sylvae,* but it can be shown to differ in organizational character from Herbert's *Temple* and Dryden's *Fables*—my reason for introducing it. Partly because its range of sources exceeds that even of *Fables,* the integrative procedures are not as extensive or as meaningful. The difference can be suggested by saying that *Sylvae* is an ordered collection occasionally integrated, whereas *Fables* is fully integrated. There is another consideration. The title chosen, *Sylvae,* recalls the *Silvae* of Statius as well as Jonson's *Forrest* and *Under-wood* (again: Jonson is included in *Sylvae*). Statius's title is a Latin version of the Greek "hylē," raw materials: that is, variety rather than order is suggested. But the classical principle of collections is basically one of variety with pleasing order. And recent studies of Jonson have shown that his major collections are ordered if not wholly integrated.[7]

Herbert offers us an example of a poet who integrates lyrics into a collection that, when read sequentially, affords a pleasure and significance not available to one who reads the lyrics separately. Dryden gives two rather different examples. *Sylvae* includes poems by a diverse, numerous set of authors, ordering them in a pleasing way if not fully integrating them. *Fables* is integrated, with the poems by the translator-author appearing early and late in crucial places. To make our range of examples suitable for further, more theoretical inquiry, we need to turn to another field, namely Japanese collections. This is important because the Japanese evidence shows that collections are intrinsically more important in that literature than in English, and because the nature of the collections differs from that of the English examples given.[8]

So "the scene is altered" when we move from one major literature to another. The most prestigious of integrated Japanese collections are twenty-one royal collections beginning around 905–20 and ending in 1439. These are mostly in twenty books or scrolls (two are in ten). They are conspicuous for various features. Like Herbert's collection, they consist of lyrics (almost exclusively of the five-line tanka form). But they differ from what we have been seeing in important respects. For one thing, each half (usually each sub-set of ten books) begins with an especially esteemed kind, the first with six books of poems on seasonal topics, and the second with four or five or so books on love topics. Other categories or topics are travel, parting, laments, congratulations, etc. Another difference is that often the compilation of the collections will involve several people. This implies an *explicit* sense of procedure. In fact there were occasional serious differences among compilers, particularly over the greatest of the collections for its poems, the eighth, *Shinkokinshū*.[9] The issue was: should only the best poems be included or should quality yield to pleasure in the whole, with good poems being set off in the sequence by lesser poems? With the *Shinkokinshū*, the issue was decided in favor of integration and varying quality.

The royal collections influenced a variety of briefer sequences more or less modeled on the larger collections. It became common to write or collect about a hundred poems integrated either on the general model of a royal collection or on one of its parts, for example, love. Two such shorter sequences have been translated with commentary.[10] From the evidence, we can select a few important features. The seasonal poems use the temporal progression of the seasons codified in various ways. Early spring poems will perhaps include a couple concerning snow on plum trees. Then, as other poems follow, the plums will bloom white among the snow, the blossoms almost indistinguishable from the snow; next the warbler, associated with the plum tree, will be introduced. Sub-progressions are also numerous. The plum blossoms may be on trees in the capital, then in nearby areas, and then—step by step—proceed to remoter areas. Association links one poem with the next. If one autumn poem tells of frost, the next may feature withered plants, so that we assume that the frost of the one has withered the plants of the next; a moon may be imagistic in one stanza and figural (for enlightenment) in the next. And so on.

It should be emphasized that these relations are established by the compilers and that if three dozen poems by a single author appear in a royal collection, they are not included in one place in the chronological order of composition. Rather, they appear throughout the sequence where their topics dictate. In some later collections, the compilers juxtapose two poems that seem to have no relation to each other. But the juxtaposition by the compilers may entail an allusion to a famous older poem whose constituents can be found in the two poems newly collected. The allusion was not made by the author of either poem but by the compilers in the act of juxtaposing. Without going further, we have enough evidence to show that Japanese collections are not only integrated differently but to a higher degree than almost all Western collections. And the principles of integration differ, as do the statuses of the compilers.

No doubt it would be useful to give a wider range of possibility.[11] But it is enough to say that varying methods of integration have been used over the centuries and in different poetic traditions. The fact and the variance are beyond question. It now remains to make some theoretical issue of the fact and the variance. The first important issue seems to me to be the literary nature of an integrated or ordered sequence. Dryden might integrate poems largely narrative in *Fables*. Herbert and the Japanese might integrate lyrics. What is the nature of the integrated product?

One of the crucial issues is whether or not an integrated collection constitutes a narrative. Dryden's poems in *Fables* may be chiefly narrative, but the issue is whether his *collection* is a narrative. Perhaps we are tempted to say that it is a narrative because of the emphasis of most of its constituents. If so, we may turn to Herbert's *Temple,* which is made up of lyric poems. Here again we may too quickly decide on narrative, because the lyric *speaker* seems to take on the role of a *narrator* on fictively going up "The Church-Porch," pausing on the threshold ("Super Liminare"), seeing "The Altar," recording the vicissitudes of a Christian soul, and at last taking holy communion in "Love" (III). This identification of a consistent speakership with narrator also tends to compromise the question. We must take recourse to the Japanese collections, especially the royal ones. The topics became traditional after the *Kokinshū* (the first of the twenty-one; but some changes occurred). The ordering was done by compilers, who usually had poems by themselves included. Since every poem is credited to an author, even if labeled anonymous, there is not the consistency of authorial/narrative voice that we find in Herbert's collection. In short, the issue comes down to this: can there be a narrative in a collection in which not only the poet but the human subject, the speaker (the "point of view"), shifts incessantly from poem to poem?

It will be obvious that our answer will depend on what our definition of narrative is. The fact that the collections we are considering may seem, at least to Western view, fictional does not therefore render them narrative. Everyone knows that there are fictions not narrative (as with the legal, lyric, and hypothetical of some kinds) and that there are narratives not fictional (as in history, reportage, etc.). The sticking point appears to be whether plot—that currently abused, despised entity—is necessary to narrative. My experience, however, has been that banished plot is too quickly welcomed home when integrated Japanese sequences are posed as a non-Western example that may be plotless narrative.

Must narrative have plot? Again, the question turns on definitions of narrative—and of plot. Our word, "narrative," was devised of course by Roman rhetoricians to designate one part of an oration, in general a relation of past facts. The most influential discussions posit three kinds of narrative. One kind is "historia," which is "exposition of actual fact" ("*in qua est gestae rei expositio*"); another is "argumentum," which "though not true, has yet a certain verisimilitude" ("*falsum sed vero simile*"); and "fabula," which "is not merely not true but has little resemblance to the truth" ("*non a veritate modo sed etiam a forma veritatis remota*").[12] Quintilian offers counterparts for each of the three kinds. For "historia," history was the obvious example. I do not find it obvious that for "argumentum" comedy was the counterpart. One can see that he must have used "fabula," as classicists believe, to designate extraordinary stories such as fill the first half or more of Ovid's *Metamorphoses*. But he also mentioned tragedy. What a mixture the counterparts are! Where would historical Lucan or scientific Lucretius fit in? It does appear that Quintilian wished to posit a spectrum for narrative that ranged from fact to fiction, and even to extreme fiction. Yet in the central section of the *Institutes* dealing with the *use* of narratives (IV, ii), he seems to ignore the fictive and use "narratio" to designate the stating of facts in court. "Fabula" is almost wholly ignored, and when he uses a word like "argumentum," it does not seem to suggest Plautus or Terence: "Then follow these arguments based on facts" ("*His subtextitur argumentatio*": IV, ii, 14). In short, although the rhetorician seems willing to allow space in theory for the fictive, in practice he thinks of "narratio" as an ordered presentation of presumed facts or events, not of something identified with a plot or story.

On the Roman evidence, we may then term ordered collections plotless narratives. But of course usage of words does not remain unchanged, and we ought to consider later evidence, say, that taken from the heyday of postclassical poetic narrative. Unfortunately, one looks long and far for traditional uses of "narrative." Kinds may be mentioned. Guillaume de Lorris and Jean de Meun write a *roman,* Dante a *commedia,* Boccaccio many *novelle,* and Chaucer *tales,* one of which (The Monk's) he also calls *tragedies.* "Narrative" is not in the indices of C. C. Smith's *Elizabethan Critical Essays* or J. E. Spingarn's *Critical Essays of the Seventeenth Century.* (Those rhetoricians are beginning to look downright helpful.) Spingarn omitted Dryden, so we can turn to George Watson's glossary in *Of Dramatic Poesy and Other Critical Essays*.[13] Dryden does use "narration" twice, although he feels far more comfortable with "relation." Yet he uses the terms for the fact as well as the act, which is what we have been looking for, not expecting, I think, that it would take so long. Much the same is true in the critical study of Chinese and Japanese literatures. Like Dryden, and long before him, Japanese used a verbal noun and verb for "relation" and "relate" (*katari, kataru*), meaning in prose. The deficiency in devising of words for "narrative" seems universal, since every initial, systematic view of literature seems to have been founded either on contact with drama as the esteemed genre (Aristotle, the West) or lyric (all other cultures).[14] Quintilian's practice shows that for an orator narrative is basically a statement of facts. Does the statement, or do those facts, entail a plot? He does not say so.

Relying on what we are pleased to call intuition, most of us could find plots in a novel, a history (of a certain kind), a biography, or a newspaper account of an athletic event. But what is a plot? We may take its minimal criteria to be continuance and development of characters in temporalities, locations, and relations with a logical system of causation, etc. Certainly we look in vain for definitions of plot in Asian criticism, although we do find the suggestion that a narrative is told by a person distinct from the audience, whereas lyrics bring poet and audience together on common ground.[15] That allows for the existence of plots without naming them. Literary narrative emerges fully developed earlier in Japan than China, and there is much evidence to show that the emphasis is the same; there is a connection with history, and the medium is prose. It seems no accident that when what are usually thought the first English novels appear, they are often specifically named histories or lives, that is, biographies.[16] Defoe goes to great efforts to be thought historically veracious and Swift, to some ironic lengths, to pretend as much. And we may recall early English uses of "story" to mean history (compare the Italian "storia"). It would not be long after when writers who spoke of plots sought to evade what they thought their conventional or tyrannical nature.

We are left with the minimal description of plot given, letting others add what they find necessary. In any event, plot is not the prime radical of literary continuity. Every work of literature, including every one with a plot, must be told in some *sequence*. A different sequence might have been used by Herbert in *The Temple,* and he might still have had an integrated collection. For that matter, another sequence could have been used by Milton in *Paradise Lost* or by Márquez in *A Hundred Years of Solitude*. The changes in sequence could be made while the works retained their plots, even if *Paradise Lost* began with creation (the obvious first temporal event) or the fall (the climactic event). If Márquez had begun with that extraordinary ascent or assumption of Remedios, the plot would still be what it is.

In other words, plot depends so much on causalities—which we can understand even if effect is given before cause—that its very logicality, even when bizarre or contradictory, can be understood in whatever sequence as long as the means to understand are given. Of course the works will differ enormously in what they mean to us if a plot is changed in its sequence. That is because, unlike plot, the sequence of a work cannot be changed without in fact, by definition, altering the sequence. We need only imagine an O. Henry story or a detective story beginning with its final revelation to see how basic sequence is. It is a radical of literature prior to plot.

A lyric of three lines like a Japanese *haiku* has its sequence, and that is true also of the one-line poem that Aeneas presents: "These arms *Aeneas* took from Conqu'ring *Greeks*" (*Aeneid,* 3; Dryden's Translation, not the same sequence as the Latin, "*Aeneas haec de Danais victoribus arma*" [line 288]). It will be clear that this leads to the argument that plot is not minimally necessary to narrative but that sequence is. Because that is the case, it must be made clear that plot as I have narrowly described it is in fact a feature of most narratives and may be grounds for great satisfaction in a narrative. Only when plots grow too conventional or people come to doubt matters like causality, personhood, beginning, and ending do plots seem contemptible. I do not hold such views, and I find that the concept has explanatory powers. These may be historical.[17] Or they may allow us to make certain analytical and descriptive distinctions of great importance. For example, acquaintance with *nō* shows that it cannot be understood without appreciating its highly narrative character ("*erzählen auf der Bühne*" was how Brecht put it), and its kind of narrative cannot be grasped without understanding how little importance plot has in it. Everyone who knows about *nō* is aware of these things, and the terms are adequate to convey important distinctions. On both logical and empirical grounds the terms do seem to make sense.

If we now suppose that an integrated collection has a narrative without the plot normally expected, what are the features of that narrative? There seem to be but two things: (of course, intelligible) sequentiality and continuousness. Sequentiality being a radical of all verbal and musical expression, it is clearly not a differentia of narrative. But when sequentiality continues in a Japanese collection for thousands of five-line poems and many more thousands of lines, continuousness takes on a dimension for which "lyric" does not seem the best description. (For obvious reasons, drama is out of consideration here.) We may well say that Japanese collective narrative has a definite lyric cast, something also posited of the Western "lyrical novel."[18]

If, however, the "cast" is only attributively lyric, what is the main thing? Since it is not drama or lyric, we may choose to call it minimal narrative.

What do we gain by taking sequential, integrated collections on narrative terms? It seems inescapable that, if the classifying is correct, we assume in theory that the basis of narrative is (sequential) continuousness rather than plot or the Asian non-identity of the compiler with the relater. Are there any benefits in practice? Not to consider modern Western antinarrative narrative as probative evidence, there is the common Renaissance assumption that satire is narrative.[19] Renaissance editions and criticism by Dryden show that agreement was widespread on satire's being narrative, even if some of Hobbes's ideas would have excited disagreement. To establish the principle, we must exclude certain satires by Horace, who has provided theorists of satire the most difficulty. The point is that he gave *plots* to many of his satires. The journey to Brundisium (*Satires,* I, 5), the experience of being accosted by a bore in the Via Sacra (I, 9), and the tale of the town and country mice (II, 6) all have plots. If Hobbes's definition is to have point for us it must be taken in terms of the non-plot satires by Juvenal and Persius. In them we find reasonably sustained continuance— in Hobbes's terms the narrative alternative to dramatic comedy. On such grounds, we also have a basis for considering as narrative *De Rerum Natura* along with Pope's *Essay on Criticism* and *Essay on Man,* not to mention many a later poem.[20]

"Minimal narrative." The category is not a very appealing one; what is maximal narrative? Well, there probably is an answer. It would be plotted, so-called third-person narrative and, for literary examples, highly fictional. Extreme fictions like *The Faerie Queene* or other normative examples such as the *Odyssey* or *The Tale of Genji* provide further evidence. Clearly these "maximal narratives" meet the minimal demands and, by definition, supply much more as well. And yet, if we accept the idea of minimal narrative, the question may now be stood on its head.

If the sticking-point earlier was the definition of narrative, we now face a comparable trial in defining a collection. The concept of collections normally used by Western classicists appears to be diverse materials arranged in some suitable fashion.[21] The problem with this definition is that, although it applies to collections very well, it does not distinguish them from *The Prelude* or *To the Lighthouse*. The advantage of the definition is that it allows us to think of collections as minimal narratives, to hold that narratives that are more than minimal add other elements. But the advantage is offset by the fact that "diverse materials arranged in some suitable fashion" does not exclude lyrics.[22] Once more, it seems, we are left to posit radical continuousness—elusive as that concept may be—as the distinction between lyric and narrative. But the distinction between lyric and narrative does not function to distinguish between collections and "maximal" narratives.

It does appear that we gain some insights into narrative by considering that a given instance is a collection—that is, that a "maximal" narrative is founded on a "minimal" with added characteristics. Homer's catalogue of the ships can hardly be construed as narrative on any other terms, and heaven knows that in modern narratives as well as Rabelais, Swift, Whitman, and others there are many passages of lists or collections that arrest the plot. Clearly, the collective principle is one that narrative often uses, at least if by collection we mean lists, pilings-up, series that do not advance the plot and in fact abate it.

At this point one can hear two kinds of emergency alarms going. One, sounding for all the world like a French horn, would hold the distinctions posited are meaningless and that texts are texts. Another, sounding like Big Ben, tells us that common sense shows that a narrative tells a story. Although as Addison memorably observed, there is something to be said on both sides, we may proceed in our labors as if the alarms were silent, trying to construct a logical path through matters that are very difficult.[23]

The problem with conceiving of the catalogue of the ships as narrative is not that we would wish to rule it out but that, to the extent that it does abate, give pause to, the main narrative, it has a counter-narrative potential. In other words, if the collective principle is to be considered narrative, it must fit with some positive conception of narrative, not with its abatement.

There is another problem, one in many ways more serious. The discussion to this point has presumed comparison between integratively collected works and the usual narrative. But it is in the nature of a collection that its constituent units have another feasible existence as separate literary integers. In fact, in many collections the authors collected had no idea that their work(s) would be collected, and even if they had hoped so, they could not have been able to conceive what the wholeness of that other collection would be like, since they could not know which works by others would be chosen. To the extent that we consider the importance of the divisible integers a central fact of collections, there is no identity of narrative with collection, although of course as *Fables* or Joyce's *Dubliners* shows, individual integers may be narrative. And although a maximal narrative may be excerpted from, as Dickens did so successfully for his public readings, it is by no means clear (as it is in a collection) where the beginnings and endings of an excerpt will fall.

The divisible or separable integers of collections are units unlike chapters, episodes, or paragraphs in an ordinary narrative. This is especially marked in *Fables* and in the Japanese royal collections, because in them we have units (poems) largely written by people other than the compiler. In a Japanese royal collection, dozens of authors may be included. In *Fables,* the range is from Homer and Ovid to Chaucer and Boccaccio and to Dryden himself.

The narrative status of a collection, or the collective status of a narrative, therefore pertains not to parts but to their articulation as a whole. We must simply give over as irrelevant to the narrative any narrative status in a collection's individual parts: *Pygmalion and the Statue* in *Fables.* This work may be narrative in itself but it has no *collective* narrative status; one integer does not make a collection. We must find the narrative element of collections, if we are to find it at all, in the principles that allow us to integrate in satisfying ways integers otherwise separable. Some of these ways have been spoken of in terms of Herbert's physical progression as into a church for worship, by subjects such as his recurrent concern with the eucharist and the vicissitudes of the soul. These are important, but if by "these" we mean worship, the eucharist, and vicissitudes of the soul, they are important to the cognitive what-ness of *The Temple.* They are not narrative procedures of continuance. If however, we consider—apart from the religious what-nesses—the principles of progression and recurrence, then we certainly have come to important procedures of continuance, principles of how, canons of how, not issues of what.

Since only things that begin can be said to continue, beginning is clearly important, and given the use (by definition) in a collection of otherwise separable pieces, the recurrence of marked beginning is more strongly emphatic in a collection than it is in noncollective narratives. Since, in order for a new thing to begin after *the* beginning, an old thing must end, endings are also important principles. And as for *the* end of the collection, that is determined by the discovery of there being no further beginning, a fact that shows that beginning is logically prior to ending. Recurrence is implied by a series of beginnings and endings. Sequentiality implies an order to the series. Progression implies a higher degree of *qualitative* order. And as with beginning, so with continuance, it is not only a principle of narrative in general but also one that must be considered pluralistically: continuances. Otherwise each beginning and ending coincide, as the jingle I remember from my childhood almost does.

> I'll tell you a story of Jack-a-Norry,
> And now my story's begun;
> I'll tell you another about his brother,
> And now my story's done.

Those various principles covered so quickly could all be examined at length. But since my proper subject is collections rather than narrative in the larger sense, we ought to consider, if possible, any principles that function in the *integration* of sequences. For without the integration, it is impossible to presume a cohesion in continuance or a narrative in a collection. What integrates the units (for example, lyrics in *The Temple*) must pertain to: (1) that joining (for example, lyric) *a* to *b*, *b* to *c*, etc.; (2) elements i, ii, and iii appearing in *a*, *b*, *d*, *g*, *h*, and *k*; or (3) that pertaining to wholeness. Both Herbert and Dryden make something of (1), very much of (2), and no little of (3). Japanese evidence is useful partly because it differs: the point will not be reached at once—but effectively, Japanese collections do not much use procedure (2). Japanese collections are also of interest because the people who made them gradually devised explicit categories and names for what they were doing, something that has only begun in the West.

In Japanese poetics, there is an explicit principle of relation, degree. This is spoken of metaphorically but understandably in both languages: "close" ("*shin*"; also "*jū*" or "heavy") and "distant" ("*so*"; also "*kei*" or "light") relation. Given the at least relative variety that collections possess by definition, and given Japanese attachment to asymmetry, both closeness and distance (and not simply in two degrees) were thought to operate. As so often, the idea was practiced well before it was explicitly expressed, but diverse relation is an important principle in describing the nature of collective integration. For that matter, it applies to plot narrative as well. To take a simple example, we would find it tedious if every Spenserian stanza covered fifteen minutes throughout *The Faerie Queene*.

Close or distant connection implies not pure formal status but cognitively grasped substantialities: connection is thought to exist only when the succession is meaningful. A green bank and a daffodil may not be as close as a green bank and a stream, but the connections are very much more natural than a green bank and a logarithm. In a plotted narrative, such connectedness is more easily followed (in the absence of trouble) because of those characters, temporalities, places, and causalities spoken of earlier. But in a collective whole we may have these very things as well—providing that the continuousness does not involve identical cognitive entities; always to have Malone and his fictionally imagined characters, his room, his passage from near death to understood death does work in Beckett's novel, *Malone Dies,* but not in a collection.

Because the discussion has been highly abstract this while, let us turn to examples. To begin with, there is *relation.* In Dryden's *Fables,* there is a very close connection between the fifteenth and the sixteenth units. The former gives all of the twelfth book of Ovid's *Metamorphoses,* which is concerned with the rise and course of the Trojan war. The latter gives the debate between "Ajax and Ulysses," which is doubly related to the preceding, one way being that it is something dividing the at last victorious Greeks (who deserves the armor of Achilles?) and another way being that it is the beginning of the next book of the *Metamorphoses.* On the other hand, the second and third units are more distantly related. The second is a version of Chaucer's Knight's Tale, and the third is a poem of address by Dryden "To My Honour'd Kinsman," his cousin John Driden. The connection is important—the search for the happy or good life—but the answers to what constitutes that ideal life are directly opposed and the relation therefore far less close.

A contrast from the eighth royal Japanese collection, the *Shinkokinshū,* will show how the principle of fluctuating relation can work when the units are not themselves narrative. As an example of close relation, here are three autumn poems from book four of the *Shinkokinshū,* poems 361–63—respectively by the poets Priest Jakuren, Priest Saigyō, and Fujiwara Teika.

Sabishisa wa
sono iro to shi mo
  nakarikeri
maki tatsu yama no
aki no yūgure.

Loneliness—
even though one sought it out
  it has not been found:
where black pines stand on the hills
the autumn dusk comes on.

Kokoro naki
mi ni mo aware wa
  shirarekeri
shigi tatsu sawa no
aki no yūgure.

Even a priest
who has schooled away desire
  knows deep feeling:
from the marsh a longbill
flies off in the autumn dusk.

Miwataseba
hana mo momiji mo
  nakarikeri
ura no tomaya no
aki no yūgure.

As I look about
what if I see no flowers of spring
  or bright autumn leaves:
the inlet with its grass-thatched huts
in the growing autumn dusk.

It will be obvious to anyone who looks at the Japanese that the last lines of the three poems are identical, that the third lines are alike in inflection (with those of the first and third poems identical), and that in each poem there is a paradox between the subjective first part and imagistic last two lines, for example, the first poet, offering what he says cannot be found.

From the same collection here are three winter poems in succession (book six, 671–73) whose relations differ. The poets are Fujiwara Teika (671, 672) and Fujiwara Ariie (673).

Koma tomete	There is no cover
sode uchiharau	where I can rein in my horse
kage mo nashi	and brush clear my sleeves,
Sano no watari no	in this region of the Sano ferry
yuki no yūgure.	where dusk thickens with the snow.

Matsu hito no	He whom I wait for
fumoto no michi wa	must find his foothills road to me
taenu ran	obliterated;
nokiba no sugi no	in the cedars by my eaves
yuki omoru nari.	the snow grows ever heavier.

Yume kayou	Even in my dreams
michi sae taenu	love visits are interrupted—
kuretake no	the Chinese bamboos
Fushimi no sato no	in the village of Fushimi
yuki no shitaore.	crack loudly underneath the snow.

Matters are not simple when we come to such actual examples. Close attention will show, I believe, that the second set of three are beautifully related in a progression: the man cannot find his way; the woman waits in vain in the evening (the trysting time in Japanese courtly love), and later one of them (no doubt the woman) finds that, although she can visit her lover in dreams (something thought feasible then), the snow that is the common problem now, at a later hour, breaks the bamboos so loudly that she wakes up. On the other hand, the three autumn poems are more given to recurrence in syntax and in specific elements—the identical last line and the very clear first-person presentation of a paradox. Since immediate recurrence (semi-repetition) is more obvious than progression, the autumn stanzas are more "closely" related than are the winter ones.

In these examples we find that the "cognitively grasped substantialities" are related, not purely formal entities. We have people, time, place (singular or plural), and causalities. Because of the heavy snow, the traveler is in distress just as the beauty of the day is about to yield to night, or love becomes impossible. (Very brief plot in a poem but not the sequence.) There is no question but that the sequences are integrated. If we were to chart the Japanese sense of the second set of three poems, for example, the anatomy would be much like this.

671. "There is no cover"
    1. Topic: winter
    2. Added topic: travel
    3. Chief image: snow
    4. Speaker: first-person male (traveler)
    5. Tone: loneliness
    6. Place/time: hills, trees, snow; dusk
672. "He whom I wait for"
    1. Topic: winter
    2. Added topic: love
    3. Chief image: snow
    4. Speaker: first-person female
    5. Tone: isolation
    6. Place/time: indoors to shelter, trees; evening
673. "Even in my dreams"
    1. Topic: winter
    2. Added topic: love
    3. Chief image: snow
    4. Speaker: first person female (?)
    5. Tone: frustration
    6. Place/time: indoors, bamboo outside from trees; middle or late night

These are cognitive constituents of narrative of any kind, but although there is continuance in the *presence* of the cognitive constituents, the *identity* of the constituents changes. This seems pretty well to offer one kind of evidence that we have in integrated collections either something like narrative or what may be termed plotless narrative. For we must understand that the closeness or distance of consecutive units is not sheer formality, simple intertextuality. These principles involve six minimal cognitively grasped elements (see the "anatomy" given earlier), elements at once subjective and objective, codified and free. If a narrative must have continuous plot, these poems do not provide that. But if a narrative need only be continuous in its sequence, using the six elements that would be sufficient for a plot, then the collection has at least a minimal narrative.

If we were to turn back to Herbert's *Temple,* we would find what is in some ways a greater degree of integration: the same Christian speaker functions throughout as a kind of sequential narrator. Yet in that collection also, the principle of shifting distance or closeness functions. After "The Church-Porch," "Superliminare," and "The Altar" comes "The Sacrifice." In it the speaker shifts—exceptionally—from the Christian to Christ himself. There are other connections, of course. As a link to "The Sacrifice," the penultimate line of "The Altar" is: "O let thy blessed SACRIFICE be mine" (Herbert's stress).

By way of comparison, let us take a comparable section from what everyone would think to be a well-made, traditional novel, Austen's *Pride and Prejudice,* beginning with the eighth of the brief paragraphs in the second chapter.

> Mrs. Bennet deigned not to make any reply; but unable to contain herself, began scolding one of her daughters.
> "Don't keep coughing so, Kitty, for heaven's sake! Have a little compassion on my nerves. You tear them to pieces."
> "Kitty has no discretion in her coughs," said her father; "she times them ill."
> "I do not cough for my own amusement," replied Kitty fretfully.
> "When is your next ball to be, Lizzy?"
> "To-morrow fortnight."
> "Aye, so it is," cried her mother, "and Mrs. Long does not come back till the day before, so it will be impossible for her to introduce him [Mr. Bingley], for she will not know him herself."
> "Then, my dear, you may have the advantage of your friend, and introduce Mr. Bingley to *her.*"
> "Impossible, Mr. Bennet, impossible, when I am not acquainted with him myself; how can you be so teazing?"

What has preceded and what follows will be as familiar to readers of *Pride and Prejudice* as what precedes and follows the two examples from the *Shinkokinshū* will be to readers familiar with that collection.

There is one difference, however. A plotted continuousness is easier to keep in the memory than an unplotted or purely sequential sequence in which speakers are constantly shifting. Otherwise, however, we observe that the principle of more close and more distant relation between units does function as a continuing principle in plotted and unplotted narrative alike. Also that the basis for establishing the continuance is that of "cognitively grasped substantialities": speakers (who shift but are present within a narrative point of view), time and place (in Austen more nearly identical than in the Japanese examples and therefore less progressive), topics or what-ness, and the rest. On this evidence, it would surely prove difficult to frame any definition, other than that of plot, of declaring one but not the other a narrative.

The narrator's voice in *Pride and Prejudice* is of course distinct from the opening onward: "It is a truth universally acknowledged," etc. In the Japanese collections even more than in Dryden's *Fables* the narrator's presence is less defined. The *Shinkokinshū* had six compilers (we know those who recommended each selection) with the retired sovereign, Gotoba, also exercising his preferences. Corporate compilation of poems composed in the first instance by dozens of poets old and new is not the same thing as a novel by Jane Austen. An early thirteenth-century Japanese collection is not the same as an early nineteenth-century English novel. Yet we have found it difficult in recent years to sort out concepts of authorship (here, also compilership), implied authorship, implied narratorship, and individual narratorship. No one could deny the fact of difference in the presenting or presenters of the examples given. All the same, it would be equally difficult to argue that the distinction is more one of kind than of degree.

We seem readier to accept the idea that integrated collections are narrative in character when the constituents integrated are mostly narratives, as in Dryden's *Fables,* or when an author integrates a series of poems personally written: Shakespeare's or Sidney's sonnets, Herbert's *Temple.* We do not have for those collections the information that we do for the Japanese collections or for Tennyson's *In Memoriam.* It is quite clear that Tennyson originally started writing the separate lyrics without thought of publication, much less of ordering.[24] And it is equally clear that in his finished work the principles of sequentiality, continuousness, and varying closeness or distance function to a degree like those of the Japanese collections. The major difference between the latter and Tennyson's most read poem/collection is that the Japanese compilers had a model to work from, that of the previous seven royal collections. Some change was possible: books or scrolls on lesser topics might be dropped or added. But the model was clear from four centuries before; here is that third principle of integration posited earlier. Given the model, the Japanese royal collections were more integrated than the Western collections mentioned, which is to say that the continuance had a more formal, unified character. It is very difficult indeed to conceive of a definition other than plot that would include *In Memoriam*—or for that matter, Wordsworth's *Prelude,* Byron's *Don Juan,* or Meredith's *Modern Love*—and exclude the Japanese collections along with *The Temple* and *Fables.* And it is also difficult to frame a definition of narrative late in the twentieth century that would make plot a necessary constituent of narrative.

If plot is necessary to narrative (to say it explicitly once more), integrated collections are not narratives. But once we have seen how sequential relation may use the same elements that plot does without creating a plot, the issue is not so simple. All other characteristics of narrative are satisfied by integrated collections. I have avoided the standard example of theorists dealing with narrative in the English novel, Sterne's *Tristram Shandy,* omitting along with them a number of seventeenth-century works of considerable interest: some of Donne's sermons, (much of) Burton's *Anatomy of Melancholy,* (all of) Browne's *Hydriotaphia,* and Dryden's *Essay of Dramatick Poesy.* If these be narratives, as I believe they are, then plot is not as important as our instinctive reactions indicate.

If it can be assumed that minimal narrative, at least, need not have a plot but must be integrated in sequential continuance, then the kind of collections we are considering are narrative.[25] As a heuristic example, we may well consider in conclusion a special kind of Japanese example, linked poetry. In its two major kinds, *renga* and *haikai,* the "collection" is part of the act of composition—surely something that takes us yet closer to narrative as we conceive it.[26] Sometimes these sequences were written by a single poet, but multiple composition is far more typical. The poets composed stanzas in some agreed-on alternation so that they might compose an agreed-on number of stanzas, one hundred (or its multiples) being typical of *renga,* and the same or thirty-six being most typical of *haikai.* There were other set lengths varying from but two to forty-four. Sometimes they were composed over a period of days or months, but normally they were written at a single sitting. To avoid sheer randomness, the poets composed their stanzas according to an extraordinarily complex set of canons. The whole sequence was to have a three-part rhythm; sheets and their sides had certain rules (a moon stanza for each side, a flower stanza for each sheet, with formal and much manipulated places for each); topics (a season or nonseason, that is, "miscellaneous"), subtopics (love, travel, Buddhism); motifs, canons of four degrees of relation (close, close-distant, distant-close, and distant; or heavy, heavy-light, light-heavy, and light); standards of impressiveness although not exactly of quality (design,

design-ground, ground-design, and ground). There were criteria for continuing topics and discontinuing or suspending use of certain words. More might be said, but it is clear that with seeming randomness in quick composition (*renga* stanzas were typically composed, checked, and written down in three minutes or less), there were elaborate rules that might well take two decades to master. There can be, then, no question about the collective nature of these sequences, even if composed at a sitting, and equally no question about the integration of the result. The only further matter requiring emphasis is that plot is utterly infeasible. That is because, like a link of a chain touching only the one before and the one after, a given stanza has continuous semantic connection only with its predecessor, which is also to say by definition a connection with its successor.[27]

To clarify what is going on in the example chosen, stanzas from the *renga*, *A Hundred Stanzas by Three Poets at Minase* (spring, 1488), one may give the stanzas paired into the discrete units that they were conceived to be (earlier plus added stanza) with information about impressiveness, relation, topics, sub-topics and motifs (if any), along with brief commentary. For appreciation of the art, the reader should read the sequence twice, the first time paying attention to the commentary and the second solely to the stanzas (or their translations). Stanza 76—the first two lines given—was composed by Shōhaku, who composed a Ground-Design stanza of Close-Distant relation to stanza 75 (not given). Although there are overtones of Summer in his stanza, no word justifies such specification, so the stanza is Miscellaneous (not on a season). There is a Plants motif.

	Uenu kusaba no	Shrubs never cultivated by the owner
	shigeki shiba no to	stand thick by the wattled door
77	katawara ni	in that vicinity
	kakiho no arata	the overgrown field by the hedgerow
	kaeshi sute	covers the neglected hoe

Sōchō
77 Ground. Close. Spring. Residences.
It is a fine stanza of close relation that yet gives development. "Kakiho" (hedgerow) refers to plants growing atop a fence or earthen wall or some other barrier enclosing the garden of the house. "Kaeshi" is a large hoe for digging in lieu of plowing.

    Katawara ni   In that vicinity
  kakiho no arata   the overgrown field by the hedgerow
    kaeshi sute   covers the neglected hoe

	yuku hito kasumu	the traveler returns drifting in haze
78	ame no kuregata	brought by twilight in light rain
	Sōgi	

78 Design. Distant-Close. Spring. Persons. Rising and Falling Things.
This magnificent stanza is superbly led up to by 77. There is some connection with 77, as if the person here is the long-gone farmer of 77. Haze rises, rain falls; the light fades as the person comes by. So the third sheet concludes.

	Yuku hito kasumu	The passer-by drifts off in haze
	ame no kuregata	brought by twilight in light rain
79	yadori sen	where can one lodge
	no o uguisu ya	unguided by the warbler on a moor
	itou ran	that it dislikes
	Sōchō	

79 Ground Design. Close-Distant. Spring. Birds.
Whether the warbler has left or is there but does not sing cannot be told, but warblers often fail to sing when desired. This is one of Sōchō's poorer stanzas. The poem recalled (*Shinkokinshū*, 1:82) is embarrassingly fine and makes comparison awkward.

	Yadori sen	Where shall I lodge
	no o uguisu ya	unguided by the warbler on a moor
	itou ran	that it dislikes
80	sayo mo shizuka ni	even the brief night holds stillness
	sakura saku kage	and cherries blossoming in dim forms
	Shōhaku	

80 Design-Ground. Distant-Close. Spring. Night. Trees.
"Sayo" (brief night) is a poetic diminutive, here for a brief night in spring, when the flowers are seen more by imagination than by eyes. The stanza relates to 79 by virtue of the assumption that one would like to lodge for the night beneath flowering boughs. This rivals Sōgi's skill in connecting stanzas. This is not a Flower stanza, because the flower is named, not simple "*hana.*"

	Sayo mo shizuka ni	Even the brief night holds stillness
	sakura saku kage	and cherries blossoming in dim forms
81	toboshibi o	with the lamp dimmed
	somukuru hana ni	the blossoms grown paler in the dark
	akesomete	take on the tint of dawn
	Sōgi	

81 Design. Close-Distant. Spring. Night. Cultivation.
Sōgi shifts the scene from a large to a smaller. To see outside better, the speaker dims the lamp, as in a line by Po Chü-i.

	Toboshibi o	With my lamp dimmed
	somokuru hana ni	the blossoms grown paler in the dark
	akesomete	take on the tint of dawn
82	taga tamakura ni	on whose arm was I pillowed
	yume wa mieken	when that lovely dream appeared
	Sōchō	

82 Design. Close-Distant. Miscellaneous. Love. Persons.
The man recalls the beauty of that love and his pillowing his head on her arm, with the flowers of 81 part of the distant time that now is a dream.

	Taga tamakura ni	On whose arm was I pillowed
	yume wa mieken	when that lovely dream appeared
83	chigiri haya	he keeps on breaking
	omoitaetsutsu	all the vows of love he promised
	toshi mo hen	and my long years pass
	Shōhaku	

83 Ground-Design. Distant-Close. Miscellaneous. Love.
Years pass. Now the woman of the dream of 82 recalls the man and his inconstancy. The lament is timeless in Japanese conceptions of the anguish of the abandoned woman.

This run of stanzas raises a question that seems unfamiliar: can there be a collection composed by poets working together at a sitting? Once again, the answer is hard to decide. But we may recall our central distinction between an integrated collection and a single work: the individual units of a collection are separable integers. It must be conceded that the integers of Japanese linked poetry are *not* entirely separable. But to repeat, they share with the poems of an integrated collection this degree of separation: no stanza is related to any other than the two that make it a poetic unit, the predecessor and successor. If stanzas 27 and 64 happen to concern a lover gazing at the moon as it rises over autumn hills, there is *no* semantic connection. A Western reader may read the sequence so, as a reader may ignore rhyme, fail to recognize a character who reappears, or read chapters in backward order. These things can be done, but they are not the suppositions of the poet.

None of the arguments advanced here is fully clear, fully conclusive. I can only hope that the grounds of my understanding them has been made fully evident. If I am close to being right, then we may posit that, although plot is usual in narrative, it is not necessary to it, and integrated collections are plotless narratives. Sequential continuousness (that is not redundant) is in any event a radical prior to plot in narrative. And the principles of that continuousness are beginnings and endings (in addition to *the* beginning and ending) that are separated-joined by continuances (as opposed to *the* continuousness). Further principles include progression, recurrence, and varying relation between the units of a collection (or plotted narration). The principles are cognitive in being knowable and mentally usable, determining the relatable continuity of elements cognitively apprehensible for their what-ness: *specific* versions of people, times, places, and causalities. The difference between plotted and nonplotted versions of narrative are illustrated by collections, in which the individual constitutive elements may also stand alone as integral lyrics, narratives, or dramatic entities.[28] These theses will need testing by a wider variety of evidence than that used here, even if the variety has been greater than usual in discussions of integrated collections or even of narrative. At a minimum, it should be clear what fruitful evidence is supplied for narrative and other kinds of literary theory by the evidence available from integrated collections in different periods and cultures.

NOTES

1. Those interested in integrated collections should consult the classic article by Jin'ichi Konishi, "Association and Progression: Principles of Integration in Anthologies and Sequences of Japanese Court Poetry, A.D. 900–1350," *Harvard Journal of Asiatic Studies* 21 (1958): 67–127.

2. Louis L. Martz, *The Poetry of Meditation* (New Haven: Yale University Press, 1954), pp. 280–320.

3. Earl Miner, *The Metaphysical Mode from Donne to Cowley* (Princeton: Princeton University Press, 1969), pp. 232–45.

4. At almost the same time, the late Judith Sloman and I individually discovered the integration of *Fables*. My first version appeared in Chapter 8 of *Dryden's Poetry* (Bloomington: Indiana University Press, 1967) and hers as "The Structure of Dryden's *Fables*," Ph.D. diss., University of Minnesota, 1968. See also her "Interpretation of Dryden's *Fables*," *Eighteenth-Century Studies* 4 (1971): 199–211. I added a few things in *Writers and Their Background: John Dryden* (London: G. Bell & Sons Ltd, 1972), pp. 259-66; and more particularly in *The Restoration Mode from Milton to Dryden* (Princeton: Princeton University Press, 1974), pp. 541-57. For other studies, see David J. Latt and Samuel Holt Monk, *John Dryden: A Survey and Bibliography of Critical Studies, 1895-1974* (Minneapolis: University of Minnesota Press, 1976). Judy Sloman's posthumous *Dryden: The Poetics of Translation* (Toronto: University of Toronto Press, 1985), edited by Anne Mc-

Whir, in part concerns Dryden's integrative methods and is an excellent study; she also left a collection of essays on Dryden's late poetry that will now be edited by Reginald Berry, with contributions by her, him, Mary E. Devine, and possibly others besides myself on *Fables*. Among the other studies there is a fine one by James D. Garrison, "The Universe of Dryden's *Fables*," *Studies in English Literature* 2 (1981): 409–23, which may be examined for citations of other recent work.

5. Sloman and I often discussed integration of Dryden's collections. I suggested to her that *Sylvae* was integrated, and in the posthumous book mentioned in note 4 she shows that she had studied the matter more deeply than I.

6. Because it is in my commentary in H. T. Swedenberg, Jr., et al., *The Works of John Dryden* (Berkeley and Los Angeles: University of California Press, 1969), 3:276–86.

7. Numerous studies have been made of the ordering of Jonson's *Epigrams* and *The Forrest*. Those familiar to me deal either with the very important and pleasurable alternation of satiric and panegyric poems in the former or with proportional or numerological structures in the collections. Neither procedure seems to me to yield integration, but rather ordering. On proportional and numerological structures of various kinds in English renaissance literature see: A. Kent Hieatt, *Short Time's Endless Monument: the Symbolism of Numbers in Spenser's Epithalamium* (New York: Columbia University Press, 1960); Maren-Sofie Røstvig, *The Hidden Sense* (Oslo: Universitets Forlaget, 1963), essays by herself and others; and Røstvig's *Fair Forms* (Cambridge: Cambridge University Press, 1975); also Alastair Fowler, *Spenser and the Numbers of Time* (London: Routledge, 1964); *Silent Poetry: Essays in Numerological Analysis* (New York: Barnes & Noble, 1970); and *Triumphal Forms: Structural Patterns in Elizabethan Poetry* (Cambridge: Cambridge University Press, 1970). Some of the studies seem rather rarified to the innumerate critic, but I think everyone finds Hieatt's work convincing (although it does not deal with a collection). And those collections with temporal numerical schemes such as the calendrical clearly are integrated.

8. This point, with others relevant here (Greek, Roman, Chinese collections; theoretical concerns; analysis; ideological implications of Japanese collections; and social concepts of self and group) are dealt with in "The Collective and the Individual: [Japanese] Literary Practice and Social Implications," in Earl Miner, *Principles of Classical Japanese Literature* (Princeton: Princeton University Press, 1985), pp. 17–62.

9. See the article by Konishi, note 1. Also, by Robert H. Brower and me, *Japanese Court Poetry* (Stanford: Stanford University Press, 1961), pp. 319–29, 403–13.

10. They are *Superior Poems of Our Time*, eighty-three exemplary poems integrated into a sequence by Fujiwara Teika (1162–1241), translated and commented on by Brower and me (Stanford: Stanford University Press, 1967); and *Fujiwara Teika's Hundred-Poem Sequence of the Shōji Era, 1200* by Brower (Tokyo: Monumenta Nipponica, 1978). Brower is the leading Teika scholar outside Japan, and this represents his mature thought about, as well as translation of, one of the very most important sequences of Japanese poems (waka) written by a single person.

11. As I try to in "The Collective and the Individual."

12. Quintilian, *Institutes,* II, iv, 2 (Loeb trans. by H. E. Butler). See also Cicero, *De Inventione,* I, xix, and the pseudo-Ciceronian, long-influential *Ad C. Herrenium de Ratione Dicendi,* I, viii. Note that nothing is said of plot.

13. The glossary appears in volume 2, 295–305. The edition was published in two volumes in London by Dent in 1962 (Everyman Library). The words discussed can be more accurately followed in the *Oxford English Dictionary.* "Narration" as a literary matter is not clear as to date from the quotations, but it had appeared by 1586. "Narrative" is first cited in literary terms in 1725 (Pope, *Homer*), although there are earlier legal and historical usages. "Plot" in the modern sense appears in 1649 (Lovelace, of a play, Dryden's usual usage). "Relation" is unclear as to first appearance: Dryden offers examples unnoticed by the *OED* (but shown by Watson); and the *OED's* earliest clear instance, Milton's *Samson Agonistes,* was published in 1671, but its date of composition is uncertain. "Story" emerges for tale or narrative about 1500, although the prime meaning was still history; for story as plot, the *OED* cites a usage of 1725.

14. I have detailed this argument in "On the Genesis and Development of Literary Systems," *Critical Inquiry* 5 (1979): 339–53, 553–68; one point is that without conceptions of drama, lyric, and narrative (though they need not be termed genres), a wide range of historical evidence from different cultures cannot be readily explained. The unusually early emergence of esteemed prose narrative in Japan makes Japanese evidence the best surrogate for a poetic system founded on encounter with narrative.

15. See Dore Jesse Levy, "A Study of Chinese Narrative Poetry from the Late Han through T'ang Dynasties," Ph.D. diss., Princeton University, 1982, chap. 2.

16. According to the *OED,* Dryden is the first to use "biography" in English; it is significant that he terms it one of three kinds of history: see Watson, *Of Dramatic Poesy,* 2:8.

17. Which is important to me (n. 14) and to a Marxist of whatever degree, as it is to Michel Foucault. But it is plain as daylight that others hold far more nominalist positions today.

18. Ralph Freedman, *The Lyrical Novel* (Princeton: Princeton University Press, 1963). It is significant that a book written with modern Western European fiction in mind should seem so appropriate to students of Japanese and Chinese narrative.

19. Hobbes is characteristically clear in his "Answer to Davenant's Preface to *Gondibert,*" J. E. Spingarn, ed., *Critical Essays of the Seventeenth Century,* 3 vols., repr. ed. (Bloomington: Indiana University Press, 1957), 2:55.

20. I stay here with poetry to avoid the contentious issues of whether there is a separate genre or mode of "prose." Earlier English evidence includes "literary" essays, sermons, and epistles dedicatory; long before them there was the Chinese *fu* (rhyme-prose, rhapsody) and Japanese *zuihitsu* (prose miscellany).

21. See, with the many references the articles provide, three essays in *Arethusa* 13 (1980): John Van Sickle, "The Book-Roll and Some Conventions of the Poetic Book," pp. 5–41; Matthew S. Santirocco, "Horace's *Odes* and the Ancient Poetry Book," pp. 43–57; and J. E. G. Zetzel, "Horace's *Liber Sermonvm:* The Structure of Am-

biguity," pp. 59–77. The essays are assessed and put in context with other points related to those here in the essay cited in note 8.

22. Of course it does not exclude drama, either. I have been presuming that the represented character of drama is its differentia, distinguishing it more from lyric and narrative than they are from each other, so requiring features of the discussion here. But see note 28, below.

23. Digression is a traditional part of narrative, and asymmetry a Japanese aesthetic ideal.

24. See Robert Bernard Martin, *Tennyson* (New York: Oxford University Press, 1980), pp. 341–43.

25. Collections arranged by chronology and similar procedures are ordered but not integrated in the senses used here, and their narrative character, if any, is altogether exiguous without further in the way of integration.

26. Various features of Japanese linked poetry are discussed, with examples translated and commented on by me, *Japanese Linked Poetry* (Princeton: Princeton University Press, 1979); and by me and Hiroko Odagiri, *The Monkey's Straw Raincoat and Other Haikai of the Bashō School* (Princeton: Princeton University Press, 1981). As this is written, these are the only books in English treating rules and theories of linked poetry, pending Steven D. Carter's revision of his Berkeley thesis. See also Konishi Jin'ichi (the surname is Konishi, but the usage for his name varies in this country), "The Art of Renga," a translation by Karen Brazell and Lewis Cook of sections of Konishi's discussion of that art in his *Sōgi* (Tokyo: Chikuma Shobō, 1971). Their work emphasizes things mine does not, although my work is greatly indebted to Konishi. (Carter follows another line and so is very valuable.) The example of *renga* quoted below is taken from the earlier book, pp. 214–17, although redone typographically and with some other changes.

27. The decorum of *haikai* being lower than that of *renga*, there are some occasions when there is definite echo: to my knowledge solely of beginnings and endings in a given work or within a given sequence or collection.

28. The importance of collections in Japan has been alluded to and mention of drama provides an opportunity for an example. Formerly five *nō* were performed on a given occasion, and they had to conform to the same *jo-ha-kyū* rhythm that *renga* had taken over from court music: that is, the first *nō* provided the stately "introduction" (*jo*), and the fifth the "fast close" (*kyū*); the middle three pieces made up the "breaking" or agitated "development" (*ha*); and a day's performance was an integrated collection. Each *nō* also possesses the *jo-ha-kyū* rhythm.

William S. Anderson
The Theory and Practice of Poetic Arrangement from Vergil to Ovid

Shortly after Augustine took up his post as professor of rhetoric in Milan in 382, he came into contact with Bishop Ambrose. Although Ambrose's influence on Augustine's eventual conversion to Christianity must be the dominant factor of their relationship, I am interested here in a few details that Augustine registers in passing, with amazement, about the bishop. When he and others would go in to talk with Ambrose, they would find him reading. Nobody interfered with them as they approached, but they were daunted by the sight of a man reading silently, and, after watching him a while in his silent activity, they departed. None of them was so bold as to dare to annoy a man so intent. "When he read," says Augustine as of an unusual practice, "his eyes moved through the pages and his heart worked out the meaning, but his voice and tongue were silent."[1] For Augustine as late as the fourth century, it was a novelty to find someone reading silently: he expected the bishop to read aloud. That would have been a surprise four hundred years earlier, in the time of Augustus, but equally amazing would have been the reading materials available to the bishop. Ambrose was silently following the writing down each page, then turning the page and continuing: he was, in short, reading a book, no doubt a parchment codex of the Bible or a commentary on some part of it. Thus, Ambrose was reading very much as we do today, but he was one important stage ahead of Augustine in reading silently, another vital stage ahead of the Latin poets and audiences that I am concerned with in this study, inasmuch as he enjoyed the advantage of a codex and pages, which could be turned easily in either direction.

The five poets whom I wish to discuss, Vergil, Horace, Tibullus, Propertius, and Ovid, in the half-century dominated by the Emperor Augustus, between roughly 36 B.C. and 14 A.D., published collections of their poems, not in books such as we use, but in successive columns on long papyrus sheets that were rolled up into scrolls.² I do not know how to estimate the importance of reading aloud upon the capacity of the reader to be aware of subtle schemes of arrangement, but I am inclined to believe that, because reading aloud is a slower process than reading silently, a reader might appreciate relationships among several continuous poems but might not recall an earlier passage seen and pronounced two hours ago or even a day or so previously. However, the negative effects of coping with a papyrus roll are more obvious. We today flip back through the pages to check on some vague recollection or to discover some correlation that we desiderate for an artful scheme of arrangement in, say, Jonson or Donne. The Roman reader of Vergil or Horace had to go through the cumbrous process of unrolling what he had already rolled onto one scroll and rolling it back on the second scroll in order to check each of his suspected echoes and interconnections. The simple fact of publication in the form of papyrus rolls tends to put a damper on elaborate schemes of poetic arrangement, as beyond the capacity of most Augustan readers to appreciate and probably beyond the interest of most Augustan poets to design.

The facts of papyrus publication on scrolls act as one important limitation on any theory of poetic arrangement in Augustan times. A second limitation arises from the absence of secondary data: we possess no comments on arrangement from any of the five poets (except Ovid) or their readers or ancient critics and scholars; we of course lack notebooks and original manuscripts that might provide clues to arrangement; and no ancient writer discussed arrangement except in the simplest terms of chronology and casual collections. Thus, we are obliged to treat the collections themselves as our primary and almost sole data and to evolve our theory in strict relation to Augustan practices. The better our theory corresponds to those practices, the more likely it is that we have approximated the actual theory that governed the planning of the poets from Vergil to Ovid.

I have stated above that Ovid alone comments on the factors that affect arrangement of his poems. Coming as he does at the end of this line of five talented and sophisticated Roman poets, Ovid should have been in the position of epitomizing the Art of Arrangement if anyone could. Alas, what he says proves a serious disappointment:

> denique materiam cum quis sibi finxerit ipse,
>   arbitrio variat multa poeta suo:
> Musa mea est index nimium quoque vera malorum,
>   atque incorrupti pondera testis habet.

> nec liber ut fieret, sed uti sua cuique daretur
> littera, propositum curaque nostra fuit.
> postmodo collectas, utcumque sine ordine, iunxi:
> hoc opus electum ne mihi forte putes.
> (*Epistulae ex Ponto* 3.9.47–54)

Finally, when someone invents his own subject-matter, the poet can vary many things according to his own judgement: my Muse is the all-too-honest witness of my misfortunes, and she has the weight of an absolutely uncorrupted informant. Besides, it was not my purpose nor my concern that a book be produced, but that each addressee receive an appropriate letter. When I subsequently collected these letters, I joined them randomly without order: do not think that selection went into this opus.

These lines come from the conclusion of the final poem in the last collection that Ovid lived to publish, in A.D. 13. As such, they aim to influence the reader's attitude; what they say about arrangement, whether somewhat disingenuous and exaggerated or not, fits in with Ovid's more general thematic stress on the special nature of his existence and the poetry he writes about it. Composing in exile on the unfriendly coast of the Black Sea, among an uncivilized people who do not even know Latin, let alone the charm of Ovidian verse, he has not been able to exercise free poetic invention—his troubles have been too oppressively present—and he has not tried to do so, because he has been writing to communicate the sense of his misfortunes and, he hopes, end his exile from beloved Rome. Thus, whereas the creative poet, working freely with his subject, can exploit the pleasure of deliberate variety, Ovid must pay the price of truth: he realizes that his undifferentiated tale of woe is monotonous. In these four lines (47–50), Ovid seems to refer to one theoretical factor that affects poetic organization: variety (*varietas*). Poets and audiences expect poems to exhibit some diversity: different subjects, different tones, different techniques of presentations, etc. In arranging a collection, the average poet would explore the several possibilities of *varietas*. Ovid continues in lines 51 and following by saying that he had no intention originally to produce a book of poems; he was writing functional letters. Thus, the letters just accumulated, and he finally put them together in random order, indeed without any order, he claims. The book and its shape are accidental results; what counts is the individual letter, the desperate effort by Ovid far away among the barbarians to communicate with his former friends in Rome, to bridge the physical distance and the psychological chasm that has been created by the political nature of his exile, a punishment personally ordered by Augustus. Here, then, we find some additional implicit factors in book arrangement. Other poets, who enjoy freer circumstances, produce poems that they expect to employ in a book, and therefore the individual poem is affected by, and itself affects, the growing sense of design they entertain of the future book as the poems accumulate, their themes and images intersect, and certain voices and ideas seem to dominate. The idea of the book modifies some of the poems at the writing stage. But then, when a sufficient number of poems has accumulated, the idea of the book can also determine the final contents as well as the arrangement of the poems. A normal book of poetry should have some order, some kind of arrangement that can be appreciated by readers as an enhancement of the separate poems. Ovid has had to forgo these advantages, and he appeals to his audience's sympathy for the unusual circumstances of exile that supposedly determine the very special quality of his book, his "unordered" collection.

It is not my purpose to expose the inaccuracies and tendentiousness of Ovid's claims for his own poetry so much as to make use of the theoretical material that he has presented in order to create an effective antithesis. I hardly need to observe that a letter in verse tends to weaken the claim to immediate, truthful communication. Others have already sketched out some ingenious principles of arrangement here.[3] So let me turn back from A.D. 13 and Ovid's last publication to the earlier Augustan poetry books to see how adequately the theories broached by Ovid fit their arrangement. We should expect a purposefully shaped book, which suggests some selectivity by the poet and some effort to consult the principle of *varietas*. Do we in fact find such books from the time of Vergil; are there other important principles that Ovid has failed to mention?

All students of Augustan arrangement agree that all the poets took cognizance of variety.[4] In the earliest surviving book, Vergil's *Eclogues,* it is obvious that the poet avoided repeating his subjects and presentational devices in adjacent poems. In fact, scholars have often claimed that he alternated his methods: Eclogues 1, 3, 5, 7, and 9 can be described as dialogues or mimes or poems in which the characters speak for themselves, as opposed to 2, 4, 6, 8, and 10, where Vergil used monologues or narratives or let the pastoral poet dominate.[5] None of the poems has the same length. Otis classifies Eclogues 2, 3, 7, and 8 as "fully Theocritean poems"; 1, 4, 6, and 9 as "non-Theocritean"; and 5 and 10 as Theocritean "with a specifically Roman, contemporary bearing."[6] Such a classification contributes to a different scheme of *varietas* in which the non-Theocritean poems frame pairs of Theocritean, and the Roman-Theocritean punctuate middle and end of the collection.

Horace's first book of *Satires* was published in 35 B.C., shortly after the *Eclogues*. It contains ten poems, too, but uses different kinds of *varietas*, not simple alternation nor continuous by-play with Horace's great predecessor Lucilius. There is no system of "Lucilian" and "non-Lucilian" satires. Instead, Horace groups his poems in triads: 1–3, 4–6, 7–9, plus a concluding programmatic poem (10). In the first three, we find an examination of a moral issue (avarice, sexual desire, friendly tolerance) in the loose manner of street-preaching or diatribe. The second triad pushes forward the character of the satirist (Horace) and his conscious principles of satiric poetry, their agreement and disagreement with the conventions associated with Lucilius. The satirist talks in the first person about himself and his strong views on literary matters; instead of Lucilius as his main inspiration, he honors his father, a lowly freedman. Then, in Satires 7, 8, and 9 he examines some narrative situations in which a character, weak, inoffensive, and somewhat comic, suffers attack and/or embarrassment from a comically malign person. The weak character, with whom we are made to sympathize—once, in Satire 9, it is Horace himself—manages to extricate himself from his "peril," not by strength or violent anger, but by his very weakness, in a humorous surprise. The dissolution of a tense conflict of personalities by comic weakness seems to be part of Horace's satiric program, and he summarizes his position in the emphatic final poem, Satire 10.[7] Still different methods of *varietas* characterize the book of ten elegies that Tibullus published a few years later.[8]

So far, I have discussed the diverse possibilities of *varietas* exhibited by three collections of ten poems, each in uniform meters. When the poet employs lyric meters, he has an added criterion for variety in the different meters he uses. Horace exhibits this criterion at work in his early collection of *Epodes*, then far more elegantly in his mature *Odes*. The *Epodes* consist of seventeen poems. In arranging them, Horace decided to group the first ten as a decade of metrically identical verse (each epode alternating iambic trimeter and dimeter) in highly diverse manners, then to display metrical as well as thematic virtuosity in the second group of seven.[9] Later, when he published his *Odes* in 23 B.C., Horace decided to issue three books of quite different proportions (thirty-eight, twenty, and thirty poems respectively) together, framing the other eighty-six poems with a pair, 1.1

and 3.30, in a meter used only for these occasions and calling attention to his exalted status as a lyric poet in the Greek tradition. Each book starts off ostentatiously with a significant metrical and thematic group. Opening the collection in book 1, Horace parades his virtuosity in nine different meters; nowhere else does he show such *varietas*. In book 2 he alternates his meters, Alcaics and Sapphics, through eleven poems, then finally introduces a new meter and considers his lyric subject matter in 2.12. To take quite a diverse tack, Horace groups six powerful poems, all in the same Alcaic stanzaic pattern, at the start of book 3; these avoid the light topics of love, drinking, and seizing the pleasant moment, which otherwise are repeatedly planted throughout the three books, and instead concentrate on the great themes of Augustan politics. Hence, they act as an emphatic unit, usually called the Roman Odes, amid the diversity; nowhere else does Horace repeat his meters and topics this way.[10]

Nobody, then, would challenge the existence of an ordering principle of *varietas*. However, a great number of scholars have been dissatisfied with mere variety and sought some more elaborate systems, without the support of Ovid or any other ancient commentator, which would go beyond small pairs or triads or metrical groups and present an aesthetically satisfying account of all the poems in a collection. Here is where controversy rages, for what one scholar passionately advances as a reasonable and aesthetically valid scheme of arrangement, inasmuch as it lacks ancient authority and rests on an individual preference and analysis of the collection, often strikes another scholar as simply preposterous. Basically, the schemes fall into two main types: in the first, a collection seems to be organized around a center, with the poems on either side linked by certain correspondences, so that the whole collection presents a pleasing impression of symmetry focused on a central poem or section; in the second, the collection seems to illustrate a thematic and/or dramatic progress in a linear direction from the first to the final poem and produces in readers a pleasing impression of complex but steady development.

Let us start with the theory of symmetrical arrangement. We should ask two questions of it: (1) Do the alleged instances of symmetrically disposed poems actually convince us? (2) Is symmetry an apprehensible and satisfactory aesthetic experience for a reader, as it is for one who looks at a picture or a building or listens to a complex piece of music? For symmetry, classical scholars put forward as their most triumphant examples two collections: Vergil's *Eclogues* (once again) and book 1 of Propertius's *Elegies*. Indeed, some of the same scholars have worked and written on such books. Let me review their data.

For a century now, the supposed symmetry of Vergil's book has received ever sharper definition.[11] Removing Eclogue 10 from consideration or treating it as a separable conclusion, many believe that Vergil organized the remaining nine poems as two groups of corresponding fours focused on the central Eclogue 5. It is obvious that Eclogues 1 and 9 deal with dispossession from the precious pastoral world; Eclogues 2 and 8 might be reduced to topics of love; Eclogues 3 and 7 feature song contests (though not about really similar themes); and Eclogues 4 and 6 are said to focus on revelation of the future (the royal baby's destiny in 4) and of the past (the mythology of the universe in 6). Those who are predisposed toward symmetry may find this scheme automatically attractive, whereas those who incline otherwise will find that these different kinds of "correspersion" (thematic, formal shape, and antithetical uses of a narrative device) seem dubious and, on closer inspection of the pairs, will decide that the brief précis used to establish corresponsion distorts the shape of individual poems.

To sharpen the analysis of corresponsion and symmetry, it is now useful to conjure with numbers. The block of Eclogues 1–4 exhibits a surprising numerical correspondence to Eclogues 6–9: 330 against 331 total verses. Moreover, if we add the total lines of the corresponding paired poems, we get another symmetry: 150 (Eclogues 1 + 9), 181 (Eclogues 2 + 7), 181 (Eclogues 3 + 6), and 149 (Eclogues 4 +6). To the "discoverer" of these numbers, they assumed a kind of mystical significance.[12] And he yielded to the temptation to improve them by hypothesizing that Vergil really sought the magical sum of 333, that hence somewhere in Eclogues 6–9 three verses had been lost, in Eclogues 1–4 two. More recently, the tendency has been to reject the hypothetical 333 as a desideratum but to assume that a good textual critic can find a place (not agreed upon as yet) where either a line might be added or another where one could be subtracted, to the great improvement of the text and the creation of absolute numerical corresponsion between the two groups of four poems.

Numbers in elaborate diagrams seem very impressive, but, when we ask why we or Vergil or his audience should add the total lines of distant poems and what the sum signifies, we must hesitate. It is not as though the line numbers of Eclogues 1 and 9 (83 + 67) correspond or those of 4 and 6 (63 + 86); only their sums come close to being identical. To demonstrate how meaningless the pursuit of such sums may be, I note that, adding the total verses of Eclogues 1 and 2 (83 and 73) and 6 and 7 (86 +70), we get the identical totals of 156; then 3 + 4 (111 + 63) and 8 + 9 (108 + 67) give the near-identical totals of 174 and 175. The numbers now suggest a "significant" corresponsion between adjacent pairs in the two tetrads around Eclogue 5. Worse still, we can do the same thing with Eclogues 1 and 3 (83 + 111) and 6 and 8 (86 + 108), which gives 194 each time, and 2 and 4 (73 + 63) and 7 and 9 (70 + 67), which gives 136 and 137. These astounding numbers prove close corresponsion among alternate pairs. In short, to make this *reductio ad absurdum* absolutely clear, we can conjure three contradictory systems of corresponsions by resorting to the irrational procedure of adding the verses of pairs of poems. Numbers have aesthetically pleasing properties for many people, but I doubt the effects attributed by Classical numerologists to these sums.

One last example of numerology connected with the *Eclogues* seems at first thought more poetically useful. Van Sickle argued that Eclogues 1–4 were given a numerical relationship, in that Vergil used the common factor of 63 verses in all of them.[13] What exactly does he mean? Well, Eclogue 4 contains a total of 63 verses. The others all have more than that, but each exhibits some sort of unit that comes to 63. That is, in Eclogue 1, we might resolve its 83 verses into 5 + 5 + 63 + 5 + 5, since the opening two speeches cover five lines each and the final ten lines consist of part of one speech and Tityrus's final comment of five lines. Unfortunately, that produces a highly arbitrary unit of 63 verses despite the seeming attraction of the symmetrical frame. In a similar manner, Van Sickle takes the 73 verses of Eclogue 2 and quickly produces a framing pair of five lines for 63, which seems cogent only so long as one studies the mere numbers and ignores Vergil's poem. Vergil gave a five-line narrative introduction to a monologue of 68 verses; it is hardly licit to break off the end of Corydon's speech and call it a part of the symmetrical frame. Even less persuasive is the analysis of Eclogue 3: its 111 lines consist of 48 verses in amoebean contest (60–107), and the "surrounding frame, a number of verses that Vergil was free to calculate for his own devices, proves to be 63 lines in length."[14] True, Vergil was free to calculate it, but I doubt that his devices were close to what Van Sickle implies; the "frame" is much more than what we have been asked to accept for Eclogues 1 and 2: it involves a long, important opening section of 59 verses that no doubt outweighs the significance of the shorter amoebean contest, then the final four lines in which the judge Palaemon refuses to award victory to either of the equally matched contestants. Since these units of 63 verses in Eclogues 1–4 fail to convince as meaningful organizing parts of their poems, it seems necessary to conclude that, even if Vergil's audience could have appreciated these esoteric figures—a supposition that I shall hereafter dispute—Vergil did not compose by 63s any more than he did by massive corresponsions over a whole book of 828 verses. The evidence for significant numerology is not adequate.

Now, let us briefly turn to the supposed numerical symmetry of Propertius's book 1. As the manuscripts transmit it to us, this book consists of twenty-two elegies. Skutsch and Otis together have developed the analysis of the book that goes as follows.[15] Elegy 20 is anomalous, a short mythological epyllion that lacks the personal amatory connection with Propertius's own love affair, so it can be ignored. Also to be omitted from consideration are Elegies 21 and 22, which can be categorized as autobiographical and funereal, not strictly related to the themes and characters of the rest of the book. Taking the nineteen other poems, we transform them to a round and divisible twenty by dividing Elegy 8 into two separate but related poems. Elegies 6 through 14 exhibit certain correspsonsions: for example, around 8A and 8B stand 7 and 9, both addressed to Ponticus in contrasting and clearly connected situations; Propertius addresses Elegies 10 and 13 to Gallus, 6 and 14 to Tullus; and there are thematic connections between the adjacent pair 11 and 12. Skutsch then concluded that Elegies 6 through 14 should be read as two corresponding pentads. (A more accurate description would have been to note two similarly organized tetrads, a pair defined by the same addressee framing a juxtaposed pair that deals with two related phases of Propertius's love affair, and both tetrads framed by a pair of poems addressed to Tullus.) Without paying much attention to the organization of Elegies 1–5 and 15–19, Skutsch proceeded to outline the tempting argument for numerical symmetry. Elegies 1–5 possess a total of 89 couplets or distichs, and Elegies 15–19 a near-identical 88; the two, when added—again, why?—produce the sum of 177. Now, add Elegies 6–9 (71 distichs) to Elegies 10–14 (70), and, since that is not striking enough in its similarity, add the total distichs in Elegies 20–22 (a very convenient 36) to achieve another wonderful sum of 177. Q.E.D.

Otis devoted his attention to the pentads Elegies 1–5 and 15–19 with the intention of demonstrating what Skutsch had omitted, that they are organized symmetrically.[16] He argued that Elegies 1 and 19 corresponded because they constitute the first and last poems of the amatory cycle about Cynthia in the book. They provide a frame, within which 2 and 15, 3 and 16, 4 and 17, and lastly 5 and 18 have their own symmetry. Otis supported his claim by his familiar use of short epitomes (three or four words) of the topics of the elegies, and he introduced a second argument, namely, the similarity of what he called the stanzaic patterns. To take the most plausible of his connections, at least at first presentation, we are told that Elegies 4 and 17, which alike contain 28 verses, both concern Cynthia's beauty, and both are organized in stanzas of 10, 4, 10, and 4 lines, and that Elegies 5 and 18, both of 32 verses, take Cynthia's cruelty as their theme and use stanzas of 10, 12, and 10 verses alike. That seemingly exact corresponsion does not stand up to scrutiny; although 4 does have something to do with Cynthia's beauty (but also with her fiery temper and an interfering fool), 17 in no way deals with that topic, being focused on the lover's self-pitying loneliness and imagination of an unmourned death, nor do the stanzaic patterns convince when examined. The topics of Elegies 5 and 18 cannot be cogently simplified to that of Cynthia's cruelty, for the poems differ radically in dramatic situation, addressee, and argument, and their structures should probably be analyzed as different, not identical merely on the evidence of stanzaic length. If even the most likely seeming corresponsions falter, we hardly need to pause over the utterly unlikely comparison of Elegies 3 and 16: in no way should they be connected just because Cynthia sleeps through much of 3 as her lover steals into her room, whereas the lover is awake in 16 and locked out. Once again, then, even apart from the question as to whether the audience could appreciate such artful corresponsion, the data used to bolster the case for symmetry lack cogency. Subject matter really does not correspond, and the numbers used to conjure with, quixotic addition of lines and now similar stanzaic patterns, either possess no true significance or lack credibility.

It is time to face the second question: is symmetry on a massive book scale an apprehensible and significant aesthetic experience for a reader (as it is for one who views a picture or a building)? If we put it in these general terms, then we must of course answer in the affirmative; the very fact that some scholars advance the claims of symmetry with enthusiasm signifies their own personal affinity for such a scheme. Some modern readers even believe that symmetrical arrangement of poems in a book of 600 to 800 verses constitutes a high point of their aesthetic experience of the poetry. But we have no such testimony for ancient scholar-readers; I have questioned the data on which the claims for Vergilian and Propertian symmetry rest, and now we must investigate the basis of the aesthetic experience. In many studies of poetic arrangement, scholars move into metaphors such as "structure" and "architecture," which imply that reading a book involves the same aesthetic process as "reading" a building or a painting; as the ancients read aloud the poetry books, they took in with their eyes and ears the parts and the whole in the same way as one assimilates parts and whole of visual art. No doubt, the tendency to accept this identification of processes and the validity of architectural metaphors is bolstered—should I say aggravated?—by the elaborate diagrams that purport to lay out the organization of the books. Numbers and connecting lines imply that an architect has been at work on the poems, planning the parts and their functional contribution to the whole "structure." Inasmuch as the most majestical Classical building was the temple, we often hear that Vergil designed the *Eclogues* to be a "temple" honoring Julius Caesar, the person supposedly figured under the guise of the dead Daphnis of Eclogue 5. Similarly, in analyzing book 4 of Propertius, among whose 13 poems Elegy 6, on the Battle of Actium, can be viewed as the numerical "center," Grimal has resorted to the temple-image and argued for a symmetry designed to adore Augustus, victor at Actium.[17]

There are two obvious problems with the general architectural analogy and the specific temple-image: (1) The ancient reader, struggling to roll and unroll his papyrus, was not in the position of the modern scholar to experience or even guess at an elaborate architectural scheme. (2) Organizing a book is not like designing a temple, and reading a book of individual poems is not like appreciating a revered temple (or an exquisite painting or sculpture). To take the first point, we do know that poets emphatically began and ended their books, prominently placing what we call programmatic poems to state and summarize some of their dominant themes and to appeal, often with selected autobiographical details, to the audience. If one designates these initial and final poems, using a metaphor from painting, as a "frame," there is no serious harm done, as long as we realize that the metaphor has no connection with visual process. I would indeed be willing to concede that the diligent ancient reader would, if he/she so desired, be in the optimal position of checking repeated and varied themes with these terminal poems, for it would be easiest of all to roll right back to the beginning of the papyrus. However, when scholars claim some intricate numerical relationship between Vergil's Eclogues 2 and 8, for instance, which supposedly depends upon not only the apprehension of the numerical distance between the poems (600 lines) but also the conscious or unconscious addition of the lines in the two poems, then, apart from the (to me) apparent absurdity of this activity in any reader, I must doubt its very possibility in the Augustan Age.

The decisive point remains: a book is not a piece of visual art, most definitely not architecture like a temple, not a carefully designed and framed painting of, say, a battle or mythological event, not a sculptured group or single figure; reading a book of eclogues, satires, odes, or elegies requires a different kind of attention and produces a different aesthetic effect from viewing art works. Symmetry in a temple is a fact, but we can well ask whether the aesthetic effect precedes or derives from structural necessity. In any event, we know that the temple as a whole takes priority over the parts in the demands of the public, in the design of the architect, in the operations of the builder, in the experience of the worshipper and the appreciation of the aesthete. Sloppy approximations of unequal columns, for example, acquiescence and even ecstasy with corresponding parts that add up to a desired total when they grossly violate exact corresponsion, and numerous other structural irrationalities that crowd the diagrams of those who lay out the "architecture" of the Augustan poetry books, well, such features would be impermissible and incredible in the mind of an architect, sculptor, or painter, let alone in an ancient temple, statue, or wall painting. The temple and statue would quite literally collapse from the structural defects, and the painting would be ridiculous. Since the architect envisages the temple as a whole from the start, he can and must make the individual members correspond precisely, oblige them to serve the function of the whole without distraction. Although symmetry need not determine the structure of all buildings, statues, or paintings, it must, when employed, be exact.

Augustan Rome did not confine its aesthetic enjoyment to symmetrical order; it combined admiration for the symmetry of Classical Greek art and the asymmetry of Hellenistic art. Its sense of poetic order owed much to the un-Classical practices of the Neoteric generation of Catullus. Thus, whereas we can find good examples of symmetrical organization of individual poems or episodes in epic poetry among the Augustan writers, we can also find clear examples of asymmetry as early as Vergil, and the technique is thoroughly established in the practices of Ovid. We have no reason to attribute to Augustan poets and audiences an automatic regard for and expectation of symmetrical organization, especially of poetry books, which by the very nature of their being would resist such a system.

Although, to be sure, some collections of poems seem to be parts of a story or a thematic cycle that has been planned from the beginning, most collections have acquired their raison d'être and their organization almost accidentally, at different points in the creative process, after some, most, *or all* the individual poems have been written. The opposite extreme from meticulous preplanning of the book and each poem to be written for it would be the situation that Ovid, in the passage earlier cited, defines for his book of epistolary poems; he never planned any book but just collected the poems without any special order after they had all been written. Pliny says much the same thing about his prose letters: "I collected them without attention to their chronological order—for I was not composing history—but as each one came to hand."[18] Chronological order is the most natural system of arrangement, and, where writers have worked in some kind of notebook, it is the easiest to check. Most poets, however, avoid an order that depends simply upon the date of composition of the individual poems, and, wherever we can date Augustan poems, we find that strictly chronological arrangement has been ignored.

Let us assume, then, that neither of the extreme cases applies to Augustan collections of poetry: neither did the poet plan the book from the beginning and subordinate all the poems to the grand plan, nor did the poet decide to collect his poems into a book *after* they were all written, indifferent to any arrangement at all or merely setting them in the order of their composition. Between those extremes lies a wide area of possibilities. The idea of a book may have come to an ancient poet after he had composed about two hundred verses, that is, several eclogues, satires, elegies, or the like. Or it may have seized him at any later point, even after all the poems he would use had been written. In any case, the extant poems determine the original nature of the book, shape the idea embraced by the poet. But once he has his idea, the poet will continue to compose under its influence; and it is quite conceivable that he will return to the poems he has completed and revise them to fit his book-conception more aptly. The adherents of numerical symmetry find their opportunity here in the hypothetical period of revision, when, according to them, the poets padded certain poems and cut others in order to arrive at the desired number of lines that would contribute to mathematical symmetry.[19] Granted, a poet could use his revisions to such an end. Nevertheless, it seems a high price to pay for a very trivial goal to distort the shape of a poem by adding or subtracting lines merely to produce a set total of verses. I know of no poet who has revised his notebooks according to such a purpose, and I find it most unlikely that Vergil or Horace or Propertius ever did so, especially since the hypothetical products of mathematical symmetry prove, on inspection, to be delusory or insignificant.

I conclude that no Roman poet of the Augustan era composed his book on principles of mathematical symmetry, that no Roman reader would have demanded an organization of such senseless fussiness or been in the position to appreciate the systems that Classical scholars today have assigned to the *Bucolics* and Propertius. If I am right, then, we must look to the alternative method of organization: a collection that seems to illustrate a thematic and/or dramatic progress in a linear direction from the first to the final poem and produces in readers a pleasing impression of complex movement. In such a collection, instead of looking at themes and numbers in distant poems that correspond, we look at situations, themes, characters, and emotions in adjacent poems that link the poems and produce a sense of movement. I have spent much time on Vergil. Even though his *Eclogues* can be shown to move like this, let me use first Horace then Ovid as illustrations.[20]

When Horace decided to compose satires, he knew that he was working in a genre that had been brilliantly defined by Lucilius some eighty years earlier, and he wanted to keep and build on the best qualities of Lucilius, but to modify or entirely abandon certain techniques that he judged defective or dated or uncongenial to his own temperament. Thus, we can imagine Horace starting out to define his position as a follower and innovator of Lucilius in one of several ways, that is, as a satirist: he could write a programmatic satire and state clearly his critical appreciation of Lucilius, his new perception of the function of the genre, and his personal goals and methods—something like what we have in Satire 1.4; he could take a topic or situation that Lucilius had earlier exploited, with admitted success, and show how he, Horace, could do it better with his techniques—something like what we have in Satire 1.5; or he could write the kind of satire he really wanted to do, with no express reference to Lucilius, the result of which would be an implicit improvement on his predecessor in numerous significant aspects as exemplified in the poem—something like Satires 1.2 or 3. Now, we are pretty sure that 1.2 and 4 are among the earliest of the collection, that 1.3 and 5 were composed shortly after. The interesting thing is that, in the final arrangement, whichever of them he actually wrote first, Horace did not choose to place it first. The initial motivations to write and demonstrate his superiority to Lucilius became modified in the course of writing, no doubt partly as the result of success among his friends and a growing feeling of confidence in his abilities and new conception of satire.

The early Satires 1.2 and 3 took the form of poetic diatribes or popular sermons on the familiar topics of irrational sexual indulgence and harsh intolerance. At some point later—some believe as the latest poem of the collection—Horace wrote another poetic diatribe that now stands as the initial poem of book 1. It takes a moral issue that seems less sensational than sex, but more central to Roman concerns than intolerance toward friends: avarice and miserliness. Like the other two, it adopts a generally Epicurean attitude toward ethical issues and toward our goals in life: we should aim at rational moderation and a kind of happiness (*vita beata*) that is characterized not by heroic virtue and magnificent self-discipline but by an escape from pain, by modest possessions and friendship. It differs from Satires 2 and 3 in its greater stress on the goal of contentment, in its restricted use of the satirist (Horace) as an illustration, in its deliberate interruption of the ethical discussion to glance at the satirical technique of laughingly telling the truth (*ridentem dicere verum*, line 24), and in the emphatic opening address to Maecenas that constitutes a dedication. Placed together, Satires 1–3 introduce us to a poet-moralist who, while being deeply concerned with ethics, is also firmly committed to the careful technical demands of poetry and to the light touch of smiling wit. Under the guise of casual conversations, he manages to say a great deal, with considerable urbanity. Lucilius was never so brief or polished.

As I suggested above, Satire 4 may be one of the first satires that Horace composed, especially because he does not name Maecenas anywhere in it and seems very intent on defining his relationship polemically toward Lucilius. However, when it came to arranging the satires in a book, Horace wisely decided to make his introduction more modest and let the three ethical diatribes speak for him, before he inserted his programmatic poem and argued his superiority to Lucilius. There are some clear connections between Satires 3 and 4 that enhance this order. In Satire 3, the satirist weighed against intolerance the creative criticism of a true friend and the self-awareness that encourages one to overlook or attenuate the gravity of others' faults. Satire 4 assesses the techniques and goals of the Lucilian satirist, which involve outspoken, often intemperate and sensational personal attacks, and Horace attempts to put forward some modifications. While he acknowledges Lucilius as his master in the genre, he invokes his own father as the model for his ethical approach, which aims not at attacking and hurting others for the purpose of attracting attention to himself, but at modestly, impersonally using others' faults and virtues as examples (*documenta*) for self-improvement. As in Satire 3, Horace sets as one of his prime goals that of being a beloved friend (*dulcis amicis* 135; compare 3.69).

In Satire 5, Horace vies with Lucilius more patently than in any other poem. Lucilius had written a much longer poem, perhaps an entire book, concerning a long trip he took from Rome to Sicily, in which he focused amusingly on the rather trivial "adventures" he experienced en route and rendered them in mock-epic. He reported the daily mileage, it appears, the kinds of travel conditions, the pleasures and difficulties of food, and other mundane events, with appealing self-irony. But it was a very long poem, and it involved only the rather egoistic Lucilius. What Horace presents as an improvement on his model is the record of an arduous trip from Rome to Brundisium, succinctly reported, where he functions as a minor companion of some important politicians who are engaged in a critical piece of diplomatic negotiation to avert civil war. He functions as the "reporter" of this newsworthy expedition, and ironically he presents himself as so obtuse to current events and so preoccupied with his daily comforts that we laugh at him in our frustration. He fails utterly as a news reporter. He exposes himself and his inadequacies, his inability to live up to the Epicurean ideals. And yet, in his patent indifference to politics and the so-called "friendships" that such leaders as Antony and Octavian formed and broke, this clumsy satirist-reporter opts for a valid Epicurean goal, personal friendships, and actually achieves it. Amid all the physical discomforts of this long trip, his one continuous consolation is the warm association of such men as Vergil and Maecenas. Thus, this proves to be a shorter and much more complex travel-poem than that of Lucilius, embodying both the art and the favorite themes of Horace as we have come to perceive them in Satires 1–4.

Satire 4 had dealt at length with Horace's conception of satiric *libertas*, free speech, and introduced Horace's father as a non-Lucilian model for his methods and goals. In Satire 6, he analyzes what might be called social *libertas*, civic freedom and social position and their ethical ramifications, and again he introduces his father as a non-Lucilian model, indeed a model designed to shock the sensibilities of many a well-born Roman. Horace's father had been a slave, had in some way acquired his freedom before Horace's birth, and Horace himself had been born a free man, but afflicted with the social stigma of having an ex-slave (*libertinus*) as father. That placed him at a social disadvantage, which particularly rankled when he was scorned by men whom he knew to be inferior to himself in intelligence, culture, ethical commitment, and poetic talent. One important man did, however, recognize the merits of this ex-slave's son, and that was Maecenas. And looking back on the many snubs and blocked opportunities that he endured and the life he now leads as poet and friend of Maecenas, Horace paradoxically *credits* it to his admired father. The old boy, far from being the liability he seemed to others, has been the source of Horace's character, achievements, and the special kind of personal freedom (*libertas*) that allows him to present his daily existence as a model of modest Epicurean pleasure.

Satires 4–6, then, go very much together, with their considerable emphasis on the personal circumstances of the satirist and the role his father and humble background have played in his life. Satires 7–9 also form a group of a distinct kind. Each of them is a narrative about a personal conflict that might have resulted in violence but is resolved amid laughter. Horace avoids his opportunity to interpret the event, to intrude as the ethical judge and teacher, and he lets the narrative continue to the end, leaving it to the audience to draw the requisite lessons. But the lessons support the ethical themes of Satires 1–6 by negative illustration; anger between people accomplishes no good, and the best way to deal with an enemy is by the healing tactic of laughter or some comic effect that shows oneself to be harmless and simultaneously undermines the other's animosity. And that, after all, is the strategy of Horatian satire, to tell the truth with a laugh, a non-vindictive, painless, self-effacing laugh. Satire 7, possibly another very early one, records an event that Horace himself may have witnessed in 43 B.C. when he enlisted with Brutus and followed him to Asia Minor. But he says nothing about himself or the political situation, concentrating rather on the intemperate hostility of two low-born businessmen (symbolic equivalents of the high-born political rivals of the Civil War leading up to Philippi?) and its laughable conclusion. Satire 8 puts forward its own engaging narrator, a wooden statue of Priapus, the garden "scarecrow" of Roman times, who recounts his hostility toward some witches, intruders in his garden, and his "heroic" vengeance against them by means of a frightened fart. Their witchery so terrified him that he farted with fear, but that sudden crack of his woodwork in turn startled and routed the witches, much to the laughter of little, inoffensive Priapus and, he trusts, of his audience (*cum magno risuque iocoque,* line 50). Once again, laughter resolves a tense, grim, unpleasant situation, and the garden, which had for a while reverted to its sinister past association with corpses and witches, returns to its happy present loveliness (a condition it owes to Maecenas and the improvements that he has made to this property that he has purchased for his city mansion).

After the relative impersonality of Satire 7 and the fictitious narrator of Satire 8, Horace returns to dominate Satire 9, with a first-person account of a minor experience of his in the Roman Forum, which he constructs with self-irony into another fearful crisis (like Satire 8) with another comical resolution. As he was walking idly through the Forum, thinking about some poetry, a man approached him, forced his company on him, and was trying to use him to gain a hold on Maecenas when fortunately an opponent in a lawsuit appeared and dragged him off to court. In dealing with this ambitious, callous political climber, Horace shows himself to be appalled but helpless, comically so, inasmuch as he eventually escapes the man's clutches. Once again, Horace implies his apolitical ethical position, and once again he defines as his positive values friendship and poetry. It is because of the climber's commitment to political fighting that he falls victim to an earlier opponent at law, and helpless Horace escapes. But with considerable irony the happy satirist exclaims that, in his mind, he has been saved by Apollo (line 78). The god has appeared to rescue him like a Homeric hero, but the reason for Apollo's intrusion is not that he is a Homeric hero; his poetry has earned him escape.

These three narratives, Satires 7–9, have glanced at the central themes of the book from a special angle, without express argumentation either as diatribe or personal apologue. By concluding the triad with a personal experience, where innocent poet was matched unequally with political climber and yet ended up "master of the battlefield," Horace prepares for a new discussion of satiric poetry and his personal position among Roman poets. Satire 10 makes no attempt to correspond to Satire 1: it refers us expressly back to Satire 4 and its discussion of satire. In that earlier poem, Horace's main purpose had been to treat the ethical function of satire, that is, his tactics and goals of personal criticism. He had raised the question of whether and in what sense satire might be considered poetic but postponed a full discussion. Now, having demonstrated fully the modest Epicurean way in which he has moderated Lucilius's outspoken vituperation, as claimed in Satire 4, and having implicitly manifested the techniques that prove his superiority to Lucilius as a poet, Horace is ready to face that postponed question. Satire 10 reviews the ways in which Horace's art supersedes that of Lucilius, places him among the revolutionary generation of poets in the 30s who are modernizing the genres, one by one, and lists the men of approved taste who value his poetry.

I think that there can be little question that Horace has given careful thought to the order of his Satires and organized a book that makes sense of his definition of satire as a thoughtful combination of nondoctrinaire Epicurean ethics and of poetic techniques and purposes. Three interrelated groups of three poems expose us by different methods to the satirist as poet-moralist (or moralist-poet), and the final poem makes clear how confident and committed Horace the poet wishes to appear. Each group has a dominant motif, but it also repeats themes (such as friendship, living happily and modestly, avoidance of ambition) that occur throughout the collection, and each group shades nicely into the next. Here we meet one solid example of artful organization by linear progression.

Before his final publication, about A.D. 14, of the three books of *Letters from the Black Sea,* whose last poems' references to organizing principles I have discussed, Ovid published a collection of short love elegies, the *Amores,* and then, much later, books of *Sad Poems* (*Tristia*) from exile, in A.D. 8–12. Originally, as he tells us in a prefatory epigram, the *Amores* appeared as five books, but he subsequently decided to revise the collection and re-issue it in three. It might be interesting briefly to compare

Ovid's techniques of arrangement at the start and end of his career, keeping in mind the careful organization of linear progression that Horace utilized in book 1 of his *Satires*.

We might expect, since Ovid pruned his collection of *Amores* and reduced it to three books, that he would also have given it a very careful organization. Editors have managed to emend the manuscripts so that this edition consists of fifteen, twenty, and fifteen poems, but nothing can be made of this specious numerical symmetry.[21] It is evident that Ovid placed programmatic poems at the beginnings and ends of books 1 and 3 but avoids such a self-conscious frame for the love poems of book 2. He groups some elegies in pairs and achieves some very successful effects thereby, but that is a sporadic device, most frequently employed in book 2.[22] He names his beloved Corinna twice in book 1, three times in book 3, but regularly in book 2. He plays in three different ways with a triangular situation involving his *puella,* her "man" (*vir,* husband or current mate), and himself, one in each book, yet at no predictable position; and the device of repeated motifs/situations recurs nowhere else over the three books.

Evidently, Ovid did not aim at the tight organization we find in Horace. For one thing, variety was a valid principle in this love-elegy. He did not intend to chronicle the rise and fall of a passionate affair with a single woman named Corinna but to portray a kind of urbane lover seeking amusement freely among the many eligible women of Rome (presumably, talented prostitutes). So in book 1 Ovid puts his lover through his paces, exposing him to a variety of situations that gradually add up to a complex portrait of an urbane lover and of love. I personally do not feel that each poem is in a necessary, sequential progression; some of the poems could easily be moved to other positions within the programmatic frame. Nevertheless, the total variety does add up to something: a light-hearted lover whose moral qualities fail to elicit our admiration, whose love is fickle, dishonest, and self-serving, who tries to gain satisfaction from an environment where men and women dishonestly exploit each other and nobody remains faithful. By and large, this lover has better success with himself, his women, and us in his audience in book 1 than in the next two; and thus we may detect a second principle beyond *varietas* in the organization of the collection: a certain dramatic progression. The long book 2 begins to undermine the urbane lover and his poetic pride; he has few successes to dramatize but many failures, much unhappiness, jealousy, and suspicion. The paired poems, especially 2.7 and 8, 13 and 14, reveal the nasty selfishness of the lover's dishonesty and exploitativeness. The last poem, instead of reiterating Ovid's poetic claims, presents his lover grotesquely addressing the man whose *puella* the lover is enjoying, asking the fool to please make it more interesting by at least trying to hinder their affair. A perverse kind of game is masquerading as love. In book 3 the lover and the poet fail, deservedly. The girl no longer trusts him and seeks her own happiness elsewhere; the lover is often deceived, rejected, and once even impotent; and the poetry seems to look outside the topoi of erotic elegy for material. Altogether, the collection strikes us as more loosely organized than Horace's *Satires,* but still organized to work with some important themes and to dramatize the progressive failure of a lover who does not understand what love really signifies.

Ovid expressly denies organization or selectivity or variety as qualities of the *Letters from the Black Sea;* instead, he emphasizes lack of plan, monotony, and mere communication as the guiding principles, if such they may be called, of the three books. Well, monotony is an important theme, which often seems more evident in Ovid's constant iteration than in the actual poems themselves. Trapped in exile among barbarians far from Rome, Ovid does not in fact let himself sink into lethargy; he actively fights the cruel monotony of his existence and the seemingly monotonous indifference of his friends, Augustus, and the once-admiring audience he possessed in Rome. He writes to many different people in Rome, each of them a distinct problem of communication. And time passes on the Black Sea, drearily but season by wretched season. Thus, these letters do exhibit modest and useful organization: general chronological development of Ovid's years along with occasional developments in Rome at the end of Augustus's reign; a quite intricate variation of addressees;[23] but above all the dramatic movements of a sensitive poet who struggles to keep up his talent, to maintain contact with Rome and his friends, and to record for the world his sense of injustice at the punishment Augustus has inflicted on him. Granted, this is the most loosely organized collection of the Augustan era, but Ovid has ordered his poems to give rich interplay to his important themes and made his supposed lack of order just one more support for his poetic purposes, one further mark against Augustus.

NOTES

1. Augustine *Confessions* 3.6.
2. The move from scroll to codex was a gradual development between the second and fourth centuries of our era. See Leighton D. Reynolds and Nigel G. Wilson, *Scribes and Scholars* (Oxford: Oxford University Press, 1968), pp. 30 ff.

3. See especially Hermann H. Frösch, "Ovids Epistulae ex Ponto I–III als Gedichtsammlung," Ph.D. diss., Bonn University, 1968.

4. The basic material on *varietas* and the principles of book-organization in Rome has long been Wilhelm Kroll, *Studien zum Verständnis der römischen Literatur* (Stuttgart: J. B. Metzler, 1924), chapter 10 on Das Gedichtbuch, pp. 225–46, and Wilhelm Port, "Die Anordnung in Gedichbüchern augusteischer Zeit," *Philologus* 81 (1925): 280–308, 427–68. To that must now be added the special issue on the subject in *Arethusa* 13 (1980), particularly John Van Sickle, "The Book-Roll and Some Conventions of the Poetic Book," pp. 5–42. In the same issue, pp. 115–127, may be found an excellent, up-to-date bibliography on Greco-Roman poetry books.

5. See Eleanor W. Leach, *Vergil's Ecologues: Landscapes of Experience* (Ithaca, N.Y.: Cornell University Press, 1975), pp. 263 ff., and Eugène de Saint-Denis, "Encore l'architecture des 'Bucoliques virgiliennes,'" *Revue de Philologie* 50 (1976): 7–21.

6. Brooks Otis, *Virgil: A Study in Civilized Poetry* (Oxford: Oxford University Press, 1964), p. 128.

7. For a provocative view of Horace's arrangement as "a coherent pattern of incoherence," see James E. G. Zetzel, "Horace's *Liber Sermonum*: The Structure of Ambiguity," *Arethusa* 13 (1980): 59–77. I analyze book 1 in greater detail below, pp. 57–61.

8. For recent analyses of Tibullus, see Barry B. Powell, "The Ordering of Tibullus Book I," *Classical Philology* 69 (1974): 107–12; David F. Bright, *Haec mihi fingebam: Tibullus in his World* (Leiden: Brill, 1978), pp. 260–68; and Eleanor W. Leach, "Poetics and Poetic Design in Tibullus' First Elegiac Book," *Arethusa* 13 (1980): 79–86.

9. For recent analyses of the *Epodes*' order, see Robert W. Carrubba, *The Epodes of Horace: A Study in Poetic Arrangement* (The Hague: Mouton, 1969); Henri Hierche, *Les Epodes d'Horace: Art et Signification,* Collection Latomus 136 (Brussels: Latomus, 1974); and Ernst A. Schmidt, "Amica vis pastoribus: Der Jambiker Horaz in seinem Epodenbuch," *Gymnasium* 84 (1977): 401–23.

10. For recent material on the *Odes*, I refer the reader to Matthew S. Santirocco, "Horace's *Odes* and the Ancient Poetry Book," *Arethusa* 13 (1980): 43–57, and his new book, *Unity and Design in Horace's Odes* (Chapel Hill: University of North Carolina Press, 1986), and Herbert Eisenberger, "Bilden die horazischen Oden 2, 1–12 einen Zyklus?" *Gymnasium* 87 (1980): 262–74.

11. See John Van Sickle, *The Design of Virgil's Bucolics* (Rome: Edizioni Dell' Ateneo, 1978), pp. 20 ff., and "Reading Virgil's Eclogue Book," *Aufstieg & Niedergang der römischen Welt* 31 (Berlin 1980): 576–603.

12. See Paul Maury, "Le secret de Virgile et l'architecture des Bucoliques," *Lettres d'Humanité* 3 (1944): 71–147.

13. Van Sickle, *Design*, pp. 22ff., based upon his earlier article, "The Unity of the *Eclogues*: Arcadian Forest, Theocritean Trees," *Transactions of the American Philological Association* 98 (1967) 491–508.

14. Van Sickle, *Design*, p. 22. I have altered the past tense of "proved" to present.

15. Otto Skutsch, "The Structure of the Propertian *Monobiblos*," *Classical Philology* 58

(1963): 238–39; Brooks Otis, "Propertius' Single Book," *Harvard Studies in Classical Philology* 70 (1965): 1–44.

16. Otis's "Propertius' Single Book" has now been supplemented by Edward Courtney, "The Structure of Propertius Book I," *Phoenix* 22 (1968): 250–58, and Joy K. King, "Propertius' Programmatic Poetry and the Unity of the *Monobiblos*," *Classical Journal* 71 (1975/6): 108–24.

17. For the temple-metaphor in connection with the *Eclogues,* see Maury, "Le secret de Virgile . . ."; for its use in Propertius IV, see Pierre Grimal, *Les intentions de Properce et la composition du livre IV des "Élégies,"* Collection Latomus 12 (Brussels: Latomus, 1953).

18. Pliny *Epist.* 1.1.1: collegi non servato temporis ordine (neque enim historiam componebam), sed ut quaeque in manus venerat.

19. Eduard Fraenkel, *Horace* (Oxford: Oxford University Press, 1957), pp. 112 and 124, suggested a variant on this theory of padded lines: he believed that Horace's Satires 7, 8, and 9 are anomalous in book 1 and that the poet inserted them largely so that he might have the desired total of ten Satires. He has not found much agreement.

20. Van Sickle, *Design,* has produced the most persuasive portrait of the *Eclogues,* arguing cogently for what he calls an "ideological order."

21. For the alteration of the total number of poems in Ovid's manuscripts, see Port, "Die Anordnung," p. 451, and Edward J. Kenney's edition of the *Amores* (Oxford: Oxford University Press, 1961), p. x. On the relation of the present three books to the original five books, see Alan Cameron, "The First Edition of Ovid's Amores," *Classical Quarterly* 18 (1968): 320–33. For recent analyses of the organization of these poems, see Gesine Lorcher, *Der Aufbau der drei Bücher von Ovids Amores* (Amsterdam: Gruner, 1975), and the review by John T. Davis, *American Journal of Philology* 98 (1977): 189–92.

22. See John T. Davis, *Dramatic Pairings in the Elegies of Propertius and Ovid,* Noctes Romanae 15 (Bern: Verlag Paul Haupt, 1977).

23. Frösch, "Ovids Epistulae," presents an elaborate diagram of symmetry on the basis of the patterning of the addressees of the elegies, p. 143. It is to be noted that, in order to make the symmetry "perfect," Frösch proposes to move 2.11 to a new position after 3.4. That would have the added "value" of making each of the three books a decade. Such are the temptations of symmetry.

S. K. Heninger, Jr.
Sequences, Systems, Models
Sidney and the Secularization of Sonnets

In 1591 Thomas Newman, one of the grubbier London booksellers, brought forth a handy volume of amorous lyrics: *Syr P. S. His Astrophel and Stella. Wherein the excellence of sweete Poesie is concluded. To the end of which are added, sundry other rare Sonnets of divers Noble men and Gentlemen.* The slim quarto contains a corrupt text of *Astrophel and Stella*, 28 quatorzains by Samuel Daniel, five songs by Thomas Campion, a twelve-line poem by Fulke Greville, and a poem of two six-line stanzas, the author of which has not been identified. Newman aimed this volume at the public that had bought the gentlemen's miscellanies of the 1560s and 1570s, and he had his eye on the prototype for this sort of collection in England, the oft-reissued *Songes and Sonettes* first printed by Richard Tottel in 1557. Any literate person picking up this little frivolity would have known immediately the sort of fare to expect.

Sidney, of course, did not intend that his sequence of sonnets make their public appearance in the company of other verse. In fact, it is unlikely that he thought of publishing the work at all, since he did not allow it to circulate in manuscript. But there is no doubt that he wrote *Astrophel and Stella* with the tradition for lyrical assortments in mind. Tottel's miscellany and its heirs, distantly echoing Petrarch, had established a set of conventions that served as a licensing code for sonneteers.

The text we know as *Astrophel and Stella* did not receive that title until Newman published his pirated edition in 1591, nine years after its composition and five years after Sidney's death. The title was then confirmed in the authorized edition of Sidney's collected works sponsored by the Countess of Pembroke and published by William Ponsonby in 1598, and it has stuck ever since. But Sidney himself assigned no title to his collection of poems.[1] In the first recorded mention of it, Abraham Fraunce in 1588, drawing upon a time-tested receipt, refers to it simply as "Songs and Sonets."[2] For Fraunce, the conspicuous feature of the work was its kind, and he thought the generic title sufficient to identify it. Again in 1591, perhaps after the publication of Newman's quarto, Sir John Harington in the commentary on his translation of the *Orlando Furioso* refers to Sidney as "our English *Petrarke*" and his work as the "sonets of *Stella*."³ To the contemporary eye, Sidney's sequence of quatorzains with the accompanying canzoni was, before all else, an exemplar of the highly visible tradition for collections of "songs and sonnets."⁴

Sidney also places the work in this familiar tradition when in the opening sonnet Astrophel reports that he has often turned the leaves of other poets hoping for inspiration in his own efforts to write love lyrics, even though to no avail. And throughout the text of the sequence there are insistent echoes of familiar voices. Sidney wants us to read his work with the poems of those amorous forebears in mind. Astrophel too is in love with a beauteous though unattainable lady, and he too undertakes to compose the rituals of her worship. He assumes a place among the legion of poetical lovers, and Stella belongs in the company of Beatrice and Laura and Fiametta and Hélène.

But *Astrophel and Stella* is not, of course, simply another sonnet sequence. Sidney goes far beyond the codes which semioticians recognize as the enabling discourse of sonneteering, and the more astute of his immediate readers—most notably Spenser, Shakespeare, and Donne—were excitedly aware of the new possibilities that his innovations allowed. Following Sidney's lead, they too drew aloof from Petrarchism while operating along the borders of its jurisdiction. They eagerly exploited the radical changes which Sidney made in the generic model.

For one thing, the lady in *Astrophel and Stella* is not ethereal. Stella is, in fact, a married woman; and though she remains a chaste wife, she is not above flirting and nocturnal rendezvous. Her honor remains intact because of some fear of scandal if discovered *in flagrante delicto* rather than because of any innate celestial virtue. For another thing, the lover in Sidney's poem, although worthy and diligent, is crushingly unrewarded. Regardless of what moralism we read into the ending of the poem, we must agree that Astrophel's efforts in wooing have failed miserably and that he renounces the pursuit of poetizing as well as the pursuit of Stella. His sonneteering comes to nought, without hope of compensation of any sort, in heaven or on earth. So Sidney redefines the experience of love and thereby reformulates the orthodox relationship between sonneteer and lady.

Finally, contrary to the common practice of his predecessors, Sidney in his sequence gives his persona a name, Astrophel, thereby objectifying him. Previous sonneteers had wooed in their own right, so the fiction of the sequence implied an autobiographical experience. As Warkentin aptly observes, "In the genre of the canzoniere from Dante to, I would venture, George Herbert's *The Temple,* the poet functions both as the maker, the *auc-*

tor of his book, and in effect as the material of the book itself."⁵ The sequence of love lyrics was the reputed record of the poet's own suit to an actual lady. But Sidney creates a fictional lover so that the poet of *Astrophel and Stella* is distinct from its titular hero.⁶ And in one instance (at the end of Song viii), albeit fleetingly, we are made very much aware that the narrator is omniscient, above and beyond the fictional characters. This is not the usual circumstance of amorous lyrics, where the poet/lover reports the progress of his own affair.

And yet, in other instances, most notably in Sonnets 30 and 65,⁷ Sidney insinuates personal information that evidently identifies him with Astrophel, supporting an autobiographical interpretation of the poem. The name of the lover, especially when spelled "Astro*phil*," also carries a personal signature. So Sidney sometimes is and sometimes is not Astrophel. This ambiguity in the relation of Sidney to Astrophel, of poet to persona, has lately caused increasing concern among critics, and rightly so.⁸ The choice between the possibilities is the interpretative decision—explicit or covert, conscious or unexamined—that most fundamentally affects how a reading of the work might go.

In *Astrophel and Stella,* then, Sidney reconstitutes the three central features of the sonnet tradition. He revises the nature of the lady so that she is no longer an untarnished vessel of beatific virtues. He revaluates the effects of love so that it is no longer comforting and exalting, even when unfulfilled. And most important for literary history, he calls into doubt the identity of the poet/lover so that a new relationship may evolve between poet and poem and reader.

To wreak these changes, however, Sidney (and his readers) had to be fully familiar with the tradition for songs and sonnets. And this they certainly were, perhaps already *ad nauseam*. On the Continent parodies had begun to appear, and Sidney himself had tried his hand at them in the *Arcadia*. A parody, of course, depends upon the recognizability of its model. It is the oppressive inescapability of the model, in fact, that calls the parody into existence. And so too of the sonnet tradition that Sidney so carefully reconstructed in *Astrophel and Stella*.

The vogue for songs and sonnets had enjoyed a lively history, and the sonnet sequence is a veritable paradigm for a system of poems in their place. It was based upon the motif of multeity in unity, which is grounded in Augustinian esthetics, and it provided the pattern for the Renaissance collection of poems. It began with Dante's *Vita nuova,* reached an early maturity in Petrarch's *Canzoniere,* continued in the popular sequences by the Italian followers of Petrarch such as Boccaccio and Serafino, received serious attention among the Pléiade, made an English appearance (albeit dismembered) in Tottel's *Songes and Sonettes,* and then rapidly degenerated into the gentlemen's miscellanies that followed. It was here that Sidney found it, although he was fully acquainted with each of its previous incarnations.

Historians in the Renaissance with their rage for order were compulsive categorizers; and especially historians of literature, with their newly acquired knowledge of the classics, organized poems according to genre and sought to identify the original practitioner of each sort. Just as Homer led the epic poets, just as Aeschylus initiated the tragedians, and just as Theocritus introduced the pastoralists, so Dante stood at the head of the sonneteers. There were Provençal *chansonniers,* Sicilian court poets, and Tuscan *stilnovisti* upon whom Dante drew and who therefore command a place of honor at the birth of the sonnet tradition; but it was Dante and Beatrice who became the prototypes of the poet/lover and his lady. The *Vita nuova* was seen as the *fons et origo* of the genre.

The *Vita nuova* comprises forty-two items, only twenty-eight of which contain verse, and it narrates the poet's love for Beatrice. The story is fully articulated in an easily followed chronology: the poet first sees Beatrice when nine years old, he sees her again nine years later, her father dies midway through, Beatrice herself dies shortly thereafter, a period of grief follows, and the work concludes with the poet resolving to write another poem more worthy of her (that is, the *Divina commedia*). What is most notable in the *Vita nuova* is the poet's fixation upon Beatrice. She is the receptacle of all values: love, beauty, virtue, godliness. And every item in the sequence is an incidence of the poet's relation to her. In fact, the poet has no personality of his own, no life—no existence—except through this relationship to Beatrice. She is unmitigatedly his raison d'être.

In order to explain the intensity of the *Vita nuova* and to understand its concentration upon Beatrice, we need to recognize the poetics from which it derives. And for that, we must look ultimately to the theories of St. Augustine, whose principles in esthetics were not seriously challenged until literary scholars resurrected Aristotle's *Poetics* in the sixteenth century. Augustine's theology had resulted in a neoplatonist cosmology, which in turn dictated a poetics that held sway until the age of empiricism.

Augustine was the Church Father who most successfully amalgamated Platonic doctrine with Christianity, and this is especially true in his theories of creation, both creation of our universe and artistic creation, which he saw as analogous processes. In accord with Plato's *Timaeus* and with the Book of Genesis, Augustine took for granted that God created our universe, with all its symmetry and harmony—in a word, with all its perfection. The creating godhead began with a *ratio,* a reason or a plan or idea or ratio (to bring in the notion of mathematics)—God began with a *ratio,* which He then projected into a continuum with dimensions of space and dimensions of time, which we know through our sense faculties as our universe. Analogously in artistic creation, the artist begins with a *ratio,* and he projects this idea into our time-space continuum by means of his artifact, which similarly we comprehend with our sense faculties. But just as the anterior and absolute truth of our universe resides in the mind of God, so the truth of the artifact resides in the *ratio* with which the artist began. And understanding the artifact proceeds from *per*ception of the sense data that the artifact provides toward *con*ception of the idea that informs the artifact—toward comprehending the idea that serves as the artifact's informing principle.[9]

Art is efficacious in this theory because there is assumed an intimate interrelationship between man, the cosmos, and God that supports the analogy between artistic creation and the deity's creation of our universe. God not only created the cosmos, which of course is an image of Himself, a projection of the *mens Dei,* but He also created man in the image of Himself, and consequently there is a correspondence between man and the cosmos, each being an *imago Dei.* Man is a microcosm, incorporating the mathematical proportions that are evident in the macrocosm and that inhere in such religious beliefs as the paradox of three-in-one residual in the Holy Trinity.

Applying these assumptions to esthetic theory, we must recall that for Augustine the purpose of art, as indeed of everything else, is to acquaint man with God, the ultimate reality. This purpose is achieved by making man aware of his own microcosmic nature so that he comprehends his correspondence to the cosmos, and thence to deity. Art should display the symmetry and harmony latent in the cosmos in order to awaken the symmetry and harmony latent in the percipient. Since man is made in the image of God, once he knows himself in his cosmic potential, he will know his heavenly maker—or at least he will know as much of God as is allowable to mortals. At the minimum, man will be acquainted with his place in the providential scheme.

In this esthetics, then, art reflects the patterns of cosmos, and the basic form of art, as of creation, is the paradox of multeity in unity. Just as God is One, a unified infinite, yet fills a finite time-space continuum with a multitude of creatures, so the poet, in imitation of the heavenly maker, creates his literary universe and populates it with a multiplicity of creatures who act out their existence in simulated space and time. Numbers provide the necessary extension and variety in the poet's artifact, just as in God's cosmos. But just as in the infinite variety of the cosmos we perceive the unifying hand of God behind natural order, so in the variousness of the artifact we perceive the unifying hand of the artificer and ultimately his original idea, his *ratio*. And as Sidney comments, "The skill of each artificer standeth in that *idea* or fore-conceit of the work, and not in the work itself."[10]

The sonnet sequence, a nonclassical genre, originated within this esthetics. Indeed, the sonnet sequence is the purest literary expression of this esthetics. The poet creates a world of passing time, a series of incidents that give the illusion of temporal dimension. There is multeity of event. But all this variety is focused on the lady, the repository of all value and therefore the unifying factor. The idea of the lady permeates and informs the sequence; she is its *ratio,* its fore-conceit, the potential that it actualizes. To use a term made current by Roman Jakobson, she is actually, not figuratively, the "dominant" of this literary system.[11] The lady is perfection personified—in Astrophel's phrase, "Perfection's heire" (*A&S*, 71.9). The several items displayed discursively in the sonnet sequence, giving the effect of temporality, are no more than the poet's means of unfolding the infinite variety that makes the lady an inclusive replica of divine perfection. That is why the sequence plumbs the depths of sorrow as well as reaches the highest joy. Extremes must be exemplified so that opposites may be reconciled in a stable order, the definition of perfection.[12] As Astrophel says of Stella, she is

> Where Vertue is made strong by Beautie's might,
> Where *Love* is chastnesse, Paine doth learne delight,
> And Humblenesse growes one with Majestie.   (48.2–4)

Consequently, by reading the sequence in its entirety, an experience in durational time, we come to know the lady in all her fulness, from the mundane to the celestial, as an image of perfection, as a reflection of the divine One. In this discernment of the mistress, there is an unfolding paralleled by an infolding. By exhausting the possibilities of multeity, we paradoxically conceive unity.

And that, in our model of the sonnet sequence, is what it is to love: to glimpse heaven through appreciating the multitudinous virtues of the lady, *Madonna*. She descends from heaven and resides for a brief period on earth so that the lover may know her within the confines of his mortality. Knowing her is the greatest joy allowable to man. Loving her is our initiation into *caritas*. Loss of her in this life is inevitable, however, the necessary outcome of the disparity between her perfection and our imperfection. Her departure *from earth* and *to heaven* is a clear-cut demarcation between mortal and divine. And therefore it leads to unbearable grief, an acknowledgment of death, of our defectiveness. The hope of rejoining her in heaven, though, the hope of eventually gaining her favor, becomes the lover's salvation. Meanwhile, he spends his remaining years on earth commemorating his love for her and the values she represents. The sonnet sequence is a literary monument consecrated to that end, and each sonnet in the sequence contributes to the collectivity, which is at once a happening and a memorial. The lover turns poet, and by creating a literary universe analogous to that of the heavenly maker, he guides his reader through the infinite variety of his collection of poems and, by exhausting earthly experience, arrives at what Sidney describes as "the highest end of the mistress-knowledge, by the Greeks called ἀρχιτεκτονική, which stands (as I think) in the knowledge of a man's self" (*Defence*, 82.35–83.1). Loving and poetizing have the same edifying aim and produce the same beneficial effect for both poet and reader.

Dante exemplifies this model exactly. The *Vita nuova* unfolds the significance of Beatrice in a series of episodes that proceeds chronologically, some joyful and some sorrowful, at first while Beatrice is alive and then after her death; and by the end of the work, we know what she means to the poet. She is his end-all and be-all. He has being only through her being. Without her, he would not have entered upon his new life leading toward beatitude. Presumably, also *we* now know what it is to love. Just as the lady renders knowable the celestial qualities by assuming a palpable form (she is a gift from God), so the poem through its discernible harmony and symmetry reveals the divine will; and both lady and poem carry us back to heaven, their source of origin.

When we come to Petrarch, we find a close adherence to this model. There are also notable modifications, however, modifications that take on added weight when we acknowledge that Petrarch was consciously writing with Dante in mind. But first, the similarities. Petrarch's *Canzoniere* in its final form comprises 366 items, and the chronology of events, as in the *Vita nuova*, is clearly marked: exactly twenty-one years elapse between the first sight of Laura and her death (see numbers 211 and 336), and there are ten more years until the end of the sequence (see number 364).[13] Moreover, some poems describe events while the lady is alive, and a final group of one hundred poems deals with the aftermath of her departure from earth. Laura, like Beatrice, is first and foremost a divine being; and after a brief sojourn on earth, she returns to heaven (295.9–11), causing the poet's intense sorrow, which is consolable only by writing poems in her praise. As in the *Vita nuova*,[14] the *Canzoniere* displays discernible patterns in the arrangement of poems which point to a liturgical referent,[15] so that the poetry is an act of worship. Petrarch takes over this much from Dante and establishes it as convention in the sonnet sequence.

There are, however, significant differences between the *Canzoniere* and the *Vita nuova*. In Dante's work, Beatrice is left very much a heavenly being, an ideal of no fleshly substance. Although Dante several times arrives in her presence, he never describes her in physical terms. He knows her as an idea only.[16] In contrast, Petrarch makes of Laura a flesh-and-blood creature who is in fact married. He lingers over her physical features, frequently describing her face, especially her sparkling eyes, her golden hair, and her bright smile. As Petrarch was mimicked in succeeding centuries, his blazon of physical attributes became a tedious cliché: the rosy cheeks, pearly teeth, coral lips, ivory forehead, and snowy bosom that the sonneteering hack bestowed upon his notably unnotable mistress.

Even more interesting, Petrarch subtly shifts the focus of the sonnet sequence. The unifying factor, the dominant, is no longer the ethereal essence of the lady herself but rather the response of the lover to her. Although in the early portions of the *Vita nuova* Dante frequently describes the debilitating effect that Beatrice has upon him, his purpose invariably is to demonstrate the awesomeness of the lady. But Petrarch seems more interested in his emotional response to Laura than in what she is in and for herself, and his poems are suffused with the tear-floods and sigh-tempests that Donne gently mocked. To encompass the extremes that the lover must embrace in order to comprehend the infinite variety of love, Petrarch is icy cold in warm weather and burning hot in cool[17]—the "freezing and frying" that the Elizabethans formulated with their delight in alliteration. Moreover, the antinomy between reason and desire, which Dante had mentioned only *en passant* as a means of extolling chastity,[18] becomes for Petrarch a serious conflict;[19] and the outcome—whether lust will prevail over reverence—is decided only by Laura's death.[20]

All of these changes are what we might expect for a humanist to make of the conservatively Christian prototype provided by Dante.[21] Petrarch is not dealing with other-worldly ideals in a religious context. A poem for him does not as a first priority lead us back to heaven, as Augustine had prescribed, but more importantly it acquaints us with the human condition on earth. As he concludes despondently in number 99, "This mortal life is like a meadow where the serpent lies among the flowers and grass, and if anything we see there pleases our eyes, the result is to enlime our souls more deeply." For Petrarch, the pleasures perceived by our senses become more real than the values conceived by our soul. The actual phenomena of everyday life assume an unwonted vividness. In consequence, his response to *Madonna* is not religious ecstasy, or even intellectual enlightenment, but bodily attraction.

Furthermore, unlike Dante, who indicates chronology in symbolic units of nine years, Petrarch obtrusively metes out chronology in terms of durational time: seven years (number 30), nine years (number 43), ten years (number 50), fourteen years (number 79), fifteen years (numbers 107, 145), sixteen years (number 118), eighteen years (number 266), twenty years (numbers 212, 221), twenty-one years (numbers 271, 364), twenty-four years (number 278), thirty-one years (number 364). His events transpire concretely within the coordinates of our time-space continuum. Although Petrarch eventually aligns his work with heaven by means of the final hymn to the "Vergine bella," this comes almost as an afterthought, and a rather desperate one at that, a contrived compensation for an obsessive world-weariness. And though he centers his poem on Laura, a lady who acts as agent of God on earth, he disperses his interests. These are, in fact, *rime sparse,* as he tells us in the opening line of the *Canzoniere*. Several of these "scattered rhymes" have nothing whatever to do with Laura, or even with the theme of love; they are addressed to contemporaries, usually aristocratic men of wealth and power, and are concerned with purely political or patronal matters.

So Petrarch orients his passion to this world, not the next, despite his lip-service to Laura as an object of worship. His readiness for death at the end is more a dissatisfaction with this life than a joyous anticipation of beatitude. He makes man, and specifically himself, the measure of his literary universe. He exhibits the self-centeredness and worldliness that became increasingly the compulsion of Renaissance poets as deference to the classical spirit secularized their work. Finally, Petrarch indulges the humanist's fascination with pagan texts, and his pages are littered with references to Vergil and Ovid. After him, the mythological allusion became a *sine qua non* of sonneteering, so that literariness assumed a prominent place in the licensing code.

Petrarch's humanism results in an ambiguous attitude toward Laura. There is ontological equivocation about whether she is heavenly or earthly,[22] as well as epistemological uncertainty about how best to know her.[23] And this ambiguity toward Laura is reflected in the verbal system of the *Can-*

zoniere. In the *Vita nuova* the actual physical experience of the poet is recorded in prose headpieces, while the lasting significance of that experience is abstracted into metrical poems. In each item that contains verse, the poetry is clearly demarcated from the historical event by the arrangement of the item, which separates the prose headpiece from the sonnet or canzone or ballata that follows. The poetry clearly exists in the higher realm of art, above the changeableness of phenomenal nature, just as Beatrice belongs to a higher order of being above the mortal poet; and this divine status of the poetry is unmistakably indicated by the fact of its metrics. It has the harmony and symmetry of the idea of cosmos. In the *Canzoniere*, however, actual events—the particular occurrences and the politics—are not set apart in prose headpieces. There is, in fact, no prose to provide a narrative continuity, but rather the actuality of event is woven into the poetic fabric itself. Literature and life are intermeddled. A metrical poem points to this world as well as to an idealized existence. There is no heaven set aside as residence for the lady.

The indissoluble this/other-worldliness of Laura is reflected also in smaller units of the verbal system. While Dante suffers and rejoices by turns, Petrarch often undergoes these contrarious emotions simultaneously. In number 122 he confides perplexedly. "When I reflect on my state, I feel in the midst of the flames a chill." In number 55 he exclaims in anguish, "Love, though I have been tardy in seeing it, wishes me to be untuned between two contraries."[24] Repeatedly, to a point that invites parody, Petrarch hopes and sorrows at the same moment. This sufferance of conflicting moods is sometimes encapsulated in an oxymoron, that rudimentary rhetorical device to express paradox. In number 240, for example, Petrarch pleads with Laura for pardon if his desire should overcome his reason, and he addresses her in neatly reversible formulations: "O my sweet suffering, my bitter delight." The unresolved conflict between carnal lust and rational reverence is conveyed effectively by the plethora of such oxymorons in the language of the *Canzoniere*. They call attention to the irremediable plight of the poet-lover, torn between two emotions, and therefore necessarily expressing himself in terms of self-contradiction. The reconciliation of opposites in the perfection of the lady, characteristic of our model for the sonnet sequence, is dangerously near disruption. Rather than symbolizing unity, *Madonna* threatens disintegration of the lover, his dissolution.

Sidney was keenly aware of this ambivalence in Petrarch. Like many of his generation, he saw Petrarch's oxymoronic stance vis-à-vis Laura as a contrived conflict, a pretense to justify the excessive emotion that the poet self-indulgently exhibits. Repeatedly, Sidney questions such an unrestrained show of passion. In *The defence of poesie* (116.27 ff.), he recognizes the potential of that "lyrical kind of songs and sonnets . . . in singing the praises of the immortal beauty," although he doubts the sincerity of its practitioners. "But truly," he opines, "many of such writings as come under the banner of unresistible love, if I were a mistress, would never persuade me they were in love"; and he continues by giving a reason for this negative criticism of the sonnet tradition: "So coldly they apply fiery speeches, as men that had rather read lovers' writings . . . than that in truth they feel those passions." Sidney's objection rests on his opinion that sonneteering is a bookish tradition with only feigned emotions.

In *Astrophel and Stella* itself, Astrophel frequently disclaims the histrionics of other sonneteers and insists that he speaks with the forthrightness of a true-born Englishman. In number 6, for example, Petrarch is the unmistakable butt of his rebuke, reprehensible especially for the excessive use of ridiculous oxymorons:[25]

> Some Lovers speake when they their Muses entertaine,
> Of hopes begot by feare, of wot not what desires:
> Of force of heav'nly beames, infusing hellish paine:
> Of living deaths, deare wounds, faire stormes and freesing fires.
>
> (lines 1–4)

Astrophel continues in this sonnet by similarly rejecting the practice of those who express their love in mythological allusions, in pastoral ditties, and in saccharine amorous complaints. And for the conclusion of the sonnet, he asserts, "I can speake what I feele, and feele as much as they"; so his mission is succinctly completed "when trembling voice brings forth that I do *Stella* love."[26] Again in number 15 Astrophel deplores those who resort to compendia of literary tropes or who consult the dictionary for words that alliterate in "ratling rowes"; and he further dissociates himself from those who repeat "poore *Petrarch's* long deceased woes, / With new-borne sighes and denisend wit." As we have noted, already in the opening sonnet Astrophel ostentatiously calls attention to his predecessors in the genre but just as ostentatiously insists that he is deviating from their practice.

Nevertheless, what Sidney takes over most directly from Petrarch is the equivocal attitude toward *Madonna*, so that Stella for Astrophel is very much a palpable creature as well as the traditional embodiment of beauty and virtue. The duality of Stella is presented concisely but unmistakably in number 52:

> A strife is growne betweene *Vertue* and *Love,*
>   While each pretends that *Stella* must be his:
>   Her eyes, her lips, her all, saith *Love* do this,
> Since they do weare his badge, most firmely prove.
> But *Vertue* thus that title doth disprove,
>   That *Stella* (ô deare name) that *Stella* is
>   That vertuous soule, sure heire of heav'nly blisse:
> Not this faire outside, which our hearts doth move.
>
> (lines 1–8)

Rather more than Petrarch, and certainly more than Dante, Sidney develops the bifurcation of the lady into temptress as well as angel, and Astrophel's persistent difficulty derives from having to deal with it. In number 71, after describing Stella as "Perfection's heire" and after assigning her the ability to draw all to love of virtue in the best Platonic manner, Astrophel concludes nonetheless by confirming her undeniable sexuality: "'But ah,' Desire still cries, 'give me some food'."

Actually, the conflict between reason and desire becomes the central issue of Astrophel's story, rising to prominence already in number 4, and it is never satisfactorily resolved.[27] When Stella rejects Astrophel, he leaves off writing further poems, resigned to his failure. He accepts the torment of unrequited love as a continuing condition. He is not reconciled to his plight by either theological doctrine or philosophical argument, and he does not pledge to commemorate the lady or her values in further poetry more worthy of her. His poems, in fact, reveal shameful passion more than chaste adoration: "Mine owne writings," Astrophel early admits, "like bad servants show / My wits, quicke in vaine thoughts, in vertue lame" (21.3–4). So his love, it seems, keeps him from heaven rather than providing the means, however circuitously, of arriving there.

In the final analysis, of course, Stella proves unavailable to Astrophel, just as Beatrice remains above Dante and Laura eludes Petrarch. But Stella is beyond Astrophel for a vastly different reason. Sidney's adaptation of the cruel mistress is novel and significant. Stella is not a celestial spirit, above the carnality of love-making—*au contraire,* she belongs in another man's bed. Stella lies just as conveniently beyond reach as does the orthodox *Madonna,* but she is no saintly virgin. She resides unremittingly in this world.

So, as Wittgenstein might have put it, Sidney plays the cultural game of writing a sonnet sequence. The lady is the dominant of his poem, and true to type she remains unavailable. But he stretches the cultural rules. She is heavenly in name only. She is capable of amorous activity[28] and indeed is presently sharing the intimacies of marriage with another man. Her carnality gives real point to the conflict between reason and desire which Astrophel feels so acutely—in fact, it makes the satisfaction of his desire a viable possibility.

If the poem were autobiographical, this possibility raises the evident question (see number 33), why did Sidney fail to express his love to Penelope Devereux before her marriage to Lord Rich? Or if Sidney did not feel this passion until after her marriage (as perhaps he suggests in number 2), why did the two lovers rule out an illicit *affaire de coeur,* especially since the marriage was an unhappy one? Seven years later, Penelope plunged into a protracted relationship of that sort with another lover, Charles Blount.[29] From considerable evidence, she was a sufficiently strong and self-willed young woman to overcome any fear of scandal.

But clearly *Astrophel and Stella* is not autobiographical in any sense of recording Sidney's thwarted attempts to seduce Lady Rich. By its openness, in fact, the poem prevents rather than invites such a conclusion. Evidence points to a composition date shortly after Penelope's marriage in November 1581, probably the following summer, and Ringler argues that the sequence was conceived and executed as a whole rather than being a reorganization or revision of earlier work.[30] If the real-life "Astrophel" and "Stella" had extricated themselves from a love affair in deference to some code of honor, it would have been indecorous, to say the least, for Sidney to broadcast the news so soon after the event. Rather, I conclude, Sidney's affection for Penelope was friendship, not lust.[31] The fact that Sidney's uncle and patron, the earl of Leicester, married Penelope's widowed mother in 1578 all but guaranteed their genial acquaintance; and probably by mutual, mischievous agreement, she became the mistress of his sonnet sequence.[32] At the time Sidney was much involved with poetic activity—during the preceding two years he had written *The defence of poesie* and the first version of the *Arcadia;* and he now wished to try his hand at the genre of sonnet sequence, which he had found so popular on the Continent. *Astrophel and Stella* was practical training in that mode, assurance that he had mastered the tenets of neoplatonist poetics. It is an exercise in amorous lyrics, a result of reading, not of actual pining in unrequited passion. So *Astrophel and Stella* contains no covert confession of Sidney's love-life. Astrophel, not Sidney, adores Stella. Penelope, the wife of Lord Rich, in the image of Stella provided a convenient *Madonna* to satisfy the sonneteer's need for a lady, and Lord Rich readily filled the role of the detested rival. But we take this triangle in the wrong direction if we locate it in historical time rather than in the fiction of literary convention.

Astrophel and Stella, however, does serve as autobiography of another sort. It records a stage of Sidney's life as a poet. He still had in hand *The defence of poesie,* a theoretical treatise that proposed to modify the time-honored neoplatonist esthetic rooted in Augustine by melding it with the new theories of Aristotelian mimesis currently touted on the Continent. Early in the *Defence,* as orator's platform, Sidney proclaims, "Poesy . . . is an art of imitation, for so Aristotle termeth it in the word $\mu\acute{\iota}\mu\eta\sigma\iota\varsigma$" (79.35–6). And this unequivocal commitment to a poetics defined by its practice of mimesis leads him soon after to reject the traditional poetics as it had been interpreted by the Florentine Platonists, a lyrical poetics of song based upon a divine frenzy inspired in the poet by the Muses—that is, a poetics of $\mu o \nu \sigma \iota \kappa \acute{\eta}$.[33] Hardly more than a year before, Sidney had also completed a draft of the *Arcadia,* a prose narrative which demonstrated that, to use his words in the *Defence,* "it is not rhyming and versing that maketh a poet . . . but it is that feigning notable images of virtues, vices, or what else" (81.33–7). Sidney lies at that node in our cultural history when poetry was sloughing off its identity as a formal art dependent upon metrification and was instead developing its potential as a narrative and depictive art. For England, Sidney is the mediator of this transition. Unequivocally, he opts for a poetics of mimesis, the production of images, rather than a poetics of $\mu o \nu \sigma \iota \kappa \acute{\eta}$, the production of measures; and the years 1579 to 1582 are the time when he works out his new theory. Never was Sidney more intensely involved with the principles of poetry.

Astrophel and Stella, then, is a testing of this new theory—an exercise in the orthodox poetics but within the frame of a fresh perspective. It is autobiographical in the sense that it records Sidney's growth as a literary artist, rather than his failure as a Casanovan lover. Astrophel's loss of Stella at the end should be construed metonymically as Sidney's disaffection with the neoplatonist esthetic. He has a nostalgic fondness for the orthodox poetics, but it is no longer viable. So *Astrophel and Stella* functions as Sidney's critique of the generic sonnet sequence.

Sidney makes clear this intention in the earliest sonnets of *Astrophel and Stella,* and several later sonnets confirm and keep active his interest in poetic theory.[34] In the opening sonnet, as we have noted, he indicates his awareness of those who had preceded him as love poets. Astrophel dutifully turns the leaves of their amatory verse and studies their *topoi.* But he can derive no inspiration from that source. "Others' feete," he says (with a pun on metrical "feet" as the measures of $\mu o \nu \sigma \iota \kappa \acute{\eta}$)—"Others' feete still seem'd but strangers in my way." Instead, he concludes, he should look in his heart and write—not that he will find there the passion that fuels his love, a Romantic reading of the line, but rather that he maintains there an image of Stella, who has replaced the Muses as his inspiration. In his mind's eye, like a good Petrarchist, he retains a concrete image of Stella as the embodiment of Beauty and Virtue.

This reading of the final line in the first sonnet is made mandatory by number 3:

> Let daintie wits crie on the Sisters nine,
> That bravely maskt, their fancies may be told:
> Or *Pindare's* Apes, flaunt they in phrases fine,
> Enam'ling with pied flowers their thoughts of gold:
>   Or else let them in statelier glorie shine,
>   Ennobling new found Tropes with problemes old:
> Or with strange similes enrich each line,
> Of herbes or beastes, which *Inde* or *Afrike* hold.
>   For me in sooth, no Muse but one I know:
>   Phrases and Problemes from my reach do grow,
> And strange things cost too deare for my poore sprites.
>   How then? even thus: in *Stella's* face I reed,
>   What Love and Beautie be, then all my deed
> But Copying is, what in her Nature writes.

In this sonnet, Astrophel systematically renounces each of the popular movements in poetry prominent at the time and finally proclaims his positive program for a poetry of Aristotelian mimesis. In the octet, allowing two lines for each, Astrophel enumerates the four most evident schools of poetry: the "daintie wits" who call upon the Muses for divine inspiration; those who, like the Pléiade, model their precious poems upon the odes of ancient Greece; those who write philosophical poems, merely versifying accepted doctrine; and those who, in the wake of Lyly, compose in the highly wrought style of *Euphues*. But Astrophel finds nothing of use in these poetic programs, as he had already stated in the opening sonnet. In the sestet, instead, he says that Stella is the only inspiration he acknowledges. Her image, carried in his heart, is the basis for his poetry.

But Stella produces in Astrophel a much more complex response than divine frenzy. In her face he sees pure Love and Beauty, divine qualities equivalent to the heavenly love and heavenly beauty that Spenser extolls in

Fowre Hymnes. The status of these two qualities as Platonic essences is suggested by their capitalization in the text. And Nature has put them in Stella's face, so that they have become palpable entities. The Platonic essences of Love and Beauty have been embodied in Stella, rendered physical and particular, so that they might appear manifest to mortal men. Stella becomes a "booke of Nature," as Astrophel says in number 71, wherein he can read the otherwise ineffable secrets of the universe:

> Who will in fairest booke of Nature know,
>   How Vertue may best lodg'd in beautie be,
>   Let him but learne of *Love* to reade in thee,
> *Stella,* those faire lines, which true goodnesse show.
>
> (lines 1–4)

So Astrophel's task as poet then becomes the act of copying this text that Stella, as book of nature, sets forth (compare 77.2). As he concludes in number 3, "All my deed / But Copying is, what in her Nature writes." Loving becomes first an act of reading, with the mistress as text, just as worship of the deity requires a reading of the evidence of His attributes, in both the Holy Scriptures and the book of Nature. And love poetry becomes an exercise in copying the mistress, of providing a verbal artifact which reproduces her meaning.

In the opening lines of number 50, Astrophel states the proposition succinctly. He is compelled to write a poem, he says, that replicates the image of Stella he carries in his heart:

> *Stella,* the fulnesse of my thoughts of thee
> Cannot be staid within my panting breast,
> But they do swell and struggle forth of me,
> Till that in words thy figure be exprest.

Love poetry of this sort, clearly, is best accomplished by Aristotelian mimesis, by the conscious and rational execution of images that convey the lover's response to the mistress, and that in turn provide an image of the mistress herself. And since the medium of the poet is language, the poem at basis becomes literally a verbal icon. As Astrophel says in the lines just quoted, "In words thy figure be exprest." Or as Astrophel describes the enterprise in the opening sonnet, "I sought fit words to paint the blackest face of woe," his state of mind as a result of loving. After his lot improves, Astrophel changes his mood, though not his means of expression: "My pen the best it may / Shall paint out joy, though but in blacke and white" (70.10–11).[35]

If in Sidney's new poetics the poem is a verbal icon—in the instance of the sonnet sequence, an image of the adored lady and the anguished lover expressed in words—it is clear that the verbal system of the poem assumes an unwonted importance. It is an entity in its own right, enjoying an autonomy and authority of its own. The language of a poem is not merely the encapsulation of some pre-existent concept such as beauty—the role of the verbal system in a neoplatonist poetics, where words are a veil through which we look to discern the truth concealed behind them. Nor is the language of a poem merely a clothing for the thought—the role of the verbal system in a poetics based upon rhetoric, where the *res* of subject matter is encoded in the *verba*. Poetry is not merely a formal art (à la Plato), whose distinctive feature is the metrification of μουσική which echoes the cosmic harmonies; nor is it merely an art of discourse (à la Cicero), whose distinctive feature is the practical statement of an author-determined meaning. Rather, in Sidney's new poetics, the ontology of a poem resides in the verbal system itself. Its mode of existence inheres primarily in its language. Like Stella, who is a page from the book of nature embodying the Platonic essences of Love and Beauty at the same time she refers to the historical personage of Penelope, Lady Rich, a word in Sidney's theory of language points to conceptual meanings of an intellectual sort at the same time it refers to facts in our phenomenal world. Like the mistress of a sonnet sequence, language leads an amphibious existence, inhabiting both the heavenly and the earthly realms. It is at once intellectual and sensible, and therefore fit to paint palpable images of concepts, such as virtues, vices, and what else.

What allowed the greatest freedom for play, however, was Sidney's dissociation of the poet himself from his putative persona, the lover. Through employing a dramatically realized character whom he distances by giving a name, Astrophel, Sidney draws a clear distinction between fictive lover and actual poet. And by means of this wedge, he makes room for irony—that is, the poet, Sidney, can watch the lover, Astrophel, in the act of loving and can make observations and insinuate inferences about his success. By the same token, Sidney can also comment upon Astrophel's practice as a poet. While Astrophel is serious about the tenets of sonneteering, Sidney need not be. For that reason, *Astrophel and Stella* often suggests a parody of Petrarchism, although it is never so coarse that it resorts to outright buffoonery. And like parody, *Astrophel and Stella* makes unusual demands upon the reader. We are invited to stand behind Sidney and watch him at his making. We must recognize and even respect the model to which Sidney points (a parody does not work if the model is already debased), while at the same time with Sidney we criticize and reject it. These conflicting demands upon the reader are new to the sonnet tradition. We cannot imagine looking over the shoulder of Petrarch while he dispassionately evaluates the performance of his persona. And Dante, as we have noted, has no authorial shoulder to look over—his poet/lover does not exist outside a relationship to Beatrice. But Sidney, by objectifying Astrophel, interposes himself between his reader and his poem, and is thereby in a position to anatomize his model for the instruction of an audience.

Spenser was one of Sidney's most ardent admirers and early in his career may have come almost as close as Fulke Greville to being a poetic collaborator. But Spenser proved notably resistant to Sidney's novel poetics of mimesis and the new hypostasis of poetry's verbal system. He never forsook metrification; instead, he clung rather old-fashionedly to the neoplatonist esthetic conducive to allegory and at least professed to seek inspiration from the Muses. The vast difference between *Astrophel and Stella* and *Amoretti* is usually expressed by modern critics as praise for the liveliness of the earlier sequence and disappointment in the conventionality of the later. But such a perception, I think, is to misread, or perhaps to under-read, *Amoretti* and to overlook its dependence upon Sidney's sonnets. Despite Spenser's heedlessness of the general thrust of Sidney's *Defence,* it is not likely that *Amoretti* would have been written if *Astrophel and Stella* had not come first.

Spenser takes even further Sidney's development of the lady as a fleshly creature available for sexual union. He, in fact, remakes the traditional relationship between lover and mistress so that it concludes in marriage, a consummation devoutly wished by the Protestant ethic. From the start in *Amoretti* the poet/lover takes for granted the likelihood of wedlock, and in large part the sequence is a paean to the sacrament of holy matrimony between willing partners: "Sweet be the bands, the which true love doth tye, / without constraynt or dread of any ill" (65.5–6).[36]

Spenser also further individualizes the lady, making her not only a particular character in the fiction—a Beatrice or Laura or Stella—but a particular historical person, Elizabeth Boyle, soon to be wed on a particular date to the poet. She quickly acquires a singular personality and an immediate presence, participating more actively and more frequently in the events of the narrative than any previous mistress.[37] She has no fictitious name with religious or mythological overtones that might lead her out of time and space; rather, in number 74, Spenser pointedly reveals her given name and her personal relationship to him, in the precise context of sharing the same name with his mother and his queen. This is a highly personal poem. And it is no distortion to claim that Spenser is using the genre of sonnet sequence for a practical purpose, for the wooing of his bride. *Amoretti* is a gesture of courtship, a wedding gift from the groom.

What is most interesting in Spenser's adaptation of Sidney's strategy as a sonneteer, however, is the development of Sidney's use of a persona. Sidney, of course, deploys the independent Astrophel, so that we readily (and necessarily) distinguish between the actual poet and his speaking voice. Inevitably we raise questions about the degree of autobiography in *Astrophel and Stella*. But Spenser does not objectify his persona in *Amoretti* by giving him a name in the fiction. The poet/lover is an anonymous first-person narrator, like the speaking voice in the sequences of Dante and Petrarch. We are left to assume that the sonneteer is the poet himself. Despite the several unmistakable references to Spenser's own circumstances,[38] however, it would be naïve to assume that the speaking voice of Spenser's sonnets is uncomplicatedly Spenser. It is, in fact, paradoxical that the autobiographical imperative is enunciated so forcefully in a work that with equal force is presented as little more than a pastiche of well-worn conventions. The very title of the work, "little love poems," announces its triteness, and the particularity of Spenser's circumstance quickly decomposes in the common solvent of Petrarchism. Spenser professes to be making a personal statement of his love for Elizabeth Boyle, but he speaks only in terms of what earlier sonneteers had already said many times over. As Sidney observed of others in the *Defence,* so coldly he applies fiery speeches, as men that had rather read lovers' writings than that in truth he feels those passions (116.35–117.9).

What Spenser is doing, of course, is carrying the autobiographical ambiguity of *Astrophel and Stella* to its logical extreme and adapting it to his practical purpose. By not giving the speaking voice an actual name in the fiction, Spenser induces a perfect equivocality. The amorous voice of *Amoretti* carefully iterates the tired conventions and thereby activates the Petrarchist system; but at the same time, the accentuated conventionality calls attention to the literariness of the work and alerts us to a sophisticated poet who is manipulating the system for personal ends. What we have, of course, is a forty-year-old husband (60.8) attempting to flatter a bride half his age. The lady would be pleased to have a fashionable sonnet sequence in her honor, and the lady of a great poet might be pleased in no other way. Therefore the poet complies as a concession to what she looks for and faithfully reproduces the system. But having learned from Sidney how to dissociate persona from poet, Spenser takes the same wry stance toward the sonneteer of *Amoretti* that Sidney assumed toward Astrophel. So the enabling codes of the sonnet tradition allow Spenser to express his love for Elizabeth, while Sidney's critique of that tradition permits him to retain his integrity as a self-aware poet.

Spenser loves his bride, to be sure, but not in the jejune terms and the stereotypical ways that his persona sets forth in the sonnets. Rather, Spenser the poet, as distinct from the persona of *Amoretti,* makes known his love for the woman who will read his poem by the very act of writing it, not by the dog-eared sentiments it expresses. Spenser wrote to please his lady, like a sonneteer should, and he was careful to run the gamut of emotions that a sonneteer should avow. But the exercise is ironical, as Spenser certainly knew, and perhaps as Elizabeth Boyle, sprightly young woman that she was, might also have surmised.[39] Spenser hints as much in number 18:

> But when I pleade, she bids me play my part,
>   and when I weep, she sayes teares are but water:
> and when I sigh, she sayes I know the art,
>   and when I waile she turnes hir selfe to laughter.
>
> (lines 9–12)

In number 54 Spenser again performs a theatrical role:

> Of this worlds Theatre in which we stay,
>   my love lyke the Spectator ydly sits
> beholding me that all the pageants play,
>   disguysing diversly my troubled wits.   (lines 1–4)

This sort of role-playing, knowingly acceded to by both lover and mistress, is given dramatic credence in a pair of sonnets beginning with number 28, when Spenser assumes the hopeful part of a Petrarchan lover who has sent his lady a sprig of laurel:

> The laurell leafe, which you this day doe weare,
>   gives me great hope of your relenting mynd:
> for since it is the badg which I doe beare,
>   ye bearing it doe seeme to me inclind.   (lines 1–4)

But by the next sonnet, Elizabeth has replied to his Petrarchan pretense by noting that the laurel is the sign of military victory as well as poetry, and therefore she re-interprets the laureate conceit as confirmation of her mastery. Feigning dashed hopes, Spenser assents to his lady's interpretation of the laurel, knowing that such subjection is the sure sign of triumph:

> See how the stubborne damzell doth deprave
> my simple meaning with disdaynfull scorne:
> and by the bay which I unto her gave,
> accoumpts myselfe her captive quite forlorne.   (29.1–4)

Spenser's poems are what he has to offer his bride—as he concludes the *Epithalamion*, they are made in lieu of other ornaments; and he gladly applies his poetical talent in the service of his lady. His gift of *Amoretti* was a real-life counterpart to his gift of Petrarch's laurel leaf in the fiction, and Elizabeth's response to the poem was in keeping with that charade. She recognized the poetic tribute as a studied gesture of praise and affection, not as a simple expression of true-felt emotion, and she accepted it as a token of Spenser's commitment to their union.

Rightly read, then, *Amoretti* is a sportive action in a serious cause, the pleasing of a bride. It is ultimately a play of wit in the manner of Serafino, the sort of self-conscious joking with the sonnet tradition that had led to anti-Petrarchism and within a few years eventuated in the sophistication of Marinism. It is Spenser's turn at playing the game of sonneteering, with Sidney's rules bent even further. While *Astrophel and Stella* is a critique of the sonnet sequence as genre, *Amoretti* becomes a fond parody of it. And like a good parody should, it replicates the original in the minutest, most telling detail.

About the same time that Spenser was writing *Amoretti*, Shakespeare was composing his sonnets, and he too extends certain principles instituted by Sidney. In Shakespeare's collection of sonnets there is no lady to provide a focus, no unifying dominant. For all his devotion to the young man addressed repeatedly, Shakespeare makes of him no cynosure of an idealized love.[40] It is true that love is a frequent topic in the poems, but the mortality of the loved one weighs more heavily upon the poet than any potential for divinity, and love itself is more often a hellish torment than a heavenly elation. So Shakespeare continues the secularization of love, bringing it even farther into the realm of fleshliness, carrying it even farther away from the integrative and uplifting experience it serves to accomplish in our original model for the sonnet sequence. Shakespeare conveys what love is like in a world of time and space where only a self-confirming assertiveness provides any protection from the ravages of mutability, the pain of separation, and the temptations of ignoble lust.

In the *Sonnets* Shakespeare himself and the speaking voice are largely indistinguishable, and the autobiographical imperative is so strong that it has driven many annotators to the brink of folly. Even more consequential than Shakespeare's treatment of the theme of love and the stance of his persona, though, is his adaptation of Sidney's attitude toward the verbal system of a sonnet sequence. Since there is no dominant lady in Shakespeare's collection of sonnets and little narrative continuity (it is hardly a *sequence* in the usual sense), each poem enjoys a great degree of independence. With Shakespeare, the concept of a sonnet sequence as a unified work begins to disintegrate. The requirement of collectivity weakens, and the individual sonnet, rather than the coherency between sonnets, emerges as the primary vehicle of meaning. After the publication of Shakespeare's collection, the sonnet is dealt with as a single poem more often than as an item in a series, and the well-defined tradition for songs and sonnets is soon ingested by the larger, more tenuous tradition of lyric poetry. Later poets, such as Milton, felt free to write individual sonnets isolated from any immediate framework, and on such topics as the poet's blindness or a massacre in the Piedmont. Shakespeare prepared for this assimilation of the sonnet to the nondescript lyric, characterized only by the incidental fact of its having fourteen lines. He effectively nullified the distinctive model for the sonnet sequence derived from Augustine's esthetics.

As the individual sonnet acquired freedom from the formal support of a sequence considered holistically, it achieved a separate identity and for its meaning became commensurately more dependent upon the language of its own restricted verbal system. Each sonnet meant only what its own words meant, without reference to the other sonnets in the conglomerate, and far removed from the prefabricated codes of the sonnet tradition. It is easy to see that the autonomy of the verbal system in a poem necessarily awaited this dissolution of the sonnet sequence into a loose collection of individual items. The equilibrium between part and whole had to shift in favor of the part before the language of a sonnet could be freed. Conversely, this greater authority bestowed upon the verbal system is an opportunity, if not a requirement, for the poet to express himself through personal language. The poem is no more than the verbal system he contrives. The poet cannot rely comfortably upon the repetition of familiar vocabulary and motifs but must invent afresh. The technical term "invention," in fact, requires a new definition. Freed from the traditional poetics, the verbal system is no longer a veil to be pulled aside in order to reveal an anterior truth nor is it merely the dress that clothes an author's thought. Rather, the verbal system of a poem becomes increasingly the product of the poet's unfettered imagination.

Shakespeare recognized this opportunity held forth by Sidney's poetics of mimesis, and he took advantage of it to produce sonnets so rich in verbal imagery that many critics consider them unmatched in the literature of any nation. Without taking away from Shakespeare's achievement or diminishing his genius, however, we can say that he profited from Sidney's validation of the verbal system in a poem and from Sidney's actual demonstration in *Astrophel and Stella* of how mimetic poetry produces images. The sonnets, for all their greatness, were Shakespeare's apprenticeship in the school of Sidney. Along with the Ovidian narrative poems, they provided a period of learning, experiment, and practice that eventuated in the great plays, where the verbal-visual imagery of Sidney's poetics is given the added physical dimension of dramatic realization on stage.

Donne, for all his metaphysical wit and his orientation toward the modern age, is most informatively characterized as an adventurous Elizabethan. Although he gave no title to his collection of amatory lyrics (nor is it certain that he considered them a "collection"), at some point in the early manuscripts they acquired the label "Songs and Sonnets."[41] Unlike Sidney and Spenser, but like Dante, Petrarch, and probably Shakespeare, Donne wrote these poems over a period of time. As Gardner dates the *Songs and Sonnets,* Donne began writing them not long after the publication of Spenser's *Amoretti,* and the last of them may be as late as 1605.[42] They are, then, roughly contemporaneous with Shakespeare's *Sonnets.*

And like Shakespeare, Donne exploited the depictive possibilities inherent in Sidney's mimetic theory of poetry, the potential for the striking image and the dramatic moment. In most of the *Songs and Sonnets,* we are very much aware of a speaking voice with strong personality and we readily discern a second-person who is being cajoled or berated, seduced or denounced. Sidney's persona in *Astrophel and Stella* may begin a poem *in media verba:* "Your words my friend (right healthfull caustiks) blame / My young mind marde" (21.1–2); but Donne opens even more explosively: "For Godsake hold your tongue, and let me love" ("Canonization," line 1). In the *Songs and Sonnets,* every poem's a stage, and at the center of it is Jack Donne, passionate lover—sometimes a sensual libertine, at other times a devoted monogamist. The persona Donne projects in this collection of love-poems has become so real that it obscures the historical figure who later wrote solemn sermons as Dean of St. Paul's. In our mind, persona takes precedence over person.

So Donne goes even farther than Shakespeare in his modification of our model for the sonnet sequence. Like the *Vita nuova* and the *Canzoniere*, the *Songs and Sonnets* displays a mixture of metrical forms. But Donne does not confine himself to a few standardized forms, such as the canzone and the ballata, and he completely avoids the quatorzain. He ranges at will wherever his ear for the actual accent of conversation takes him. And he is more willful in his rhetoric as well as in his metrics. The ontology of the poem rests even more compellingly in its own verbal system. The sounds of his speaking voice are so distinct, in fact, as to seem colloquial, dialogue in a vignette. There is little narrative—only drama.

Donne, of course, flauntingly rejects more of our model than he adopts. With Sidney, he looks askance at the "whining Poëtry" of the sonneteers;[43] and though he agrees with the neoplatonists that "Loves mysteries in soules doe grow," he adds knowingly, "But yet the body is his booke" ("Extasie," lines 71–72). In consequence, he is unabashedly sexual. And often he is unabashedly promiscuous. He has no Beatrice or Laura, no Stella or even Elizabeth, no lady of any name. Furthermore, his poems are not always in praise of the mistress but often snarlingly reprehend her as a member of the faithless sex. Donne has, in fact, turned our model upside down, producing what has come to be called a "countergenre."

When we consider *Songs and Sonnets* as a countergenre of the sonnet sequence, a number of important points can be made. In Donne's work, the lady of the traditional sequence is evidently fragmented, or rather replaced by several paramours *en passant*, thereby debasing her. Furthermore, the sex partner of any particular occasion is allowed no identity of her own; she exists only as a requisite counterpart in the sex act. While Stella is necessary as the object of Astrophel's adoration so that Sidney can produce a sonnet sequence, the women in the *Songs and Sonnets* are only incidental. They appear only in relation to the poet/lover. Donne has in fact reversed the relation of poet to mistress that Dante posits: rather than the poet being defined in terms of the lady, the female partner in Donne's scheme has no existence beyond meeting the needs of the male. It is *his* moods that prevail, that determine. Moreover, unlike Petrarch, who always loves despite his freezing and frying, Donne enlarges the range of emotional attitudes. On monogamistic occasions he expands love into a cosmic optimism that verges on Platonic serenity, secure in a providential orderliness; on other occasions, he denies even the possibility of love and fills with hate, lashing out at the world like a cynical malcontent. He too reaches the heights and depths of emotion in the best tradition of the sonnet sequence, but he goes beyond the confines of the theme of love. The usual conflict between lust and restraint becomes metonymically for him an irresolvable contention between cynicism and belief. The opposites that Donne postulates as his extremes are the widest possible poles of human response.

Donne is saying more, of course, than merely what it is to love. He attempts to say what it is to be human, what it is to live in this world. He describes, in the best humanistic fashion, the parameters of man's potential, and thereby defines the limits of the individual "I." What unifies Donne's *Songs and Sonnets* is no hypothetical lady but rather his honest, relentless search for selfhood. The dominant of the work is the definition of the poet as a sentient entity. Donne resorts to the string of mistresses as a means of learning about himself in a variety of situations, ranging from love to hate, from faith to despair. In the *Songs and Sonnets,* then, taken as an integrated work, the poet identifies himself by means of what he has learned from loving, both from the annihilation of self through submitting to a mistress and from the exaltation of self through rejecting her. It is the most intensely human, and perhaps the richest, of the sonnet sequences.

In retrospect, it was Sidney who acclimated the sonnet sequence to English soil. He showed Spenser how to employ it for innuendo and wit, turning its conventions into the sort of *double entendre,* embracing both the personal and the universal, which is the hallmark of Spenser's genius. He provided a poetics of liberated language that Shakespeare could apply in the production of vivid imagery to express his sensitive perception of human relationships under the unremitting pressure of fleeting time. He offered Donne the model of a poetic voice that is obsessed with love, but only as a narcissistic exercise toward self-knowledge. Fortunately, despite his own reservations about it, Sidney transplanted the genre of sonnet sequence with roots intact so that English off-shoots drew sustenance from the luxuriant Continental tradition. But he also added native nutrients and cross-pollinated with the mimetic theory of Aristotelians, accomplishing a mutation that resulted in a distinctive English strain. Thanks in large part to Sidney's husbandry, the sonnet sequence in England flourished and soon burst forth in a dazzling display of our most poignant poetry.

NOTES

1. See William A. Ringler, Jr., ed., *The Poems of Sir Philip Sidney* (Oxford: Clarendon Press, 1962), p. 458. Citations of *Astrophel and Stella* will be made by reference to item and line numbers in this edition.

2. *The Arcadian Rhetorike,* ed. Ethel Seaton (Luttrell Society, Oxford: Blackwell, 1950), facsimile of original title page inserted facing p. 1.

3. *Ludovico Ariosto's "Orlando Furioso,"* trans. Harington, ed. Robert McNulty (Oxford: Clarendon Press, 1972), p. 183 [comm. on book 16].

4. It should be remembered that these words "song" and "sonnet" were actually synonymous. Their regular pairing resulted from some persistent urge in English to link two alliterative synonyms, apparently for reinforcement—for example, "might and main," "time and tide," "toss and turn." It was George Gascoigne who in 1575 first attempted to limit the meaning of "sonnet" in English to a poem of fourteen lines: "Some thinke that all Poemes (being short) may be called Sonets, as in deede it is a diminutive worde derived of *Sonare,* but yet I can beste allowe to call those Sonnets whiche are of fouretene lynes, every line conteyning tenne syllables" ("Certayne Notes of Instruction Concerning the Making of Verse or Ryme in English," in *Elizabethan Critical Essays,* ed. G. Gregory Smith, 2 vols. [London: Oxford University Press, 1904], 1:55).

5. Germaine Warkentin, "The Form of Dante's 'Libello' and Its Challenge to Petrarch," *Quaderni d'italianistica* 2 (1981): 162. For helpful comments about the narrative assumptions of Dante and Petrarch, see Sara Sturm-Maddox, "Transformations of Courtly Love Poetry: *Vita Nuova* and *Canzoniere,*" in *The Expansion and Transformations of Courtly Literature,* ed. Nathaniel B. Smith and Joseph T. Snow (Athens: University of Georgia Press, 1980), pp. 128–40.

6. Sidney could have found a noteworthy precedent for giving the lover a name in George Turbervile's *Epitaphes, Epigrams, Songs and Sonets* (London, 1567). In this twice-reprinted collection of miscellaneous short poems, modeled on Petrarch's *rime sparse,* Turbervile provides an overarching framework in a passionate but unsuccessful tale of love related in disconnected amorous lyrics, what he calls on the title page "a Discourse of the Friendly affections of *Tymetes to Pyndara* his Ladie." Turbervile adapts the sonneteer's convention of writing in honor of his own lady by opening and closing his collection with a poem in fulsome praise of his dedicatee, Lady Anne, Countess of Warwick (incidentally, Sidney's aunt by marriage).

In Turbervile's work, however, equally influential as the sonnet tradition was the romantic story of classical lovers, such as Paris and Helen, whom Turbervile uses as the basis for an extended similitude in an introductory poem entitled "The Argument to the whole discourse and Treatise following" (fol. 3–3ᵛ: cf. fol. 5ᵛ, 60, 117, 122, 138ᵛ), and Troilus and Cressida, whom Turbervile recalls repeatedly (cf. fol. 6ᵛ, 30ᵛ, 32, 49ᵛ, 61ᵛ, 71–71ᵛ, 91, 139–40ᵛ). Other hapless couples whom Turbervile mentions include Hero and Leander (fol. 26, 122ᵛ), Dido and Aeneas (fol. 63ᵛ, 99, 103–104ᵛ), and Pyramus and Thisbe (fol. 123ᵛ–24). Tymetes and Pyndara belong to this company. And when Thomas Newman printed Sidney's collection of poems as "Astrophel and Stella," he was probably thinking of the work, at least in part, as yet another example of star-crossed lovers such as these.

7. In number 30, Astrophel mentions the governorship of "my father" in Ireland, and in number 65 he claims to share with Cupid the heraldic emblem of an arrowhead, which was the armorial device of the Sidneys. Stella also, of course, is unmistakably identified in various ways as Penelope, Lady Rich, in numbers 13, 24, 35, and 37.

8. See Alan Sinfield, "Sidney and Astrophil," *Studies in English Literature* 20 (1980): 25–41; and Arthur F. Marotti, "'Love is not love': Elizabethan Sonnet Sequences and the Social Order," *ELH* 49 (1982): 396–428.

9. See my "The Semantics of Symmetry in the Renaissance," *Hebrew University Studies in Literature and the Arts* 11 (1983): 284–316.

10. *A Defence of Poetry*, 79.7–8, in *Miscellaneous Prose of Sir Philip Sidney*, ed. Katherine Duncan-Jones and Jan van Dorsten (Oxford: Clarendon Press, 1973). Citations of Sidney's *Defence* will be made, as here, by reference to page and line numbers in this edition.

11. "The dominant may be defined as the focusing component of a work of art: it rules, determines, and transforms the remaining components. It is the dominant which guarantees the integrity of the structure" ("The Dominant," in *Readings in Russian Poetics: Formalist and Structuralist Views*, ed. Ladislav Matejka and Krystyna Pomorska [1971; rpt. Ann Arbor: University of Michigan Press, 1978], pp. 82–87).

12. George Puttenham was well aware of the exhaustive range of moods the sonneteer must encompass in his need to reconcile opposites. In a chapter entitled "In what forme of Poesie the amorous affections and allurements were uttered," Puttenham comments:

> It requireth a forme of Poesie variable, inconstant, affected, curious and most witty of any others, whereof the joyes were to be uttered in one sorte, the sorrowes in an other, and by the many formes of Poesie, the many moodes and pangs of lovers, throughly to be discovered: the poore soules sometimes praying, beseeching, sometime honouring, avancing, praising: an other while railing, reviling, and cursing: then sorrowing, weeping, lamenting: in the ende laughing, rejoysing & solacing the beloved againe, with a thousand delicate devises, odes, songs, elegies, ballads, sonets and other ditties, mooving one way and another to great compassion.

(*The Arte of English Poesie* [I.xxii], ed. Gladys D. Willcock and Alice Walker [Cambridge: Cambridge University Press, 1936], p. 45).

13. Citations of the *Canzoniere* will be made by reference to item and line number in *Petrarch's Lyric Poems: The "Rime Sparse" and Other Lyrics*, ed. and trans. Robert M. Durling (Cambridge, Mass.: Harvard University Press, 1976).

14. See Charles S. Singleton, *An Essay on the "Vita Nuova"* (reprint ed.; Baltimore: Johns Hopkins University Press, 1977), esp. pp. 78–80.

15. See Thomas P. Roche, Jr., "The Calendrical Structure of Petrarch's *Canzoniere*," *Studies in Philology* 71 (1974): 152–72.

16. In contrast to the *Divina commedia,* which is often almost overpoweringly sensuous, there is a notable lack of sensory detail in the *Vita nuova*. There is negligible description of place, of time, or of personal appearance. Mark Musa draws the incontrovertible conclusion: "This extreme concern with the abstract implies an extreme concern for the spiritual, which means a concern for the essential" (*Dante's "Vita Nuova": A Translation and an Essay* [Bloomington: Indiana University Press, 1973], p. 105).

17. See, for only a few notable examples, numbers 132, 150, 182.

18. Cf. *Vita nuova,* numbers 38 and 39. At an early point, Dante firmly renounces the passionate element in his love: "Though her image, which remained constantly with me, was Love's assurance of holding me, it was of such a pure quality that it never allowed me to be ruled by Love without the faithful counsel of reason" (number 2; quoted from *Vita nuova,* trans. Musa, p. 4).

19. See numbers 101, 140, 236, 240, 360.

20. See numbers 264, 270, 289. But see also numbers 315–17, where Petrarch claims that he was beginning to reconcile his passion with Laura's chastity just as Death snatched her away; and by number 347, abetted by a convenient memory, he asserts to Laura's spirit, "I never wished anything from you but the sunlight of your eyes." By this point, however, the *Canzoniere* is suffused by a maudlin *contemptus mundi*.

21. Perhaps the strongest argument for reading the *Vita nuova* as an exposition of Christian belief is mounted by Singleton; see *Essay on "Vita Nuova,"* esp. pp. 55–77.

22. See, for example, numbers 156–59, 213, 248, 297. For a precise demonstration of Petrarch's ambivalence toward Laura, see Robert M. Durling, "Petrarch's 'Giovene donna sotto un verde lauro'," *Modern Language Notes* 86 (1971): 1–20.

23. See, for example, numbers 90, 173, 191.

24. Cf. number 102: "If at any time I laugh or sing, I do it because I have no way except this one to hide my anguished weeping." Cf. also numbers 127, 134, 178, 224.

25. Astrophel, however, is not above the use of oxymorons; see, for example, *A&S,* 21.7, 41.4, 42.6, 48.13, 60.11, 61.2, 80.3, v.8, viii.20, 103.8, 103.13, 106.1.

26. Cf. *A&S,* numbers 28, 44, 55.

27. Cf. numbers 5, 10, 14, 18, 19, 21, 25, 33, 39, 47, 52, 56, 61, 62, 68, 69, 71, 72, 100, 107, 108.

28. Cf. numbers 66, 67, 76–81, iv, viii, 87, 100, 102.

29. See Ringler, ed., *Poems of Sidney,* pp. 444–46.

30. Ringler, ed., *Poems of Sidney,* pp. 435–40.

31. After centuries of searching and speculating, the only external evidence to suggest that Sidney felt a carnal attraction to Penelope Devereux lies in a recently recovered manuscript account of his death ascribed to George Gifford (*Miscellaneous Prose of Sir Philip Sidney,* ed. Katherine Duncan-Jones and Jan van Dorsten [Oxford: Clarendon Press, 1973], Appendix III; see 169.25–7). But I concur in Duncan-Jones' suspicion that this report "is basically a piece of pious myth-making" (p. 162), hardly to be credited in its details. It is evidently the work of a moralistic preacher who would

not miss an opportunity of impugning *Astrophel and Stella* and the love poems that followed its example.

32. In any case, she felt no embarrassment in acknowledging her identification with Stella; see Ringler, ed., *Poems of Sidney*, p. 436.

33. In number 55, Astrophel expressly renounces the poetics of divine inspiration: "Muses," he says with disappointment, "I oft invoked your holy ayde, / . . . / But now I meane no more your helpe to trie" (lines 1, 9).

34. Esp. numbers 6, 15, 28, 32, 34, 44, 45, 50, 55, 58, 70, 71, 74, 84, 90.

35. Cf. also "paint" in 2.14, 81.7, 93.3, 98.10. To accomplish his painting, of course, the poet has at his disposal the "colors" of rhetoric. This phrasing had become commonplace in English sonneteering; cf., for example, Turbervile's "Aunswere of a woman to hir Lover, supposing his complaint to be but fayned," which begins: "You want no skill to paint / or shew your pangues with Pen" (*Epitaphes, Epigrams,* fol. 31).

36. Quotations from *Amoretti* are taken from *The Poetical Works of Edmund Spenser*, ed. J. C. Smith and Ernest de Selincourt (London: Oxford University Press, 1912).

37. See, for example, numbers 11, 12, 16, 18, 29, 48, 54, 71, 75.

38. See numbers 33, 60, 74, 80.

39. Long ago Louis L. Martz published this opinion and supported it with much documentation from the text; see "The *Amoretti*: 'Most Goodly Temperature'," in *Form and Convention in the Poetry of Edmund Spenser*, ed. William Nelson (New York: Columbia University Press, 1961), pp. 146–68. See also Judith Kalil, "'Mask in Myrth Lyke to a Comedy': Spenser's Persona in the *Amoretti*," *Thoth* 13.2 (1973): 19–26.

40. Yet, in deference to the tradition Shakespeare speaks of him as his Muse and, similar to what Astrophel says of Stella, claims him as his inspiration:

> Be thou the tenth Muse, ten times more in worth
> Than those old nine which rhymers invocate;
> And he that calls on thee, let him bring forth
> Eternal numbers to outlive long date.
> If my slight Muse do please these curious days,
> The pain be mine, but thine shall be the praise.   (38.9–14)

(*The Riverside Shakespeare,* ed. G. Blakemore Evans *et al.* [Boston: Houghton Mifflin, 1974], p. 1756).

41. See John Donne, *The Elegies and the Songs and Sonnets,* ed. Helen Gardner (Oxford: Clarendon Press, 1965), p. 151. All quotations from Donne are taken from this edition.

42. Donne, *Elegies and Songs and Sonnets,* ed. Gardner, pp. lvii–lxii.

43. "Triple Foole," line 3. For other instances of Donne's reproving attitude toward the excessive emotionality of Petrarchism, see "Valediction: Forbidding Mourning," line 6; "Canonization," lines 10–15; and "Loves Infiniteness," lines 3–4.

Annabel Patterson
Jonson, Marvell, and Miscellaneity?

'Tis not, what once it was, the World,
But a rude heap together hurl'd;

. . . .

Your lesser World contains the same.
But in more decent Order tame;

There are two questions to be asked of any collection of poems by a single author: is the arrangement authoritative? And what, if anything, does it signify? In the seventeenth century these questions are both difficult to answer with certainty and peculiarly demanding of inquiry. Several of the volumes we most value—the poems of Donne, Herbert, Marvell, Jonson's *Under-wood*, were all published posthumously. Yet there is as much evidence of ordering in these volumes as in those of their contemporaries who saw to the publication of their own work, like Robert Herrick or Milton; and from all indications, the concept of significant order was culturally available, something that writers could count on intelligent readers to look for.

It has not, however, been equally recognized by modern editors and critics. The original order of Herbert's *The Temple,* as published in 1633, was replaced in 1905 by the hypothetical chronology of George Herbert Palmer's *English Works of George Herbert.* Since being restored in the definitive Oxford edition by F. E. Hutchinson,[1] the apparent blend of architectural, liturgical, and autobiographical structures has provoked several decades of lively controversy.[2] By contrast, it was not until the mid-1960s that the original order of the 1645 *Poems of Mr. John Milton* received critical attention. Since the chronology of Milton's work can be much more reliably reconstructed, often with the help of his own dating, than is the case with Herbert, modern editors have usually adopted that principle; but, as Louis Martz has shown, the order of the 1645 text, actually a pair of volumes, implies a more subtle narrative. Not only did Milton choose not to include all of his early work, but a roughly chronological (historicist) principle of arrangement is counterpointed by a formal principle of sorting by kinds: Latin poems are separated from English ones, devotional poems from secular, sonnets from pastorals. In the English volume, the devotional poems come unmistakably first by metaphysical primacy; and first among them, as a statement of vocational intent, is the *Ode on the Morning of Christ's Nativity.* The last of the secular poems is not *Lycidas,* written in 1637 and clearly pointing ahead to "pastures new," but the 1634 *Maske at Ludlow.* The result is a complex record of the "rising poet," a retrospective arranged at the age of thirty-seven with the wisdom of hindsight and, as Martz suggests, a "farewell to the pleasures and attitudes of youth."[3]

There is another issue here, opened, but not, I think, closed by Martz's essay. The 1645 title page hints at both chronology and deliberate arrangement: the poems, "Compos'd at several times," are "Printed and publish'd according to ORDER." This double entendre refers also, of course, to the Printing Ordinance of 1643 that Milton had just magnificently challenged in *Areopagitica* (1644). This irony may partly explain why a writer who had been publicly supporting the Presbyterians in the first years of the Long Parliament now published a volume with seemingly royalist affiliations; for the title page also defers ostentatiously to "Mr. Henry Lawes Gentleman of the Kings Chappel, and one of His Maiesties Private Musick." Martz saw other signs that the edition constituted a "bland ignoring, or bold confronting, of the political situation" and read them as an attempt to assert "the transcendent values of art."[4] Yet to assert the right to make "Private Musick" in 1645 was not to transcend the historical moment. More probably, it was intended as a reactionary gesture, in defiance of those who had reinstated the censorship of the old regime; and the placing of the *Maske at Ludlow* last, explicitly redated "Anno Dom. 1645," was in that structure to show his continued pride in it, a significant act of impenitence.[5]

We should keep this possibility in mind when considering Herrick's *Hesperides.* Although Herrick almost certainly saw to the publication of his own poems in 1648, and although the original order has never been tampered with, critics are deeply divided as to whether there is a discernible principle of arrangement. Although *Hesperides* contains poems that refer directly to events in the civil war and can therefore be dated, the volume resists solution by even a rough chronology;[6] and because of the epigrams that, for some readers, so rudely interrupt the volume's lyric charm, it encourages readers to fall back on the principle of variety and contrast, or "Delight in Disorder," as Herrick himself put it in the title of one of his most appreciated poems.[7] Others, encouraged by the fact that Herrick himself lists "Time's trans-shifting" among the "arguments" of his book, suspect that even, or especially, a distorted chronology may carry significance.⁸ One principle of order Herrick clearly observed: the separation of his *Noble Numbers,* or devotional verse, however childish, from his subtly pagan lyrics, however implicitly Laudian.⁹ The volume as we have it, with the *Noble Numbers* at the end, contrasts both with Milton's 1645 *Poems* and with the 1633 edition of Donne's poems, where the devotional sonnets were placed first;¹⁰ and it also reverses the strategy of Herrick's friend Mildmay Fane, whose *Otia Sacra* was also published in 1648. Yet the 1647 date on the title page of *Noble Numbers* suggests a change of plan.

It is not entirely impossible that Herrick changed his plan in order to avoid too obvious a comparison with his friend. *Otia Sacra* was also divided into two books, of sacred and secular pastoral verse, in that order. And the second book is prefaced by an explanation of the structure, in verse (of a sort). The first part, we are told, "bears a stamp Divine, / And so may pass for currant Coin."¹¹ That is, it would appear on a cursory reading to be highly acceptable to a Presbyterian censor. In the second part, however, the poet will be "Adorn'd with modest Loyaltie; . . . under a shade / Of such Security" as is provided by the pastoral metaphor.¹² Within the much shorter second part, poems of Stoic retreat modeled on Horace, Martial, or Vergil's second Georgic alternate with comments on the political situation, in which Fane discreetly conveys his commitment to the Stuarts, a hope most easily embodied in the young prince Charles.¹³ In this, too, *Otia Sacra* matches *Hesperides,* which was dedicated to "the most Hopefull Prince, Charles, Prince of Wales." And so also was the 1648 edition of Sir Richard Fanshawe's translation of *Il Pastor Fido,* a reissue of the 1647 edition but with a new collection of Fanshawe's own poems, suggesting by their arrangement a lyric history of the Caroline era. If we add to these Richard Lovelace's *Lucasta,* intended for 1648 but delayed for a year by the Long Parliament's restraint of its author,¹⁴ we may see another dimension of what it means to consider poems in their places. All four volumes were immediately identifiable as royalist in their effect and intent. All four addressed a historical moment defined by the king's imprisonment at Hampton Court in 1647,¹⁵ by the Vote of No Addresses at the end of that year, by which Parliament tried to complete his isolation, and perhaps by expectation of the second civil war in the summer of 1648. If we wish to understand the arrangement of *Hesperides,* we will also have to take into account this larger structure, this possibly coordinated wave of "literary" royalism, designed unmistakably to promote solidarity for the crown at a crucial moment in the revolution, while distracting the attention of the unsympathetic by the apparent neutrality of lyric form and convention.

This last long paragraph should have made it clear that there is a third question, more interesting than the two elementary ones with which we started, to be asked of any collection of poems. To what extent does the existence of authoritative and significant order in a volume depend on the predisposition of the reader to find it or to find it absent? In the case of *Hesperides* there is a marked tendency for readers to divide on ideological lines, according to whether they hold an idealist or an historicist theory of poetry (especially lyric poetry). Among the long-term effects of the old New Criticism, the general demotion of the author and of authorial intention has obviously inhibited any respectful attention to "original" order; and the supremacy of the reader-critic has merged with pedagogic necessity to legitimate the modern anthology. My own preference is for retaining (or returning to) the order as originally published, even in posthumous volumes, unless (as is the case with Donne's 1633 *Poems*) there is manuscript evidence to the contrary. And if the original order of a volume should prove to be *capable* of meaning, one might reasonably construe such a finding as evidence of authorial control; that is, if one were predisposed to the principle of intention.

That this argument is circular need not deter us. It will stand or fall on the quality and interest of the information it produces when applied to specific problems. I offer here a reading of Ben Jonson's *Under-wood* and Andrew Marvell's *Miscellaneous Poems* as coherent structures whose very coherence argues authorial design. Both volumes are alike in asserting an idea of miscellaneity, Marvell's in its title, Jonson's in a prefatory note to the reader, an idea that, I shall argue, was originally intended to distract some part of the expected audience from the actual principle of arrangement. This strategy seems, however, to have totally misled readers of our own century. The definitive edition of *Under-wood* by Herford and Simpson has left us with its order intact, but modern criticism has ignored it; and almost all readers of Marvell approach him via Margoliouth's edition, which drastically rearranges his poems. Whereas Jonson's volume gradually reveals a powerful and subtle chronology, Marvell's was clearly organized by theme. Yet this was invisible to Margoliouth (or so we must suppose), since he reorganized the volume as far as possible on a chronological principle.

In the 1640 folio of Jonson's *Works*, published under the supervision of Sir Kenelm Digby, *The Under-wood* was preceded by the following note "To the Reader":

With the same leave, the Ancients call'd that kind of body Sylva, or
῞γλη, in which there were workes of divers nature, and matter congested; as the multitude call Timber-trees, promiscuously growing, a Wood, or Forrest: so am I bold to entitle these lesser Poems, of later growth, by this of Under-wood, out of the Analogie they hold to the Forrest, in my former booke, and no otherwise.

Ben. Io[h]nson.¹⁶

Taken at face value, this statement suggests that Jonson, toward the end of his life, had "at least begun to arrange" his poems for a new collection;[17] that he regarded it as inferior in some way to his first collection of lyrics and verse epistles, mostly to members of the Sidney family, published in 1616 as *The Forrest*; and that the principle of order in the new collection was the absence of order. All aspects of this self-presentation are peculiar, if not disingenuous. Even within the conventions of modesty *topoi*, it would have seemed odd for him to designate his poems to Charles I, to the queen and to Treasurer Weston as "lesser" than his tributes to the Sidney family; and his stress on the "congested" or promiscuous (indiscriminate) character of the classical sylva appears to be eccentric.

In Statius, the sylva is simply a collection of shorter poems in the epideictic mode—acts of praise or compliment, in which variety and contrast are supplied by the range of subjects praised. When Julius Caesar Scaliger summed up for the late sixteenth century all that was known of classical rhetoric and poetics, he provided a list of what a sylva might contain: marriage songs, birthday songs, prayers to avert an event or for its success, well-wishings before a departure, thanks to our teachers, and all the different forms of consolation to the bereaved.[18] He made no suggestion that a lack of arrangement was part of the tradition. Jonson frequently made use of Scaliger when compiling *Timber, or Discoveries*, a work obviously linked by its title to his governing sylvan metaphor.

Also, despite Drummond of Hawthornden's malicious comment that Jonson cited Ronsard without being able to "understand French,"[19] it is most unlikely that he developed his tree structure in ignorance of Ronsard's *Bocage Royal*, published in the *Oeuvres* of 1584. The *Bocages* carried a preliminary definition of the sylva:

> Comme un Seigneur praticq & soigneux du mesnage
> Regard en sa forest ou dedans son bocage
> Mille arbres differents de fueilles & de fruict:

> L'un pour l'ouvrage est bon, l'autre indocile fuit
> La main de l'artizan: l'autre dur de racine
> Tantost va veoir la guerre, & tantost la marine:
> L'autre est gresle & chancelle, & l'autre spacieux
> Ses bras durs & fueillus envoye jusqu'aux Cieux:
> Ainsi dans ce Bocage on voit de toutes sortes
> D'arguments differents, comme tu les apportes,
> O Muse![20]

Ronsard, who reminded his readers that it was "Stace entre les Romains [qui] nous en monstra la voye" in the sylva, clearly accepted the principle of variety and contrast; but there is no sign in his text of any idea of promiscuity or disarray, the *bocages* themselves being carefully arranged by the rank and political importance of the addressees.

There is, in fact, evidence of equally careful arrangement in *Under-wood*, on a much more interesting principle. The main body of the collection, consisting of eighty-seven occasional poems, is set in a double frame. Three Christian hymns (the first to the Trinity) at the beginning, and a group of short translations from the classics at the end, establish the two main sources of authority in Jonson's poetics. Both the first hymn and the last translation of Martial's epigram on the quiet life (10:47) look forward to death, from distinct but compatible perspectives, the Christian poet looking forward to rest among the saints, the Stoic determined neither to "feare his latest day, nor wish therfore" (*Works*, 8:128, 295). The inner frame consists of "A Celebration of Charis in Ten Lyrick Peeces" and the ten-part elegy, "Eupheme," for Lady Venetia Digby, in second and penultimate place. In their place, these matched but contrasting tributes acquire symbolic force, personifying, as Grace and Fame respectively, two different ideals to which the lyric of praise might strive. Within the volume's closed structure, whose limits are mortality, present grace or youthful eroticism is ultimately rendered trivial by the concept of "Faire Fame left to Posteritie," as Jonson's subtitle for "Eupheme" puts it, a concept that bears on his motives in collecting, for the record, his occasional poems written over more than three decades. Jonson's Fame is a historicising principle,

> . . . ordain'd to crowne
> With ever-greene, and great renowne,
> Their Heads, that Envy would hold downe
> With her, in shade

>   Of Death, and Darknesse; and deprive
>   Their names of being kept alive,
>   By THEE, and CONSCIENCE, both who thrive
>   By the just trade.   (8:272–73)

Adjusting the memory; setting the record straight; these functions specific to elegy are also, as we shall see, central to Jonson's concept of Historia, or historiography; and *Under-wood,* I shall argue, was designed to do for Jonson himself what elegy or history could do for others.

Within this double frame, then (a metaphysical frame of reference), Jonson's career as a writer is exposed to view. Eighty-seven poems record his experiences with the stage, the state, friends, politicians, other men's publications. A contemporary reader would have recognized dimly that the first two-thirds of these poems belong to Jonson's personal history under James I; and when he came to "An Epigram to K. Charles for 100. pounds he sent me in my sicknesse" (8:235), he would discover not only that the king had changed but that the poem is ostentatiously dated in the margin. More dates follow; and those that can be reconstructed for the preceding poems confirm the discovery of a roughly chronological order. There are exceptions. The poem on "Lord Bacons Birth-day" (8:225), which celebrates Bacon's elevation to Viscount St. Albans in his sixtieth year, must be dated 1621; but it follows a group of poems whose references to the German wars and the Spanish Match (James's failed attempt to marry Charles to the Spanish Infanta) belong to the years 1623–25. Yet both the occasional anomaly and the reader's retroactive grasp of the structure are appropriate to a volume in which collection is also so emphatically recollection.

There is, however, one striking disturbance of the system that is impossible to ignore as a slip of the memory, provocative to consider. The pindaric ode to James Fitzgerald, Earl of Desmond, was "Writ," as its title proclaims, "in Queene Elizabeths Time, since lost, and recovered" (8:176). A principle of order is thus admitted, by pointing to its disruption; and the reader is encouraged to wonder about the motive for the poem's "recovery" and location here.

"Here" means, most precisely, immediately after an extraordinary poem whose tone and statement is significantly linked to "Eupheme." "The Mind of the Frontispice to a Booke" was originally written in 1614, to commend to the public Sir Walter Raleigh's *History of the World.*[21] For a poem of compliment its tone was, however, disturbing:

> From Death, and darke Oblivion, (neere the same),
> The Mistress of Mans life, grave *Historie,*
> Raising the World to good, or Evill fame,
> Doth vindicate it to *Æternitie,*
>
> High Providence would so: that nor the good
> Might be defrauded, nor the Great secur'd,
> But both might know their wayes are understood,
> And the reward, and punishment assur'd.

The poem's purport was to explicate Raleigh's emblematic frontispiece showing Historia in all her aspects and to provide an orthodox definition of the historian's role. The last two lines, translating Cicero's *De Oratore* (2:36), praise Historia and, by extension, Raleigh as "Times witnesse, herald of Antiquitie, / The light of Truth, and life of Memorie."

But there was another, darker reading of Jonson's poem. In 1614, Raleigh was in prison, a hostage to James's negotiations with Spain. The *History* had to be published anonymously and was shortly afterwards removed from circulation by royal order. Jonson's poem, discreetly unsigned, suggests a world in which it is necessary to "vindicate" men's reputations because of that threatening distinction between "the good" and "the Great." Relocated in *Under-wood,* the poem's somber tone was itself vindicated in the light of subsequent history. In 1618 James had succumbed to pressure from the Spanish ambassador Gondomar and agreed finally to have Raleigh executed as a traitor. To include the poem in *Under-wood* was, therefore, an act of limited defiance, even though its connection with Raleigh was left for the reader to remember and its text slightly modified.[22]

It is not hard to see, then, why the Fitzgerald ode should follow. In it, Jonson aspired to "Pindar's Muse" in order to raise his "intention" to an appropriate level:

> High, as his mind, that doth advance
> Her upright head, above the reach of Chance,
>   Or the times envie: (8:176)

Fitzgerald was also a notable victim of political injustice, though under Elizabeth, not James. His father had been executed for treason in 1583. He himself had been sent to Ireland, and kept a prisoner in Dublin Castle from 1579 to 1584, in the Tower of London from 1584 until 1600. To Jonson he was therefore a stoic hero, his integrity created by default; and the original purpose of the poem was, apparently, to encourage the earl to remain loyal to the crown in the hope that Elizabeth would relent and release him:

> Then shall my Verses, like strong Charmes,
> Breake the knit Circle of her Stonie Armes,
>   That hold[s] your spirit:
>   And keepes your merit
> Lock't in her cold embraces, from the view
>   Of eyes more true,
> Who would with judgement search, searching conclude
>   (as prov'd in you)
> True noblesse. Palme growes straight, though handled
>   ne're so rude.
>
>   Nor thinke your selfe unfortunate,
>   If subject to the jealous errors
> Of politique pretext, that wryes a State,
>   Sinke not beneath these terrors:
>   But whisper; O glad Innocence,
> Where only a mans birth is his offence,
> . . . .
> Of then (my best-best lov'd) let me importune,
>   That you will stand
> As farre from all revolt, as you are now from Fortune.

Since Desmond was in fact released in 1600, the poem's restrained optimism was initially justified; but by the time it was "recovered" for *Underwood* Fitzgerald was long dead, dead at the age of thirty-one, his health having been undermined by his twenty-one years in prison. The ode's darker side, its potential alienation from the power structure to which its author paid deference, was therefore retroactively manifest.

In sequence these two poems offer an ironic, indeed cynical, brand of exegesis, not only for themselves, but for the poems that surround them. It is a form of intertextuality to which only knowledge of the historical circumstances can give full access; but in this volume the act of historicising is explicitly rendered problematic by the act of recollection, by the fact that time does not stand still. Chronological order here means something more subtle than arrangement by date of composition; and as Jonson's initial motives and "intention" in writing for Fitzgerald in the late 1590s and for Raleigh in 1614 must have been replaced by different imperatives in the late 1630s, so the poems in their new location acquire meanings that are equally intentional, equally "original," *found* meanings accreted in hindsight, but surely found by Jonson.

There are many other ironic or disturbing juxtapositions in *Under-wood*, too many to be explored here.[23] But one of the most characteristic occurs at the point where James's reign is seen to give place to Charles's. That apparently first of the Caroline poems "An Epigram To K. Charles for a 100. pounds he sent me in my sicknesse," is dated 1629, the opening year of Charles's "personal rule," or the Eleven Years' Tyranny, as others would call it. Jonson's reference to "the Peoples Evill" in the last line of his otherwise flattering poem indicates his awareness of the king's recent struggle with the House of Commons and his unwilling acceptance of their demands in the Petition of Right. Read in isolation, this poem could all too easily categorize Jonson as a sycophant, playing on the royal cure for the King's Evil (scrofula) in the hopes of a cure for the "Poets Evill, Povertie" (8:235). But such a reading will not stand up to the discovery that the preceding poem is an attack on "all the games of Fortune, plaid at Court" (8:234). It is, further, a praise of an unnamed bishop whose removal from court office has made him, in Jonson's eyes, another one of those heroic victims of the system:

> That you have seene the pride, beheld the sport,
> And all the games of Fortune, plaid at Court;
> View'd there the mercat, read the wretched rate
> At which there are, would sell the Prince, and State:
> That scarce you heare a publike voyce alive,
> But whisper'd Counsells, and those only thrive;
> Yet are got off thence, with cleare mind, and hands
> To lift to heaven: who is't not understands
> Your happinesse, and doth not speake you blest,
> To see you set apart, thus, from the rest.

As a text, the poem queries the epigram to Charles, in its emphasis on the "holy gifts of grace / Annexed to his Person, and his place"; but when we also think we know who the bishop was, the voice of ironic interrogation is unmistakable.

The bishop was almost certainly John Williams, bishop of Lincoln, who had been selected by James to take on the Lord-Keepership after Bacon's fall. In 1625, shortly after his accession, Charles removed him from office, ostensibly to separate the functions of church and state, but more likely to rid himself of an advisor with strong parliamentarian principles. Williams had played an important role in the House of Lords during the debates on the Petition of Right, a fact that postdates the composition of the poem but surely influenced its placement here, for his aim was to strengthen the Petition, specifically by the inclusion of a clause against arbitrary imprisonment.[24] He belonged, then, in Jonson's system of values, with those arbitrarily imprisoned figures, Raleigh and Williams; but Jonson himself, caught in the less visible trap of the "Poets Evill, Povertie," was condemned to lead a double life and speak with a double voice. If his juxtaposition of compliments to Williams and Charles works, in painful retrospect, to the latter's disadvantage, it also implies a criticism of himself; and as the sylva tradition depends on a societal idea of poetry, on those public assumptions without which praise is literally unspeakable, so Jonson depended on the sylva to allow him to reflect out loud on those public assumptions and especially on those political and financial exigencies that marked the limits of his own freedom.

The structure of *Under-wood* is, then, neither "matter congested" and "promiscuously" assorted, nor a banal and mechanical chronology. It is essentially a narrative structure, an elliptical history of the Jacobean and Caroline era, informed by Jonson's concept of Historia as rectification of the memory. The story is told partly by the poems in their places, partly by the silent operations that time has performed on them and they on each other; and the autobiographical pressure on the volume is intensified by poems like the "Ode: To himselfe" or "An Epistle answering to one that asked to be Sealed of the Tribe of Ben," poems of self-definition in which Jonson explored the costs and compensations of his chosen profession.

This same pressure informs, finally, the most famous poem in *Under-wood,* so often read out of its sequence in the Caroline poems of 1629, so often subjected to a purely idealistic reading: the wonderful pindaric ode "To the immortall memorie, and friendship of that noble paire, Sir Lucius Cary, and Sir H. Morison." Reading the poem between an epigram on court flattery and the self-abasing "Epistle Mendicant" to Treasurer Weston, we are more likely to notice, alongside the titular heroes, Jonson's portrait of the corrupt elderly statesman who stooped "To sordid flatteries, acts of strife" and the fact that Jonson aligns himself with those old men whose idealism the age has spoiled. "Goe now," he told himself,

> . . . and tell out dayes summ'd up with feares,
> And make them yeares;
> Produce thy masse of miseries on the Stage,

> To swell thine age;
> Repeat of things a throng,
> To shew thou has beene long. (8:244–45)

The historiographical import of the language here—telling out days, summing up, repeating—consists with the memorial function of the poem as a whole; but the emphasis on fears and miseries, on the complicity of the self in societal decadence, reminds us that fame, as in Raleigh's emblematic title page, has two aspects, one fair, the other decidedly spotted. We do Jonson an injustice, then, if we ignore what the order of the *Under-wood* poems can suggest. The evidence as presented in 1640 argues that his idealism was not empty, his venality and servility not unselfconscious, his stand, finally, not without courage. Whatever else his note "To the Reader" tells us, it surely declares his intention to own and publish these poems, to assert his authorship, and to take responsibility, in them, for the record of his past.

When Marvell's *Miscellaneous Poems* appeared in the spring of 1681, about two and a half years after his death, it too carried a note "To the Reader." If Jonson's was disingenuous, this was, in one respect, a downright lie:

> These are to Certifie every Ingenious Reader, that all these Poems, as also the other things in this book contained, are Printed according to the exact Copies of my late dear Husband, under his own Hand-Writing, being found since his Death among his other Papers, Witness my Hand this 15th day of October, 1680.
>
> Mary Marvell.

In 1726 Thomas Cooke stated that the volume was "published with no other than a mercenary View, and indeed not all to the Honour of the deceased, by a Woman with whom he lodged, who hoped by this Stratagem, to share in what he left behind him. He was never married."[25] And in 1938 F. S. Tupper established that Mary Palmer's claim to Marvell's name was indeed a fiction, part of a ploy involving Marvell's business associates, and discovered rival claims on a bond for £500 that was tied up in his estate.[26] It was merely an inference, however, that the publication of the poems was also motivated by greed, a "mere move in the game of obtaining credence for the widowhood."[27] And there seems to have been a further inference that, as Mary Palmer was an uneducated woman, the arrangement of the volume was both unsupervised and unreliable. Margoliouth, in consequence, felt free to restructure the volume, on what it must be admitted are inconsistent principles. On the one hand, he worked by genre, trying to get the pastoral dialogues together, moving four prose epitaphs to the end of the volume and the single letter to his second volume, with the rest of Marvell's correspondence; on the other, "satirical, commendatory, and political poems" were "collected together and arranged in chronological order" (1:225).

We do not, however, need to go this route. Whether Mary Palmer carried to the printer a single manuscript or a bundle of papers, someone not without intelligence arranged the contents of the *Miscellaneous Poems* in a way that belies their title. And there are other facts about the volume and the circumstances in which it appeared that deserve reconsideration. Not the least of these is the extraordinary fact that the "Cromwell poems"— "An Horatian Ode upon Cromwel's Return from Ireland," "The First Anniversary of the Government under O. C.," and "A Poem upon the Death of O. C."—were canceled while the volume was actually in press, surviving only in two known copies. The motives for publication and for cancellation cannot be unconnected; between them lies the question of the volume's arrangement and its possible significance.

There are, also, two connected points of emphasis in the volume's front matter. One is the reminder, on the title page, that the author was "Late Member of the Honourable House of Commons"; the other is "Mary Marvell"'s specification of the date: 15 October 1680. What links them is the recent history of the English Parliament in its struggles to survive as an institution, as a constitutional force, against the will of Charles II, who would have much preferred to rule without its interference. In that conflict Marvell had played a part, by publishing in the winter of 1676–77 his *Account of the Growth of Popery and Arbitrary Government,* which, though published anonymously, was widely suspected to be his.[28] Between then and October 1680, English political history had been permanently scarred by the Popish Plot (which seemed to confirm many of the suspicions held by Marvell and much of the nation) and its consequence, the Exclusionist bills in parliament, by which Shaftesbury and his followers hoped to disable the Roman Catholic James, Duke of York, from the succession. The further consequences of the Exclusionist crisis were two dissolutions of parliament and several prorogations, with the result that, on 21 October 1680, that assembly was due to meet for the first time since mid-May 1679.[29] It is impossible that a volume of any kind, appearing less than a week before this hotly anticipated event, and advertised as by a "Late

Member of the Honourable House of Commons," should not have been expected to play some part in the political imagination.

There was also another side to the business dealings uncovered by Tupper, in that both Thompson and Nelthorpe, the bankrupt bankers whom Marvell, with the assistance of Mrs. Palmer, concealed in secret lodgings in the spring of 1678, were connected to political activists on the side of Shaftesbury;[30] while Robert Boulter, who printed the *Miscellaneous Poems*, was actually arrested in July 1681 for seditious talk, saying that "he did not question to see the monarchy reduced into a commonwealth and very speedily."[31] These facts make it most unlikely that Mary Palmer's motives were purely (or rather impurely) mercenary; more probably she collaborated with Thompson and Boulter in a decision to publish Marvell's work at a moment calculated to assist the cause to which he had devoted the last ten years of his life. Certainly the volume was of particular interest to Shaftesbury's party; as Anthony à Wood reported, Marvell's poems "were taken into the hands of many persons of his persuasion, and by them cried up as excellent."[32]

Before attempting to explain why this could have happened, it is worth noting that "Mary Marvell" addresses herself to "every Ingenious Reader." While every reader may, even then, have regarded himself as ingenious, the word happened to be of peculiar significance in Marvell's personal lexicon. For him it meant a complex of values derived from the classical *ingenium*, and perhaps particularly associated with Cicero: natural talent, verbal wit, genius, political intelligence. In 1676 he had published a prose pamphlet in which he articulated the task of the religious polemicist, "to whom the bishop shall commit *omne et omnimodum suum ingenium*" (absolutely all his wit);[33] and at the very beginning of his career as a writer, he had equated being ingenious with "speaking well," both with a culture that the civil war threatened to destroy. The occasion was the publication, finally, of Richard Lovelace's *Lucasta* in 1649, on which we have already briefly focused, and Marvell's commendatory poem took the position that what threatened ingenuity was the confusion of literature and politics; that the author's difficulties in getting his poems before the public were the result of his royalist activism:

> Our times are much degenerate from those
> Which your sweet Muse which your fair Fortune chose,
> And as complexions alter with the Climes,
> Our wits have drawne th'infection of our times.

That candid Age no other way could tell
To be ingenious, but by speaking well.
Who best could prayse, had then the greatest prayse.
(italics added)

Now, on the contrary:

> The barbed Censurers begin to looke
> Like the grim consistory on thy Booke;
> . . . .
> Some reading your *Lucasta* will alledge
> You wrong'd in her the Houses Priviledge.
> Some that you under sequestration are,
> Because you write when going to the Warre,
> And one the Book prohibits, because *Kent*
> Their first Petition by the Authour sent.[34]

So Marvell in 1649 had played with the notion that a book of lyric poems ought to be immune from political censorship, a neutral event to be read independently of its author's political reputation. Yet he must have known even then (and the wit shows it) that the ideal of literary neutrality was a fiction. When the *Miscellaneous Poems* appeared in 1681, its title may actually have connived at the same fiction, with the same mixed success, since the Cromwell poems did not survive censorship, whether actual or merely anticipated.

The new parliament did not last long. On 10 January 1681, it was prorogued in the middle of an attempt to pass the second Exclusion Bill and then dissolved on 18 January. The *Miscellaneous Poems* were offered for sale on 20 January. According to Pierre Legouis, it was this defeat of the Whigs that probably led the printer to lose his nerve and cancel the Cromwell poems; and the result was a volume in which, "sous le titre sans prétention," the public received all of Marvell's work that "la censure la plus soupçonneuse devait déclarer inoffensifs."[35] I am not so sure that the title was without pretence, nor that the remaining contents of the volume were quite so inoffensive; the original order of the poems both supports such a hypothesis and allows, on closer investigation, messages to emerge that would have been highly acceptable, possibly even helpful, to the temporarily frustrated Opposition.

The most obvious fact about the original order is that of grouping. The volume opens with a group of eight devotional poems: the most unequivocally inoffensive category of lyric at any time, one might suppose, although the recent paranoia about "popery" had rendered the style of devotion problematic. It was characteristic of Marvell, but it was also wise, to confuse initially the question of where the author stood on the place of asceticism and aestheticism in the religious life, for example. Several of the group have apparently Roman Catholic texts or genres as models or analogues: "On a Drop of Dew" derives from Henry Hawkins's *Partheneia Sacra,* "A Dialogue between the Soul and Body" from a Jesuit emblem book,[36] "Eyes and Tears" recalls the Counter-Reformation "poetry of tears," with its focus on the Magdalene. Yet "Bermudas" celebrates the escape of Puritan settlers in the New World from "Prelat's rage," a poem more obviously appropriate to Marvell's Nonconformist connections. Very close readings may determine that these poems rewrite or modify the positions from which they seem to start, creating a delicate structure of objectivity, if not of non-alignment; and the cursory reader would certainly find nothing he could certainly approve or disapprove, nothing to alarm him. It is quite startling, however, to see what happens to the group in Margoliouth's edition. For after "Clorinda and Damon," clearly a spiritualized eclogue, a mini-drama of conversion, both of the speakers and of the pastoral metaphor, Margoliouth inserted "A Dialogue between Thyrsis and Dorinda" on the grounds that it was "misplaced" in the folio and belonged with "the other poems of its kind" (1:247). A preliminary distinction between spiritual and secular pastoral is thus destroyed but not, however, for the sake of another kind of consistency, since another pastoral dialogue, "Ametas and Thestylis making Hay-Ropes," was left in its original place.

That place is within the second obvious grouping, a set of twenty poems, all of which (with one major exception) deal in some form with attraction (usually sexual) to the things of this world (predominantly female). The effect of the group is complicated by the opening and closing poems, "The Nymph complaining for the death of her Faun" and the two versions of "The Garden," English and Latin, respectively; for the nymph's language always trembles on the brink of allegory, the speaker in the garden is poised for longer flight, and both poems powerfully suggest the liminality of categories of experience, the difficulty of categorization. Yet the overall effect of the grouping is of a harmless blend of "metaphysical" and "cavalier" modes of poetry, perfectly acceptable to a Restoration audience, and, from a Modernist perspective, revealing Marvell at his best.

There is no getting away, however, from the fact that the group contains one shocking anomaly, "Tom May's Death." The subject of this poem is the actual death of the poet-historian Thomas May in 1650 and his imagined descent into the underworld, where he is condemned by the ghost of Ben Jonson as a "servil' wit, and Mercenary Pen," who has destroyed his credibility as a writer by becoming too partisan, by turning "the Chronicler to Spartacus," or the Puritan revolutionaries. Much has been written about the apparent inconsistencies between this poem and Marvell's "Horatian Ode," presumably composed at the same time and adopting a very different political stance, not to mention indulging in the same kind of "Romane cast similitude" for which Jonson's ghost blames May.[37] And the canonical status of the poem has been seriously thrown into question by the discovery that it was carefully excised from the "Popple" manuscript of Marvell's poems, a manuscript that almost certainly derives from the family of William Popple, Marvell's beloved nephew, and appears to be a copy of the *Miscellaneous Poems* amended in preparation for a new edition.[38]

Margoliouth, who would have perceived no anomaly since he saw no groupings, removed "Tom May's Death" to that new group of his own, the "satirical, commendatory and political poems" for which some date could be ascertained or conjectured. I am alternatively drawn to the radical solution of the Popple manuscript, which solves a number of problems at once, and required to consider what the effect of the poem in its original place would have been. Certainly its impact, immediately following "The Picture of little T. C. in a Prospect of Flowers," would have been shocking, alerting the reader to a much larger set of issues and the responsibility of the poet to preside over times of historical crisis:

> When the Sword glitters ore the Judges head,
> And fear has Coward Churchmen silenced,
> Then is the Poets time, 'tis then he drawes,
> And single fights forsaken Vertues cause.
> He, when the wheel of Empire, whirleth back,
> And though the World['s] disjointed Axel crack,
> Sings still of ancient Rights and better Times.[39]

It is an effect largely dispersed when the poem is read *after* the "Horatian Ode," when the reader's attention is drawn instead to the contradictions between the two.

There follows in the original a group of poems that were obviously difficult to categorize by theme or mode of experience, yet that share a certain literariness: the Latin response to the graphologist Joseph de Maniban, who had somewhat crudely analysed Marvell's handwriting; the satire on

Richard Fleckno, author of "hideous verse" inflicted on Marvell during a visit to Rome; the Latin and English compliments to Dr. Robert Witty on his translation of the *Popular Errors* in medical thought; the wonderful poem "On Mr. Milton's Paradise Lost"; and a handful of Latin epigrams. The group ends with a translation of a famous chorus from Seneca's *Thyestes* (act 2, end) which resembles in its Stoicism and its sense of finality Jonson's translation of Martial on the quiet life. Its rejection of court life and the "publick Stage" is equally Jonsonian and equally a pose, or at least a wish that the real career denied:

> In calm Leisure let me rest;
> And far of the publick Stage
> Pass away my silent Age.
>
> .   .   .   .   .
>
> Who expos'd to others Ey's,
> Into his own Heart ne'r pry's,
> Death to him's a Strange surprise.   (p. 64)

Its chief function here, I infer, is to introduce the next grouping, a series of epitaphs, in prose and verse, to members of Puritan families and the letter consoling Sir John Trott for the death of one of his sons.

These six pieces, all completely dispersed in Margoliouth's edition, supply the credo that was only barely discernible in the opening devotional section. They are all, of course, tributes to Puritan virtues and values: Jane Oxenbridge's "antiqua modestia," the "Honesta Disciplina" that Edmund Trott acquired from his parents, the unnamed young man who was "Chearful without Gall, Sober without Formality, Prudent without Stratagem; and Religious without Affectation"; and the unnamed young woman whose life was a reproach to "this Age loose and al unlac't." All these make explicit (even if in Latin) what was only implicit in "Bermudas" but fully developed in Marvell's prose pamphlets of the 1670s, especially *The Rehearsal Transpros'd*: that the Nonconformists were not narrow-minded zealots, but culturally worthy of respect. It is interesting to note, too, that the young John Trott is described as having been "Ingeniosus supra Fidem," enhancing faith with wit. And if we wonder why the letter to his bereaved father appears here in such splendid *formal* isolation (made more splendid by the hugely bold type that introduces it), the answer may lie in a peculiarly ingenious form of topicality.

When Marvell originally wrote the letter in 1667, he was obsessed, as we know from his satires, by the debacle of the Second Dutch War and the role in that disaster of Edward Hyde, then Chancellor, later Earl of Clarendon. It was that preoccupation that no doubt explained his peculiar illustration of bereavement by the story of Eli who "had been Chancellor, and in effect King of Israel, for so many years":

> he heard that Israel was overcome, that his two Sons Hophni and Phineas were slain in one day, and saw himself without hope of Issue, and which imbittered it further without succession to the Government, yet he fell not till the News that the Ark of God was taken. I pray God that we may never have the same paralel perfected in our publick concernments. (p. 68)

One has to wonder what consolation Sir John was supposed to derive from this dubious "paralel" to his own situation. But when the letter was published in 1681, the nature of the parallel had significantly altered. The king was without legal issue, the problem of the succession was foremost in everyone's mind, and the reference to "publick concernments" would have leaped from the page, in a context of sternly Puritan idealism.

It is not without preparation, then, that the volume proceeds to the character and contributions of another Puritan family—Thomas Lord Fairfax and his wife and daughter, to whom Marvell acted as tutor in 1651–53. The three Fairfax poems retained their natural connection to each other in Margoliouth's edition, excluded, perhaps for want of confident dating, from his chronological reorganization. What they offer, in ascending order of complexity, is an analysis of the competing ideals of the quiet life and of political responsibility, as exemplified by a family that had had singular opportunity to explore them both. The "Epigramma in Duos montes" and still more its English counterpart, "Upon the Hill and Grove at Bill-Borow," are studies for the long apology, in "Upon Appleton House," for a revolutionary leader who abandoned "publick concernments" for the pleasures of retirement on his country estate. And the point of *this* grouping is made clearer when we come to the last section of the *Miscellaneous Poems,* where a political imperative is massively reinstated.

In the surviving uncensored copies of the volume, the last section contained, with one exception,[40] poems devoted to the praise of English republicanism, with Cromwell as its presiding genius. The group begins with naval imperialism, in "On the Victory obtained by Blake over the Spaniards . . . 1657"[41] and "The Character of Holland," written early in 1653 as propaganda for the First Dutch War. It ends, appropriately, with "A Poem upon the Death of O. C." International diplomacy is represented by the poem on Oliver St. John's embassy to the United Provinces, the Latin

"Letter to Doctor Ingelo, then with my Lord Whitlock, Ambassador from the Protector to the Queen of Sweden," and two Latin epigrams on the portrait of himself that Cromwell sent to Queen Christina. The role of Cromwell as the possible founder of a dynasty is suggested not only in the final elegy but also in the "Two Songs at the Marriage of the Lord Fauconberg and the Lady Mary Cromwell," pastoral dialogues carefully segregated by their location from their *formal* analogues in the first and second sections of the volume. When the three major "Cromwell poems" were canceled, these songs became the volume's conclusion. Yet their representation of Cromwell as the patriarch shepherd Menalca[s] was no less ideological, given what preceded it, than the final elegy would have been. Indeed, in 1681 some of the lesser poems in this group might have been even more significant, at least in terms of topical possibilities, opportunities for re-reading in the light of later events such as those presented to the audience in Jonson's *Under-wood*. The two poems on Anglo-Dutch relations acquire a certain irony in the knowledge that the First Dutch War had been followed by the Second, in 1664–68, and by the Third in the 1670s; in the knowledge that Marvell had come to take a very different position toward the Dutch, both in his *Last Instructions to a Painter* in 1667, and especially in his *Account of the Growth of Popery*, by which time he had become convinced that the Third Dutch War was merely a ploy to conceal the sinister dealings between Charles II and Louis XIV of France. Similarly, the epic alliance that Marvell had envisaged in 1653 between Cromwell and Queen Christina was to have had as its objective an anti-Catholic campaign in Europe. The difference between those hopes and the facts of 1681 was all too apparent.

It is worth noticing, finally, that the Latin epigram on Oliver St. John's mission to the Dutch reintroduces "Mary Marvell"'s mode of address to the reader. "Ingeniosa Viris contingunt Nomina magnis," Marvell had written in 1651, intending to play ingeniously on the ambassador's name, especially its fortuitous connection with Oliver Cromwell. But the epigram also assumes, interestingly, a principle of encoding. "Chance," Marvell continued, "covers truth under a prophetic name"; and since the republic has entrusted its diplomacy to a man so mysteriously named,

> Non opus Arcanos Chartis committere Sensus,
> Et varia licitos condere Fraude Dolos.
> Tu quoque si taceas tames est Legatio Nomen
> Et velut in Scytale publica verba refert. (p. 130)

It is not necessary to commit arcane meanings to paper, and to conceal licit stratagems with multiple deceit. Even if you say nothing, your name is an embassy; and, just as in Scytale [an ancient Spartan form of code] it carries public significance.

I think we could probably say the same for the naming that appeared on the title page of the 1681 folio: "*Miscellaneous Poems* By Andrew Marvell, Esq; Late Member of the Honourable House of Commons"; and as in the art of Scytale the message could only be read when wound on a staff of a particular shape and size, so the meaning of the 1681 folio depends in part on its structure. In fact, as the relationship between *respublica* and *publica verba* is an extraordinarily complex one, not only in English political history, but also in language theory and ideas of representation, one might venture the larger statement, however rhetorically crude, that the original order of the volume *was* its meaning in 1681. This is not to devalue Margoliouth's edition, the object of which was to show as far as possible the shape of Marvell's career as a poet and hence the importance of chronology, when determinable; nor does it resolve the central ambiguity in my use of the term "original." But if Marvell did not himself arrange his poems in this way, leading his readers through different categories, different imperatives, until they arrived at active republicanism, it was done by someone who knew his work and its import extremely well.

NOTES

1. F. E. Hutchinson, *The Works of George Herbert* (Oxford: Oxford University Press, 1941), pp. lxvii–lxix.

2. John R. Roberts, in *George Herbert: An Annotated Bibliography of Modern Criticism, 1905–1974* (Columbia and London: University of Missouri Press, 1978), lists twenty-seven items relating to the structure of *The Temple*. Amy Charles, however, in "The Williams Manuscript and *The Temple*," *Renaissance Papers* (1971): 59–70, doubted whether anyone except Herbert could ever explain the order.

3. Louis L. Martz, *Poet of Exile: A Study of Milton's Poetry* (New Haven and London: Yale University Press, 1980), p. 37. The argument was first made in "The Rising Poet, 1645," in *The Lyric and Dramatic Milton*, ed. Joseph Summers, Selected Papers from the English Institute (New York: Columbia University Press, 1965), pp. 3–33.

4. Martz, *Poet of Exile*, p. 34. He cites as other evidence Moseley's association in his preface of Milton with Waller, recently exiled for a royalist plot against the Long Parliament, and the reprinting from the 1637 edition of the *Maske at Ludlow* of Lawe's dedication to "a young nobleman with strong royalist associations."

5. This assumes that the masque was unequivocally regarded as a court form, mor-

ally suspect and wastefully expensive, an attitude expressed in William Prynne's *Histriomastix* (1633) and consistent with Puritan suspicion of all drama. Milton's *Masque* was, of course, already a reformed and chastened example of the genre.

6. See L. C. Martin, ed., *The Poetical Works of Robert Herrick* (Oxford: Oxford University Press, 1956), pp. xxxvi–xl. Martin followed Floris Delattre, *Robert Herrick* (Paris: Bruges, 1912), pp. 490–91, in believing in the presence of a rough chronology of composition; but his table of datable poems shows several striking anomalies.

7. See, for example, J. Max Patrick, ed., *The Complete Poetry of Robert Herrick* (New York: New York University Press, 1963), p. viii; and Louis L. Martz, "Marvell and Herrick: The Masks of Mannerism," in *Approaches To Marvell*, ed. C. A. Patrides (London: Routledge & Kegan Paul, 1978), pp. 194–202. For a strictly formal account of the arrangement, see John L. Kimmey, "Order and Form in Herrick's *Hesperides*," *Journal of English and Germanic Philology* 70 (1971): 255–68.

8. I defer here to the work in progress of Ann Baynes Coiro, who finds in the placing of the epigrams the key to Herrick's *recollected* account of the Caroline era.

9. See Leah Sinanoglou Marcus, "Herrick's *Hesperides* and the 'Proclamation made for May'," *Studies in Philology* 76 (1979): 49–74.

10. They were, however, preceded by the "Progresse of the Soule," probably on account of its deceptively spiritual title.

11. *Otia Sacra* (1648), facsimile ed. Donald M. Friedman (Delmar, New York: Scholars' Facsimiles & Reprints, 1975), p. 125.

12. This strategy is also projected by the frontispiece, engraved by William Marshall, who was also the artist of Herrick's frontispiece. Both show pastoral landscapes; but Fane's strategically misquotes Vergil's first eclogue to place himself not "lentus" but "*tutus* in Umbra."

13. *Otia Sacra*, p. 158:

> . . . .Your return will bless
> The Brittish Islands with new cheerfulness:
> Be pleas'd no longer therefore, Sir, to tarry,
> Lest a whole Gleek of Kingdomes should miscarry;
> But You that are the Blossom of all hope,
> Dispell the Mists from off this Horiscope;
>
> . . . .
>
> And place Your Royall Father where he was.

14. *Lucasta* was granted a license on 4 February 1648 but not registered for actual publication until mid-May 1649. The delay was obviously caused by his arrest in April 1648 by the parliamentary forces led by Fairfax. He was finally released on 10 April 1649, and the sequestration of his estate remitted by the House of Commons on 5 May.

15. Compare Herrick, "To the King, Upon his welcome to Hampton-Court"; Fane, "Upon King Charles's meeting with . . . his three children at Maidenhead, the 15 of July, 1647"; and Lovelace's ecphrastic poem on Sir Peter Lely's portrait of Charles I and the Duke of York, painted during the Hampton Court imprisonment (*Lucasta*, pp. 57–58).

16. Ben Jonson, *Works*, ed. C. H. Herford and Percy and Evelyn Simpson (Oxford: Oxford University Press, 1947), 8:126.

17. *Works*, 11:47–48.

18. Julius Caesar Scaliger, *Poetices Libri Septem* (Heidelberg, 1561), pp. 156–69.

19. From Jonson's "Conversations" with Drummond, in *Works*, 1:134.

20. *Les Oeuvres de Pierre de Ronsard* (1587), ed. Isidore Silver (Chicago, London and Paris: University of Chicago Press, 1967), 4:225.

21. See M. Corbett and R. Lightbown, *The Comely Frontispiece: The Emblematic Title-Page in England, 1550-1660* (London: Routledge & Kegan Paul, 1979), p. 135, for the text of the poem as published in 1614, and an account of the circumstances of its publication.

22. In *Under-wood* the threatening reference to rewards and punishments was replaced by the more conventional line, "When Vice alike in time with vertue dur'd." The change, qualitatively for the worse, may have been dictated by caution. On the other hand, it may simply reflect a later admission that there *was* no justice.

23. There is an extended account of *Under-wood,* incorporating the poems to Bacon, Coke and Weston, in my *Censorship and Interpretation: The Conditions of Writing and Reading in Early Modern England* (Madison: University of Wisconsin Press, 1984).

24. See B. Dew Roberts, *Mitre & Musket: John Williams, Lord Keeper, Archbishop of York* (London: Oxford University Press, 1938), pp. 94–117.

25. Thomas Cooke, *The Works of Andrew Marvell Esq.* (London, 1726), 1:36.

26. F. S. Tupper, "Mary Palmer, Alias Mrs. Andrew Marvell," *PMLA* 53 (1938): 367–88.

27. H. M. Margoliouth, ed., *The Poems and Letters of Andrew Marvell* (1927; rev. Pierre Legouis, Oxford: Oxford University Press, 1971), 1:242.

28. See my *Marvell and the Civic Crown* (Princeton: Princeton University Press, 1978), pp. 250–51.

29. For details, see David Ogg, *England in the Reign of Charles II* (Oxford: Oxford University Press, 1934), 2:584–602.

30. Tupper, "Mary Palmer," pp. 368, 372n. Tupper observed that Marvell's connection with Thompson, Nelthorpe and Major Braman, Thompson's brother-in-law, "reputed to be a great fanatick," put him "more intimately into the group of anti-Royalist plotters than we had realized."

31. Margoliouth, *Poems and Letters,* 1:241. Cited from Calendar of State Papers, Domestic, 1680/1, pp. 382, 385–86.

32. Anthony à Wood, *Athenae Oxonienses,* ed. Philip Bliss (London, 1813–20), 4:239.

33. *Mr. Smirke: Or, The Divine in Mode* (London, 1676), in *Complete Works,* ed. A. B. Grosart (1875, rpr. New York: AMS, 1966), 4:8–9.

34. Margoliouth, *Poems and Letters,* 1:2–3. The poem alludes to the sequestration of Lovelace's estate and his involvement in the first Kentish Petition.

35. Pierre Legouis, *André Marvell: poète, puritain, patriote, 1621–1678* (Paris and London: Didier, 1928), p. 428.

36. For the relationship between Marvell's dewdrop and one of the sacred emblems in *Partheneia Sacra* (Rouen, 1633), see Rosalie M. Colie, *"My Ecchoing Song": Andrew Marvell's Poetry of Criticism* (Princeton: Princeton University Press, 1970), pp. 115–17; for the "source" of his soul-body debate in Hermann Hugo, *Pia Desideria* (Antwerp, 1624), another Jesuit emblem book, see Kitty Scoular Datta, "New Light on Marvell's 'Dialogue between the Soul and Body,'" *Renaissance Quarterly* 22 (1969): 242–55.

37. That is, comparisons between English and Roman history, especially with respect to their periods of civil war. It is well known that Marvell actually opens the "Horatian Ode" with echoes of May's 1627 translation of Lucan's *De Bello Civile*.

38. The status of the Bodleian manuscript, Eng. poet. d. 49, remains a matter of debate. For the most recent discussion, see Warren L. Chernaik, *The Poet's Time: Politics and Religion in the Work of Andrew Marvell* (Cambridge: Cambridge University Press, 1983), pp. 206–209.

39. Andrew Marvell, *Miscellaneous Poems (1681)*, facsimile ed. (Menston, England: The Scolar Press, 1973), p. 37.

40. The exception is "Thyrsis and Dorinda." It is interesting to note that this poem was also carefully excised from the Popple manuscript, and that recent scholarship has discovered manuscript versions of it too early for Marvell's authorship. See Chernaik, *The Poet's Time,* p. 207.

41. This poem was also deleted from Popple.

John T. Shawcross
The Arrangement and Order of John Donne's Poems

It is axiomatic that any group of items will be placed in some kind of arrangement when presented together, even if the group be only two. Once that presentation is repeated, fully or partially, certain significant relationships among the items, among subgroupings of the items, and among the parts and the whole will emerge. Variations of positions or order, omission, and addition will alter at least some of those relationships. In addition, the seeming nonexistence of overall arrangement sets up other connotations. While what does exist will lead to reader-response, what does not exist may also lead to reader-response when the reader has been led through some experience to expect that which is not given. The arranger of a volume of poems may be the author or a fiction—a composite involving author, copyist, editor, and/or printer. And of course arrangement and order may be purposive or incidental.

John Donne's poems offer one of the first examples of one kind of arrangement that has become somewhat commonplace for collected poems and partially in other collections, that is, the generic.[1] Tottel's Miscellany (1557), Barnabe Googe's *Eglogs, Epytaphes, and Sonettes* (1563), and Ben Jonson's *Epigrammes* (1616) printed poems with attention paid to types and genres. *Songes and Sonettes, written by the ryght honorable Lorde Henry Haward late Earle of Surry, and other* (Apud Richardum Tottel)[2] generally groups by author, but within groupings poems are sometimes arranged by type or genre (description, complaint, sonnet, satire, little songs) and sometimes ordered with nonauthorial but appropriate headings added; for example, 1:68–71, "Charging of his loue as vnpiteous and louing other," "A renouncing of loue," "The louer forsaketh his vnkinde loue," "The louer describeth his restlesse state," "The louer lamentes the death of his loue," "The louer sendeth sighes to mone his sute," "Complaint of the absence of his loue," "The louer blameth his loue for renting of the letter he sent her," and so forth. Clearly a narrative is being developed and we are on our way to an emulation of Petrarch's *Rime in Vita e Morte di Madonna Laura*.[3] "Complaint" is preceded by a number of fourteen-line sonnets, "The louer describeth his restlesse state" being a double sonnet, and is followed by various "little songs." (The poem immediately before "Complaint" has a somewhat different rhyme scheme from the others.) Indicated is one element that will creep into such "sonnet" sequences as Sir Philip Sidney's "Astrophil and Stella": not every poem in a sequence is necessarily a sonnet of the standard variety. Googe's volume, which should be examined as an organized volume—a book—rather than simply as a collection, first prints some balanced preliminary material (a commendatory poem, a prose dedication, a prose and verse preface) and then begins its poetry with Eclogue 1 on p. [23]. Eight eclogues are presented (to p. [80]), followed by four epitaphs (pp. [81–89]), thirty-one "sonnets" (that is, "little songs," pp. [90–140]),[4] and a longer narrative poem, "Cupid Conquered," pp. [140–72]. Arrangement is thus by types or subgenres. In *The Workes* Ben Jonson included both a generic collection of *Epigrammes* and a sequence, "The Forrest." Richard C. Newton comments on *The Workes:* "The culmination of this growth-as-unfolding-rather-than-development is presented in the form of a book-within-the-works, in *Epigrammes. I. Booke,* that famous 'ripest of my studies, my *Epigrammes'*."[5] On the other hand, the collections of Donne's poems have been viewed as a "halfway response to Jonson's (re-)invention of the book" since they "appear to be manuscript miscellanies on the older model" and as such "unanalytical and textually unreliable" (Newton, p. 47). Yet there have been critics who have tried to view the songs and sonnets (or some of them) as a fairly unified collection, and this has been something of a commonplace approach to the Holy Sonnets.[6]

At least Donne's satires and perhaps the elegies and the epigrams had been circulated in manuscript groups,[7] it would seem, prior to January 1615 when he called in his poems for publication before his ordination.[8] They would seem to have been worked into a manuscript grouping by genres and types. The Group I MSS apparently derive from such a manuscript,[9] and the nature of that collection is basically the nature of other manuscripts and of the printed editions. The second edition of the *Poems* in 1635, while based on the prior edition in 1633, is a thoroughgoing generic collection with section headings: "Songs and Sonets," p. 1; "Epigrams," p. 68; Elegies," p. 71; "Epithalamions, or Marriage Songs," p. 103; "Satyres," p. 123; "Letters to Severall Personages," p. 148; the Anniversaries, p. 211ff., with a running head thereafter, "Funerall Elegies," and a section heading, "Epicedes and Obseqvies Vpon The deaths of sundry Personages," p. 251, the running head continuing; "Letters," p. 275, that is, prose letters except for the inclusion of a Latin verse letter; "The Progress of the Sovle," p. 301, that is, "Metempsychosis," the prose letter attached to it having been printed as a kind of foreword before the "Songs and Sonets"; and the "Holy Sonnets," p. 327, with a running head, "Divine Poems." "Elegies upon the Author," as the running head has it, begin on p. [389] in an unpaged gathering. The label "Songs and Sonets," which Donne's poems became and still are generally known by, is, of course, playing off against the title and celebrity of Tottel's Miscellany; there is no sonnet of the usual form in that grouping. Indeed many of the generic groups of Donne's poems—the verse letters, for example—are little attended to by commentators. We must thus ask, what importance does generic grouping acquire? and conversely, what does it deny? The evidence is mixed but Donne himself may have grouped some types but not others. Perhaps some poems of a single genre written about the same time were placed together, but others, later or separated, were not put together until later and until some editorialism was exerted (earliest around 1620?).

This essay contemplates two issues: a description of the collections of Donne's poems in manuscript and in print, and the advantages of the generic grouping and its effects. From this discussion should emerge some "new" readings of specific poems but also denial of some frequently heard beliefs about specific poems and dates and about Donne as their conscious author. The aim of the essay is to indicate the importance of generic arrangement and order for our reading of a poem and of a group of poems and to re-view the reliability of arrangement and order of Donne's poems specifically. We do read those poems in some order; are they then indeed poems in their place?

Recently I discussed the problems of the grouping of Donne's poems by reference to the three epithalamia and the five satires.[10] Satires 1–5 are generally grouped together and in that order in the manuscripts and in print. One of the epithalamia—a mock poem, "Epithalamion Made at Lincoln's Inn"—would seem to have been attached at one time to the epigrams and thus perhaps should not be grouped with other epithalamia. Grouping with the epigrams, of course, implies a direction to the reader to stress its mock quality, its satirization, for Donne's epigrams generally fall into that modal classification. Some are witty without much intended barb—like "Hero and Leander" or "A Burnt Ship"—but many poke fun—like "An Obscure Writer" or "Raderus." Connected to the other epithalamia, "Lincoln's Inn" does not lead the reader to a contextual reading of parody. The poem was written for a midsummer revels in June 1595, by all accounts, with an enactment of it by the men at the Inn. Not only does the poem pun on the patricians, the sons of wealthy senators, and the country men who people the Inn as hermaphrodites, since they study (in this community of men) and "play" (in sexual community with women),[11] but the "bride" and the "Daughters of London" in attendance were actually men in drag. The poem travesties Edmund Spenser's beautiful and well-wrought "Epithalamion," published earlier in 1595, and we can understand the schoolboy antics of putting down the national poet of The Faerie Queene (books 1–3 having been published in 1590). Compare, for example of parodic poetizing, the imagery of the sunbeams bidding the bride to leave her bed: the "Daughters of London, you which bee / Our Golden Mines, and furnish'd Treasurie" (the sexual double entendre is similar to that in "Love's Alchemy") with Spenser's "Tell me ye merchants daughters did ye see / So fayre a creature in your towne before?"; and "Thy two-leav'd gates faire Temple'unfold" and Donne's ensuing lines evoking labia and vagina with Spenser's seriously literal "Open thy temples gates vnto my loue, / Open them wide that she may enter in." But even more, Spenser's last stanzaic line "The woods shall to me answer, and my Eccho ring" (or its variant) and then its transcendence, "Ne let the woods them answer, nor theyr eccho ring" (or its variant), the change occurring at the golden section (that is, at a position roughly .618 and .382 within the poem) and the comma within the line breaking it at the golden section should be remembered as we read Donne's "To day put on perfection, and a womans name," which transcends into "To night put on perfection, and a womans name," at midpoint in the poem although the comma of the line maintains a golden section. "Put on" in the later line, of course, has an anatomical implication and stresses a male chauvinism.

Arranging this epithalamion as appendant to the epigrams is more meaningful for a reader than grouping it with the two others of that genre, which are almost consistently ordered by chronology; that is, "An Epithalamion, or Marriage Song on the Lady *Elizabeth,* and *Count Palatine* Being Married on St. *Valentine*'s Day," 14 February 1613, precedes "Eclogue . . . [and Epithalamion] at the Marriage of the Earl of Somerset," 26 December 1613. The first edition of Donne's collected poems in 1633 grouped the three together, with "Lincoln's Inn" last, and therefore that has been the usual arrangement in later editions, although the early poem is often given first through chronological ordering.

I shall in this part of the essay present evidence of and for arrangement and order of Donne's poems by their genre. Some discussions will reaffirm general editorial practice and some will call certain practices into doubt, at times with corrective suggestions. Only a listing of the specific poems in their order will allow the reader to comprehend the variations observable, particularly since the range of orderings is often wide. To facilitate reading I have placed lists in the appendixes.

The epigrams appear as a group in many manuscripts, and one or more are copied incidentally into other manuscripts.[12] Their order in 1633 is generally observable in the manuscripts except for "Mercurius Gallo-Belgicus," which, probably because it has eight lines rather than the more usual two, is given second to last in 1633; see appendix A. Five other epigrams, two of which have not always been accepted as Donne's ("The Juggler" or "Manliness" and "Faustus"), and two Latin epigrammatic book inscriptions complete this subgenre. Of the three epigrams accepted into the canon, "Cales and Guyana" and "Sir John Wingefield" (which occur only in O'F and W[13]) should be placed on the evidence of the manuscripts after "A Lame Beggar," and "The Liar" (which occurs in twelve manuscripts) should be placed after "Disinherited."

This ordering of the epigrams suggests that their critical treatment would best be directed toward looking at them as (1) three "classical" subjects, (2) "war" subjects ("A Burnt Ship" through "Sir John Wingefield"), and (3) satirized "types" ("A Self-Accuser" through "Ralphius"). Perhaps "Mercurius Gallo-Belgicus" and "Raderus" should be examined as specific satiric statements, but their potential as types—as this ordering suggests—should not be overlooked critically.

The love elegies are also grouped in the editions; see appendix B for the order in 1633. However, the grouping is also interrupted by other poems, three of which are non-love elegies,[14] and two of which should not be classified as love elegies.[15] Of the other intervening groups, 1635 repositions them so that "The Comparison," etc., follows "Nature's lay idiot" directly. After the epicede "Language, thou art too narrow," 1635 adds "Not that in color it was like thy hair" ("The Bracelet"); a spurious poem;[16] "Since she must go, and I must mourn, come night" ("His Parting from Her") in an abbreviated text; two spurious poems followed by "To make the doubt clear," the last love elegy in 1633. The 1635 edition also prints "By our first strange and fatal interview" ("On His Mistress") among the epicedes. The elegies of 1635 and their positioning are repeated in 1639, 1649, and 1650, except that 1650 adds "The heavens rejoice in motion, why should I" ("Variety") as the second to the last poem in the full collection (six poems, one of which is spurious, are appended in 1650.) The 1654 and 1669 editions duplicate 1650, except that 1669 prints a full version of "Since she must go" and adds two elegies after "To make the doubt clear":

"Whoever loves, if he do not propose" ("Love's Progress") and "Come, madam, come, all rest my powers defy" ("Going to Bed"). That leaves only one accepted love elegy, "Till I have peace with thee, war other men" ("Love's War"), unpublished in the early editions. It was published by F. G. Waldron in *The Shakespearean Miscellany* (London, 1802), "Elegy XX," pp. 1–2. 1633 printed only eight elegies in the first grouping (including "Sorrow, who to this house") rather than thirteen because the licenser of the volume (as recorded in the Stationers' Register, 13 September 1632) objected to the "first, second, Tenth, Eleventh, and Thirteenth Elegies" in the manuscript submitted by the publisher John Marriott. These five excepted elegies, as comparison with the Group I MSS collections shows, were, respectively: "Not that in color," "Come, madam, come," "Till I have peace," "By our first strange," and "Whoever loves." Of the other elegies appearing in 1633 in separated groupings, "The Comparison" through "The Expostulation" do not appear in Group I MSS; and "No *Spring*, nor *Summer*" and "Image of her" appear among songs and sonnets. Implied, of course, is that the text of 1633 derives from a member of the Group I MS tradition, augmented by one or more other manuscripts. ("Since she must go" and "The heavens rejoice" are also not included in Group I.)

Group II MSS present the elegies in partial grouping but generally interspersed with various other poems; the order is quite different from that in Group I MSS. All omit "Since she must go" and "The heavens rejoice." There are differences of inclusion between two of the manuscripts and two others; see appendix B. Additional MS 18647 (British Library) and its cognate, the Puckering MS (MS R.3.12, Trinity College, Cambridge), omit "Not that in color" and "To make the doubt clear," whereas the Norton MS (English MS 966.3, Norton 4503, Harvard University) and its cognate, MS 877 (Trinity College, Dublin), have "Not that in color," "The Storm," and "The Calm" immediately preceding "Marry, and love thy *Flavia*"; "You that are she" following "Language, thou art too narrow"; and "To make the doubt clear" amidst various poems following the epicede and before "Whoever loves."[17]

Group III MSS generally have a full grouping of love elegies, but in varying order and in different order from that in 1633, Group I, and Group II. Stowe MS 961 (British Library) does not have "Nature's lay idiot," but poems that would have been numbered 74–77 are missing, and this elegy may have been one of them. A few other poems are interspersed in the grouping of this manuscript with two others fairly well separated from the group and from each other ("Here take my picture" and "Not that in color"). The Dobell MS (English MS 966.4, Harvard University), does not include "Here take my picture," "Whoever loves," or "Since she must go"; and "Not that in color" is separated from the rest by the three epithalamia, and then after a number of intervening poems comes "Fond woman." *O'F* and the Luttrell MS (now in Cambridge University Library) are, for the most part, cognates; however, *Lut* does not have "As the sweet sweat," which follows "Metempsychosis" in *O'F* (and is thus first of the elegies), perhaps because *Lut* omitted "Metempsychosis" and in so doing inadvertently also omitted the elegy. The elegies are collected as a group. See appendix B for the order in *O'F*.[18]

The elegy "The heavens rejoice" had also been added in *O'F*, appearing on now-missing pages 157–60. It has often been alleged that 1635 and *O'F* have a relationship; they do both include "Not that in color," "Since she must go," and "To make the doubt clear" (these three appear at the end of the *O'F* grouping or separated from it, and are added to the 1633 collection by the 1635 editor). But 1635 gives a short text of "Since she must go," whereas that in *O'F* is complete; it does not add "Whoever loves" or "Come, madam, come" although they appear in this manuscript; it prints "By our first strange" among the epicedes; and it does not include "The heavens rejoice," though that would have been in the manuscript at that time. (Similar observations will be made for other generic groups.) Rather 1635 would seem to derive its text from 1633 and a manuscript akin to the Group III tradition, the editor of this second edition quite thoroughly revising the order of the groups of the poems (which is often confused in 1633) and firmly creating generic arrangement and adding subheadings.[19]

W has an order similar to that in *O'F*, with "Not that in color" appearing first and "Marry, and love thy *Flavia*" in slightly different order. While the arrangement is different from that in Group I, we perhaps should note that the "Elegy on the L. C." is included here after "Here take my picture" as it is in Group I MSS. (The epicede is not included in Group II MSS, and *S961* places it elsewhere, *Dob* omits it, and *O'F* and *Lut* have it with other epicedes.) Omitted, besides "Image of her" and "No *Spring*, nor *Summer*" (perhaps because they really should be classified as songs and sonnets, and *W* gives only one of that type, "A Jet Ring Sent," which is added later at the very end of the manuscript), are "Whoever loves," "Since she must go," "To make the doubt clear," and "The heavens rejoice," only the first of which appears in Group I MSS.

Other collections and miscellanies also include various elegies usually grouped and in differing orders. Among these we might instance the Bridgewater MS (MS EL 6893, Huntington Library), the Stephens MS (English MS 966.6, Harvard University), the John Cave MS, and the Utterson

MS (English MS 966.7, Harvard University). (Reference: *B, S, JC, Ut.*) The first three are classified as Group V MSS by Gardner (V.c, V.c, and V.b) and the last, collation indicates, has affinities with a Group III tradition. While Group V MSS often furnish quite differing texts of poems from the other groups and among themselves, there is sometimes a closer relationship with Group III MSS than with the others and many of them seem to be "early"; that is, dated somewhere in 1619–23 perhaps. *JC,* for example, has a notation of 3 June 1620, well before Group II and Group III MSS were written down. *B* has all the elegies except "The heavens rejoice," but they are generally scattered, except for a grouping of six with three intervening poems. *S* groups, labels, and numbers the elegies: it omits "Since she must go" and "The heavens rejoice," and includes other "elegies" ("Sorrow, who to this house," "You that are she," "Language, thou art too narrow," "Death, I recant," as well as two verse letters, "Reason is our soul's left hand" and "Man is a lump," all of which are labeled "Elegia"). This manuscript's grouping, labeling, and order of elegies has had much influence on nineteenth- and twentieth-century editors and commentators. (See appendix B for its very different order.)

JC, as noted before, groups and numbers the elegies. The separate group has thirteen that interestingly are almost the same ones found in Group I, but in a different order—an order that is quite close to that in *O'F.* It includes "As the sweet sweat," which is omitted in Group I, and omits in this grouping "Whoever loves." The latter elegy, however, is included in the "Miscellanea" as "An Elegie on Loves Progress" (counted as number 14 but not so designated). "No *Spring,* nor *Summer*" appears some poems later (counted as number 15 but not so designated) as "Elegie Autumnall"; the verse letter "Man is the world" is included (counted as number 16 but not so designated) as "An Elegie on ye Ladie Markham"; "Elegia 17th" is "The heavens rejoice"; "Eleg. 18th" is "Sapho and Philaenis"; and "Elegi. 19th" is only a title, the rest of the manuscript being blank. One cannot speculate on what was intended here, since there are a few love elegies it could have been and it might have been a funeral elegy or even a verse letter. "Image of her" is also included but not as an elegy.

Ut is typical of a number of manuscripts and of 1633 in that poems are often mixed in terms of genre and yet there are stretches of poems grouping basically one generic form. It has songs and sonnets through most of its pages until we come to "La Corona" and "Good Friday," followed by five verse letters (plus an elegy and two spurious poems), the five satires (plus two spurious satires), and the elegies (with five non-Donnean poems), except that the songs and sonnets are punctuated by other types, including seven epigrams together (plus a spurious epigram), and divine poems, epithalamia, verse letters, and elegies. The final grouping of poems in this manuscript is headed "Elegies," but as reference to appendix B makes clear, the manuscript has been misbound and whatever was "Elegie 7th" is now missing. Again we observe the mixing of love and funeral elegies. The order we see is similar to that in O'F and JC, and therefore we can conclude that the missing seventh elegy was "Come, madam, come." Previously among the songs and sonnets the writer had transcribed "Image of her," "Not *Spring,* nor *Summer,*" lines 29–56 of "Marry, and love thy *Flavia,*" "By our first strange," "Whoever loves," and "Not that in color"; none is labeled "Elegy." Thus Ut has all the elegies except for "Since she must go" and "The heavens rejoice," which also do not appear in Group I or Group II, and the latter is not given in Group III except for its addition (now missing) in O'F. Perhaps Ut, like many of those in Group V, is earlier than Group III MSS and similarly related to them.

I have taken much time in describing the arrangement and order of the elegies to indicate the problems that Donne's poems pose for any attempt to determine how they should be presented to a reader. Other generic groups will also be reviewed, but somewhat more briefly. Our examination of the elegies leads to five conclusions, which can be extrapolated for other genres.

1. There is a strong tradition of grouping the elegies. While 1635 established such grouping with formal generic subheads, the manuscript tradition seen in Groups I, III, IV, and some V or other manuscripts had previously recorded generic groupings, despite transcription of additional poems. Some manuscripts, in fact, like JC and Ut, formally present generic designations. The basic groupings may have been a result of the circulation of generic collections, like the Satires. Incidental transcriptions of others of a specific kind may have occurred because those poems were encountered in some other manuscript, either in a group which was differently constituted from the basic group that had been copied, or as separated poems. Such additional elegies may have been added to the basic group or separately and incidentally recorded.

2. The order of the elegies was not constant. While some groupings might copy exactly or almost exactly some other grouping, a line of transmission thus being suggested, the evidence indicates that there were varying basic groupings, altered from time to time by a scribe. The order of the elegies can be justified but not unquestionably argued as one of two possibilities: that of W, augmented, or that of the Group I MSS, augmented (that is, of 1633 and 1635, altered and augmented).

3. A number of explanations may be offered for the separation of some elegies from the group, like "As the sweet sweat," which does not appear in Group I although it leads off or is at the beginning of the grouping in W, JC, Ut, and O'F, or like "Not that in color," which is removed in the Ut and Group III MSS, although it leads off the grouping in Group I, W, and JC. In the first instance, "As the sweet sweat," before being united with "Once, and but once" and others, was an incidental poem as suggested by its omission from Group I and its separated appearance in B, P, O, S962, HM 198 (Book I), and C.[20] We might further conclude that these Group V MSS derive their texts, as miscellanies, from earlier manuscripts than the tradition reflected in Groups I, II, or III. In the second case, the Group II MSS suggest that "Not that in color," with its satiric proportion and continental references, was attached to and circulated with "The Storm" and "The Calm" and was thus recorded with them in N and TCD, all three together being omitted in A18 and TCC. An inference is that Group II MSS did not receive their texts in any fairly direct line of transmission from the Group I tradition or from that of such Group V manuscripts as B.[21]

4. Scribes and traditions often combined non-love elegies with the collection, including epicedes and verse letters. Some modern commentary has wasted effort in discussing the classification of these poems because of a lack of textual awareness.

5. Some poems—notably "Not *Spring*, nor *Summer*" and "Image of her"—have inaccurately been grouped as elegies by modern commentators because of that classification in 1635, despite the evidence to the contrary of Group I and 1633, W, Ut, P, O, and S962, and of Group III and JC for "Image of her." S, HM 198, and Group II do cast these poems as elegies; B's ordering is ambiguous; and C includes neither poem.[22]

"Metempsychosis" is in certain ways an anomaly in Donne's poetry since it is such a different kind of poem, one that is difficult to place generically and one that has sometimes been considered unfinished. Probably it should be published as a separate category—it did circulate by itself[23]— although it surely has a satiric dimension. It appears first in 1633 before the holy sonnets, but while 1635 retained the prose epistle in first position in the volume since the printer's letter (omitted in 1635) intervened, it followed the epistle by songs and sonnets and gave the poem itself after the epicedes and prose letters with the holy sonnets again following. 1633 was copying what may have been the Group I tradition, recorded only in C57. The four Group II MSS also place it before the holy sonnets but precede it by other divine poems. Perhaps its "biblical" narrative made the connection for some early transcriber. It more logically appears after the satires and before the elegies in *O'F*.

The Anniversaries—that is, "An Anatomy of the World," "A Funeral Elegy," and "Of the Progress of the Soul" (although the middle poem is often forgotten about)—were published during Donne's lifetime, the first two in that order, even though "A Funeral Elegy" was composed before "The First Anniversary," in 1611, and "The Second Anniversary" added in 1612. They are printed in differing roman and italic type to enhance the contrast between the two long poems and the shorter middle one. The 1633 edition took its text from the edition of 1625; there is no manuscript tradition.[24] The poems are given in 1633 amidst songs and sonnets; they are repositioned in 1635 after the verse letters and at the beginning of the epicedes, which are separated from them by a generic main heading. However, there is a running head, "Funerall Elegies," that is continuous for both the Anniversaries and the epicedes.

The epicedes often appear in confused arrangement and order in the manuscripts and 1633, as is obvious from our former references to "Sorrow, who to this house," "Man is the world," "Death I recant," and "Language, thou art too narrow," as well as "You that are she," which is more usually classified today as a verse letter. See appendix C for the grouping in 1635, which includes the love elegy "By our first strange." It would seem that for the 1635 editor "Elegie on His Mistress" was governed by such words as "fatal," "remorse," "When I am gone," "o my love is slain," "stabbed, bleed, fall, and die."[25] Among the elegies is "Language, thou art too narrow"; among the verse letters is "You that are she"; and among the divine poems is "An Hymn to the Saints and to Marquis Hamilton." Some tradition like that reflected in Group II (where it follows a love elegy), *S*, or *S961* must have placed "Language, thou are too narrow" as an elegy for the 1635 editor; the placement of "You that are she" in such a manuscript as *O'F* probably influenced its position here; and any poem titled "Hymn" was to be classified as a divine poem. Thus the collection and order of the eight or nine epicedes is not certain. The evidence cited in appendix C manifests this uncertainty. A generic grouping for the epicedes (including the Anniversaries) seems justified by such groupings of other kinds and by the "tradition" of *O'F* and 1635, but the order is clearly confused, and in these two latter collections random. Generally, however, "Man is the world" and "Death I recant" travel together, as do "Language, thou art too narrow" and "You that are she," except for *O'F* (and *Lut*) and 1635, and except that sometimes only one of these latter poems may appear in a manuscript.

Two specific poems raise individual problems. "Epitaph on Himself" is found in two versions, lines 1–16 and lines 7–24, with varying titles ("Elegy," "On Himself," "Epitaph," "Omnibus," and others). It is not always grouped with other epicedes (rather often with songs and sonnets), and of course it is quite different in tone and context from other epicedes. Perhaps it should be removed to some kind of nongeneric gathering.[26] The classification of "You that are she" has created a critical dilemma of context, tone, rhetorical stance. It is called "Elegie *to the Lady Bedford*" in 1633, but only "*To the Lady Bedford*" in 1635 (the title of *O'F* as well), having been added to the collection of verse letters by the editor along with "Sapho and Philaenis" and three spurious verse letters. In *N* and *TCD* it appears with other funeral elegies and some love elegies among songs and sonnets. *C* places it with other epicedes; *Ut,* calling it "Elegie to La. Bedford," and *S* put it with the elegies; *H40*, with songs and sonnets; *P* and *O*, in a mixture of elegies, songs and sonnets, and verse letters; *HM 198*, in a mixture of kinds (including songs and sonnets), a verse letter preceding it and an epicede, two love elegies, and "Sorrow, who to this house" following it; and *L74,* after songs and sonnets and an epicede, and before a verse letter, other epicedes, and a mixture of love elegies and songs and sonnets. The classification of "You that are she" must rest, it seems, on one's reading of it,[27] although the textual evidence is strongly in favor of classifying it as an epicede.

Only a few additional texts of a few divine poems have been discovered since Helen Gardner's first edition of them in 1952.[28] I cite the divine poems by short title and number,[29] considering all the holy sonnets as a unit for the time being. Almost consistently "La Corona" (2) precedes the holy sonnets (3): Group I, Group II, *Dob*, 1633–69. It precedes but is separated from them by "Hymn to God the Father" (13) in *Lut* and *O'F*; it follows them in *W*. Only in *B* and *S961* are the two sonnet groups really separated. "La Corona," but none of the holy sonnets, is copied into *Ut, S*, and *K*; neither group is found in the Group I MS, *Lec*.

The earliest divine poems that appear in the manuscripts are "Corona" (2), "Cross" (4), "A. and P." (5), "Litany" (6), and "Friday" (7), dated between July 1607 (2) and April 1613 (7). Four of these are found in *Ut*; all five, in *S*; and all five, between *K* and Additional MS 25707 in the British Library. *JC* and *Ned* have two poems; *HM 198*, three. No poem in these manuscripts, which may have been put down in the period 1619–23 to 1625, is dated after August 1614. The Laing MS (MS III.493, ff. 88a–109a, Edinburgh University Library), whose latest datable poem is August 1609, although two songs may have been composed within the next two years, includes two of these poems. (See appendix D for detailed listings.) Thus we find 4, 5, and 6 often in proximity to each other alongside the earlier 2 and the later 7. Number 4 was written presumably in 1607–1608; 5, in March 1608; and 6, perhaps autumn 1608. It is possible that 6 appears first among the divine poems in some of these manuscripts because of its length.

Group I MSS, apparently deriving from a manuscript prepared for a prospective collection around the beginning of 1615, present the same five poems of these Group V MSS, plus the sonnets. *H49, C57,* and *Lec* all have the same order for four of them, but *H49* has "Corona" (2) and "Sonnets" (3) immediately following; *C57* has them immediately preceding; and *Lec* omits them. On the other hand, *D* and *SP* collect the divine poems without a break, with these two poems preceding the others and with the last two reversed: 2, 3, 4, 5, 6, 7.

Other Group V MSS—*B, P,* and *O*—add to these early divine poems "Lament" (11) and "H. Christ" (12), the second of which is dated May 1619. Again we see "Cross" (4), "A. and P." (5), and "Litany" (6) traveling together (remembering that *P* is now misbound and has lost some pages), with the two sets of sonnets appearing in *B*, though differently ordered, just as we have observed that poems in other generic groups are often in a different order from their kind in this manuscript. *B*, like others of the Group V MSS, also includes "Friday" (7), while *P* and *O* for some reason do not. Significantly 11 and 12 have been added to the group although 11 does not appear in *P*. The date of "Lament" (11) would thus seem to lie after April 1613 (the date of "Friday"), perhaps nearer that of "H. Christ" (12) (May 1619), and before September 1621, the earliest date for "Psalms" (9). Gardner has conjectured (*Divine Poems,* pp. 103–104) that "Lament" was written around 1620–22, but near the composition of "Psalms." The textual evidence suggests a date closer to "H. Christ," and perhaps that could be, therefore, before May 1619.

Group II MSS (perhaps dated around 1625) have some differences between their two subgroups, but they present the "later" divine poems along with the "early" ones. *TCD* and *N* give "Lament" (11); *TCC* and *A18* omit "A. and P." (5); but all four include "H. Christ" (12). Additionally all four Group II MSS transcribe "Resurrection" (8) and "H. Father" (13) into the collection. Clearly "Corona" (2), "Sonnets" (3), and "Lament" (11), "Litany" (6) became separated as the scribe of *DC* copied from his Group II MS or had been separated, and various other poems intervened, and somehow he lost "H. Christ" (12), "H. Father" (13). "E. of D." (1) is found in the midst of verse letters. The placement of 11 and the relationship of 12 and 13 reinforce the suggestion that Number 11 may be dated earlier than Number 12.

Group III MSS present a rather full and grouped collection of divine poems. Oddly *S961* omits "Cross" (4) from the "early" poems found in Group V and Group I MSS, which otherwise appear together, and adds the three hymns (12, 13, 14). "H. Christ" (12), as we have noted, occurs in some Group V and Group II MSS; "H. Father" (13), in Group II MSS; and "H. God" (14) appears for the first time, not being found in others of this manuscript group. In fact, Number 14 is found otherwise only in Additional MS 34324 (British Library; the only Donne poem in it) and partially in Rawlinson Poetical MS 142 (Bodleian Library; it includes three other Donne poems, all of which are separated from each other), and in the editions of 1635–69 and partially in Walton's *Life of Donne*. Walton dated the poem 23 March 1632, shortly before Donne's death, and Sir Julius Caesar (in Additional MS 34324) said it was written during Donne's grave sickness of December 1623. If Caesar was correct, it seems strange that it should not appear in other manuscripts and particularly not in conjunction with Number 13.[30] (Beal dates Caesar's papers only as early seventeenth century, and Rawlinson Poetical MS 142, ca. 1630s–40s.)

Dob has all six "early" divine poems together at the beginning of the grouping, and adds "H. Christ" (12) and "H. Father" (13), which occur in Group II, although it does not include "Lament" (11) or "Resurrection" (8) found in Group II. For the first time we encounter "Tilman" (10), written perhaps in December 1618, or more likely in March 1620 when Tilman became an Anglican priest; it also is included in *O'F* and was printed in 1635.[31] The poems are given in the same order as in *TCD*, suggesting an ultimately common source to which *Dob* added Number 10 and to which *TCD* added 11 and 8. None of these three appear in *S961*, suggesting the same ultimately common source to which it added Number 14.[32] *Lut* and *O'F* are, as noted before, generally cognate collections, except that *O'F* is fuller, with various additions and corrections. For some reason *Lut* does not continue its collection of divine poems with 11 and 10 as *O'F* does. With the addition of "Psalms" (9) and then of "E. of D." (1) amid verse letters, *O'F* offers all the divine poems[33] except for Number 14, perhaps thus corroborating the possibility that it was not written in 1623. The poems in *Lut* are those in *TCC* in a similar order, despite the separation into two gatherings, except that it includes "A. and P." (5). *O'F* records those in *Lut* plus 11, found in *TCD;* 10, found also in *Dob;* 9, which occurs in no other manuscript; and 1, classified as a verse letter as it is in *DC, W,*[34] and Additional MS 23229 (the Conway Papers, British Library).[35]

Number 1 is printed in modern editions with the divine poems because it was written to accompany six "songs," a seventh having "still some maim." It is unlikely that these "songs" were the seven sonnets of "La Corona," written July 1607, for the first six sonnets of the poem by themselves would not allow artistic sense. If the "songs" are holy sonnets, then intended might be the first six as printed in 1633 and either "Wilt thou love God, as he thee" or "Father, part of his double interest." If the sonnet is addressed to the Earl of Dorset, it was written after February 1609, the date when he assumed the title. Conjectural dates for the holy sonnets are not in disagreement with a time somewhere around this date. There is no connection with Donne's ordination. However, in a forthcoming article, Dennis Flynn argues for a different recipient and a different interpretation of "songs," thus placing the date of the holy sonnets into question. In any case, Number 1 is a verse letter and should be printed in that generic category.

The inclusion of "Resurrection" (8) in Group II MSS only, from which it apparently was picked up by *Lut, O'F,* and 1633, raises a question of dating. The fact that the poem is incomplete ("*Desunt caetera*") may account for its lack of inclusion in Group I, IV, and V MSS. There is a likeness to "Elegy on the Lady Markham" ("Man is the world"), dated May 1609, and thus it may have been composed around Easter of that year. But any date would seem to be a guess, and thus the textual evidence may lead us to a date after "Friday" (7) (that is, after April 1613) and even perhaps after August 1614, when the verse letter "To the Countess of Salisbury" ("Fair, great, and good") was written. This is the latest datable poem in Group I and manuscripts of Group V discussed first before. The other divine poems not included in Group I or V (excluding Number 1, classified as a verse letter) cannot be dated earlier than August 1614. Number 8 is added to the "earlier" divine poems in Group II along with the two hymns, Numbers 12 and 13 (which are dated 1619 and 1623).

Printed in 1633 is the same collection as in *TCD* but in a different order. It is not unlike *C57,* beginning the same way with "Metempsychosis" and "Corona" and "Sonnets," but followed by a different generic grouping, except that it adds four poems not found in Group I MSS. The 1635 edition uses 1633, gathering the divine poems and adding Numbers 9, 10, and 14. Only two of these were available in *O'F* but in a different position. Thus the divine poems might best be arranged as follows: the sonnet to Magdalen Herbert and "La Corona," which accompanied it, followed by the holy sonnets and then by the other poems: x, 2, 3; 4, 8, 5, 6, 7; 10, 12, 11, 9, 14, 13. The order is generally chronological, except that there are questions of date for Numbers 8, 10, 11, and 14, and in general agreement with 1633 and 1635, except for the reversal of Numbers 6 and 7 (but see B, Group II, and Group III) and the repositioning of 9 (because of possible date). This arrangement differs from Gardner's on three counts (aside from the removal of Number 1). First, she prints "Litany" (6) immediately after the holy sonnets because she separates it from "Occasional Poems." Second, she places "Lament" (11) in a separate position although apparently under "Occasional Poems." Third, the three hymns are grouped by themselves. It differs from my edition[36] by placing Number 11 after Number 12, as in 1633 and 1635, whereas I had printed it in a possibly earlier chronological position (I also retained Number 1 in this category.) If the arguments for redating Numbers 8, 10, 11, and 14, are valid, however, then the generally chronological arrangement might be: x, 2, 3; 4, 5, 6, 7, 8; 11, 12, 10, 9, 13, 14.

The holy sonnets present a special problem of ordering.[37] 1633 prints twelve sonnets[38] which are given in the same order in Group I and Group II (*DC* has only the first eight); 1635 adds four more[39] which it intersperses among the former ones. *B*, *S961*, and *Dob* all have the same holy sonnets in the same order: they omit four found in Group I and II (7–10) but add four others interspersed (13–16). The order of these sonnets in these manuscripts is different from that in Groups I and II: *13*, 1, *14*, 12, 2, 3, *15*, 4, 5, *16*, 6, 11. *Lut*, *O'F*, and *W* repeat the collection in these three manuscripts exactly, but add 7–10 in that order. The 1635 edition does not employ the order of these five manuscripts but instead simply inserts the four additional sonnets into the 1633 ordering: *13*, 1, *14*, 2, *15*, 3, 4, *16*, 5, 6, 7, 8, 9, 10, 11, 12. It is not certain, I think, that 1635 took the additional sonnets from *O'F* since they were available in other manuscripts of Group III (or such as *B* in Group V with its affinities to Group III) and since their insertion has differences of order. *W* adds three more sonnets which appear nowhere else; they were first printed by Edmund Gosse.[40] Gardner argues, quite rightly, I believe, that the sonnets fall into four groups: 1–6 and 7–12; 13–16; and the three quite individually distinct sonnets in *W*. The interspersing of *13–16* arises, it would seem, from such a manuscript as *B*, a manuscript whose order for other subgenres can be seen frequently to be haphazard and in opposition to evidence of ordering other manuscripts. Sonnets *13–16* should probably be considered in that order, although Gardner argued for a reversal of *14* and *15* (*Divine Poems*, pp. liii–liv), and I previously followed her ordering. The argument rests on content interpretation and thus goes to the heart of the present volume of essays: *Poems in Their Place* explores certain seemingly significant relationships among poetic items and thus it is clear that the order of those items will define relationships. I shall later take up both arrangements (*13, 14, 15, 16* and *13, 15, 14, 16*) to determine the differences in reader-response and meaning each affords.

Donne's verse letters fall into two groups: early ones (probably before 1604) addressed to various male friends and later ones (probably after 1603) addressed to various more aristocratic friends. Included in the first group are "The Storm" and "The Calm," although they are in various ways different from what we might generally classify as a verse letter. We have remarked already that at times they travel with the elegy "Not that in color." The sonnet to the E. of D. was also placed in this category, as we have remarked, and the poem "You that are she" appears as both an epicede and a verse letter. See appendix E for the printing of the verse letters in 1633. The 1635 edition gives the same verse letters in the same order, dropping out the three Donne poems of other generic classification, except that after "Honour is so sublime perfection" it adds "That unripe side of earth, that heavy clime" ("To the Countess of Huntingdon") and a spurious poem, then continues with the next three verse letters of 1633 and adds others. The poems added to the end of the 1635 gathering are "You that are she," "Sapho to Philaenis," and three spurious poems. There seems little reason to construe "You that are she" and "Sapho to Philaenis" as verse letters on the basis of textual evidence, as we have seen. "That unripe side of earth" is found in manuscript only in *P, O,* and the miscellany collection appended to *TCD*; it is not recorded in proximity to other verse letters, but it has now been accepted into the canon.[41]

It is clear that 1633 took its collection from a Group I MS up to "Man is a lump" (including the three non-verse letters), which then gave two divine poems and "Here where by all" and "Fair, great, and good." The intervening poems 1633 took from a Group II MS. *TCD* has "The Storm," "The Calm," "Like one who'in her third widowhood," and "Here's no more news" with an elegy ("Marry, and love thy Flavia") intervening early on, and then "Sir, more than kisses" later, followed by a spurious poem and "The Primrose," and the collection of verse letters in an almost exact order as 1633 except for the inclusion of some of the poems that 1633 took from Group I and the omission of the sonnet to the E. of D. and "Though I be dead" (see appendix E). That is, *TCD* records "All hail" through "After those reverend papers"; then "Who makes the past" and "Man is a lump" found in Group I; "Mad paper, stay"; "Reason is our soul's left hand" found in Group I; "Honour is so sublime"; "You have refin'd me" found in Group I; "To'have written then" through "Man to God's image," the preceding being placed first in 1633 after the Group I collection; and then "Fair, great, and good" and "Here whereby all." "Though I be dead" appears only in *DC* and *O'F* where it is with the verse letters. The order in *O'F* and other Group III MSS is quite different from that in Group I or II, as is that in *W*, where the four additional poems are given with other early ones to male friends. *W* does not include any verse letter datable after 1603 (unless the E. of D. sonnet continues to be associated with Dorset) and its collection omits "The Calm." The order in which to consider the verse letters might be that of 1635 or of Group II MSS, with the four additional poems added as in *W*, or revised to group the early ones, basically as in *W*, and the later ones as in 1635, with perhaps some revision to accord with what seems to be a better chronological order. This is also to say that order does not seem to depend upon thematic relationships in the poems but that a possible influence of grouping by recipient may obtain.

The designation by which John Donne's poems are often known, Songs and Sonnets, is, as noted before, a conscious effort to recall Tottel's Miscellany, and perhaps the 1635 editor was suggesting that Donne's poems were the source of another poetic outpouring. For such an outpouring of verse had surely occurred through the influence of manuscript collections and miscellanies of his work. This influence is the reason for the plethora of manuscripts, which total well over 230, and for the overwhelming number of ascriptions and imitations. However, there is not a single sonnet of the usual variety in the group (or even the "little song" such as one finds in Googe's poetry), and there are only two songs: "Go and catch a falling star" and "Sweetest love, I do not go," neither of which falls into the usual form of the song, iambic tetrameter quatrains, rhyming a b a b or, at times, a a b b. (Other poems had, of course, been set to music.) The verse patterns, stanzas and/or meters, are different in all fifty-seven poems in this category (including "The Autumnal" and "Image of her") except for four which are in the song form, iambic tetrameter quatrains, rhyming a a b b or a b a b: "The Bait," "A Valediction Forbidding Mourning," "A Fever," and "The Extasie." We could, of course, call this group *lyrics* as opposed to the elegies, epicedes, epigrams, satires, and some of the divine poems, and differentiated from the other lyrical forms, the epithalamia and the verse letters, as well as other of the divine poems. In other words, the generic classifications under which Donne's poems have been printed and known are in certain ways different from what one might have meant by generic classification; the critical angle from which Donne's poems have been viewed involves, for the most part, content rather than form, and treatment rather than intention.[42] This brand of epireading (that is, the reflection of the speaker in the literary work) is concerned with an I/you *content* relationship, whereas genre in its more traditional meaning as defining "kinds" stresses the author as conscious writer writing.[43] While one kind or another may be more adapted to certain content than some other kind and while treatment may be suggested by content, genre itself stresses form (and structure if we differentiate that as a more physical term) and certain characteristics and an I (writer)/*poem* relationship which evokes a you (reader)/*poem* relationship. By *poem* here is meant the literary artifact per se, not the "thought" content of the poetical piece.

Interesting for the songs and sonnets is a note by William Drummond (who not only had recorded conversations with Ben Jonson that are often cited for remarks about Donne's poetry, but who was the orthographer of the Hawthornden MS, dated by Beal 1613?–33), himself a well-known poet, somewhat in the Spenserian mold. Under "Bookes red by me anno 1613," found in MS VII (catalogued as MS 2059 in the National Library of Scotland), f. 366a, Drummond listed "Jhone Dones Lyriques." This list and others, their dates of writing being uncertain, contain only printed works published before or in the year noted with the exception of this one reference to Donne and three notations of "Ben Jhonsons epigrames" (once under 1612, f. 365a, and twice under 1613). For example, the Donne notation appears with "Dratons Poluolbion," which was published in 1612 and 1613, with Sir John Davies's "Epigrammes" (1590?) and his "Nosce Te Ipsum" (1599, 1602, 1608), which is entered twice, with "lamentations of Jeremie & prophetic" (perhaps the 1606 or 1608 edition), and with "campions Ayres" (1610 or 1612?).[44] To give weight to Drummond's implication that what he read was a printed edition is an entry in the Stationers' Register by John Stepneth for May 15, 1612: "Entred for his Copy under th'andes of master Nydd and Thwardens, A Booke called, Ben Johnson his Epigrams." The evidence seems to point to a printed edition of Jonson's epigrams, though none is known, yet no poem in the 1616 collection can be dated after 1612. And similarly we have the possibility of a printed edition of lyric poems (songs and sonnets?) by Donne. Perhaps there is a connection with Drummond's reference to "Anacreontic lyrics," of which he found no author equal to Donne, in *A Character of Several Authors*, written c. 1612–16.[45] It is unlikely that the progenitor of Group I MSS would have been called "Lyriques" although forty-six songs and sonnets (including "The Autumnal" and "Image of her") should have appeared in it. Group I begins with satires, except for *C57*, which first has "Metempsychosis" and the divine poems before the satires.

What are the possibilities? (1) Drummond may have referred to a manuscript book of Donne's lyrics, but since the list otherwise consists of printed books (except for the Jonson reference), this is suspect. (No extant manuscript seems capable of the label manuscript book of lyrics, if "lyrics" was being used correctly.) (2) Drummond may have misremembered the date of reading the lyrics, placing it too early, his reference being to a nonexistent edition in 1614–15 before Donne took Anglican orders on 23 January 1615. But then "lyrics" is surely a misnomer, and this possibility becomes unlikely. (3) Drummond may have read a printed edition of the lyrics, published sometime before 1613, although no copies now seem to be extant. The reference in the letter to Goodyer, cited earlier, denies the likelihood of this, even though the statement in the letter is somewhat inaccurate in implication since nine of Donne's poems had appeared in print before that time, most notably, of course, the *Anniversaries*. If the collection referred to in 1614 was to emphasize the divine poems and the farewell to poetry in "Obsequies to the Lord Harrington" as Gardner has suggested, perhaps it was needed to counteract not just the manuscript versions of the songs and sonnets which had circulated among those in important positions whom Donne now wanted to impress with his dedication to the clerical life. Perhaps he had developed a wider reputation for "*Loose* raptures," as Thomas Browne called them in his commendatory verses printed in the 1633 edition of the collected poems, through an earlier publication of his lyrics. With our present knowledge we can only pose these three possibilities without conclusion. The first, that this was a manuscript collection, is the most frequent inference.

But to return to the matter at hand. As in other groupings, 1633 took its primary text of the songs and sonnets from a Group I MS but with various differences:

1. "The Autumnal" and "Image of her" are printed before the group begins with a number of other Donne poems intervening.
2. After the first poem of the collection, "The Message," 1633 inserts "A Nocturnal upon St. Lucy's Day" (written after the progenitor of Group I was compiled) and "Witchcraft By a Picture," neither of

which occurs in Group I, except that the latter is added in *Lec* by a different hand.
3. "Lecture upon the Shadow" is omitted, probably either through compositorial error or through its erroneous omission from the copy-text; it appears in all extant Group I MSS.
4. After "Woman's Constancy" 1633 inserts "The Undertaking" (without title) and omits "Image of her," which it had given earlier. "The Undertaking" appears in Group I MSS later in their gathering.
5. It omits "The Prohibition" after "Break of Day" probably because it was omitted in its copy-text; it does not appear in *C57* or *Lec*. It is given later along with other songs and sonnets taken from some other source.
6. It omits "The Autumnal" after "A Valediction of my name in the window" since it had printed it previously.
7. It omits "Epitaph on Himself" after "Twicknam Garden" probably because it was omitted in its copy-text; it does not appear in *C57* or *Lec*.
8. After "The Curse" it inserts the *Anniversaries* and then returns to the Group I collection with "The Extasie" but omits "The Undertaking," printed earlier, and continues with "Love's Deity" through the end of the Group I gathering ("The Damp").

Thus 1633 followed a Group I source but with some repositioning, some omission, and some addition. Forty-four of its songs and sonnets derive from Group I in almost the same order, and it omits three which are usually found in Group I MSS. It adds seven more songs and sonnets, six immediately after "The Damp," the seventh "The Paradox" (without title) after "Language, thou art too narrow," "You that are she," and "To make the doubt clear." These, plus the two other added poems ("A Nocturnal" and "Witchcraft"), would have been found in the Group II MS that 1633 also seems to have employed, but in a different order with other songs and sonnets. Group II has "The Paradox" (without title) with other songs and sonnets but immediately after "To make the doubt clear" and well separated by other kinds from the run of songs and sonnets that 1633 adds. "Lecture upon the Shadow" is also recorded in Group II MSS, among other songs and sonnets, but well separated from both "The Paradox" and the other added poems. The 1633 editor simply seems to have missed this poem in his collation. "Epitaph on Himself" is also omitted in Group II MSS, and thus could not have been picked up by the editor.

The 1635 edition repeats 1633 with a few changes. It begins with "The Flea," delays the first seven poems in 1633, but follows it exactly from "The Good Morrow" down to "The Curse" (omitting "The Flea" which had appeared immediately before this poem in 1633), adds the first seven poems in exact order, and then continues through the 1633 collection, omitting the three non-lyrics before "The Paradox." Next there is a spurious poem, then "Farewell to Love," another spurious poem, and finally "Lecture upon the Shadow." ("Epitaph on Himself" is given with the epicedes; "The Autumnal," "Image of her," "Language, thou art too narrow," and "To make the doubt clear" with the elegies; "You that are she" with the verse letters.) Therefore, the only songs and sonnets omitted from 1635 are the dubious "Sonnet. The Token" (first published in 1649) and "Self Love" (first published in 1650).

The order given in 1633 with some slight changes is perhaps the most defensible; that in 1635, less defensible. Changes to the 1633 text would involve the inclusion of "The Autumnal," "Image of her," "Lecture upon the Shadow," and "Farewell to Love"; perhaps the order of "A Nocturnal," "Witchcraft," "The Prohibition," and "The Undertaking"; and, of course, the repositioning of the *Anniversaries,* "Language, thou art too narrow," "You that are she," and "To make the doubt clear." The classification of "Epitaph on Himself" and the authenticity of "Sonnet. The Token" and "Self Love" (as well as "When my harte was mine owne") are debatable questions. Gardner prints the first two as Dubia, along with John Dowland's version of "Break of Day" ("Stay, O sweet, and do not rise"), and dismisses "When my harte was mine owne." A different kind of order is presented by Gardner, who divides the songs and sonnets into two sets, those written prior to 1600, those written after 1602, and orders them differently according to theme, form, or style. (See her discussion, *Elegies and Songs and Sonnets,* pp. li–lxii.) Such reordering creates meanings for the poems and has not been well received by various commentators.

In what order should all these generic categories be printed in a collected edition? One approach might be that of some manuscripts of Group I, except that *H49* is somewhat different and *C57* is quite different from the rest: satires, elegies, verse letters, divine poems, songs and sonnets, epithalamia, but this omits the epicedes which are variously placed and of course "Metempsychosis" and the epigrams which are omitted from Group I. ("Metempsychosis" does appear in *C57.*) Most manuscripts are so diverse in placement of groups and often incomplete in their grouping, as is 1633, that they offer little evidence for conclusion. On the other hand

1635 gives an order, listed before, that was followed by Grierson even though there is no textual manuscript basis for the arrangement. Beginning the volume with Songs and Sonnets in 1635, of course, capitalizes on that title and the frequent practice in modern editions may be for a similar celebrity, as in A. J. Smith's edition (New York: St. Martin's Press, 1974).

What is Donne's presence or lack of presence in the arrangement and order of his poems? By authorial presence I mean those matters of text that are the result of the author's writing activity and attention and which persist in the volume and individual poems we read. It is manifest that a concrete poem or one of e. e. cummings's "arranged" poems shows authorial presence; a strictly reader-response approach, when it denies authorial presence, is an evasion of consideration of the author's craft. But authorial presence also looms as one moves from one grouping to the next and from one poem to another in each grouping. For instance, Grace Schulman's *Burn Down the Icons* (1976) has five groupings: "Double Vision," "Waiting for a Comet," "Names," "Written on a Road Map," and "Burn Down the Icons." Each group has several poems, the last, "Recovery," "Burn Down the Icons," "Cold Fire," "Moon," and "Letter to Helen." The poems and groupings lead the reader to induce relationships of meaning and theme; here in these last five poems the reader is overwhelmed by the author's presence:

> Love, there is a world of pain
> where sun fires bricks and glass
> slowly as a season.
>
> What happened to Cassandra? She who cried
> In me 'Love is war!' has died, loving.
>
> How could I know
> . . . That fire
> Ungoverned by gravity
> Caught, blazing
> Through morning's haze . . . .
>
> If I do not feed flames,
> . . . for brief moments
> I cover the sun.

There is the possibility of nonauthorial influence (from an editor, for example), of course. An editor may indeed be a kind of contributing author for the text—even that of the disembodied poem and its style and its craft when that editor has encouraged an altered word or replaced punctuation mark. For Donne's poetry we cannot be sure of the full extent of the author's presence in his work since we have in his own hand only one poem (the verse letter to Lady Carey and Mrs. Riche) and two epigrammatic book inscriptions. The texts of individual poems are derived from scribal copies and printed versions (almost all, at least, based on scribal copies), and their accuracy is thus suspect; it is clear that the order of the poems is suspect too. Of the arrangement, we are emboldened to believe that generic groupings of at least the satires, elegies, and epigrams had been produced with his cognizance and even, perhaps, original contribution, and manuscript evidence suggests that some of the verse letters, divine poems, and songs and sonnets were often collected as well, or at least grouped together. With the epicedes we are on unsure ground, except that some two or three seem to have travelled together. Perhaps Donne thought of the poems in generic groupings, and perhaps, within generic groupings, of certain poems together. The order within groups by all accounts was either iteratively transcribed, being drawn perhaps from manuscripts with affinities to Donne, though not always transcribed without change, or incidental. We cannot with any reliance talk of an authorial presence in the order except for noting what seem to be relationships of some poems (like "Love's Deity" and "Love's Diet," or "The Blossom," "The Primrose," and "The Relique," or "The Storm" and "The Calm"). More certain would seem to be the nonauthorial presence of a number of scribes and at least two editors (those of 1633 and 1635).

Generic grouping has advantages and drawbacks. The generic grouping of Donne's poems, as pointed out before, involves content rather than form and treatment rather than intention. Genre in the broad sense implies a form or structure and certain characteristics that are not necessarily exclusive to the genre and not necessarily fully in evidence. It does not demand a certain content despite the appropriateness or inappropriateness of a specific genre for certain content (inappropriateness may lead to satiric proportions). While critics have often required certain characteristics to exist before allowing a label to be attached to a work, such characteristics may exist in part only or in sharp variation from the "normal" without obviating a classification. At the same time there are three levels of generic classification that are unfortunately confounded rather than integrated: the broad divisions of narrative, dramatic, and lyric (which emphasize the nature of presentation and at times *but not necessarily* the form a literary work will take); the modal-generic categories of tragedy, comedy, satire, and the like (which emphasize the effect of the work on the audience—both visual and auditory audience);[46] and specific forms that seem to take on certain characteristics, such as epic, villanelle, romance, farce, *Bildungsroman*. That forms may overlap can be seen in, typically, Donne's "Thy friend, whom thy deserts to thee enchain," a sonnet, which is addressed to his friend Christopher Brooke. As verse letter (and lyric, of course), its classification in manuscripts and in print, it directs the reader to recognize form, tone, and intention (as well as possible personal and hidden thoughts). Its form tells us it will include an introduction (the salutation), the body (which may involve a statement of personal circumstances of the addressee or the writer and present news or dwell on matters of thought), and a leave-taking. In this poem one melds into the other. The salutation proper appears as the title "To C. B." The introduction and the entry into the body of the verse letter constitute lines 1–4:

> Thy friend, whom thy deserts to thee enchain,
> Urged by this unexcusable occasion,
> Thee and the Saint of his affection
> Leaving behind, doth of both wants complain.

The body extends through line 14, with a leave-taking being only implied through tone in lines 12–14:

> Yet, love's hot fires, which martyr my sad mind,
> Do send forth scalding sighs, which have the Art
> To melt all ice, but that which walls her heart.

The body of the verse letter describes the author's concern about the addressee's attitude toward him because the author has been forced, through some "unexcusable occasion," to absent himself. Also invoked is "the Saint of his affection," from whom he likewise must separate. He wishes to make sure that the addressee realizes his love for the addressee, a love that is not abated by the circumstances of his separation "to where stern winter aye doth wonn." The last three lines imply that his impassioned love for his "Saint" has caused him this divisive martyrdom, and yet she has not yielded, at least fully, to him.

Another aspect of the verse letter is the rhetorical relationship between the writer and the recipient.[47] The epideictic (or usually demonstrative) exhortation offers praise and example, being concerned with the present and just vaguely suggestive of future action. This poem seems determined to insure that the recipient realize nothing untoward is felt for him ("No blot, nor maim"), but while it praises, it has moved into a forensic aim: something of the past, arising from action of the friend, the saint, and the writer, has caused this division, but the I has not recanted and will not. The body of the poem becomes a plea for exoneration of his action, the forensic always being concerned with justification of the past in the present. But is there a tinge of the paraenetic here also? Is, perhaps, the writer hoping that his argument that he is perceptionally true to his "love's hot fires" (which come from his heart but which martyr his mind) will move the friend to alter his loved one's coldness? His friend is to be an emissary advocate. Thus we would seem to range through rhetorical relationships of writer/recipient, with the real aim of the poem underlying the leave-taking. (Indeed, Donne's verse letters—say, that to the Countess of Bedford beginning, "You have refin'd me," which has been discussed only as a praise—should not be read on one level only. Here, while he sincerely employs the epideictic in writing to his patroness, he is really concerned that her favors continue. In the very center of the poem he says he will not "sacrifice" to the "Deity which dwells in [her]" since that would be *petition,* not *hymn.* Yet he's made his point, which is petition. The golden section of the poem is in lines 44–45: "You as you are virtue's temple, not as she, / What walls of tender crystal her enfold." He is contrasting the countess's virtue with Nero's temple to fortune in Rome, and again the personal aim, though submerged, can be discerned.

It is tempting to see the poem to C. B. as reflective of Donne's surreptitious marriage to Ann More in December 1601, since Brooke had been a confidant in the elopement, since Donne was dismissed as Sir Thomas Egerton's secretary soon afterward (Egerton being Ann's uncle), and since he was imprisoned in the Fleet in February 1602 on the warrant of her father, Sir George More. The sunless prison would in this reading be the referent of line 11: "Going to where stern winter aye doth wonn." Ann's coldness would thus be construed as her succumbing to her father's will and not standing by her husband. (The marriage was ratified by the Archbishop of Canterbury in April 1602.) The suasion becomes clear: he is trying to urge Brooke, by precept, of the rightfulness of his action, and in turn to have Brooke persuade Ann. Whether this biographical construction is valid, the rhetorical strategies employed in this familiar verse letter (to which we are clued by its arrangement among the verse letters) lead to a cogent understanding of what is going on in the poem.

I doubt that we might be as ready to view the poem thus were it classified by its different generic level, that is, as sonnet. Its fourteen iambic pentameter lines, rhyming a b b a a b b a c d d c e e, with the volta at line 8, is a paradigm of the usual sonnet structure and form. Further, it is strongly Petrarchan in its language (for example, the oxymoronic "amorous pain") and imagery (the "scalding sighs" that can "melt all Ice, but that which walls her heart"). Alongside other sonnets we would probably stress these generic characteristics and the literary tradition.[48] As verse letter we observe another level of craft—of authorial presence; the rather thick overply of "poeticness" suggests not merely an exercise in poetizing common to the coterie poet, but a sense of satiric irony. The I of the poem (Donne?) is not going to knuckle under as if he were but an upstart romantic philanderer, eager for advancement. If I'm supposed to be this kind of mooning opportunist, he seems to be saying, then I'll act that way, but I won't give in. The ornamentation and exaggeration that were commonplace with verse letters are accomplished here with a satiric vengeance. After all, though the Petrarchisms are related to the loved one, this is a sonnet about love for a woman addressed to a man; the displacement of decorum is wide. This view underlines the forensic quality of the poem, for it becomes not a poem of seduction or thwarted seduction, but one of defense for action of the immediate past.

We are thus brought to the further element of genre definition: authorial intention. The "Epithalamion Made at Lincoln's Inn" is treated as an epithalamion, but its intent is satiric. We can label it generically as a satire in verse, cast as an epithalamion. "To Mr. C. B." is generically a sonnet, but it is treated as a verse letter. "Go and catch a falling star" is called "Song," but it is a specific kind of lyric called the impossibility poem. The three verse letters "Man is a lump," "Man to God's image," "Here where by all," often ordered together, are written in contrasting forms: iambic pentameter couplets, quatrains rhyming a b a b, and triplets in one rhyme. These typical poems illustrate the ways in which genres may be integrated; one aspect is the outer form, such as the epithalamion, the sonnet, the song, the verse satire (we must remember that "Man is a lump" was written in answer to Sir Edward Herbert's "Satire 1: The State Progress of Ill"), the philosophical poem (in quatrains),[49] the lyric (in tercets). The differences in the ways of looking at the poems generically involves treatment and intention. And the writer's intention is paramount whether he chooses to write in one genre or another, or in no common generic kind, or whether he chooses to employ one form and treat it differently from the supposed intentionality of that form. In the arrangement of Donne's poetry the 1635 editor and modern editors have followed the pattern of treatment and thus certain members of a group may exhibit differing intentions. The divine poems, for instance, can be so grouped because they are treated (by editors, if not assuredly by Donne himself) as statements of devotional attitudes about subjects that have a religious aura about them. They may be sonnets or they may be hymns, both of course in the family *lyric,* although a greater emphasis on lyric rather than on devotional may lead us to see some of the sonnets as much less personal and much more ironic in their treatment of religious themes. They may be verse letters cast as sonnets like "To the Lady Magdalen Herbert, of St. Mary Magdalen" or a verse letter in iambic pentameter couplets like "To Mr. Tilman." They may be such occasional poems as "The Cross," "Resurrection, imperfect," "The Annunciation and Passion," "Goodfriday, 1613. Riding Westward," although these poems in heroic couplets should also be classified as process poems. (I find it impossible to call them lyrics.) "The Litany," "The Lamentations of Jeremy," and "Upon the Translation of the Psalms" do not fall under any standard poetic generic kind, the last being a prayer rather than an encomium.

"Authorial intention" as related to genre means the author's attitude toward the poem he is writing *qua* poem; it does not suggest any modal effect or content. It basically answers such questions as "Why does the author choose this form?" (for example, a sestina, of which there are numerous examples with varying modal effects and varying subjects). "Why (and thus also how) does the author choose to vary the form, or structure, or characteristics from some other of its kind?" (as, for example, the use of the blazon in the elegy "Love's Progress," or the dichotomy of two voices in Satire 1, the mind [or soul] and the body, or the seven-line stanza capped with a septenary in "A Hymn to Christ"). The treatment given a poem, as opposed to the genre or its variation, may also, of course, denote a part of the authorial intention, and it may employ, as we have seen, a generic kind which is different from the genre form in which it is cast. The treatment may involve, too, such nongeneric matters as effect (or mode) or content-oriented materials.

The examples discussed previously in this paper point to one major reason why generic arrangement is advantageous; the reader is directed to look at the poem as an example of the form, structure, and characteristics of the genre to which it is assigned, determining what is drawn from the standard and how, if at all, it is altered from the standard, all with a view toward levels of meaning. A sonnet like "I am a little world made cunningly" recalls such Petrarchan imagery as *tears* and *fire,* and the reader plays this personal, devotional lyric against that tradition:

> Pour new seas in mine eyes, that so I might
> Drown my world with my weeping earnestly,
> Or wash it if it must be drowned no more:
> But oh it must be burnt; alas the fire
> Of lust and envy have burnt it heretofore,
> And made it fouler. (lines 7–12)

These lines could just as well have been taken from a love sonnet of the day. Although its beginning and ending lines declare that the You of the poem is God, the petitioning, thwarted lover breaks into our recognition to make us see the I as an actor, indeed, an agonist in all the meanings of that word including one who is not necessarily without dissimulation. Is the poem really directed to God and his omnipotence, or to the I who may have reinspirited himself by his self-analysis to mend his life? The sonnet preceding or following, "O might those sighs and tears return again," comments on this sonnet and in turn derives meaning from it. But does "O might those sighs" precede, as in the manuscripts (see before) or follow, as Gardner has rearranged them? It is clear that the Petrarchan *sighs* and *tears* are here, as well as *breast, eyes, mourn, in vain, mine Idolatry, showers of rain, griefs*, a *rent Heart, pain* (lines 1–8).[50] Gardner revised the order because "I am a little world" "is a general meditation, with a very short *compositio loci*" (that is, a place or situation envisioned by the imagination) and "O might those sighs and tear" "specifies a particular sin, 'Sufferance'" and "expands the *compositio* to fill the whole sonnet" (*Divine Poems*, pp. liii, liv). Read as argued by Gardner, the I of the poems requests God to create the tears and fire and then prays that the sighs and tears, "which I have spent," "return again"; the "showers of rain" and "griefs" have been of the past. The movement within these four penitential sonnets, so ordered, is from a statement of sinfulness and need of God's grace to prevent Satan's art, to a plea to God to bring the destruction of his world (himself) by that analogous to Noah's flood or by that analogous to the conflagration of 2 Peter 3:10; then to a prayer that his grief (sufferance) be granted visible show, now nonexistent because such show (fruit) has been used up in vain in the past, and finally to an address to his soul to turn to God rather than be seen as a weeping, mourning, idolatrous lover who conjures Jesus's name and dissembles devotion. This ordering of the sonnets, it now seems to me, obviates the reader's understanding that the "iron heart" of the last line of the first sonnet is the reason for the prayer of "O might those sighs and tear," the first line of the second sonnet. The hard-heart is doctrinally eased by repentance. We wonder what the idolatry of this latter sonnet is. The first has stressed body; this latter one likewise stresses bodily sufferance and bodily reaction. Even the comparatives of "the hydroptic drunkard, and night-scouting thief, / The itchy Lecher, and self tickling proud" emphasize a bodiliness. The idolatry is that which has "feebled [his] flesh"; "all [his] pleasures are like yesterday" but he has no "remembrance of past joys." Then proceeding to "I am a little world," the poet relates himself to a world that has two parts, his body and his soul. He now wishes not a return of sighs and tears but "new seas" and new flames that replace those "of lust and envy . . . heretofore." He wants that world destroyed by blood or fire, through which he will be restored anew. The Petrarchan language of this sonnet implies former bodily idolatry, to be replaced by new and quite different seas and fire through "fiery Zeal" of God. He surely understands doctrinally that the grace of God is needed to effect such zeal, but he recognizes that any act must involve himself. The final sonnet coming immediately after this one underlines such recognition. The Petrarchist I the poem recalls is an agonist and a dissembler; but is the new I still? "Well," says the last sonnet, stressing soul ("faithful souls," "father's soul," "our minds to these souls be descried," "my mind's white truth," "pensive soul"), "my truth will be tried (tested) as my soul turns to God." He will then be seen not to be the idolatrous lover, weeping and mourning, as in "O might those sighs and tears" or the potentially reformed lover using his old strategies, nor as a conjurer or dissembler. He valiantly "o'restrides hell's wide mouth": he has felt God's grief in his breast (coming now back to the imagery of the first sonnet). God will add this commendation under his name to the book of life "even to full felicity." (Ironically, the background is Revelation 22:18: "For I testify unto every man that heareth the words of the prophecy of this book, If any man shall add unto these things, God shall add unto him the plagues that are written in this book.")

We have, of course, combined generic meaning with meaning through order. The order of these four sonnets in the manuscripts adds meaning in content and interpretation through its linkages and development. Such linkages delineate Donne's craft and his presence. In Gardner's order a great stress is put upon sufferance as particular sin, whereas the manuscript order lessens that emphasis and places a stress instead on I's new fiery zeal "Of thee and thy house." Clearly the order of poems is of major importance in establishing meaning and craft.

If we look at the elegies as a group, we recognize that we are dealing with various situations, presented through heroic couplets linked together as groups of lines, allowing the individual poem to progress until some point of closure.[51] The stopping point is not particularly the result of an artistic development. Witness "The Bracelet," which in its 114 lines wanders over countries, puns on gold and money, mocks religious ardor, and imprecates the finder of the lost chain. The poem becomes occasion for epigrammatic satiric barbs (couplets and quatrains of this nature were excerpted in commonplace books) and offers as backdrop a circumstance which might occur in some love relationship. In contrast is the elegy entitled "Jealousy" or that well-known one called "Going to Bed," which are directly and primarily interested in a man/woman narrative (although a recent view of the latter sees a political substruct). In the first the stance is observer of a "Fond woman" and her husband; in the second the stance is that of male waiting for his female companion to undress. We call up contrasts and comparisons among the individual poems and see Donne's wit in fuller range, even when there may have been some biographical kernel out of which the full treatment came (such as in "His Picture"). Examined this way, under such generic characteristics, "Image of her" (which Grierson classified as "Elegy X" and called "The Dream," following 1635) cannot be an elegy: it is in three eight-line stanzas, rhyming a b a b c d c d, plus a final couplet. It treats a love situation, contributing to the range of the songs and sonnets, but it is not elegiac: it has form and structure rather than being open-ended. The love elegy has a kind of narrative substruct, presented somewhat linearly (for example, "On His Mistress"). The song and sonnet may imply some "story" or "story element" (such as in "The Primrose"), but it is not the concern of the poem. The concerns lie, on the one hand, in depiction and development of an attitude or emotion or thought and, on the other, in the lyric expression, built on interrelated forms and imagery and language. The stance in the lyric purports to envelop the I, perhaps in a kind of soliloquy. However, something like "The Flea," as witty seduction poem, is directed to a female auditor; the stance is not much different from that in "Going to Bed." The form and structure distinguish the generic category; the subject matter and treatment distinguish the poems.

Interrelationship can be induced among runs of songs and sonnets: "Song" ("Sweetest love, I do not go, / For weariness of thee") can be seen to link with "The Legacy" when the poet writes, "When I died last, and, Dear, I die / As often as from thee I go," and then in contrast "O do not die, for I shall hate / All women so, when thou art gone" ("The Feaver"). If the conjunction of these three poems in manuscripts and print is meaningful, it suggests that all three or none of the three is biographically oriented. The first was assigned by Izaak Walton to Donne's leaving his wife Ann when he went to the continent with Sir Robert Drury, and thus "The Legacy" may refer to those absences that took Donne to London and

Twickenham, and "A Fever," to some time when Ann was seriously ill (perhaps at childbirth). But if we discard a biographical interpretation for the first—and that is not impossible—then the poems can be viewed as lyrics presenting an I who takes differing stances toward a nonspecific You, each poem being another serious excursion into another aspect of love. Since immediately preceding this group are "The Triple Fool" and "Love's Infiniteness" and immediately following are "Air and Angels" and "Break of Day" (where the speaker is a woman), this latter view appears cogent. Of course, all of this is speculative and built upon the assumption that the poems were ordered in this way purposefully and that they interrelate on the same level. At least one can say that these poems read together in their place in 1633, 1635, and the manuscripts (as well as other such fairly assured groupings) will lead to this kind of reader-response, that is, will produce a reader in the poems who is different from the reader in the same poems differently arranged.

APPENDIX A: EPIGRAMS

Hero and Leander
Pyramus and Thisbe
Niobe
A Burnt Ship
Fall of a Wall
A Lame Beggar
A Self-Accuser
A Licentious Person
Antiquary

Disinherited
Mercurius Gallo-Belgicus [repositioned on the basis of the manuscripts]
Phryne
An Obscure Writer
Klockius
Raderus
Ralphius

APPENDIX B: LOVE ELEGIES

1633
"Fond woman which would'st have thy husband die" ("Jealousy")
"Marry, and love thy *Flavia,* for, she" ("The Anagram")
"Although thy hand and faith, and good works too" ("Change")
"Once, and but once found in thy company" ("The Perfume")
"Here take my Picture, though I bid farewell" ("His Picture")
["Sorrow, who to this house scarce knew the way"]
"Oh, let me not serve so, as those men serve"
"Nature's lay idiot, I taught thee to love"
[numerous poems]

Arrangement and Order of Donne's Poems | 151

"As the sweet sweat of roses in a still" ("The Comparison")
"No *Spring,* nor *Summer* beauty hath such grace" ("The Autumnal")
"Image of her whom I love, more than she"
[numerous poems]
["Language, thou art too narrow, and too weak"]
["You that are she, and you that's double shee"]
"To make the doubt clear, that no woman's True" ("The Expostulation")

Group II MSS: A18 and TCC	Group II MSS: N and TCD
[omitted]	"Not that in color"
[omitted]	"The Storm"
[omitted]	"The Calm"
"Marry, and love thy *Flavia*"	[same]
[two verse letters]	[same]
"As the sweet sweat"	[same]
"Once, and but once"	[same]
"Although thy hand"	[same]
"Nature's lay idiot"	[same]
"The Autumnal"	[same]
"Image of her"	[same]
[four other poems]	[same]
"Oh, let me not serve"	[same]
[seven other poems]	[same]
"Till I have peace"	[same]
"Language, thou art too narrow"	[same]
[omitted]	"You that are she"
[various poems]	[various poems including "To make the doubt clear"]
"Whoever loves"	[same]
"The Blossom"	[same]
"Come, madam, come"	[same]
[several poems]	[same]
"Fond woman"	[same]
"By our first strange"	[same]
"Here take my picture"	[same]
[other poems]	[same]

Group III MS: O'F	Group IV MS: W
[omitted]	"Not that in color"
"As the sweet sweat"	[same]
"Once, and but once"	[same]
"Fond woman"	[same]
"Oh, let me not serve"	[same]

"Nature's lay idiot"   [same]
"Till I have peace"   [same]
"Come, madam, come"   [same]
"Although thy hand"   [same]
"By our first strange"   "Marry, and love thy *Flavia*"
"Here take my picture"   "By our first strange"
"Marry, and love thy *Flavia*" "Here take my picture"
[in different place]   ["Sorrow, who to this house"]
"The Autumnal"   [*omitted*]
"Whoever loves"   [*omitted*]
"Since she must go"   [*omitted*]
[two spurious poems]   [*omitted*]
"To make the doubt clear"   [*omitted*]
[eight spurious poems]   [*omitted*]
"Self Love"   [*omitted*]
"Not that in color"   [positioned as above]

Group V MS, V.c: S
"Fond woman"
"Here take my picture"
["Sorrow, who to this house"]
"As the sweet sweat"
"By our first strange"
["You that are she"]
["Reason is our soul's left hand"]
"Oh, let me not serve"
"Whoever loves"
["Image of her"]
[one spurious poem]
"Although thy hand"
"Nature's lay idiot"
"To make the doubt clear"
"Till I have peace"
"Not that in color"
"Marry, and love thy *Flavia*"
"Come, madam, come"
["Language, thou art too narrow"]
["Death, I recant"]
[two spurious poems]
["Man is a lump"]
["The Autumnal"]
"Once, and but once"
[one spurious poem]

Undesignated: Ut
"As the sweet sweat"
"Once, and but once" (numbered 2)
"Fond woman" (numbered 3)
"Oh, let me not serve" (numbered 4)
"Nature's lay idiot" (numbered 5)
"Although thy hand" (numbered 8)
"Here take my picture" (numbered 9)
"Marry, and love thy *Flavia*" (incomplete, 11. 1–28; numbered 10)
["You that are she"]
"To make the doubt clear" (titled only "Elegie")
[a spurious elegy]
["Man is the world"]
[a poem by Francis Beaumont]
"Till I have peace" (numbered 6)
[four other elegies, one of which is incomplete and two of which are by Richard Corbett]

APPENDIX C: EPICEDES AND OBSEQUIES

1635	*O'F*
"Elegy on Prince Henry"	"Epitaph"
"Obsequies to the Lord Harrington"	"Man is the world"
"Man is the world"	"Sorrow, who to this house"
"Death I recant"	"Death I recant"
"By our first strange"	[a spurious poem]
"Epitaph on Himself" ("Elegie")	"Language, thou art too narrow"
[a spurious poem]	[two spurious poems]
"Sorrow, who to this house"	"Obsequies"
	"Hymn"
	"Prince Henry"
	[Donne's epitaph on his wife Ann]

1633: "Prince Henry," "Obsequies," "Hymn" are placed with other kinds.
Group I: "Obsequies," "Man is the world," "Death I recant" are placed with other kinds. "Epitaph" is among the songs and sonnets; "Sorrow, who to this house" is among the elegies.
Group II (*N* and *TCD* only): "Prince Henry," "Obsequies," "Hymn" are placed with other kinds. "Man is the world," "Death I recant," "Language, thou are too narrow," "You that are she" are among the songs and sonnets.

154 | *John T. Shawcross*

APPENDIX D: DIVINE POEMS

1. To E. of D. (E. of D.)
2. La Corona (Corona)
3. Holy Sonnets (Sonnets)
4. The Cross (Cross)
5. Annunciation and Passion (A. and P.)
6. The Litany (Litany)
7. Good Friday (Friday)
8. Resurrection
9. Upon the Translation of the Psalms (Psalms)
10. To Mr. Tilman (Tilman)
11. Lamentations (Lament)
12. Hymn to Christ (H. Christ)
13. Hymn to God the Father (H. Father)
14. Hymn to God my God (H. God)

N.B.: a dash indicates a spurious poem or more; brackets, one or more Donnean poems.

Ut: 6, —, 4, [ ], 2, 7
S: 6, 2, 4, 5, [ ], 7
K: 5, 2, [ ], 6
A25   7, [ ], 4
JC: 6, [ ], 4
HM198:   6, [ ], 5, [ ], 4
Laing: 5, [ ], 4

H49:   4, [ ], 5, 7, [ ], 6, 2, 3
C57:   2, 3, 4, [ ], 5, 7, [ ], 6
Lec: 4, [ ], 5, 7, [ ], 6
D, SP: 2, 3, 4,   5, 6,   7

B: 4, [ ], 11, 3, 5,   —, 6, 7,   2, 12
P: 12, [ ], 5, [ ], 4
O: 12, [ ], 11, [ ], 4, [ ], 6, —, 5

TCD, N: 2, 3, 11, 6, 7, 5, 4, 8, 12, 13
TCC, A18:   6, 7,   4, 8, 12, 13, [ ], 2, 3
DC: 2, 3, [ ],   7, 5, 4, 8, [ ], 1, [ ],   11, 6

S961: 3, 7, —, 2, 5, 6, 13, 12, 14
Dob: 2, 3, 6, 7, 5, 4, 12, 10, 13
Lut: 6, 7, 4, —, [ ], 8, 5, —, 2, 13, 3, 12, [ ]
O'F   6, 7, 4, —,   8, 5, —, 2, 13, 3, 12, 11, 10, —, 9, [ ], 1

1633: 2, 3, [ ], 4, [ ], 8, [ ], 5, 7, 6, [ ], 12, 11, [ ], 13
1635: 2, 3, —, 4, —, 8, [ ], 5, 7, 6, 9, —, 10, 12, —, 11, [ ], 14, 13

APPENDIX E: VERSE LETTERS

1633
"The Storm" (Group I)
"The Calm" (Group I)
"Sir, more than kisses" ("To Sr. Henry Wotton"; Group I)
[three other Donne poems] (Group I)
"Who makes the past a pattern" ("To Sr. Henry Goodyer"; Group I)
"Like one who'in her third widowhood" ("To Mr. Rowland Woodward"; Group I)
"Here's no more news than vertue" ("To Sr. Henry Wotton"; Group I)
"Reason is our soul's left hand" ("To the Countess of Bedford"; Group I)
"You have refin'd me" ("To the Countess of Bedford"; Group I)
"Man is a lump" ("To Sr. Edward Herbert"; Group I)
"To'have written then, when you writ" ("To the Countess of Bedford")
"This twilight of two years" ("To the Countess of Bedford")
"Man to God's image" ("To the Countess of Huntington")
"All hail, sweet poet" ("To Mr. T. W.")
"Haste thee, harsh verse" ("To Mr. T. W.")
"Pregnant again with th'old twins" ("To Mr. T. W.")
"At once, from hence, my lines and I depart" ("To Mr. T. W.")
"Thy friend, whom thy deserts to thee enchain" ("To Mr. C. B.")
"O thou which to search out" ("To Mr. S. B.")
"Is not thy sacred hunger" ("To Mr. B. B.")
"If as mine is thy life" ("To Mr. R. W.")
"Of that short roll of friends" ("To Mr. I. L.")
"Blest be your north parts" ("To Mr. I. L.")
"To the E. of D."
"After those reverend papers" ("To Sir H. W. at his Going Ambassador to Venice")
"Mad paper, stay" ("To Mrs. M. H.")
"Honour is so sublime perfection" ("To the Countess of Bedford")
"Though I be dead and buried" ("To the Countess of Bedford")
"Here where by all saints invoked are" ("A Letter to the Lady Carey, and Mrs. Riche"; Group I)
"Fair, great, and good" ("To the Countess of Salisbury"; Group I)

Group II (TCD) [at times with intervening poems]
"The Storm" (also Group I)
"The Calm" (also Group I)
"Like one who" (also Group I)
"Here's no more news" (also Group I)
[other poems]
"Sir, more than kisses" (also Group I)
[a spurious poem]

["The Primrose"]
"All hail, sweet poet"
"Haste thee, harsh verse"
"Pregnant again"
"At once, from hence"
"Thy friend, whom thy deserts"
"O thou which to search out"
"Is not thy sacred hunger"
"If as mine is"
"Of that sweet roll of friends"
"Blest are your north parts"
"After those reverend papers"
"Who makes the past" (also Group I)
"Man is a lump" (also Group I)
"Mad paper, stay"
"Reason is our soul's left hand" (also Group I)
"Honour is so sublime"
"You have refin'd me" (also Group I)
"To'have written then"
"This twilight of two years"
"Man to God's Image"
"Fair, great, and good" (also Group I)
"Here whereby all" (also Group I)

NOTES

1. For example, one arrangement for John Dryden's poems has been: Poems, Historical, Political, and Controversial; Epistles and Complimentary Addresses; Elegies and Epitaphs; Songs, Odes, and Lyrical Pieces; Prologues and Epilogues; Translations from Chaucer and Boccaccio; Translations of Latin Hymns and Minor Miscellanies. At times a small volume will have a section grouping types; for instance, Edna St. Vincent Millay's 1923 *The Harp-Weaver and Other Poems* prints "Sonnets" as Part Four and "Sonnets from an Ungrafted Tree" as Part Five.

2. The most convenient edition is that by Hyder E. Rollins, 2 vols. (Cambridge, Mass.: Harvard University Press, 1966).

3. Poetic sequences are created on the basis of narrative, on the basis of metaphoric, image, or other literary pattern, and on the basis of conceptual (thematic) relationships among their parts; George Meredith's "Modern Love," George Gascoigne's "Memories: IV," and Walt Whitman's "Song of Myself" are respective examples. The latter two general types are particularly often given over to varying (contrasting) literary forms; Wallace Stevens's "Peter Quince at the Clavier" is an obvious instance. A developed sequence is to be construed as a single work, whether so planned from its inception (like

W. H. Auden's "In Memory of W. B. Yeats") or created by bringing together separate poems with or without augmentation by additional parts (like Ben Jonson's "A Celebration of Charis").

4. Included also are two answers by L. Blundeston and three by Alexander Neville.

5. Richard C. Newton, "Jonson and the (Re-)Invention of the Book," in *Classic and Cavalier: Essays on Jonson and the Sons of Ben,* ed. Claude J. Summers and Ted-Larry Pebworth (Pittsburgh: University of Pittsburgh Press, 1982), p. 38.

6. For example, see Dwight Cathcart, *Doubting Conscience: Donne and the Poetry of Moral Argument* (Ann Arbor: University of Michigan Press, 1975), and Jay Parini, "The Progress of the Soul: Donne and Hopkins in Meditation" *Forum for Modern Language Studies* 13 (1977): 303–12, respectively. A similar forcing of sequence has been applied to John Milton's various sonnets by William McCarthy, "The Continuity of Milton's Sonnets," *PMLA* 92 (1977): 96–109, and Anna K. Nardo, *Milton's Sonnets: The Ideal Community* (Lincoln: University of Nebraska Press, 1979). Milton does have a sonnet sequence, the Italian poems, Sonnets 2–6 and a Canzone.

7. See for examples of grouped generic poems: British Library, Harleian MS 5110, which records Satires 1–3; Queen's College (Oxford) Library, MS 216, which has Satires 1–5, plus "The Storm," "The Calm," and "The Curse"; Victoria and Albert Museum, Dyce Collection, Neve MS, Cat. No. 17, MS 25, F16, which gives Satires 1–5 plus "The Storm" and "The Calm"; and the Heneage MS (in private hands), which likewise copies Satires 1–5 and "The Storm" and "The Calm." Ben Jonson's Epigram XCIV, "To Lucy, Countess of Bedford, with Mr. Donne's Satyres," implies such a generic collection, as well.

The Lawson MS in the Bodleian Library, English Poetical MS e.14, has "The Bracelet," "The Comparison," "The Perfume," "Love's War," "The Anagram," "On His Mistress," and "The Autumnal," as well as six other Donne poems; Emmanuel College (Cambridge) Library, MS I.3.16, James 68, includes "The Comparison," "The Perfume," "The Anagram," "Love's Progress," "His Parting from Her," and "The Autumnal," as well as eight songs and sonnets.

The Burley MS now in the Leicestershire Record Office, MS DG7 / Lit. 2, has "Hero and Leander," "Pyramus and Thisbe," "Niobe," "A Burnt Ship," "Fall of a Wall," "A Lame Beggar," "A Self Accuser," "A Licentious Person," "Antiquary," "The Juggler," "Disinherited," "The Liar," "Mercurius Gallo-Belgicus," "Phryne," "An Obscure Writer," and "Klockius," plus five other poems; the Hawthornden MS XV in the National Library of Scotland, MS 2067, copies "Hero and Leander," "Pyramus and Thisbe," "Niobe," "Fall of a Wall," "A Lame Beggar," "A Self Accuser," "A Licentious Person," "Antiquary," "The Juggler," "Disinherited," "The Liar," "Phryne," "Klockius," "Ralphius," and "Faustus," plus twelve other poems (I have modernized titles, first lines, and quotations of Donne's poems throughout.).

8. See his remarks in a letter to Sir Henry Goodyer, dated 20 December 1614: "I am brought to a necessity of printing my Poems, and addressing them to my L. Chamberlain.... I must do this, as a valediction to the world, before I take orders" (*Letters to Several Persons of Honour* [1651], pp. 196–97).

9. Margaret Crum in "Notes on the Physical Characteristics of Some Manuscripts of the Poems of Donne and Henry King," *The Library* 16 (1961): 121–32, has shown that this manuscript probably consisted of separable parts, or "books," such as I have mentioned for the satires and the elegies, as well as other manuscript poems on other sheets. For the grouping of manuscripts generally today, see Helen Gardner's introduction to her editions of *The Elegies and The Songs and Sonnets* (Oxford: Clarendon Press, 1965), especially pp. xcvii–xcix, and the second edition of *The Divine Poems* (Oxford: Clarendon Press, 1978), pp. xcvii–xcviii, and Peter Beal's discussion in *Index of English Literary Manuscripts* (London: Mansell, 1980), Volume I, Part 1. These groupings are in need of revision and refinement, with some currently unattached manuscripts being classified as at least adjunct to one group or another. The list of sigla in Gardner's *Divine Poems* does away with any Group V listing, and it should be noted too that curiously Gardner does not print the Westmoreland MS as "Group IV," only as "IV," and "Group V," only as "V."

10. John T. Shawcross, "A Text of John Donne's Poems: Unsatisfactory Compromise" *John Donne Journal* 2 (1983): 11–13. See pp. 11–12 and n. 19 for a full listing of all known texts of the epithalamia, and p. 13 and nn. 24 and 25 for that of the satires.

11. The lines are: "Yee of those fellowships whereof hee's [the groom's] one, / Of study'and play made strange Hermaphrodits, / Here shine" (29–31). "Play" as sexual intercourse is commonplace; cf. Exodus 32:6: "And they rose up early on the morrow, and offered burnt offerings, and brought peace offerings; and the people sat down to eat and to drink, and rose up to play [*saheq*]." In coition, as well, the couple are hermaphroditic.

12. A full listing of manuscript copies would be unnecessarily long and not useful here. The primary collections appear in Group II and III MSS, the Westmoreland MS (Berg Collection, New York Public Library), Stowe MS 962 (British Library), the Burley MS, the Hawthornden MS, and MS Grey 7 a 29 (South African Public Library, Capetown). Future reference, respectively: *W, S962, Bu, Haw, Grey*. Group I MSS do not record any of the epigrams or the Lincoln's Inn epithalamion. Group I MSS are: Dowden MS, MS English Poetical e.99 (Bodleian Library); Harleian 4955, Harley Noel MS (British Library); Cambridge Balam MS, Additional MS 5778(c) (Cambridge University Library); Leconfield MS, Percy MS (now in Cambridge University Library); MS 49 B43 (St. Paul's Cathedral Library). Reference: *D, H49, C57, Lec, SP.*

13. The O'Flahertie MS, a Group III MS, is English MS 966.5 in Harvard University Library. Reference: *O'F. W* is listed by Gardner as the only manuscript in IV.

14. "Sorrow, who to this house scarce knew the way," called "Elegie on the L. C." in 1635 and correctly repositioned among the epicedes; "Language, thou art too narrow, and too weak," which should be classified as an epicede; and "You that are she, and you that's double shee," which 1635 repositions among the verse letters. "Language" follows "You that are she" immediately without intervening poems in 1635.

15. "The Autumnal" should be placed among the songs and sonnets as it is in Group I MSS. In 1633 "The Comparison," "The Autumnal," and "Image of her whom I love,

more than she" appear after and before obsequies. However, since H. J. C. Grierson (*The Poems of John Donne* [Oxford: Clarendon Press, 1912], 1:92–94) placed it among the elegies and called it "Elegie IX," following 1635, it has been so classified and discussed by most editors and commentators. "Image of her" is not a love elegy; it should have been grouped with the songs and sonnets, as the manuscripts and most twentieth-century editors except Grierson do.

16. Titled "Eleg. XIII," "Come, Fates; I feare you not" appears in various collections of Donne's poems, often grouped with authentic elegies. The spurious poems which I note in this essay usually evidence a similar persistence. This particular poem does not appear in Groups I, II, III, or IV MSS, although it does in the adjunct miscellanies Harleian MS 4064 (Group I) and Lansdowne MS 740 (Group II). Reference: *H40, L74*.

17. *TCD* has lost some pages and has been misbound, thus affecting the texts of "Oh, let me not serve" and "To make the doubt clear." An adjunct manuscript *L74* and Dolau Cothi MS (National Library of Wales), in the Group II tradition, confounded by some other tradition, have some of the elegies in differing orders. Reference for Group II MSS respectively: *A18, TCC, N, TCD, DC.*

18. *Lut* has only six spurious poems before "Self Love." Reference for Group III MSS, respectively: *S961, Dob, Lut, O'F.*

19. *JC* (Arents Collection, New York Public Library) may have taken its poems from various separately generic manuscripts; at least Cave arranged the poems by groupings with separate title pages. First, there is "Five Satyrs: The Letanie: The Storme, and Calme" (compare note 7); then "Elegies:" and "Epigrammes:". But there are no epigrams given; instead the verso of the leaf on which he transcribed the end of "Sorrow, wch to this house" reads: "Miscellanea. Poems Elegies Sonnetts" and these are numbered.

20. The Phillipps MS (English Poetical MS f.9, Bodleian Library) is classified as V.a by Gardner; its cognate, the Osborn MS (MS b148, James Osborn Collection, Yale University), V.a; *S962*, unclassified; MS HM 198, book I (Haslewood-Kingsborough MS, Huntington Library), unclassified; and the Carnaby MS (English MS 966.1, Harvard University), V.a.

21. We should note that *JC* and *Ned* have "The Storm" and "The Calm" immediately preceding "Not that in color," although separated by the generic divider; that *P* (despite confusion in its current binding) has the three as in Group II and O records the two verse letters, three other poems (one spurious), and then "Not that in color"; that *DC* gives "Not that in color," two other elegies, and then the two verse letters; that MS Ee.4.14 (Cambridge University Library) records the elegy, four poems (two spurious) and then the two verse letters; and that 1633 prints "The Storm" and "The Calm" immediately after the collection of elegies. The upshot is, the three poems may have been associated in some manuscript tradition other than that observed in Group I, and "Not that in color" was separated from other elegies in that tradition. *Ned,* a duplicate of *JC,* is MS D25, F17, the Nedham MS, in the Dyce Collection of the Victoria and Albert Museum.

22. I have not considered here the two clearly non-Donnean elegies which often

appear with authenticated poems: "Julia" ("Harke newes, o envy, thou shalt hear descry'd") and "A Tale of a Citizen and his Wife" ("I sing no harme good sooth to any wight"), both first printed in 1635. Gardner gives them as Dubia. The first is found in *Lut, O'F, B, HM198* (book I), and Lawson; the second, in *Dob, Lut, O'F, B,* Wase, and Rawlinson. (Wase: Rawlinson MS 117, Bodleian Library; Rawlinson: Harleian MS 3991, British Library.) Gardner also includes as Dubia "To make the doubt clear," "Since she must go," and "The Heavens rejoice," as well as "Sapho to Philaenis," which will be noted later. But "To make the doubt clear" is given in 1633, Groups II and III, and a number of other manuscripts, including Group V; "Since she must go," in 1635, Group III and a number of others including Group V; and "The heavens rejoice," in 1650, *O'F* (now missing), *HM198* (books I and II), *JC, Ned,* Additional MS 10309 (British Library), and MS Don.b.9 (Bodleian Library).

23. See the Gosse MS, MS V.a.241, in the Folger Shakespeare Library, and ff. 154–67 in Harleian MS 3998 (British Library), which has no other Donne poems. Only the manuscripts mentioned in this paragraph contain the poem except for a three-line excerpt in one miscellany with a text taken from 1635 or 1639.

24. Some lines of "A Funeral Elegy" and a couplet from "The Second Anniversary" are entered in a miscellany with the text taken from 1635 or 1639, and "A Funeral Elegy" appears complete in one other manuscript.

25. The placement of this love elegy is indicative of the 1635 editor's concerns, revisions, and *errors.* There seems to be no precedent for his including this poem in this category, and we cannot conclude that what occurs in 1635 necessarily has any authority.

26. W. Milgate prints it as a verse letter in *The Satires, Epigrams and Verse Letters* (Oxford: Clarendon Press, 1967).

27. Grierson suggested that it is a covering letter for "Language, thou art too narrow." The two poems appear together (and with another epicede) in Additional MS 30982 (British Library).

28. Incidental texts need not be listed here. The sonnet "To the Lady Magdalen Herbert" appears only in Izaak Walton's *The Life of George Herbert;* it has been joined to "La Corona" because the sequence has been identified with "these *Hymns"* in the last line of the sonnet.

29. See appendix D for a listing of the divine poems by number and short title.

30. See also Gardner's discussion in *Divine Poems,* appendix E, pp. 132–35.

31. Only two other manuscripts record the poem: the Welbeck MS (MS PwV 37, Duke of Portland Library, University of Nottingham) and MS V.a.276 (Folger Shakespeare Library, lines 1–14 only). Welbeck has twelve other Donne poems, none of them divine poems, and the Folger MS (a late seventeenth-century manuscript) has only this one, probably from a printed edition. Allen Barry Cameron argues for classification of this poem among the verse letters in "Donne's Deliberative Verse Epistles" *English Literary Renaissance* 6 (1976): 398–402.

32. The poetical miscellany *S962* contains three divine poems all found in extant

Group II MSS in the same order: 6, 4, [ ], 13. *Grey* has affinities with Group II, and includes 4, 8, 7, all of which appear in the Group II MSS in a similar order.

33. Other poems have been printed in modern editions as divine poems: "To the Lady Magdalen Herbert," mentioned before; "To Mr. George Herbert, with one of my Seals, of the Anchor and Christ," partially given in Walton's *Life of John Donne* and in the editions of 1650–69; and "Translated out of Gazaeus," published in 1650–69.

34. *W* followed the verse letters with "Sonnets" (3) and "Corona" (2) only.

35. Only "Friday" (7) is now found in this manuscript, which may date from around the time of Donne's departure for Germany in 1619. The manuscript has lost a number of leaves, but probably once contained other "early" divine poems.

36. John T. Shawcross, *The Complete Poetry of John Donne* (Garden City: Anchor Books, 1967).

37. See Gardner's discussion in *Divine Poems*, pp. xxxvii–xliii. For the argument for a different order (that of *W*), see Patrick F. O'Connell, "The Successive Arrangements of Donne's Holy Sonnets," *Philological Quarterly* 60 (1981): 323–42.

38. I number these for easier reference:
   1. "As due by many titles I resign"
   2. "Oh, my black Soul! now thou art summoned"
   3. "This is my play's last scene, here heavens appoint"
   4. "At the round earth's imagin'd corners blow"
   5. "If poisonous minerals, and of that tree"
   6. "Death be not proud, though some have called thee"
   7. "Spit in my face, you Jews, and pierce my side"
   8. "Why are we by all creatures waited on?"
   9. "What if this present were the world's last night?"
   10. "Batter my heart, three person'd God; for, you"
   11. "Wilt thou love God, as he thee! then digest"
   12. "Father, part of his double interest"

39. These are:
   13. "Thou hast made me, and shall thy work decay"
   14. "O might those sighs and tears return again"
   15. "I am a little world made cunningly"
   16. "If faithful souls be alike glorified"

40. See Edmund Gosse, ed., *Jacobean Poets* (London, 1894), p. 59, for "Since she whom I loved hath paid her last debt"; and Gosse, *The Life and Letters of John Donne* (London, 1899), 2:371, for "Show me dear Christ thy spouse, so bright and clear," and "Oh, to vex me, contraries meet in one."

41. *W* gives four additional verse letters, two of which occur also in *A23; A25* and *Bur* each have one verse letter not found elsewhere. These are, respectively: "Zealously my Muse doth salute all thee" ("To Mr. R. W."), "Muse not that by thy mind thy body'is led" ("To Mr. R. W."), "Even as lame things thirst their perfection, so" ("To Mr. E. G."), "Kindly'I envy thy song's perfection" ("To Mr. R. W."), "A Letter written by Sir H. G. and

J. D. alternis vicibus," and "H. W, in Hiber. belligeranti." Often added in modern editions are a Latin poem to Doctor Andrews (printed in 1635) and the commendatory verses on Jonson's *Volpone*.

42. One might compare W. R. Johnson's emphasis on content for generic definition in *The Idea of Lyric, Lyric Mode in Ancient and Modern Poetry* (Berkeley: University of California Press, 1982) with Alastair Fowler's rejection in *Kinds of Literature: An Introduction to the Theory of Genres and Modes* (Cambridge, Mass.: Harvard University Press, 1982).

43. There is, of course, a world of criticism on the question of what genre is and isn't, much of it ill-informed or merely vague or, worse yet, so exasperated that the critic throws up his/her hands and says it is not important since there is nothing distinctive. One problem that has led to confusion is the difference between the synchronic and the diachronic alteration of generic terms; for intelligent views of this matter see Fowler, *Kinds of Literature*, as well as Thomas L. Kent, "The Classification of Genres," *Genre* 16 (1983): 1–20. A good general survey of genre and the history of genre theory is Heather Dubrow's *Genre* (London: Methuen, 1982).

44. The 1612 statement citing Jonson is referred to by C. H. Herford and Percy and Evelyn Simpson in their edition of the *Works* (Oxford, 1947), 8:16.

45. By "Anacreontick" Drummond apparently meant a love lyric not in a Petrarchan style and did not imply meter. See Robert H. MacDonald, *The Library of Drummond of Hawthornden* (Edinburgh: Edinburgh University Press, 1971), p. 32, n. 2.

46. These terms do *not* indicate that a tragedy, for example, must be a play, or that a satire must be a poem. We have correctly begun to talk about and differentiate verse satire and prose satire. We should continue this taxonomic analysis to recognize, for example, that a novel may be a tragedy, a comedy, or other. By *modal* I mean that which partakes of a specific mode, and mode, opposed as it were to genre, implies the effect of the literary work on the audience. Genre has nothing to do with effect; it is always substantive. Mode has everything to do with effect; it is always adjectival.

47. See also Cameron's discussion of "Donne's Deliberative Verse Epistles," pp. 369–403.

48. About all that Milgate says about this poem rather begrudgingly is, "The vocabulary of the poem comes from the conventional Petrarchan stock. . . . Donne here takes the trouble to achieve a genuine sonnet" (*The Satires, Epigrams, and Verse Letters*, p. 215).

49. This designation would seem to move us into content, but as generic label I use the term to indicate the treatment (as a characteristic) rather than the subject. The treatment suggests "process poem" as an alternate label; philosophical poems are process poems, though other kinds would also fall under that category.

50. Other holy sonnets employing tears, drowning, or flood are "At the round earth's imagined corners," "If poisonous minerals," and "What if this present were the world's last night?"; only "At the round earth's imagined corners" talks of fire. But these uses have no Petrarchan relationships. "Batter my heart," while strongly sexual, uses the word *burn* with quite different connotation. The last sonnet in this added group of four,

"If faithful souls are alike glorifi'd," to be taken up in a minute, has the line "They see idolatrous lovers weep and mourn" (line 9).

51. "Sapho to Philaenis" fits this definition and should probably be classified as an elegy. It is sometimes associated with one or more elegies in the manuscripts (see Group II, *DC, Ut, JC,* and *HM198*). It does not appear in Group I. It follows verse letters, however, in *TCD* and is amongst them in *O'F.*

Joseph Anthony Wittreich, Jr.
"Strange Text!"
"Paradise Regain'd . . . To which is added *Samson Agonistes*"

The wisdom of putting these works together in the same volume is the commerce that is thus established between them. . . . Perhaps we have misread Samson Agonistes *so ineptly because we have not fully acknowledged the interrelationships of the two works. . . .*
—John T. Shawcross

How little in the impressive outpouring of Milton scholarship bears explicitly on this problem" of intertextual connection between *Paradise Regained* and *Samson Agonistes,* writes Balachandra Rajan.[1] The poems in Milton's 1671 volume, for a long time, seemed resistant to the sort of criticism that both Shawcross and Rajan would sponsor; for on the one hand, they clearly embody radically different states of mind, in the words of A. S. P. Woodhouse are "so different . . . in doctrine, temper, and tone," and on the other hand, as William Riley Parker remarks, *Samson* seems "a bitter poem, a dark poem . . . a relapse" from *Paradise Regained.*[2] Still, this tired hypothesis should not be allowed to cancel out the livelier, more daring one, shared by Shawcross and Rajan alike, that Milton placed these poems together because he wished to make a statement through the juxtaposition—meant for these poems to be mutually reflective and illuminating and thus interpretively significant for one another, with *Paradise Regained* providing a fractional gloss on the poem that succeeds it. Milton regularly thinks in terms of such juxtapositions "opposing," as he does in *A Treatise of Civil Power,* "truth to error, no unequal match; truth the strong to error the weak though slie and shifting" (*Prose Works,* 7:261).

The juxtaposition of these poems and the ensuing dialogue between them suggest that they are not autonomous but dependent upon one another for their meaning. Milton's poems are always a plurality of other texts that help to unravel their meaning; their intertextuality, whether overt or covert, provides access to their meaning, with *Paradise Regained* and *Sam-*

son *Agonistes* internalizing the usual presuppositions about intertextuality and then moving between themselves in the same way that texts, usually of different authorship, through the same elusive presuppositions become involved with one another. It is as if Milton were using explicit intertextuality between *Paradise Regained* and the Gospels, between *Samson Agonistes* and the Book of Judges, to signal a hidden intertextuality between the poems themselves, with *Samson* relating to *Paradise Regained* as each poem relates to its biblical context and thus as text relates to pre-text. An intertextuality achieved through allusion masks an elusive intertextuality, with the presuppositions governing the former now transferred to and providing the controls for the latter. Surface intertextuality, at least in *Paradise Regained* and *Samson Agonistes,* holds the reader within the confines of inferential meaning whereas, in these same poems, a covert intertextuality leads the reader into the realm of specified but subversive meanings. Interpretation of both these poems will proceed when we begin to ask, with Jonathan Culler, how does a text establish a pre-text, and then provide, as Culler urges, "an account of how texts create presuppositions and hence pre-texts for themselves and how the ways of producing these presuppositions relate to ways of treating them."[3]

MILTON'S HABIT

The signals of a hidden intertextuality in Milton's 1671 poetic volume are various; one can point to the habit of composition evident in such precursors as Spenser and Donne, Herbert and Marvell; and, more, one can point to Milton's own habit of composition evident in his early poems and prose works alike. This method of composition engages all these poets in certain strategies devised to secure intertextual connection: typological patterning, generic organization, self-quotation and echo, imagistic and thematic repetition, a common subtext, all of which are conspicuously evident in Milton's 1671 volume. *Paradise Regained* and *Samson Agonistes* have not a separate but shared syntax; these poems together form a totality, with the individual poems themselves becoming like fragments. The volume, that is, becomes the poem; *its* syntax, not that of the separate poems, governs the meaning; and the meaning itself derives from the concatenation. Beyond these shared devices for signaling and securing relationships, there is the device, distinctively Miltonic, of making arrangements mirror a dialectical interplay between poems; Milton's poems do not exist in peaceful cohabitation but are joined in strife, engaged in contention. Containing its own inner polemic, the entire volume takes energy from this opposition.

The fact that *Paradise Regained* and *Samson Agonistes* were published together tells us something about how they were intended to be read and about how they *were* read for a full century after their original publication. Not until 1779 was either poem published separately. This particular pairing of poems is sufficiently odd that the oddity itself alerts us to the ways in which normal expectations would have been dashed: first, the obvious connection, and interplay, between *Paradise Lost* and *Paradise Regained* is eschewed by the decision to separate the poems in publication; second, the natural order of works is disregarded in the decision to publish *Samson Agonistes* after, and as an appendage, to *Paradise Regained*. This frustration of expectations may, in fact, signal that Milton is employing surreptitious strategies in order to bypass difficulties with the newly institutionalized censorship; and the very effectiveness of such strategies is testified to by the fact that *Paradise Regained* regularly, but seldom *Samson Agonistes,* was perceived as a challenge and threat to orthodoxy—a challenge and threat mitigated by the apparent movement in this volume from the unconventional to the conventional, from wildly speculative theology to platitudinous Christianity. The movement is illusory, probably deliberately so; but the sheer power of the illusion is registered in the history of criticism where, for a full century, Milton is portrayed as a poet converting back to the supposed orthodoxies of his early poetry, and consequently where little attention is given to the possibility that *Paradise Regained* provides a deliberately widened context in which to read *Samson Agonistes*.

Where there is censorship, poets must circumvent its restrictions by devising new—and devious—means of expression. With *Paradise Regained* and *Samson Agonistes,* it is not enough to look at mere words on a page to arrive at an interpretation and not enough, either, to segregate poems for interpretation that are themselves integrated through their publication. Various detouring operations for poets writing under the intimidation of censorship—the use of "safe" genres to convey "unsafe" ideas, the concealment of radical content within a subtext, the appropriation of biblical stories as a screen on contemporary history, the depersonalizing of unsettling convictions, the avoidance of responsibility for dangerous opinions by investing them in dialogue, the signaling of heresies in the deep structure of a poem by the flickering unorthodoxies on its surface, the severing of contexts in order to make innocent what, if bound together, might be too provocative, the establishment of a meaningful connection between poems through casual, seemingly idiosyncratic placement of them—these very strategies for detouring censorship, now extrapolated from Renaissance texts and so finely elucidated by Christopher Hill and Annabel Patterson, are all operative in Milton's 1671 poetic volume.[4]

An argument for the interrelationship and deliberate counterpositioning of *Paradise Regained* and *Samson Agonistes* is all the more plausible now that Milton's critics have sensitized us to the collective design of his poems and to the wholeness of his canon, the impulses toward which are evident early on: in the role accorded *Lycidas* both in *Justa Edovardo King Naufrago* (1638) and in *Poems of Mr. John Milton* (1645), in the organizational patterns and intertextual relationships tested in the former volume, then transferred to the 1645 *Poems;* and even in that gathering of prose works which, though it be an afterthought, Milton seeks to capture within the overarching conception of freedom—domestic, civil, and religious. The other poems in *Justa Edovardo King Naufrago* are related to one another as *Lycidas* relates to them, through a carefully plotted mental and emotional progression and also through a system of echoing, as well as of corresponding yet contending images. The 1645 *Poems* are disposed in such a way as to chart the course of a rising poet, figured by generic progression within "a unifying and developing vision of the transforming power of poetry,"[5] its thrust beyond pagan toward Christian truth and its grasping for the prophetic strain. The attainment of the prophetic strain is not only the climax of the volume but the culminating moment in the companion poems, *L'Allegro* and *Il Penseroso*, which, like the volume as a whole, almost the volume in miniature, arrive at the prophetic moment through an elaborate generic progression. The twin lyrics are bound together, their relationship sealed, by structural and imagistic mirroring, which allows always for the perception of difference within the apparent likeness.

The poetic volumes to which Milton contributed, or which he composed, have their own logic and rhetoric, then, and their own deliberate, distinctive architectonics. Milton's conception of the poetic volume does not alter, although the principles for intertextuality do become muted owing to the circumstances in which *Paradise Regained* and *Samson Agonistes* are published and concerning which Annabel Patterson is altogether too reticent:

> We still do not know whether Milton turned to biblical reinterpretation [in these poems] in order to transcend his political experience, now seen as failed and useless, or whether in the Restoration poems

he was still operating in the tradition articulated by James I before he became king: "Ze man . . . be war of wryting any thing of materis of commoun weill, or uther sich grave sene subjectis (except Metaphorically . . .) . . . they are to grave materis for a Poet to mell in."[6]

Milton's last poems are probing and powerful political statements; they are of a piece with the 1645 *Poems* and yet a significant advance upon Milton's earlier concerns. A biblical poet, such as Milton has now become, might be expected to appropriate biblically sanctioned oppositions between positive and negative images—between prophetic idealisms and historical actualities. If the earlier poems reach for the prophetic moment, these last poems, an embodiment of that moment, turn their attention to the formation of the prophetic character, with *Paradise Regained* and *Samson Agonistes* scrutinizing the evidence for and excesses of such characters, as well as the perils of prophecy and its burden. Not only is *Paradise Regained* anticipated in the last books of *Paradise Lost,* but so too is the very problem that will be sorted out in *Samson Agonistes:* of those

> . . . feigning . . . to act
> By spiritual [power], to themselves appropriating
> The Spirit of God, promised alike and giv'n
> To all Believers

and of all the turmoil in history issuing from that "pretense" (XII, 517–20).

Milton's earlier efforts, in poetry and prose alike, are but harbingers of what has been called the "intense interrelatedness"[7] of Milton's last poems which, as a trilogy, reveal the extent to which one poem reaches out to others and defines itself in relation to them. The poetic volume of 1671 specifically raises the problem of relationship on a title page where *Paradise Regained*, as Arthur Barker notices, appears in an "emphatic typeface" and *Samson Agonistes,* in a "smaller, and perhaps hesitantly insignificant, type." According to Barker, in raising the problem of interrelationship, this title page raises the whole question of intersignificance:

> . . . does the collocation represent the imperfectly resolved conflict of the later Miltonic moods which we can discern in the poetic difficulties we encounter in the two pieces? Does not the first poem express, or move toward the expression of, the tuningly harmonious vision of spirituality towards which Milton was always striving to make his way and

needed all the more after being diverted into national revolutionary efforts and defeated in them? And does not the second poem chiefly represent the painfully guilty despair of defeat and the difficulty of struggling out of that towards vision? Should not Samson's fallen, if ultimately, in some sense, rescued, experience rather precede Christ's making possible the regaining of Paradise for all mankind? . . . Or is there some deep significance in the apparently inept reversal? Can we interpret our poems in a way which will demonstrate that . . . they are properly sequential?

In short, are the two poems . . . to be regarded as companion or rather as contrasting pieces?[8]

Milton's is a poetry not only of allusion but of contexts, both extrinsic and intrinsic, with the oeuvre having as much "connective life" and being as fully designed certainly as the contexts of either genre or milieu.[9] Hence, both *Paradise Regained* and *Samson Agonistes* harken back to *A Masque* and *Lycidas;* and both contain richly textured, finely pointed allusion to *Paradise Lost: Paradise Regained* in its opening lines and *Samson* in its initial soliloquy. The poems are companion but contrasting pieces, as well as the second and third items in a trilogy, with *Paradise Regained,* by virtue of its backward glances and forward gaze, subordinating *Paradise Lost* and *Samson* to itself and thereby achieving the status of centerpiece. There is, moreover, the often avoided yet still obvious context that each of these poems provides for the other. These are poems, as Coleridge might say, that "answer and provoke each other's songs,"[10] with the pairing itself enabling criticism to unmold the essence of each poem.

The principle of opposition is essential to Milton's volume and is essentially corrective of those who see in *Samson Agonistes* a repetition of *Paradise Regained* in a finer tone instead of a more bellicose version of that poem and even to those who, aware of opposition, define it in terms of defeatism and noble defiance instead of perceiving in both poems a call for staying the course and a joint exploration of how and why that matters. In Milton's poems, as later in Byron's and Shelley's, opposites meet—find a point of convergence—in their respective encounters with apocalypse. The Apocalypse is their subtext, and the ideologies at different times attributed to that book their point of reference and concern. It has been said that "if *Paradise Regained* can be thought of as leading into the Gospels, *Samson Agonistes* leads into the Epistles,"[11] which is but to say that what we witness in both poems is Milton's effort to square scriptural myth with historical reality. For this reason especially, these poems also lead away from the Gospels and Epistles into the Book of Revelation and the alternative myths of deliverance therein, with one myth being invalidated by the other.

THE TYPOLOGICAL CONNECTION

Interrelated by allusion and echo, and by genre (both poems are *visionary* epics, records in part of *visionary* experience), *Paradise Lost* and *Paradise Regained* are nevertheless unrelated to the usual typology that correlates the Fall in the garden with the Redemption on the cross. This is not to say that there is no typological connection between the two epics. On the contrary, the two temptation cycles are interconnected by anticipation in the concluding book of *Paradise Lost* and through retrospection, especially in the proem to *Paradise Regained* and additionally by insistent, pointed reference to the forty days both Moses and Elijah spent in the same "barren waste" (I, 352–54; compare II, 266–72, 312–15) which Jesus now travels and to which Adam and Eve were exiled. Furthermore, the forty days Jesus spends in the desert, as John Evans has shown, were thought to parallel those forty days Adam spent in the garden before the creation of Eve, a parallelism deriving from the Book of Jubilees and developed by Iraneus and Gregory the Great. Moreover, according to Evans, "the Pelagian view of the Fall as the first example of sin implies a view of the Redemption as the first example of goodness." In such a scheme, resistance to temptation dwarfs the remedy of the Cross; or as Evans argues, Adam's Fall is "neutralized not on the Cross but in the desert. It is in this typological tradition that *Paradise Regained* had its origins."[12] A similar, and similarly unexpected, typology forges a link between Milton's brief epic and tragedy.

In the 1671 poetic volume, the forty days spent by Jesus in the wilderness are made to preface an Old Testament story, but one with which the Passion story was consistently paired and through which the drama of the Crucifixion was regularly glimpsed. Viewed in terms of the two Testaments, *Paradise Regained* and *Samson Agonistes* may seem discontinuous and disjunctive, but viewed in terms of a crucial phase in the liturgical calendar the poems are perfectly continuous. Both poems also contain temptation cycles, are centered in the tradition of good temptations, with the Father's words in *Paradise Regained* providing an equally apt epigraph for either poem:

>   . . . this man born and now up-grown,
> To shew him worthy of his birth divine
> And high prediction, henceforth I expose
> To Satan. . . .   (I, 140–43)

While a good temptation is intended to "proveth" a man, as William Cowper remarks, it may have the opposite effect of "snar[ing] him, or manifest[ing] some weaknes in him."[13] It may in fact be used to unmask hypocrisy. Thus out of their shared experience emerge decidedly different heroes: one who is "far wiser" than to be lured "to the bait of women" (II, 204–5), the other who is tempted and twice succumbs to their allurement; one who conquers through weakness, the other by strength; one whose forté is mental, the other's physical might. The sense of discrepancy between the heroes of the two poems is much stronger than any sense of analogy so that, instead of thinking that "the central theme of *Samson Agonistes* is the reconstruction of . . . Samson's heroism,"[14] we should begin to talk about that poem as engaged in the deconstruction of Samson's supposed heroism.

It was once thought that "the connexion between *Paradise Regained* and *Samson Agonistes,* originally accidental, is not kept up"; that the lack of connection between these poems is nonetheless compensated for by the planned continuities between Milton's epics, with *Paradise Regained* relating to *Paradise Lost* as "its sequel."[15] This peculiarity, even perversity, of poetic placement is accompanied by an unobserved and no less curious paradox of interpretation; typological tradition, almost always frustrated and even sometimes subverted in these poems, provides the logic of connection between them, affirming their status as companion pieces—the twin halves, legitimate if not identical, of a single poetic statement.

Typological tradition yields important supporting props for the argument that the connection between these poems, their placement together in the same volume, the tragedy subordinated to the brief epic, is neither accidental nor capricious but a deliberate, deft calculation on Milton's part. This is not to say that typological connections sanction typological readings of either poem, only that such connections are a bond between these poems in which the ironies of those connections are dissuasive to such readings, at least those that stress similitudes rather than discrepancies, simple equivalents over multivalencies. Nor is this to say that *Paradise Regained* does not exhibit obvious, and obviously important, links with *Paradise Lost,* only that those with *Samson* are of equal interest and, interpretively, perhaps of more importance. Typological tradition itself accounts for the fact, as Rajan notices, that interconnections between these poems "both play against and play upon each other."[16] Samson may not be mentioned in *Paradise Regained* nor Jesus in *Samson Agonistes*, but the two figures are nevertheless made to face one another in the 1671 poetic volume and in such a way as to pit an emergent against a failed prophet and the bright light of vision against the darkness of the subjected plain.

As the once secure link between Samson ending the lives of the Philistines and Christ coming to end life on earth is broken, the Samson story, losing its analogy with the Second Coming, is correlated all the more insistently with the First Coming; and then as the analogy between Samson's final days and Christ's loses its potency, another correlation, this time between Samson's trials as a judge and those of Jesus in the wilderness, achieves prominence. A new set of analogies secures this linkage, behind which stands the typologist's tendency to correlate temptations in the Old Testament with those of Jesus in the New, comparing a whole complex of previous temptations, one with the other, and thereupon contrasting them all with those experienced by Jesus in the wilderness. Thus Lancelot Andrewes observes, "that which was in the Olde Testament the temptation of *Meribah*, is here in the new Testament the Temptation of the Wilderness: and that which was there the Temptation of *Massah*, is here the temptation of the Pinacle." Later, Andrewes conjoins the pinnacle temptation to Samson's hurling down the pillars, Samson in this regard representing the foolish in the world, those who "have begun in the spirite" but who "will ende in the flesh," in contrast with Jesus who, overcoming the flesh, triumphs in the spirit.[17] From this analogy others eventually are spun.

The episodes at the pillars and on the pinnacle had been explained in terms of divine impulsion but could also be used to differentiate true from false inspiration, as well as to illustrate the propositions that God never leads men to a stage or theater but only to the Word, that nothing is ever lost by waiting upon divine providence.[18] The episode at the pillars and the kingdoms temptation had also become linked within a perspective from which each was regarded as illusory: "I finde, although a man have the strength of *Sampson* . . . all are nothing, all are but fantasticall . . . to the eye: as those Kingdomes which the *Divell* offered to Christ."[19] In Samson's rending of the lion is seen Jesus in the wilderness subduing the devil, Samson here emerging as "a notable type of Christ vanquishing and triumphing over Satan the roaring Lion . . . by the sole virtue of his own power."[20] Samson and Jesus are equally prisoners in this life, and each is shown—Samson with the lion, Jesus in the desert with Satan—being exercised during "initiatory encounters," although for all their similarity, this typecasting eventually yields to the perception that Jesus, a "spiritual Samson," is "the better *Nazarite*,"[21] a stronger, more perfect, hence more glorious Samson—a victorious not a defeated hero, a spiritual warrior rather than one to blood enured.

These sorts of analogies are cited with growing frequency to emphasize, through Samson, the humanity of Jesus; and each of these figures, in his tearing down the bar and opening the gates into paradise, is regarded as a deliverer, Samson commencing what is left for Jesus to complete.[22] The situations of Samson and Jesus reinforce such analogies, with Jesus in the wilderness and Samson at Gaza both being isolated and alone in their suffering and from that posture inviting reflection upon their private and public persons, the natural and the spiritual man, the nature and proof of divine authority, the prospects for apocalyptic deliverance, and the efficacy of millennial expectations. Often the product of such reflections is a Samson motivated by private desire, a natural man whose claims to divine impulsion are unwarranted, an agent in a broken apocalypse who himself provides a profound critique of millenarianism. Such a Samson, in turn, emerges as a foil for the heroism of Jesus. The false and fallen prophet stands against Jesus, the agent of divine vision and the spirit of true prophecy.

The wilderness episodes—Samson's temptations and those of Jesus—become linked, it seems, only for the purpose of differentiating them and, in the process, of neutralizing the Samson story by subordinating it to Christ's. In *Eikon Basilike,* for example, the author correlates his own experiences with those of Job, Jonah, David, and Solomon and, more interestingly and importantly, with those of Samson and Christ. "The solitude they have confined Me unto, adds the wildernesse to my temptations," writes Charles's spokesman, who has already analogized Charles's experiences with those of Christ on the mountain and pinnacle and drawn from those analogies the lesson that the kingdoms are not worth gaining—nothing is worth gaining—by wrong and violent means. The Samson story is thereupon alluded to in order to instance that one just does not, should not, readily submit to others: "This were as if *Sampson* should have consented, not only to binde his own hands, and cut off his haire, but to put out his eyes, that the *Philistins* might with the more safety mock, and abuse him; which they chose rather to doe, then quite destroy him."[23] The Samson story is at once a positive and a negative example: follow Samson in not submitting to the enemy, but follow the enemy rather in mocking without destroying; now be like Samson and now be like his Philistine oppressors. Nothing is to be gained by wounding in order to heal, Milton himself states in *A Treatise of Civil Power,* and also there stipulates his belief that the ultimate gesture, always, is not "to destruction, but . . . to a final saving" (*Prose Works,* 7:267, 269).

Commonly in the seventeenth century, whenever the Samson legend disagrees with that of Jesus, it is subordinated to, then corrected by, the New Testament story. That Milton has this sort of contrastive relationship in mind is suggested by the intertextual connections involving *Paradise Regained* and *Samson Agonistes* and the ironies attending them. Milton's brief epic casts a beam of light through the gloom of history as it is figured in *Samson Agonistes.* From one perspective, Samson contains the sad reality, the elemental despair that issues forth from the failed idealisms of *Paradise Regained;* but from another perspective, it is as if *Samson* contains the illusion and *Paradise Regained* the true reality. *Samson,* that is, transforms the historical reality into an illusion, while *Paradise Regained* would wrest from history its potentiality and thereby transform idealisms into the reality of history. Neither poem reduces to an ideology, but both strike a relationship with an ideology of which each is more than a mere reflection. Both poems, that is, foster a perception of their opposing ideologies, each looking at a distance upon the other, and, as Terry Eagleton claims of analogous forms of ideological confrontation, "contribute to our deliverance from ideological illusion."[24]

INTERTEXTUAL RELATIONSHIPS

Typology is a habit of mind—sometimes a vital part, other times not, of the consciousness of a culture. In the seventeenth century, typology was very much a part of that consciousness, so much so that an audience of readers would have discerned in *Paradise Regained* implicit reference to the Samson story and, conversely, in *Samson Agonistes* reference to the wilderness temptation of Jesus. There is, however, explicit connection between these poems, for in Milton's brief epic Jesus refers to the people of Dan taking up with idols in the aftermath of Samson's tragedy, and in the Preface to *Samson Agonistes* Milton himself sets the view of tragedy expressed here within the perspective afforded on the same genre both by the Jesus and Satan of *Paradise Regained.* The two poems are interconnected in these instances by allusion but more often by an elaborate system of echoing. Such allusions are the equivalent of scholia transferred from the margins into the text itself. These allusions, but even more emphatically the "rebounds of intertextual echo," as John Hollander theorizes, "distort the original voice," in the instance of these poems, the voice of Jesus, "in order to interpret it." Each poem is an echo chamber for the other with "language answering language" and in "a kind of phonetic mimicry," which, again to quote from Hollander, produces "analytic irony" out of this dramatic and typological play.[25]

It has been said that "Milton's return to the Old Testament allows him to incorporate the Jesus and the Satan of *Paradise Regained* within his new, and for him more inclusive, hero."[26] And it is true that these two poems are interconnected but in subtler, more confounding ways: not by quotation and paraphrase but by allusion and echo that, creating dissonances and discontinuities, call for differentiations between heroes, with Samson emerging from such contrasts not as a more encompassing but as a diminished version of the Jesus of *Paradise Regained*. In fine, Samson is less like Jesus than Satan and perhaps still more like the Adam of *Paradise Lost* who, to whatever glories born, in the words of Milton's brief epic, falls "Degraded by himself" (IV, 311). In turning from *Paradise Regained* to *Samson Agonistes,* Milton, as he had previously done, must change his notes to tragedy and present an action deemed by Luther and others unworthy of imitation. If *A Treatise of Civil Power* is an accurate reflection of his sentiments, Milton himself would have to judge Samson's actions unworthy of imitation: "it is unlawfull for the civil magistrate to use force in matters of religion," for God's glory is never promoted by "unwarrantable means, much less by means contrarie to what he hath commanded" (VII, 255, 266). God never countermands his own commandments.

Samson the judge and Jesus the king are both represented as images but of a decidedly different deity, the one whose law is vengeance, the other whose only law is love. Others in Milton's century had been preoccupied with ruling in the style of God, but here Milton's concern is with an anterior question: what is, or should be, God's style? The sinister, squabbling gods of *Samson Agonistes*—"thou shalt see, or rather to thy sorrow / Soon feel, whose God is strongest, thine or mine" (lines 1154–55)—are so personated as to make not only Dagon but Samson's "God" seem ridiculous (compare PR IV, 342). In the face of Jesus are to be found "glimpses of his Fathers glory" (I, 93), is to be seen the "True Image of the Father" (IV, 596). In the figure of Samson, the Chorus discovers only "The Image of [God's] strength" (line 706), the image of a snarling, combative deity. That is, Jesus reveals the totality, is in every respect the similitude of deity, while Samson is but an aspect, a manifestation of the dark side of a deity; and it is a deity who prosecutes through Samson the claims for justice which express themselves in vengeance and violence, the very qualities that the God of

Milton's epics cannot brook. It is of some moment that, in *Paradise Regained,* Satan tempts Jesus to fashion himself in what will be the image of Milton's Samson so "that all the world / Could not sustain thy Prowess, or subsist / In battel" (III, 17–19) and to employ force (a means Satan has already rejected [I, 97]) to deliver his people from servitude (IV, 380–84)—a means that Jesus himself now rejects as "argument / Of human weakness rather than of strength" (IV, 401–2). "For Milton there is no strength except spiritual strength, and no conflict except mental conflict," says Northrop Frye; "hence the prophecy that the Messiah will defeat the serpent can only be fulfilled in a dramatic dialogue."[27] Representations of temptation and strife can only be inward, with both poems belonging to a species of prophecy.

The trials of Jesus and Samson alike are centered in a mental theater. Before Jesus goes to the temple he is afflicted with a swarming multitude of thoughts (I, 196–97), and then enters the wilderness, journeys into himself "with holiest meditations fed" (II, 110), achieving finally an "untroubl'd mind" (IV, 401). Not the Jesus but the Satan of *Paradise Regained* anticipates the mental and emotional state of Samson. Like Satan who is "inly rackt" (III, 203), "Perplex'd and troubl'd" (IV, 1), and eventually "swoln with rage" (IV, 499), Samson's mind is a turmoil of "restless thoughts, . . . like a deadly swarm / Of Hornets arm'd" (lines 19–20), with the patience he seems later to have won exploding into the rage that produces the temple holocaust. Samson's is "a troubl'd mind," tumored and festering with wounds (lines 185–86). Jesus may cause the "fiery Serpent" to flee his path as he enters the wilderness (I, 312), but as we learn from Genesis and its commentators, and as Milton remembers in *Samson Agonistes* in the image of the "ev'ning Dragon" (line 1692), "Dan [or Samson] shall judge his people . . . Dan shall be a serpent in the way, a horned snake in the path" (Genesis 49:16–17).[28]

Jesus and Samson both make signally important appearances at a temple, the one as a youth and later as an adult, the other only as an adult. The experience at the temple, the initiation of Jesus's career, contributes to the formation of his public posture fully achieved atop another temple. In the case of Samson, however, the same experience terminates a public career and involves a juxtaposition of the public good with private motives. Jesus commits himself to the former, whereas Samson subordinates the former to the latter. The liberation of their people, the deliverance of their respective nations, is an issue foregrounded in both poems, but in such a way as to discriminate the finer moral tones of Jesus from the crude sensibility of Samson. Commencing his public life by going to the temple ostensibly to learn but actually to teach, Jesus eventually goes atop the temple to learn; he finds himself where Samson loses himself, defines and discovers himself where Samson, even if inadvertently, destroys himself.

In *Paradise Regained,* Jesus avers:

> I went into the Temple, there to hear
> The Teachers of our Law, and to propose
> What might improve my knowledge or their own;
> And was admir'd by all, yet this not all
> To which my Spirit aspir'd, virtuous deeds
> Flam'd in my heart, heroic acts, one while
> To rescue *Israel* from the *Roman* yoke,
> Then to subdue and quell o'er all the earth
> Brute violence and proud Tyrannick pow'r,
> Till truth were freed, and equity restor'd:
> Yet held it more humane, more heavenly first
> By warning words to conquer willing hearts,
> And make perswasion do the work of fear;
> At least to try, and teach the erring Soul
> Not wilfully mis-doing, but unware
> Misled; the stubborn only to subdue.   (I, 211–26)

If Jesus goes from the temple to the desert and later from the temple top returns to civilization as a deliverer of the oppressed, Samson goes from the temple to his death, at the temple surrendering his own role as a deliverer of his people. *Samson Agonistes* begins with a recollection that "Promise was that I / Should *Israel* from *Philistian* yoke deliver" (lines 38–39) and proceeds into the irony that "this great Deliverer" Samson now finds himself "Eyeless in *Gaza* at the Mill with slaves, / Himself in bonds under *Philistian* yoke" (lines 40–42). Unlike Jesus who commits himself to mental fight, Samson, even at the end, is defying others "to the trial of mortal fight" (line 1175). His "fist is free" (line 1235), ready to engage in "the force of Conquest" (line 1206) in order to effect "The desolation of a Hostile City" (line 1561). "*Mortal fight*" is just "another phrase of chivalry"[29] in this poem, another component of the romance tradition of which the Satan of *Paradise Regained* is so enamored and Jesus so dismissive.

At the temple, Samson declares:

> Now *of my own accord* such other tryal
> I mean to shew you of my strength, yet greater;

> As with amaze shall strike all who behold . . .
> . . . those two massie Pillars
> With horrible convulsion to and fro,
> He tugg'd, he shook, till down they came and drew
> The whole roof after them, with burst of thunder
> Upon the heads of all who sate beneath,
> Lords, Ladies, Captains, Councellors, or Priests,
> Thir choice nobility and flower . . .
> Samson with these immixt, *inevitably*
> *Pull'd down the same destruction on himself;*
> The vulgar only scap'd who stood without.
> (lines 1643–59; my italics)

What Samson does, by his own admission, is done of his *own accord:* he kills; and killing, we are told, is an act never coming from God but "meerely from Satan."[30] The Semichorus, not Samson, attributes his action to divine impulsion: "With inward eyes illuminated / His fierie vertue rouz'd" (lines 1689–90). The action is performed impulsively, without reflection on liberation and deliverance and without regard for the authority of inspiration such as is displayed by Gideon in another of the in-set narratives in the Book of Judges. And if Samson's final act is performed subsequent to "warning words" they are not of the sort meant "to conquer willing hearts, / And make perswasion do the work of fear" (*PR* I, 222–23). That anyone escapes the catastrophe, mindlessly wrought upon the multitudes, is Milton's, not Samson's, devising. *Paradise Regained* ends with Satan bringing Jesus to his "Fathers house" (IV, 552) and with Jesus, here becoming one with his father, "Home to his Mothers house private return[ing]" (IV, 639), ready now to enter upon his ministry and "begin to save mankind" (IV, 635). *Samson Agonistes,* on the other hand, concludes with a Samson who, having failed in his divine mission, is returned publicly, by "funeral train / Home to his Fathers house" (lines 1732–33) where he is crowned not with immortal but with earthly fame, not with amaranthus but with laurel, and thereupon built an earthly monument.

The fame won by Samson is the same fame extolled by Satan in *Paradise Regained* but rejected by Jesus:

> For what is glory but the blaze of fame,
> The peoples praise? . . .
> This is true glory and renown, when God

> Looking on the Earth, with approbation marks
> The just man, and divulges him through Heaven
> To all his Angels, who with true applause
> Recount his praises. . . .   (III, 47–48, 60–64)

On earth, says Jesus, "glory is false glory, attributed / To things not glorious, men not worthy of fame" (III, 69–70). The hero of Milton's tragedy is a "secular bird" (line 1707), his fame and glory recounted on earth as the people's praise and won by means just the opposite of those recommended by Jesus: "without . . . violence; / By deeds of peace, by wisdom eminent, / By patience, temperance" (III, 90–92). While his body dies, Samson's fame survives—in time, in history; it is a secular fame generated by a people who now legendize the dead Samson, making of him an earthly idol. On this matter Milton is emphatic: idolatry is opposed in both the Old and New Testaments.

Manoa, having through most of the play forgotten about Samson's mission, may at its end proclaim that Samson has brought freedom to his people (lines 1714–15); but we know from the Book of Judges that Samson has brought no freedom at all, and we learn this too from *Paradise Regained*:

> Should I of these the liberty regard,
> Who freed . . .
> Unhumbl'd, unrepentant, unreform'd,
> Headlong would follow; and to thir Gods perhaps
> Of *Bethel* and of *Dan?* no, let them serve
> Thir enemies. . . .   (III, 427–32)[31]

Later on, Jesus explains why all of Samson's efforts, including his exertions at the temple, must be judged untimely:

> What wise and valiant man would seek to free
> These thus degenerate, by themselves enslav'd,
> Or could of inward slaves make outward free? (IV, 143–45)

Timely delays amount to an avoidance of brute violence and are a way of keeping faith in time of trouble. The cause was too good to have been fought for.

Central to both poems are their respective heroes' claims to divine authority and their commissions to the cause of liberation. The narrator of *Paradise Regained* speaks of the "Spirit who ledst this glorious Eremite/Into the Desert" (I, 8–9), and Jesus recalls the same moment:

>   . . . I knew the time
> Now full, that I no more should live obscure,
> But openly begin, as best becomes
> The Authority which I deriv'd from Heav'n,
> And now by some strong motion I am led
> Into this Wilderness. . . .   (I, 286–91)

Jesus continually invokes that "Authority" who brought him hither and will bring him hence (I, 335–36). The aforementioned speech by Jesus finds a counterpart in Milton's tragedy:

>   . . . I begin to feel
> Some rouzing motions in mee which dispose
> To something extraordinary my thoughts.   (lines 1381–83)

What those extraordinary thoughts are we are never told but can surmise that, nurtured by Samson's desire for revenge, they involve some program for its execution. When Jesus "on was led" he was also disposed to

>   . . . thoughts
> Accompanied by things past and to come
> . . . as well might recommend
> Such Solitude before choicest Society.   (I, 299–302)

"How to begin, how to accomplish best / His end of being on Earth, and mission high" (II, 113–14) of deliverance is a matter about which Samson thinks less than, and differently from, Jesus—a matter which becomes a preoccupation for him not from the moment he enters upon his judgeship but in the moment when, blinded, he is placed in prison and for all practical purposes relieved of his judgeship. Then he thinks of times past and the present, "what once I was, and what now am" (line 22), tardily remembering the "Promise . . . that I / Should *Israel* from *Philistian* yoke deliver" (line 39). He does not initially recall that his charge is to *begin* the work of deliverance but assumes that in his own lifetime he is to accomplish a full deliverance.

If in *Paradise Regained* the prophetic narrator confirms that Jesus goes into the desert, "the Spirit leading" (I, 189), the prophetic poet responsible for composing "The Argument" to *Samson Agonistes* allows no more than that Samson was "perswaded inwardly" that the call to the temple "was from God"; the Chorus urges Samson on, *hoping* "the Holy One / Of *Israel*" will be his guide, that the same spirit which "first rusht" on Samson will be "in thee now at need" (lines 1435–36). Manoa declares unequivocally, but only in the aftermath of the tragedy, that "all this" was accomplished "With God not parted from him, as was feared" (lines 1718–19). What casts doubt on such claims at the end of the play are Samson's own seemingly mindless claims early on in the play: "what I motion'd was of God . . . I thought it lawful from my former act" (lines 222, 231); and such doubts are compounded by the contexts in which such claims are made, of Samson's patently unlawful marriages, of his indiscriminate slaughtering not once but many times. The dubious character of Samson's early assertions is accentuated by Manoa himself: "thou didst plead / Divine impulsion . . . / . . . I state not that" (lines 421–22, 424). There may be folly in following the individual conscience when supposedly divine commands are at odds with God's law. In such circumstances, Milton implies in *De Doctrina Christiana,* to abrogate the law is to go down into Egypt and into the house of bondage. For Samson the judge to abrogate the law is curious indeed, for "the Judges were a sort of Magistrate inferior to kings, and could neither make new laws, nor impose any tributes, but were the supreme Executors of Gods Laws and Commands."[32] Or as Milton explains in *De Doctrina:* "It is quite unthinkable that Christ should expunge from the Mosaic law any provision which could sanction the extension of charity towards the wretched and the afflicted" (VI: 380). The "high exploits" Samson credits himself with having performed, while "Full of divine instinct" (lines 525–26), are without exception unlawful under the Old Dispensation and are of the sort ridiculed by Jesus in *Paradise Regained*. Although he comes to displace the law, Jesus never breaks the law; subject to the law, Samson repeatedly transgresses it, confusing a physical for a spiritual stimulus and mistaking an internal impulse for a divine prompting. Helen Damico understands the situation exactly: "in both origin and consequence, . . . the heroes' 'motions' in *Paradise Regained* and *Samson Agonistes* differ markedly and may be seen as representative of the generative and destructive aspects of inspiration."[33]

I was led—the very language is crucial by virtue of its presence in the one poem and virtual absence from the other. The Spirit leads, it never drives, and never does it compel a man to violence. There is the suggestion here that Jesus, not Samson, is being led on, a little further onward by each temptation, into a world of vision, the very word "led" being "expressive of a prophetic afflatus and illumination" and serving, as a code word, to authenticate the inspiration, making clear it is of God and not Satan.[34] In the words of Lancelot Andrewes, "Christ was not hastie, but stayed Gods good time" and was thus able to realize and complete his mission.[35] The dialectic within *Paradise Regained* that pits the false against the true prophet operates intertextually as well. It is Samson, like Satan, who abuses prophecy and follows it "to his fatal snare" (*PR* I, 441). Jesus, in contrast, stands as "an inward Oracle" (I, 463) and, led himself, leads others into the truth of the divine vision, away from which Samson was often thought to have fallen.[36] Samson, within the perspective afforded by *Paradise Regained* and the evidence provided by Milton's tragedy, never "reigns within himself, and rules / Passions, Desires, and Fears" (II, 466–67); in fact, by such standards he must be numbered among those unfit to rule because they are "head-strong . . . / Subject . . . to Anarchy within, / Or lawless passions" (lines 470–72).

Paradise Regained and especially *Samson Agonistes* dwell upon the annunciation of their respective heroes' births by way of focusing on their respective commissions for deliverance. Immediately, Samson asks "wherefore was my birth from Heav'n foretold / Twice by an Angel" (lines 23–24); and upon seeing the forsaken Samson, Manoa asks "For this did the Angel twice descend" (line 361). Samson remembers again that his "birth from Heav'n [was] foretold" by a "Heav'nly message twice descending" (line 635); and when Samson has gone forth to the temple the Chorus recollects "the Angel of thy Birth," who brought "his message . . . / Of thy conception" (lines 1431, 1433–34). The birth narrative in the Book of Judges, no less than these recollections of it in Milton's poem, prepare us, as Charles Burney has noticed, "for a Gideon or a Samuel, keenly alive to the fact that he holds a divine commission, and upheld in his performance of it by consciousness of the divine support. Samson, however, proves to have no commission at all, and recognizes no higher guide than his own wayward passions."[37] Through the Chorus's remembrance of the great theophany of Samson's birth at the crucial moment that he goes forth to the temple, Milton juxtaposes the beginning and end of Samson's story, his life and death, his one-time divine commission and his own impetuous act of hurling down the pillars of his "own accord" (line 1643). A life that began in marvel is thus shown by Milton to have ended in tragedy.

In contrast with Samson who affects public life to perform a private act, Jesus, while "Affecting private life" (III, 22), fixes his attention upon the "public good" (III, 204),

> Musing and much revolving in his brest,
> How best the mighty work he might begin
> Of Saviour to mankind.   (I, 185–87)

The prophetic narrator announces that "the time is come" and pleads with the God of Israel to arise and vindicate his glory: "free thy people from thir yoke" (II, 43, 48; compare II, 35–36). Neither Jesus nor Satan ever forgets the commission of deliverance; they simply disagree on when the time for deliverance will be, on the conditions under which it can be pursued, and on the methods by which it can be won. It remains an irony that Satan's own insistence that Jesus proceed without delay, despite the fact that the people are not ready and with physical force as the means, anticipates the attitudes of Samson that Jesus himself feels obliged to resist. The only way of finally crediting Samson as a deliverer is to adopt the casuistry of T. S. K. Scott-Craig and then argue for "the equivalence of ransom and redemption," for ransoming as a symbolic form of deliverance.[38]

Early on in *Samson Agonistes,* Milton's protagonist remembers, apparently after having for some time forgotten, his commission to liberate his people from their oppressors (lines 38–40, 225–26, 368–72); yet the very idea of Samson as a deliverer gets swallowed up in a double irony: that in subduing Samson, Dalila has delivered the Philistines from this deliverer (lines 982–86) and that in presenting Samson to his enemies, the Israelites have delivered themselves of their own deliverer. The issue throughout most of the play becomes, again ironically, "To prosecute the means of [Samson's] deliverance" (line 603; compare lines 1453–54) with Manoa first, then Dalila, functioning as the principals in a plan necessitating that Samson surrender his role as deliverer, even self-deliverer, and eventuating in Death's becoming Samson's deliverer (lines 1571–73). Only after his death is Samson proclaimed a deliverer (lines 1661–63, 1714–15) by those for whom deliverance is a delusion, as their subsequent history shows. *Samson Agonistes* begins with "The breath of Heav'n fresh-blowing, pure and sweet, / With day-spring born" (lines 10–11), which by the end of the poem "proves / Abortive as the first-born bloom of spring / Nipt with the lagging rear of winters frost" (lines 1575–77). Wounded in the immortal part in the conclusion of *Samson Agonistes,* Samson's life is here rendered as a tragedy and Samson himself as one of those who, while they may think like a revolutionary, feel as a Philistine.

GENERIC REGRESSION

Samson Agonistes breathes ironies, but none of them so confounding as the irony emerging from the fact that Milton presents his "Tragedy," along with his encomium of tragedy as "the gravest, moralist, and most profitable of all other Poems," against the backdrop of *Paradise Regained*. In this same preface Milton singles out Aeschylus, Sophocles, and Euripides as "the three Tragic Poets unequall'd yet by any," having just gone out of his way to have the Satan of *Paradise Regained* praise the Greek drama of which Jesus himself is so dismissive. "*Lyric* Odes," along with poems "higher sung" by Homer (IV, 257–58), precede Satan's offer of

> . . . what the lofty Tragoedeans taught
> In *Chorus* or *Iambic,* teachers best of moral prudence, with delight received
> In brief sententious precepts, while they treat
> Of fate, and chance, and change in human life;
> High actions, and high passions best describing. (IV, 261–66)

Not only is there an inversion of what are usually the second and third items in a generic triad with Satan seeming to value tragedy over epic—that is, the order of experience which, through his fall, he introduces to the Christian cosmos; hence the literary genre of which he is the originator and still the chief sponsor—but there is a continuing fixation with the very topics that consume the literary interests of the devils and are the object of Milton's parody in *Paradise Lost* (II, 546–61). Jesus, on the other hand, subordinates the classical ode to the Christian hymn, epic poetry and classical oratory to Christian prophecy, thereby privileging what is "God inspir'd" over what Satan inspires, even as he praises the efficacy of Satanic tragedy "where moral vertue is express't / By light of Nature" and hence all is not quite lost (IV, 350–52). There is, then, no small irony in the generic representations and arrangement of the 1671 poetic volume: an epic-prophecy singing the virtues of the Christian deity sits alongside a tragedy exposing the vices of such deities as are personated by the Philistines no less than by Samson; a poem that is God-inspired huddles with a poem, the source of whose revelation is the "light of Nature"; a prophecy anticipatory of apocalypse is teamed with a tragedy functioning as a warning prophecy.

The generic movement in this poetic volume is from epic and prophecy to tragedy, from composite genres to tragedy now purged of its comic mixture. The movement from *Paradise Regained* to *Samson Agonistes*—from a New to an Old Testament subject, from a Christian prophecy to a classical tragedy—constitutes a regressive maneuver, and implicit in it is the suggestion that any man, any age, is capable of either comedy or tragedy. These are not different forms but competing ideas in, variant aspects of history, which seems forever, and especially in Milton's own time, to be veering away from its potentiality and falling over again into the old reality. Like scriptural history, real history should exhibit the superseding of law, justice, and bond by grace, mercy, and forgiveness—an expected progression that Milton presents as a reversal, the lechery and violence of *Samson Agonistes* supervening love and peace and thus blocking the emergence of the new world anticipated by *Paradise Regained*. The temptations of Samson and Jesus, especially on the pinnacle and at the pillars, are encounters with a future shut down by Samson but opened by Jesus. As such, *Samson* represents the dominant ideology of Milton's age, one that served as an obstacle to a Revolution's success and that *Paradise Regained* would invalidate.

Only for those (and Milton is not among them) who read the Judges narrative as if it were an Old Testament Book of Revelation verging on a divine comedy, and then read *Samson Agonistes* in like fashion, will it seem that Milton's poem is "unlike other tragedies" because "it is tragedy beyond tragedy" as surely as is *The Tempest*.[39] As it happens, Milton's poem *is* unlike other tragedies because its tragic vision is more inclusive than that of most such poems: *Samson* is a human tragedy recounting the tragedy of civilization and of its supposedly civilizing religions. In the fullest sense, *Samson Agonistes* is a *Christian* tragedy. In one way, G. Wilson Knight is right to credit Milton with surpassing his dramatic rivals "since his religious assumptions enable him to create a semi-superman of appalling realism," although even this observation is askew insofar as Milton himself would perceive that Samson as the creation of others' (and of what ought to be outmoded) religious assumptions. Still further askew is Knight's extension of this observation: "That said, we must admit that many subtleties are bypassed; there is naturally no facing of Christian love, nor any involvement in the more complex problems of statesmanship; and the final emphasis is on wrath and destruction." In this, Knight concludes, Milton is unlike Racine who perceives a deeper connection, a fairer balance, between religion and statecraft, an achievement won by Racine through the placement of *Athalie* within the perspective of New Testament prophecy.[40] There is no love in *Samson,* just odious hypocrisy on both sides, and "despotic power" (line 1054). There *is* love in the 1671 poetic volume, however. In *Samson,* the final emphasis is on destruction, *human* destruction; but the poem is also set within a perspective that takes account of the complex interplay between religion and politics and that assimilates such concerns to New Testament prophecy, especially the drama of the Apocalypse. While the prophetic promise of a new paradise may be dashed in the tragedy of history, there is still an interrogation of that tragedy, an emergent understanding of failed history, out of which is born an improved, an enlarged consciousness that eventuates in the restoration of hopes for regaining paradise if not beyond history, then on earth, precisely on earth, and if not now, then in future history. The driving energies toward apocalypse, which are released in *Paradise Regained,* may be frustrated and forestalled by the retreat of *Samson,* and of Milton's own age, into the world of tragedy. Yet *Samson Agonistes* remains a drama of regeneration, but only in the special sense that it would effect regeneration through the representation of degeneration.

MYTHS OF DELIVERANCE

Milton must have understood, as Northrop Frye has now alerted us, that the historical books of the Bible are no more history than the Gospels are biography; history just does not possess the neat patterns that a book like Judges would impose upon it. Not history *per se,* Judges is more exactly an envisioning of history or a fictive history, investing repetition with significance and structure with meaning. In this kind of history, man is presented "as under a trial and subject to judgement": a program of action is offered that, "while it cannot afford to ignore history, may often set itself in opposition to history. This," says Frye, "is most obvious with myths of deliverance"[41]—separate, discrete, contending myths of deliverance—that Milton poses against one another in his poetic volume of 1671. There is drama within each poem and a drama of perspectives generated by their juxtaposition. The one poem speaks of peace, the other urges defiance and wreaks devastation. Within these contending perspectives, moreover, alternative courses of action are set forth, one that binds men down to the cycles of history, another that would liberate them from those cycles; one that conceives of history as a divine comedy, another that perceives in history a rehearsal for all the events of human tragedy.

Paradise Regained and *Samson Agonistes* are both reflections on history, projecting different scenarios for it and representing, through their separate protagonists, different phases of it. According to the tripartite conception of history, popularized by commentators on the Book of Revelation, history under the rule of nature is displaced by history under the rule of the law and, eventually, of grace. Commonly, the birth of Samson was used to mark the beginning of the second phase, while Christ's nativity inaugurated the final phase of history.[42] Samson and Jesus are juxtaposed in history, then, just as in parallel fashion they will be juxtaposed in the 1671 poetic volume.

It has been said that "Nothing could be less like the Book of Revelation than *Samson Agonistes,* and yet *Samson Agonistes . . .* has for its subject a prototype of the underside, so to speak, of the Book of Revelation."[43] In their respective structures, however, both *Paradise Regained* and *Samson* mirror the Book of Revelation and derive important aesthetic features from it.[44] But of more importance perhaps is the analogy that might be drawn between the historical setting of Milton's poems and of the Book of Revelation, which, as Barclay Newman reminds us, "must be sought in the conflict of ideologies":[45] pristine Christianity being locked in combat with later perversions of the faith. Once hidden from, God is now revealed in history through the similitude of the Son but also through distorted, antithetical images that are revelations of what he is sometimes thought to be, but is not. And there is one singularly important artistic strategy that Milton's poems share with the Apocalypse: contending visionary panels are set alongside one another in such a way that the first item in a series, once deciphered, provides a perspective from which the next item can be interpreted. There is progression within the apparent redaction; for in the Book of Revelation the reformation of the Church is a prologue to the renovation of history. With Milton, who believed that every man is a sect of one, the inaugural event is the regeneration of the individual who, in turn, becomes a renovator of history.

Milton identifies St. John's high and stately tragedy as his prototype in the Preface to *Samson Agonistes,* does so in the understanding that here is the tragedy of Antichrist and of all those who resemble him in history;[46] yet if here we have the underside of the Apocalypse, sitting alongside and as a headpiece to it is the apocalyptic promise of a paradise to be regained both in future history and at the end of time. The presence of *Paradise Re-*

gained in the volume and the corrective, interpretive functions it assumes in relation to *Samson Agonistes* remind us, as Jacques Ellul might say, that "the last word is not left to destruction and death. The *truth* is not that of nothingness; it is life, it is the world related to God, it is the transcendence of death."[47] The truth begins in an apocalypse of mind that becomes the prologue to an apocalypse in history. *Samson* records the tragedy of hope: "Nor am I in the list of them that hope," says Samson; "Hopeless are all my evils, all remediless" (lines 647–48). The aftermath of his tragedy is the loss of hope by and for the Israelites, for as he had done with Samson, God now departs from them. In this, *Samson Agonistes* opposes itself to the apocalyptic myth with which *Paradise Regained* is aligned, a myth that survives only because within history there remains hope and liberty for mankind. The time of temptation is time in the wilderness both for Jesus and Samson; it is their time of testing. Ellul states the case exactly: "The issue here is knowing if man is going to follow Jesus, is going to enter the plan of God, is going to accept this unity with God."[48] Or alternatively, in the instance of *Samson Agonistes,* the issue is whether man will once again follow in the way of Samson, act of his own accord, isolate himself from God, and thereby subvert God's plan for history.

Samson Agonistes, along with the poem with which it is published, mirrors both the violent revolutionary content of the apocalyptic myth and the cooling off of such religious and political activism into apolitical quietism. Yet instead of veering from one pole to another in this particular dialectic, Milton steers a middle course and, by posing alternatives, offers a way out of an either-or situation. If it is not, finally, an invitation to militancy, *Samson* emits political signals nonetheless. Neither this poem nor *Paradise Regained* is simply a repudiation of millenarianism; rather both poems, from very different perspectives, revive apocalyptic yearnings by revising apocalyptic expectations, revealing what mankind can and cannot do as they seek to establish the millennial kingdom in history. James Harrington's *Aphorisms Political* may very well have been formulated as both an expression of and expansion upon Milton's own attempt, once the Revolution had failed, to break loose from those millenarians who still vested their faith in some divinely inspired reign of the saints.[49] Realizing that God may ordain the building of a New Jerusalem, as previously he had ordained the building of the temple, both Milton and Harrington are also quick to acknowledge that the temple was built (and now the New Jerusalem will be built) by masons. The creation of the people when they have become a nation of prophets, the New Jerusalem, then, will be built not only by God but by man.

It has been understood since the nineteenth century that "Milton passed through a revolution, which, in its last stages and issue, was peculiarly fitted to damp enthusiasm, to scatter visions of hope, and to infuse doubts of the reality of virtuous principle"; and usually it has been conjectured that *Paradise Regained* and *Samson Agonistes* are Milton's songs of sorrow, effusions of resentment, instead of, what seems more likely, a chief evidence that "the ardour, and moral feeling, and enthusiasm of his youth came forth unhurt, and even exalted from the trial."[50] Milton's last poems are like the Book of Revelation in the profoundest sense. It was written during a dark hour of history, it broke upon history with its glimmer of hope, it imaged the very darkness that it would disperse. The Book of Revelation represents the despair it would steel mankind against, urging that people keep faith in time of trouble. Like Milton's last poems, it is an enabling book: bringing light out of darkness, joy out of sorrow, its affirmations restore hope to the defeated, raise expectations that have been dashed, and repair a broken world by pointing not beyond history but to a history radically transformed. The battered present is redeemed in the process, for it is the present that makes the future possible.

It is one thing to argue, as Mary Ann Radzinowicz does, that Milton "discerned a pattern in history and contemporary affairs of which the life of Samson was paradigmatic" and quite another matter to argue, again with Radzinowicz, that "Milton saw Samson as the historical example of how men should conspire with God to bring about the New Jerusalem." What is compelling about Radzinowicz's argument is that its premises are acute and nearly always right: (1) that in *Samson Agonistes* Milton prophesies "a potential movement through the educative power of tragedy"; (2) that Milton read Scripture as we should read his poem, "attentive to progressive relevancies" and "unfolding revelation"; and (3) that *Paradise Regained* and *Samson Agonistes* should be read together and interpreted by repeated reference to one another by virtue of the repeated, although muted, references that these poems make to each other.[51] On the other hand, what is curious here is that Radzinowicz puts forth a conclusion, that Samson is a positive example, that is at odds with those premises and ultimately eroded by them. As interpretive fictions, Milton's last poems are how-to-live and how-not-to-live poems.[52] They demystify their biblical stories, interrogate the ideologies that had accrued to them, and reverse what had become their accepted message in Milton's age. *Paradise Regained* is no permanent withdrawal from the active life, only a retreat into contemplation as a prologue to action; *Samson Agonistes* is no sabre-rattling poem but rather an inquiry into why sabre-rattling should cease. The greatness of both poems resides not in the fact that they transcend their age but in the fact they bear its imprint so deeply.

It is of some interest to, and perhaps even a piece of corroborating evidence for, the foregoing argument that, while *Paradise Lost* is an informing context for the major long poems of the Romantic period, *Paradise Regained* and *Samson Agonistes* enjoy the status of subtexts sometimes within the same work, as in Wordsworth's *The Prelude* and Mary Shelley's *Frankenstein,* but more often in related, even interrelated, works such as Blake's *Milton* and *Jerusalem,* Byron's *The Prophecy of Dante* and *Marino Faliero,* Shelley's *Prometheus Unbound* and *The Cenci,* or even Blake's early sketches, or prose-poems, "Samson" and "Then She bore Pale desire." This is no place to stretch out such a thesis, or to follow out its implications; but this is an occasion for reflecting upon the logic of conjoining works by employing *these* Miltonic poems as subtexts. Through their own intense interrelatedness, *Paradise Regained* and *Samson Agonistes* can assert and sanction not only the interrelatedness of other works, but a special kind of interrelatedness: dialectical in nature, with contending perspectives that, instead of sitting side-by-side, are subdued the one to the other.

If the most exacting analogues to Milton's poems are provided by *Prometheus Unbound* and *The Cenci,* that is because they comprehend most completely, and thus focus most strikingly, the logic of interrelatedness in Milton's 1671 volume. The model for presentment afforded by these poems is different from the one offered by the 1645 *Poems of Mr. John Milton,* which has its own rationale and rhetoric and which, in any event, stands behind other Romantic volumes, most notably *Songs of Innocence and of Experience* and *Lyrical Ballads*. What *Paradise Regained* and *Samson Agonistes* together offer is a model for dialectical opposition figured in generic strife and figuring forth different modes and extents of consciousness: that of Samson and Beatrice Cenci on the one hand, and that of Jesus and Prometheus on the other. There are distinct modes of prophecy, both Milton and Shelley seem to be saying, distinct stances for the prophet to assume, and decidedly different modes of consciousness exhibited by him. There is Samson and Beatrice, Jesus and Prometheus; but there is also the poet, imbued with the consciousness of the former and aspiring to that of the latter. This double consciousness—its discrepant awareness and binocular vision—is the crucial feature of Milton's 1671 poetic volume and its chief contribution to a visionary poetic. These poems in conjunction bring us to the awareness that, like the poets themselves, their protagonists are sometimes prophets and sometimes fakes. The Danites, Northrop Frye has said, "see only as far as the old dispensation allows them to see."[53] Jesus, Milton, and Milton's audiences (both contemporary with the poet and now) see further—*and beyond.* That is finally where such a poetic leads: each poem has its own integrity but also looks beyond itself, while the poems collectively and simultaneously impress themselves upon human consciousness, which they stretch, and press upon human history, which they would salvage.

NOTES

This essay was completed during a research leave provided by the Graduate School of the University of Maryland. All citations of Milton's poetry are given parenthetically within the text and, unless otherwise indicated, are (for the poetry) to *The Works of John Milton,* ed. Frank Allen Patterson, 18 vols. (New York: Columbia University Press, 1931–38) and (for the prose) to *Complete Prose Works of John Milton,* ed. Don M. Wolfe et al., 8 vols. (New Haven: Yale University Press, and London: Oxford University Press, 1953–83). For Milton's last poems, I have used the standard abbreviations: *PL* (*Paradise Lost*), *PR* (*Paradise Regained*), *SA* (*Samson Agonistes*). The title of my essay derives from Hilaire Belloc's *Milton* (Philadelphia: J. B. Lippencott, 1935), p. 280.

1. Balachandra Rajan, "To Which Is Added *Samson Agonistes*," in *The Prison and the Pinnacle: Papers to Commemorate the Tercentenary of "Paradise Regained" and "Samson Agonistes",* ed. Balachandra Rajan (London: Routledge and Kegan Paul, 1973), p. 96. The epigraph for this essay derives from Shawcross's piece, "The Genres of *Paradise Regain'd* and *Samson Agonistes:* The Wisdom of Their Joint Publication," in *Composite Orders: The Genres of Milton's Last Poems,* ed. Richard S. Ide and Joseph Wittreich (Pittsburgh: University of Pittsburgh Press, 1983), p. 240.

2. See A. S. P. Woodhouse's *The Heavenly Muse: A Preface to Milton,* ed. Hugh MacCallum (Toronto and Buffalo: University of Toronto Press, 1972), p. 293, and William Riley Parker's *Milton: A Biography,* 2 vols. (Oxford: Clarendon Press, 1969), 2:909.

3. Jonathan Culler, *The Pursuit of Signs: Semiotics, Literature, Deconstruction* (1981; rpt. Ithaca, N.Y.: Cornell University Press, 1983), p. 118.

4. See Christopher Hill, *The Collected Essays of Christopher Hill: Writing and Revolution in Seventeenth-Century England* (Amherst: University of Massachusetts Press, 1985), pp. 32–71, and Annabel Patterson's *Censorship and Interpretation: The Conditions of Writing and Reading in Early Modern England* (Madison: University of Wisconsin Press, 1984), pp. 44–119.

5. William A. Oram, "Nature, Poetry, and Milton's Genii," in *Milton and the Art of Sacred Song,* ed. J. Max Patrick and Roger H. Sundell (Madison: University of Wisconsin Press, 1979), p. 48. The fullest discussions of these early poetic volumes and of the crucial place of *Lycidas* in them are provided by Louis L. Martz, *Poet of Exile: A Study of Milton's Poetry* (New Haven: Yale University Press, 1980), pp. 31–59; Raymond B.

Waddington, "Milton Among the Carolines," in *The Age of Milton,* ed. C. A. Patrides and Raymond B. Waddington (Manchester: Manchester University Press; Totowa, N.J.: Barnes and Noble, 1980), pp. 338–64; and Joseph Wittreich, *Visionary Poetics: Milton's Tradition and His Legacy* (San Marino, Calif.: Huntington Library, 1979), esp. pp. 79–117.

6. Patterson, *Censorship and Interpretation,* p. 20.

7. John F. Huntley, "The Images of the Poet and Poetry in Milton's *The Reason of Church-Government,*" in *Achievements of the Left Hand: Essays on the Prose of John Milton,* ed. Michael Lieb and John T. Shawcross (Amherst: University of Massachusetts Press, 1974), p. 113. See also the "Postscript" to the important study by Arnold Stein, *Heroic Knowledge* (1957; rpt. Hamden, Conn.: Archon Books, 1965), pp. 203–13.

8. Arthur Barker, "Calm Regained through Passion Spent: The Conclusion of the Miltonic Effort," in *The Prison and the Pinnacle,* ed. Rajan, pp. 13–14.

9. See Balachandra Rajan, "The Cunning Resemblance," *Milton Studies* 7 (1975): 30, and also *The Lofty Rhyme: A Study of Milton's Major Poetry* (Coral Gables, Fla.: University of Miami Press, 1970), p. 10.

10. "The Nightingale," in *Lyrical Ballads 1798,* 2nd ed., ed. W. J. B. Owen (London: Oxford University Press, 1969), p. 39.

11. Barker, "Calm Regained through Passion Spent," p. 47.

12. John Evans, *"Paradise Lost" and the Genesis Tradition* (Oxford: Clarendon Press, 1968), pp. 92n, 104.

13. William Cowper, *Three Heavenly Treatises, Concerning Christ* (London: Printed for John Budge, 1612), p. 129.

14. Andrew Milner, *John Milton and the English Revolution: A Study in the Sociology of Literature* (Totowa, N.J.: Barnes and Noble, 1981), p. 207.

15. *The Poetical Works of John Milton,* ed. David Masson, 3 vols. (London: Macmillan, 1882), 3:2, 4.

16. Rajan, "To Which Is Added *Samson Agonistes,*" pp. 90–91.

17. Lancelot Andrewes, *The Wonderfull Combate (for Gods Glorie and Mans Salvation) betweene Christ and Satan* (London: Printed by John Charlwood, 1592), pp. 43, 74.

18. See, e.g., David Dyke, *Michael and the Dragon, or Christ Tempted and Satan Foyled* (London: Printed by John Beale, 1635), pp. 216, 355.

19. Edward Vaughan, *A Plaine and Perfect Method for the Easie Understanding of the Whole Bible* (London: Printed by T. S., 1617), p. 3.

20. I quote from the anonymous *Annotations upon All the Books of the Old and New Testaments,* 2 vols. (London: Printed by Evan Tyler, 1657), no pagination: note to Judges 14:6. See also John Trapp, *Annotations upon the Old and New Testament,* 5 vols. (London: Printed by Robert White, 1662), 1:84.

21. See Joseph Hall, *Contemplations on the Historical Passages of the Old and New Testaments,* 3 vols. (Edinburgh: Willison and Darling, 1770), 1:331, 340, 351; see also 1:361; Joseph Salmon, *A Rout, A Rout, or Some Part of the Armies Quarters Beaten Up* (London: Printed for G. C., 1649), p. 30. See also Thomas Taylor, *Christ Revealed: or the*

Old Testament Explained (London: Printed by M. F., 1635), p. 56, and Trapp, *Annotations upon the Old and New Testament*, 1:89.

22. See, e.g., Samuel Pordage, *Mundorum Explicatio . . . a Sacred Poem* (London: Printed for Lodowick Lloyd, 1661), pp. 233–34.

23. *Eikon Basilike* (n. p.: n. p., 1648), pp. 206, 77; see also pp. 31, 72, 208, 211.

24. Terry Eagleton, *Marxism and Literary Criticism* (Berkeley and Los Angeles: University of California Press, 1976), p. 19.

25. John Hollander, *The Figure of Echo: A Mode of Allusion in Milton and After* (Berkeley and Los Angeles: University of California Press, 1981), pp. 111, 21, 24.

26. G. Wilson Knight, *The Golden Labyrinth: A Study of British Drama* (New York: W. W. Norton, 1962), p. 127.

27. Northrop Frye, *Spiritus Mundi: Essays on Literature, Myth, and Society* (1976; rpt. Bloomington: Indiana University Press, 1983), p. 202.

28. See *The Complete Poetry of John Milton*, rev. ed., ed. John T. Shawcross (Garden City, N.Y.: Doubleday, 1971), p. 618, n.30. From Luther onward, Samson was customarily identified as the serpent in the way, the viper in the path; see *Luther's Works*, ed. Jaroslav Pelikan *et al.*, 54 vols. (St. Louis: Concordia Press, 1955–76), 9:281–82.

29. *The Poetical Works of John Milton*, 5th ed, ed. Henry John Todd, 4 vols. (London: Rivingtons, 1852), 3:287.

30. Dyke, *Michael and the Dragon*, p. 219.

31. "The sense seems to be this," says Todd quoting Charles Dunster: "'Who, if they were freed from that captivity, which was inflicted on them as a punishment for their disobedience, idolatry, and other vices, would return to take possession of their country, as something to which they had long been unjustly deprived, without shewing the least sense of God's goodness in pardoning and restoring them. This change in their situation would produce none whatever in their conduct, but they would retain the same hardened hearts, and the same wicked dispositions as before, and most probably would betake themselves to their old idolatries and other abominations'," which as Jesus knows is precisely what the Israelites do in the aftermath of Samson's tragedy; see *The Poetical Works of John Milton*, ed. Henry John Todd, 7 vols. (London: Rivingtons, 1801), 4:216.

32. Matthew Poole, *Annotations upon the Holy Bible*, 5 vols. (London: Printed by Robert Roberts, 1688), no pagination: "Argument" to Judges. See also Henry Robinson, *A Moderate Answer to Mr. Prins Full Reply* (London: Printed for Benjamin Allen, 1645), pp. 19–24.

33. Helen Damico, "Duality in Dramatic Vision: A Structural Analysis of *Samson Agonistes*," *Milton Studies* 12 (1979): 105.

34. I quote from Hugh Farmer, *An Inquiry into the Nature and Design of Christ's Temptation in the Wilderness* (London: Printed for A. Millar, 1761), p. 42; see also pp. vi, 36, 40–41; and see, too, Joseph Hall, *Contemplations upon the Remarkable Passages in the Life of the Holy Jesus* (London: Printed by E. Flesher, 1679), p. 64.

35. Andrewes, *The Wonderfull Combate*, p. 98.

36. In *The Sealed Book Opened* (London: Printed for Anthony Williamson, 1656), William Guild identifies Samson with the third angel of the Apocalypse, the star called wormwood, who, falling away from the divine vision, Samson-like, burns up the teachings of God (p. 65). On the other hand, in *Gods Love-Tokens, or the Afflicted Mans Lessons* (London: Printed by Richard Badger, 1637), John Trapp identifies Samson with the Beast's party and hence with those rebuked in Revelation 3:19 (p. 114).

37. Charles Burney, *The Book of Judges with Introduction and Notes* (London: Rivingtons, 1918), p. 337.

38. T. S. K. Scott-Craig, "Concerning Milton's Samson," *Renaissance News* 5 (1952): 47; see also p. 48.

39. Knight, *The Golden Labyrinth*, p. 128.

40. Ibid., pp. 128–29.

41. Northrop Frye, *The Great Code: The Bible and Literature* (New York: W. W. Norton, 1982), p. 49. See also Frye's *The Myth of Deliverance: Reflections on Shakespeare's Problem Comedies* (Toronto and Buffalo: University of Toronto Press, 1983).

42. Wayne Dynes elaborated this point in his fine lecture delivered as part of the Ohio State University Conference on Medieval and Renaissance Apocalyptics (Columbus, Ohio; March, 1980).

43. Frye, *Spiritus Mundi*, p. 215.

44. See Frye, ibid., and Wittreich, *Visionary Poetics*, esp. pp. 191–212.

45. Barclay Newman, *Rediscovery of the Book of Revelation* (Valley Forge, Pa.: Judson Press, 1968), p. 110.

46. See Barbara K. Lewalski, "*Samson Agonistes* and the Tragedy of the Apocalypse," *PMLA* 85 (1970): 1050–62.

47. Jacques Ellul, *Apocalypse: The Book of Revelation*, trans. George W. Schreiner (New York: Seabury Press, 1977), p. 50.

48. Ibid., p. 90.

49. For this suggestion and an elaboration, see *Complete Prose Works*, ed. Wolfe et al., 8:518–19.

50. W. E. Channing, *Remarks on the Character and Writings of John Milton*, 2nd ed. (London: Printed for Edward Rainford, 1828), p. 27.

51. Mary Ann Radzinowicz, *Toward "Samson Agonistes": The Growth of Milton's Mind* (Princeton: Princeton University Press, 1978), pp. 88, 91, 167, 245.

52. See Irene Samuel's elaboration of this idea, at least with reference to *Paradise Regained*, in "The Regaining of Paradise," in *The Prison and the Pinnacle*, ed. Rajan, p. 126.

53. Frye, *Spiritus Mundi*, p. 226.

Vincent Carretta
"Images Reflect from Art to Art"
Alexander Pope's Collected *Works* of 1717

"my works will in one respect be like the works of Nature, much more to be liked and understood when consider'd in the relation they bear with each other, than when ignorantly look'd upon one by one"
—Pope to Swift, 16 February 1732/3

In the poetic career of Alexander Pope, 1717 may justly be called an *annus mirabilis*. Within a few weeks of his twenty-ninth birthday on 21 May, Pope established himself as a poet, a translator, and an editor. On 3 June he published simultaneously, through Bernard Lintot, *The Works of Mr. Alexander Pope* and volume three of his translation of Homer's *Iliad* (books 9–12). Six weeks later, on 13 July and again through Bernard Lintot, Pope published anonymously *Poems on Several Occasions,* a miscellany by various hands that included many of Pope's unacknowledged minor poems and juvenilia, which had been excluded from the earlier *Works*.[1]

To observe Pope performing his roles as poet, translator, and editor, we need look only at his *Works*. No one has yet dealt with this collection *as* a collection to see in what ways the whole may be greater than the sum of its parts or to consider how the arrangement of poems creates a sort of dialogue among the separate pieces. Nor has anyone attempted to identify the possible principles by which Pope organized his *Works*. And, finally, no one has treated the organizing role the illustrations play in the quarto *Works* (only the finepaper folios are illustrated).[2] Unfortunately, hard evidence is scanty of how actively Pope controlled the arranging and illustrating of his *Works,* but several comments in his correspondence suggest that Pope took at least as much interest in the preparation of his most significant publication to date as we would expect of a man who, as Samuel Johnson said, "hardly drank tea without a stratagem."[3]

The strongest evidence we have of Pope's involvement in the production of his *Works* appears in a letter to William Broome in which he asks Broome to pass on to the printer specific instructions about the size of an illustration and several editorial matters. In another letter that clearly predates 3 June 1717, Pope writes to Thomas Parnell about his *Works*. Pope's characteristically false humility does not conceal his recognition of the significance of the collection's appearance:

> I shall very soon print an entire collection of my own madrigals, which I look upon as making my last will and testament since in it I shall give all I ever intend to give, (which I'll beg your's and the Dean's [Jonathan Swift's] acceptance of) you must look on me no more a poet, but a plain commoner, who lives upon his own, and fears and flatters no man. I hope before I die to discharge the debt I owe to Homer, and get upon the whole just fame enough to serve for an annuity for my own time, though I leave nothing to posterity.[4]

Pope's last surviving reference to his *Works* in his correspondence, in a 7 June 1717 letter to John Caryll, again demonstrates his involvement with the books' production as well as his pride in its appearance:

> ... the various employments Mr. Lintot engages me in of correcting the press, overlooking verses, and managing with my subscribers, have robbed me of all pretence to quiet and philosophy. At length my *Works* are out, of which I will not say a word to you (tho' an author may reasonably be allowed to be at least as full of his *Works,* when they come out in a new Edition as a lady of a new suit of clothes). The Preface will tell you everything to a tittle that I think of 'em. (*Correspondence,* 1:410–11)

The preface to the *Works* has drawn some recent, perceptive attention from Maynard Mack and Dustin Griffin. Mack calls the 1717 Preface "an exercise in image-making" while Griffin sees it as "assertive-defensive" and finds in it a "blend of confidence and polished ease on the one hand and of diffidence, humility, and even mild anxiety on the other—a mixture so characteristic of Pope's early verse. . . ."[5] Although Griffin usefully discusses several of the poems in the *Works*—the *Pastorals, Windsor Forest, An Essay on Criticism, The Temple of Fame,* and *The Rape of the Lock*—in relation to the theme of *Fame,* he does not discuss the order in which they appear in the *Works.* Rather, he chooses to deal with them as discrete poems, not as parts of a whole. Mack and Griffin emphasize that in the Preface Pope "is taking the high road of sober reflection" and that "Sensitive as he was to criticism, nowhere in this Preface (the longest he wrote to any volume of his original works) does he respond to a specific critic or charge."[6] Mack points out that specific references to critics, such as one to

John Dennis, in the manuscript do not find their way into print. As we shall see, however, Pope manages to respond indirectly to many of his critics' particular charges in the title, format, organization, and illustrations of his *Works* of 1717.

Among those charges were accusations by John Dennis in *Reflections Critical and Satyrical, Upon A Late Rhapsody, Call'd, An Essay Upon Criticism* (1711) and by Charles Gildon in *A New Rehearsal, Or Bays the Younger* (1714) that Pope was presumptuous and self-promoting. How offended they must have been by Pope's choice of the title *Works* for his collected poems! *Works*, in early eighteenth-century publishing, normally designated either collected poems of Classical authors, or collected poems by late Modern authors whose place in literary history was considered established, or collected poems by living authors near the end of their careers and whose literary reputations were thought to be assured. Pope's reference to his *Works* as his "last will and testament" in the letter to Parnell quoted above indicates that the twenty-nine-year-old poet believed he had already established a canon worthy of being labeled *Works*. Pope's contemporaries, and especially his critics, had to have seen him as placing himself in very illustrious company. Briefly consider recently or soon-to-be published *Works* against which Pope implicitly asked his own to be measured: among the editions of Classical authors were John Dryden's *Workes of Virgil* (1697); George Sewell, et al., *The Works of Anacreon and Sappho* (1713); Richard Maitland's *The Works of Virgil* (1718); and George Dart's *The Works of Tibullus* (1720). Recently or soon-to-be published *Works* by late Moderns included those of Dryden (1701), Boileau (1711–13), Shakespeare (1714), Spenser (1715), Chaucer (1721), and Pope's own edition of Buckingham's *Works* (1723). Among the very few *Works* by living authors were those of Dryden (1695) and of Wycherley (1713).

A less confident poet would have chosen the more appropriate title *Poems on Several Occasions* for the first collection of his own poems. *Poems on Several Occasions* was the usual title for a collection by a living author whose reputation was not yet established—Elijah Fenton (1717), John Gay (1720), Walter Harte (1727); or for a collection by an author whose reputation was not dependent primarily upon his verse—Nicholas Rowe (1714); or for a posthumous edition of a minor poet—John Philips (1720), Pope's own edition of Thomas Parnell (1722). The title frequently indicated that the collection included juvenilia, as in the editions of Thomas Fletcher (1692) and Sarah Fyge Egerton (1706).

Poems on Several Occasions commonly denotes a miscellany by a single author who demonstrates his talents on a variety of subjects through a range of genres. It is purposely eclectic. Although the volume Pope published in July might more accurately have been called a *Miscellany* than a *Poems on Several Occasions* because it contains poems by more than one author, in it Pope demonstrates his recognition of the demands of the form. The volume is constructed around a core of his own minor verse, poems denied canonical status by exclusion from the *Works* and by anonymous publication. I can detect no significant organizing principle of the volume or of Pope's own poems within it.[7]

As significant as the choice of title for Pope's first collected edition was the format in which the *Works* appeared. Pope's decision to publish both his translation of Homer and his own *Works* in quarto as well as folio was unusual because, as David Foxon notes, "the traditional format in England for an author's collected works, from Chaucer, through Ben Jonson, Drayton, and Shakespeare, had been folio. . . ."[8] Foxon suggests that Pope may have sought to associate his own *Works* with the elegant quarto format found in French editions of La Fontaine (1668) and Boileau (1674), as well as in the editions of Classical authors *in usum Delphini*.

Another way in which Pope associated his own *Works* with the great tradition of Western literature and with the highest contemporary literary authorities was through the use of illustrations in the quarto and finepaper folio (most of the folios lack illustrations). Many of the engraved initial letters in the *Works* had earlier appeared in the first two volumes of the *Iliad* (1715, 1716), the third volume of which, we must remember, was published simultaneously with the *Works*. Other engraved initials had earlier appeared in Joseph Trapp's *Praelectiones Poeticae* (1711, 1715, 1719), also published by Bernard Lintot. Trapp was the first holder of the post of professor of poetry at Oxford from 1708 to 1718.

The evidence for saying that Pope had control over the illustrations in his *Works* is circumstantial rather than conclusive. But that evidence makes it highly probable that Pope used the engraved initials and headpieces to help organize the volume. All the illustrations were engraved by Simon Gribelin, who had been Lintot's engraver since the initial publication of Trapp's *Praelectiones* (1711).[9] Certainly the choice of Gribelin and the decision to take engraved initials from the editions of Trapp and Homer must have been dictated at least in part by economic considerations, but we shall see that many of the initials are not taken from the earlier works. Of those that had earlier appeared, the consistent appropriateness of their repetition in Pope's *Works* indicates that their use is deliberate and not merely convenient. The headpieces are all original designs of the *Works*.

We have documentary evidence that Pope was responsible for the choice of illustrations in his translation of the *Iliad*. His publication agreement with Lintot, dated 23 March 1713 (O.S.), stipulates that the subscribers' copies of the *Iliad* translation "shall have Head Pieces and Tail Pieces and initial letters at the beginning and end of each Book and of the Notes engraven on Copper in such manner and by such Graver as the said Alexander Pope shall direct and appoint."[10] Foxon emphasizes that Pope's interest in illustration was strong at the time this contract was signed because he had been studying painting with Charles Jervas for the past year. Foxon gives Pope credit for "another revolutionary departure for the English book," the substitution of "a long narrow headpiece in place of the traditional upright plate."[11] Given Pope's control over the *Iliad* engraving, his interest in painting, and his likely role in the transformation of English book illustration, the probability is extremely high that he would take at least as great an interest in the illustrations of his own poems in 1717 as he had taken earlier in those of another poet. The most explicit piece of evidence we have of Pope's involvement with the illustrations to his 1717 *Works* is in the letter to Broome mentioned above:

> I desire, for fear of mistakes, that you will cause space for the initial letter to the Dedication to the Rape of the Lock to be made of the size of those in Trapp's Praelectiones. Only a small ornament at the top of that leaf, not as large as four lines breadth. The rest as I told you before. (*Correspondence*, 1 : 394)

When we consider the *Works* as an organized collection, we must discuss the role the engravings play.

Studying Pope's illustrations is one way to understand the significance to Pope of his own *Works*. The headpiece to the preface of the *Iliad* depicts the traditional Ovidian figure of *Tempus edax Rerum*, "time devourer of all things." At the center of the print is winged Time destroying architectural columns with his scythe. Time is moving to the viewer's left in the engraving; behind him, on the viewer's right, the landscape is strewn with ruins. The image might have been used to illustrate some of Pope's own early verses, such as "To Mr. Addison, Occasioned by his Dialogues on Medals" (published 1720 but drafted perhaps as early as 1713): "See the wild Waste of all-devouring years! / How Rome her own sad Sepulchre appears" (lines 1–2).[12] In the headpiece, only the arts, verbal and visual, withstand the ravages of Time. The visual arts are represented by a statue of a poet, presumably Homer, and the unbroken medals ("The Medal, faithful to its charge of fame, / Thro' climes and ages bears each form and name." "To Mr. Addison," [TE, 202.31–32]). The verbal arts are represented by the papers the poet holds. The statue is protected from Time by Fame with her trumpet. What we see is an emblem of the Horatian notion that Man can create "monuments more durable than brass, and more conspicuous than pyramids."[13]

Pope, in his preface to the 1717 *Works*, clearly hopes that his *Works* is another example of the Horatian monument: "In this office of collecting my pieces, I am altogether uncertain, whether to look upon my self as a man building a monument, or burying the dead." We need only recall Milton's reference to Shakespeare's "livelong Monument" in *An Epitaph on the Admirable Dramatic Poet W. Shakespeare* (1632) to recognize how conventional Pope's metaphor is. That this image is a convention, however, does not diminish the strength of Pope's belief. Pope's edition of Buckingham's *Works* (1723) makes the image of a monument even more explicit: its frontispiece is an engraving by John Cole of the Duke's funerary monument in Westminster Abbey. Dominating the sculpture is Father Time holding medals of the Duke's deceased children, but the dedication opposite the frontispiece reminds us of his more permanent creations: "These [his Works] His More Lasting Remains (the Monument of His mind, and more Perfect Image of Himself)."[14]

Pope's frontispiece and title page illustration to his own *Works* somewhat more subtly make his claim to glory. The frontispiece to Pope's literary monument had been engraved by George Vertue in 1715 after a painting by Charles Jervas. The frontispiece of Homer in the first volume of the *Iliad* translation (1715) had also been engraved by Vertue from a design by Jervas. Pope's over-sized, fold-out frontispiece calls attention to itself, as does what may have been its model—the over-sized, fold-out frontispiece of Dryden, engraved by Nicholas Edelinck after a painting by Sir Godfrey Kneller, that had appeared in the 1701 edition of Dryden's *Works*. The likely visual associations of Pope with Homer and Dryden enhance his literary prestige and serve as the first of many examples of Pope's "image-making" in the *Works*.

The frontispiece also represents Pope as a handsome young man, "the modish modern author" he refers to in a letter of 16 August 1714 to Jervas (*Correspondence* 1:243). Such a representation is especially important for two reasons: first, because Love, along with Fame, is a major subject of the *Works* and Pope's attractive appearance makes him a credible expert on the subject; and second, because Pope had repeatedly been ridiculed about his body.[15] In 1711 Dennis had described Pope as being "a young, squab, short Gentleman," whose person delighted Dennis: "So delighted, that I have

Frontispiece to *The Works of Dr. Alexander Pope,* 1717
(courtesy of the William Andrews Clark Memorial Library,
University of California, Los Angeles)

lately drawn a very graphical Picture of it; but I believe I shall keep the *Dutch* Piece from ever seeing the Light, as a certain old Gentleman in *Windsor-Forest* [Pope's father] would have done by the Original, if he durst have been half as impartial to his own Draught as I have been to mine."[16] This passage, with its threat of visual abuse, is noted in Pope's own copy of *Reflections Critical and Satyrical.* Another attack occurs in *Guardian* 92 (26 June 1713): "Nay, to that Perfection is he arrived, that he *stoops* as he walks. The Figure of the Man is odd enough; he is a lively little Creature, with long Arms and Legs: A Spider is no ill Emblem of him. He has been taken at a Distance for a *small Windmill.*" Inevitably, Pope became the target of a satiric engraving that depicted his warped body. Vertue's 1715 engraving, the first publicly available portrait of Pope, apparently served as the basis for what I believe is the earliest engraved attack on Pope, the title page engraving of John Durant Breval's *The Confederates,* advertised 30 March 1717 in the *Evening Post.* The handsome, upright man of Vertue's print becomes a hunch-back whose dwarfish stature is accentuated by the figures of John Arbuthnot on his right and John Gay on his left. The frontispiece to the *Works* should be seen as Pope's attempt to associate himself with the glorious heroes of literature, Homer and Dryden, and as his attempt to retake control of his "image" as both poet and man.

Pope's "image-making" in response to his critics continues on the title page, in its epigraph and engraving. At first, the epigraph taken from Cicero's "Speech on Behalf of Archias the Poet" seems appropriate simply because it was one of the most frequently quoted Classical justifications of literature:

> but this [reading] gives strength to our youth and diversion to our old age; this adds a charm to success, and offers a haven of consolation to failure. In the home it delights, in the world it hampers not. Through the night-watches, on all our journeying, and in our hours of country ease, it is our unfailing companion. (Loeb Classical Library translation)

But Pope, whose patriotism had repeatedly been questioned because of his Roman Catholicism and his Tory friends, surely recognized the additional aptness of the context of his epigraph to his own situation—Cicero was defending Archias against a challenge to his Roman citizenship by proclaiming the value of poetry and its ability to grant Fame and thus defeat Time. Like Archias, Pope found his own Fame to be a mixed blessing because his prominence made him an obvious target for literary and political enemies.

THE
CONFEDERATES:
A
FARCE.

By Mr. GAY.

Rumpantur ut ilia CODRO.

Thefe are the Wags, who boldly did adventure
To club a Farce by *Tripartite Indenture* !
But, let 'em fhare their Dividend of Praife,
And wear their own *Fool's Cap*, inftead of *Bays*.
                                    Prol. *to the* Sultanefs.

LONDON: Printed for R. BURLEIGH, in *Amen-Corner.* 1717. [*Price* 1 s.]

Title page of *The Confederates: A Farce,* 1717
(courtesy of the William Andrews Clark Memorial Library,
University of California, Los Angeles)

THE
WORKS
OF
Mr. *ALEXANDER POPE.*

CICERO pro ARCH.

Hæc studia adolescentiam alunt, senectutem oblectant; secundas res ornant, adversis perfugium & solatium præbent; delectant domi, non impediunt foris; pernoctant nobiscum, peregrinantur, rusticantur.

LONDON:
Printed by W. BOWYER, for BERNARD LINTOT between the *Temple-Gates.* 1717.

Title page of *The Works of Dr. Alexander Pope,* 1717 (courtesy of the William Andrews Clark Memorial Library, University of California, Los Angeles)

The two-sided nature of Fame is expressed in the title page engraving. Fame was frequently personified with two trumpets, one of good and one of bad report. The lyre of course is an emblem of poetry, and the laurel represents the glory it can bring. The engraving is the first explicit visual representation of what Samuel Johnson calls "Pope's voracity of fame," a subject that comes up repeatedly in the words and illustrations of the Works.[17] This title page engraving had earlier appeared in Trapp's *Praelectiones*, later as the tailpiece to the Preface to the *Iliad*, and then reappears in some of the quarto Works as the tailpiece to the *The Rape of the Lock*.[18]

The theme of Fame is repeated in all the commendatory poems by John Sheffield, Duke of Buckingham, Anne, Countess of Winchelsea, William Wycherley, Fr. Knapp, Elijah Fenton, Thomas Parnell, and Simon Harcourt. Parnell's lines are representative: "Ev'n here I sing, when *Pope* supplies the theme. / Shew my own love, tho' not increase his fame." The inclusion of verses by Wycherley in praise of Pope's *Pastorals* acts as a swipe against critics like Dennis and Gildon who had accused Pope of writing praise of himself under Wycherley's name. The publication of the *Works* itself demonstrates that earlier predictions of Pope's success have proven true.

The table of contents indicates the organization of the *Works* proper. It is divided into three sections: an untitled section of previously published original poems; "Translations"; and "Miscellanies," which includes previously published and unpublished original poems. In the first section we find the *Pastorals* (first published in 1709), including *Messiah* (1712); *Windsor-Forest* (1713); *An Essay on Criticism* (1711); *The Rape of the Lock* (1712–1714); and *The Temple of Fame* (1715). Why are these poems not arranged chronologically, in order of their previous publication dates? Their ordering reflects more closely the dates of composition Pope attributed to each poem. But if date of composition is the principle of organization, why is the *Messiah* linked with the *Pastorals,* and why does the first part of *Windsor-Forest* have precedence in dating over the second part but the same rule not apply to *The Rape of the Lock?* Why end with *The Temple of Fame?*

The juxtaposition of poems in the *Works* reveals relationships among them difficult to perceive when they are considered as discrete items rather than as parts of a whole. One thing we may note is that the poems in the first section retrace the historical development of poetry from Greek pastorals to Virgil to the Hebrews to Horace and finally to the native English contribution of the dream-vision of Chaucer. On a large scale, we may say that the poems move from pastoral to prophecy, a movement mirrored on a smaller scale in several of the separate poems. The movement from pastoral to prophecy, from the *Pastorals* to *The Temple of Fame*, parallels Virgil's poetic career that began with the *Eclogues* and ended with the *Aeneid*. Section one culminates with Pope's monument in verse, *The Temple of Fame*, to celebrate the great tradition of poetry and Pope's individual achievement within it. This organizing principle of Pope's own career as a kind of *Imitatio Virgili* is anticipated by several of the commendatory poems:

> Live, and enjoy their [Pope's critics] spite!
>   nor mourn that fate
> Which wou'd, if *Virgil* liv'd, on *Virgil* wait;
> Whose Muse did once, like thine, in plains delight;
> Thine shall, like his, soon take a higher flight.   (Wycherley)

> Oh cou'd thy *Virgil* from his orb look down,
> He'd view a courser that might match his own!   (Fr. Knapp)

> In Fame's fair Temple o'er the boldest wits,
> Inshrin'd on high, the sacred *Virgil* sits,
> And sits in measures, such as *Virgil's* Muse,
> To place thee near him, might be fond to chuse.
> . . . .
> Be hush'd, ye winds! while *Pope* and *Virgil* sing.   (Parnell)

    The words and pictures of the preface, too, remind the reader of the great tradition of which Pope's individual talent is now a part. The headpiece shows Apollo, god of poetry, crowned with laurel and playing a lyre amidst the nine Muses. The central oval is flanked by visual allusions to the quarto's title page engraving. Fame is gained through poetry inspired by Phoebus Apollo, a theme anticipated by Buckingham's commendatory verse. The 1717 *Works* thus become a monument to poetry as well as to Pope. And by using the same headpiece to introduce the first and third sections of his *Works*, those which contain his original poems, Pope invites the reader virtually to identify Pope with Apollo. John Gay had already done so in "On a Miscellany of Poems" (in Lintot's *Miscellaneous Poems and Translations* [1712]), when he observed that ". . . early in the Youth the God appears." The scene in the oval of the headpieces to the "Preface" and the "Miscellanies" section may well have been inspired by Fenton's commendatory verses:

PREFACE.

Am inclined to think that both the writers of books, and the readers of them, are generally not a little unreaſonable in their expectations. The firſt ſeem to fancy that the world muſt approve whatever they produce, and the latter to imagine that authors are obliged to pleaſe them at any rate. Methinks as on the one hand, no ſingle man is born with a right of controuling the opinions of all the reſt; ſo on the other, the world has no title to demand, that the whole care and time of any particular perſon ſhould be ſacrificed to its entertainment. Therefore I cannot but believe that writers and readers are under equal obligations, for as much fame, or pleaſure, as each affords the other.

Every

Headpiece and engraved initial "I" of "Preface"
(courtesy of the William Andrews Clark Memorial Library,
University of California, Los Angeles)

> When *Phoebus,* and the nine harmonious maids,
> Of old assembled in the *Thespian* shades;
> What Theme, they cry'd, what high immortal air,
> Befit these harps to sound, and thee to hear?
> Reply'd the God . . .
> . . . .
> With less regret my claim I now decline,
> The World will think his *English Iliad* mine.

Pope's desire to be seen in the Classical literary tradition is reiterated by the engraved Pegasus-Helicon initial letter of the "Preface," which Mack rightly sees as "calculated to invest the author with authority and respectability."[19] The initial had been earlier found in Trapp's *Praelectiones* and Pope's translation of the *Iliad*. Pope offers himself as the latest imbiber of the spring of Hippocrene, inspiration of poets, struck from the rock by Pegasus. In Roman times, Pegasus became a symbol of immortality, or, in Pope's case, the Fame he expects to win by publishing his *Works*.

The engraved initial letters of "Spring," "Summer," and "Autumn," all drawn from the *Iliad,* continue Pope's attempt to gain "authority and respectability," a visual attempt reinforced by the words of "A Discourse on Pastoral Poetry," first published in the *Works*. The "Discourse" identifies the organizing principle of the theme of Time in the *Pastorals* and acknowledges Pope's poetic debts:

> Of the following Eclogues I shall only say, that these four comprehend all the subjects which the Critics upon *Theocritus* and *Virgil* will allow to be fit for pastoral; That they have as much variety of description, in respect of the several seasons, as *Spenser's:* That in order to add to this variety, the several times of the day are observ'd, the rural employments in each season or time of day, and the rural scenes or places proper to such employments; not without some regard to the several ages of man, and the different passions proper to each age.
>
> But after all, if they have any merit, it is to be attributed to some good old Authors, whose works as I had leisure to study, so I hope I have not wanted care to imitate.

This notion of faithful imitation of a noble predecessor by a humble follower is carried over into the words and headpiece of the *Pastorals*. In "Summer" Pope identifies himself as Spenser's heir:

> That flute is mine which *Colin's* tuneful breath
> Inspir'd when living, and bequeath'd in death;
> He said; *Alexis,* take this pipe, the same
> That taught the groves my *Rosalinda's* name.   (20; 39–42)

The headpiece is essentially illustrative rather than interpretive, depicting the singing contest between Strephon and Daphnis judged by Damon. The theme of Love is alluded to by imagery conventionally associated with "Celestial *Venus* [who] haunts *Idalia's* groves" (15; 65): the seashells on the top and bottom of the oval and the flowers flanking it refer both to the pelagic birth of Venus and to her power on both sea and land.

Pope's assertions of faithful imitation are repeatedly qualified by his poetic practice, especially when he adds the *Messiah. A Sacred Ecologue, In Imitation of Virgil's Pollio* to the *Pastorals.* Martin Battestin has superbly shown that the *Messiah* should be seen as the completion of Pope's intellectual design for the *Pastorals,* hence Pope's decision in 1717 to include the poem under that heading.[20] Battestin discusses the transcendence and transformation of time and the Golden Age in the Classical *Pastorals* by the Judeo-Christian prophecy of the True Shepherd, Jesus. As E. Audra and Aubrey Williams point out, Pope even alters his couplet form from the *Pastorals* to *Messiah* to express the radical difference in subject matter.[21] The transformation of Nature that plays so great a role in the prophecy of the new Christian Golden Age is expressed in the engraved initial Y of *Messiah,* which combines images from several lines of the poem to depict "God's eternal Day" (42; 104):

> Then palaces shall rise; the joyful Son
> Shall finish what his short-liv'd Sire begun;
>
> .   .   .   .
>
> To leafless shrubs the flow'ring palms succeed,
>
> .   .   .   .
>
> And boys in flow'ry bands the Tyger lead;
>   (40; 63–64, 75, 78)

The engraved initial also answers the question asked by Audra and Williams about whether the last line "has flowery bands of youths leading tigers, or perhaps . . . youths leading tigers by flowery bands" (p. 106).

Transformation, indeed transcendence, as a theme applies not only to

MESSIAH.

A

Sacred Eclogue,

In imitation of VIRGIL's POLLIO.

E Nymphs of *Solyma!* begin the song:
To heav'nly themes sublimer strains belong.
The mossy fountains and the sylvan shades,
The dreams of *Pindus* and th'*Aonian* maids,
Delight no more----O thou my voice inspire
Who touch'd *Isaiah*'s hallow'd lips with fire!

Rapt

Engraved initial "Y" of *Messiah*
(courtesy of the William Andrews Clark Memorial Library,
University of California, Los Angeles)

subject matter and couplet form but to generic conventions as well. By linking *Messiah* to the *Pastorals,* Pope demonstrates at once the flexibility of the eclogue genre in his hands and the limitations of Virgil, who had been denied the truth of Christian prophecy.[22] Pope does far more than imitate his model, Virgil's "Pollio"; he improves upon it to make way for himself in the literary tradition. Like Milton before him in the ode *On The Morning of Christ's Nativity,* Pope demonstrates the limitations of Classical authors by stressing the superior subject matter of Christian poets.

The divine, atemporal apocalypse of the *Pastorals-Messiah* unit is followed by the secular, temporal apocalypse of *Windsor-Forest,* which moves from a Miltonic "*Arcadia*" (58; 159) to a prophecy of "the fair fame of *Albion's* golden days" (71; 424). The Christ of *Messiah,* who initiates the transformation and transcendence of the pastoral setting, becomes an anti-type of Queen Anne, whose language indicates the divine sanction for the new world she makes possible: "At length great *Anna* said—Let discord cease! / She said, the World obey'd and all was Peace! (66; 327–28). Words and pictures further link *Windsor-Forest* to the *Pastorals-Messiah* unit. The engraved initial T *Windsor-Forest* shares with "Winter" reinforces its tie with the earlier poem, as does Pope's echoing the first line of the *Pastorals*—"First in these fields I try the sylvan strains"—in the last line of *Windsor-Forest*—"First in these fields I sung the sylvan strains." The juxtaposition of the poems in the 1717 *Works* underscores the links between them. As a result we see the *Pastorals-Messiah* and *Windsor-Forest* as forming a sub-group of prophecy in the pastoral mode within the first section of the *Works.*

The prophetic nature of *Windsor-Forest* is illustrated in its synoptic headpiece, freely adapted from the poem as if to express the freedom with which Pope adapts his Classical and Modern models. Father Thames, amongst the "sylvan Maids" (49; 3) unlocking their springs, strikes a pose that reflects the poem's place in the prospect tradition:

> The God appear'd; he turn'd his azure eyes
> Where *Windsor*-domes and pompous turrets rise;
> Then bow'd and spoke.   (68; 351–53)

The headpiece also anticipates the opening of canto 3 of *The Rape of the Lock:* "Close by those meads, for ever crown'd with flow'rs, / Where *Thames* with pride surveys his rising tow'rs. . . ."

Although the scene in the oval of the headpiece is not strictly faithful to the letter of the poem, it and its surrounding illustrations are certainly rep-

WINDSOR-FOREST.

To the Right Honourable

GEORGE Lord LANSDOWN.

HY forests, *Windsor!* and thy green retreats,
At once the Monarch's and the Muse's seats,
Invite my lays. Be present sylvan Maids!
Unlock your springs, and open all your shades.
Granville commands; your aid O Muses bring!
What Muse for *Granville* can refuse to sing?

H The

Headpiece and engraved initial "T" of *Windsor Forest* (courtesy of the William Andrews Clark Memorial Library, University of California, Los Angeles) resentative of the spirit of *Windsor-Forest*. The oar Father Thames holds is an emblem of the arts of civilization needed in a post-lapsarian world, and the small boat in the middle distance is an emblem of the commerce resulting from the Peace of Utrecht celebrated in the poem. The trumpets and laurel on the top of the oval are richly suggestive as emblems of the Peace, Glory, and Fame for England prophesized in the poem. We are reminded of the title page engraving—just as Britain will gain Fame and Glory from the Peace of Utrecht, so will Pope from his poetic celebration of Britain's triumph. At the same time the entwining of the trumpets by the laurel probably reflects the image of the end of war expressed in the phrase "The trumpets sleep" (69; 373). The traditional association of the Phythian laurel with prophecy is particularly appropriate to *Windsor-Forest*. The themes of Fame and Glory are repeated in the images of the burning lamps flanking the oval. The flowers and cornucopiae are emblematic of the "Peace and Plenty [that] tell, a *Stuart* reigns (51; 42).

The reader of the 1717 *Works* moves directly from the explicit prophecy in *Windsor-Forest* of Britain's political and commercial supremacy to the implicit prophecy in *An Essay on Criticism* of her literary and critical supremacy. Fame and glory on a political level in *Windsor-Forest* are paralleled in *An Essay on Criticism* on a literary level, just as the recounting of political history is paralleled by the recounting of literary history. The central role Anne plays in *Windsor-Forest* anticipates the role Pope himself takes in poetic tradition in *An Essay on Criticism*.

Pope's role is illustrated in the headpiece and engraved initial T of *An Essay on Criticism*. Bordered by laurel and oak(?) leaves, the synoptic scene in the oval of the headpiece, like that in the headpiece of *Windsor-Forest*, reflects the spirit more than particular lines of the poem it illustrates. Fame, identified by her trumpet, directs the humble, aspiring poet to the busts of Homer and Virgil, where "Still green with bays each ancient altar stands, / Above the reach of sacrilegious hands" (85; 181–82), as if to tell him,

> Be *Homer's* works your study, and delight,
> Read them by day, and meditate by night,
> Thence form your judgment, thence your notions bring,
> And trace the Muses upward to their spring.
> Still with itself compar'd, his text peruse;
> And let your comment be the *Mantuan* Muse. (82; 124–29)

AN ESSAY ON CRITICISM.

IS hard to say, if greater want of skill
Appear in writing or in judging ill;
But, of the two, less dang'rous is th' offence
To tire our patience, than mislead our sense.
Some few in that, but numbers err in this,
Ten censure wrong for one who writes amiss;

L 2   A fool

Headpiece and engraved initial "T" of *An Essay on Criticism* (courtesy of the William Andrews Clark Memorial Library, University of California, Los Angeles)

The Muses' spring can be seen in the background, where Pegasus appears "High on *Parnassus'* top" (80; 94). The reverence due the ancients is reflected in the burning altars flanking the oval. Placement of the busts of Homer and Virgil in an outdoor setting enlightened by Apollo, the sun, reminds us that the aspirant needs inspiration as well as models and that "To copy nature is to copy them" (83; 140). Furthermore, the poet must

> First follow Nature, and your judgment frame
> By her just standard, which is still the same;
> Unerring Nature, still divinely bright,
> One clear, unchang'd, and universal light,
> Life, force, and beauty, must to all impart,
> At once the source, and end, and test of art. (79; 68–73)

The engraved initial T had first appeared in Thomas Parnell's "An Essay on the Life, Writing, and Learning of Homer" in the first volume of Pope's *Iliad* translation (1715). The theme of reverence is repeated as the aspiring young poet, illuminated by inspiration and whose innocence is symbolized by his nakedness, meditates upon the bust of Homer. The headpiece and initial combine to offer a flattering image of Pope as heir to Homer and Virgil. The illustrations, moreover, are a response to Pope's critics, who had long accused him of slavish imitation of the ancients and plagiarism of the moderns. Pope's response is a visual reiteration of his reverence towards the ancients and his desire to be measured by their achievements.

More specifically, the engravings act as a response to those like Dennis and John Harris who had charged Pope with plagiarizing Boileau.[23] Pope, in a kind of inside joke, proudly associates himself with Boileau through his headpiece for *An Essay on Criticism*. Gribelin probably adapted Hendrik Hulsbergh's illustration "To front ye Art of Poetry" in *The Works of Monsieur Boileau,* vol. 1 (Edmund Curll, 1712). The Hulsberg engraving, itself adapted from an illustration engraved by Guillaume Vallet after Antoine Paillet in Boileau, *Oeuvres Diverses* (1685), shows Apollo, garlanded and with a lyre, with one foot on a pile of books next to Hippocrene and pointing to busts of Homer and Virgil in an outdoor setting. An aspiring poet must combine inspiration, learning, and imitation if he is to "follow Nature." Gribelin replaces Apollo with a humble poet, in keeping with the self-image of Pope displayed in the *Pastorals, Windsor-Forest,* and *An Essay on Criticism*. Through the illustrations we are directed to Pope's literary exemplars, just as we are by his words.

Having established the literary history and proper standards of poetry

Frontispiece of Boileau's *Art of Poetry*, 1712
(courtesy of the William Andrews Clark Memorial Library,
University of California, Los Angeles)

in *An Essay on Criticism,* Pope offers his readers his most successful poem, itself about Fame, to demonstrate the validity of his own claim to Fame. And like its predecessors in the *Works, The Rape of the Lock* ends with a prophecy: "This Lock, the Muse shall consecrate to fame, / And 'midst the stars inscribe *Belinda's* name!" (155; 5: 149–50). Of the poems in the 1717 *Works, The Rape of the Lock* has the most illustrations: a headpiece plus engraved initials for the dedication and each canto. It is also the only poem in the collection that has a previous history of illustration; the 1714 edition of *The Rape of Lock* included six plates designed by Louis Du Guernier and engraved by Claude Du Bosc, as well as two headpieces, one to the dedication and the other to canto 1, by Simon Gribelin, two unattributed engraved initials for the dedication and canto 1, and an unattributed tailpiece.[24] Of all these illustrations only two reappear in the *Works*: the initial I of the 1714 dedication is used as the I of the preface; and the tailpiece of the 1714 *Rape* is the title page engraving of the 1717 *Works*. For the 1717 quarto *Works,* as Robert Halsband notes, Gribelin adapted Du Guernier's octavo frontispiece as the headpiece for *The Rape of the Lock*.

The changes Gribelin made are significant. Here is part of Halsband's description of the Du Guernier frontispiece:

> Immediately recognizable . . . is the architectural backdrop, the East Front of the Wren palace, with (on the left) one of the two ornamental, decorated urns that stood in front of the facade. A group of putti, meant to suggest sylphs, float in air; one points up to the comet in the sky, directing the viewer's eye to the apotheosis of both the raped lock and the poet's fame. Another putto drops, by accident or design, a cascade of playing cards. Centered in the main cluster of figures, the seated female looking into the mirror suggests a Venus-like Belinda adoring the cosmetic powers; her mirror is held before her by a putto, a common motif exemplified in Titian's and Velasquez's famous paintings of Venus adoring her reflection in the mirror held by Cupid. Her exposed leg is a highly erotic gesture. Biblical and later moralists link the mirror and exposed leg as marks of a lustful woman; and since the figure is obviously intended to represent Belinda, the illustration emphasizes with a more serious tone the coquetry so elegantly mocked by Pope's couplets.[25]

Halsband rightly also calls our attention to the satyr-figure holding a mask in the lower-right corner that indicates the poem's "satiric purpose" and "erotic content."[26] The mirror, besides being an emblem of vanity, is an emblem of satire. We recall that Jonathan Swift says "Satyr is a Sort of

Frontispiece to *The Rape of the Lock*, 1714
(courtesy of the Henry E. Huntington Library)

Glass" in "The Preface of the Author" to "The Battle of the Books" (1704). The association of satire and mirrors can be seen as late as 1783 in the engraving *Veluti in Speculum,* where a satyr directs a group of politicians to peer into the mirror of truth, which, like the satirist, uses a tilted (or distorted) reflection to reveal the truth behind the mask of hypocrisy. The headpiece and initial to Trapp's lecture on satire (1715) show the conventional association of masks, mirrors, and satyrs with satire.[27] The woman's pose, like that of Belinda in the Du Guernier frontispiece, "denotes Idleness, which foments Lust," as shown in the emblem of Lust in Caesar Ripa's *Iconologia* (London, 1709).

Gribelin's 1717 headpiece is quite different, especially in tone, from his Du Guernier model. Halsband describes the headpiece:

> In the illustration itself the center medallion shows, again, the East Front of the Wren palace at Hampton Court, more accurately drawn than in Du Guernier's plates. As in the 1714 frontispiece a sylph directs our attention to the heavenly body—a star this time rather than a comet. Other sylphs are engaged in various activities mentioned in the poem; playing cards (around a square rather than a triangular table), gazing into a mirror (vanity), waving a fan (coquetry), holding up a mask (pretence). And in place of the smallish satyr of the 1714 frontispiece two large satyrs dominate the design, on either side of the medallion, each peering at the scene through one mask and holding another (comedy and tragedy). The helmet and wings at the top of the cartouche symbolize Mercury, the Roman divinity who protects traders and thieves. He is invoked here to protect the ravisher of the lock of hair.[28]

If, as Halsband argues, Pope controlled the choice of illustrations in the 1714 edition, I think he recognized that the frontispiece was rhetorically inappropriate for his comic poem and had the design altered accordingly for the 1717 *Works*. Halsband calls the 1714 frontispiece "provocative"; I think "offensive" is a better description.[29] It over-emphasizes the poem's eroticism, inaccurately reflects its comic tone, and supports the charges of Dennis, Gildon, and John Oldmixon that the poem was indecent.[30] Except for the frontispiece, all the evidence, such as the dedication, the machinery, and Pope's correspondence, suggests that Pope sought to handle the poem's erotic content more delicately, not grossly, in the changes he made between the 1712 and 1714 editions. In addition, Pope had aesthetic reasons for replacing the 1714 plates; as Halsband remarks, Du Guernier's designs are often clumsy, "literal, unimaginative, [and] uncomplicated."[31]

PRÆLECTIO
DECIMA SEPTIMA,
ET
DECIMA OCTAVA.

De Satira.

FELICES sane Scriptores, qui Argumentum ab aliis multoties eventilatum tractantes, quicquid ab iis præclare vel inventum est, vel explicatum, in breve quoddam & accuratum compendium redegerint; novum etiam aliquod de suo non improbandum insuper adjecerint. Utrum hoc à me hujusce Tractatus

Headpiece and engraved initial "F" of Trapp's lecture on satire, 1715 (courtesy of the William Andrews Clark Memorial Library, University of California, Los Angeles)

THE
RAPE *of the* LOCK.

CANTO I.

HAT dire Offence from am'rous caufes fprings,
What mighty contefts rife from trivial things,
I fing----This verfe to *C---*, Mufe! is due:
This, ev'n *Belinda* may vouchfafe to view:
Slight is the fubject, but not fo the praife,
If She infpire, and He approve my lays.

                       R   Say

Headpiece and engraved initial "W" of *The Rape of the Lock*, 1717 (courtesy of the William Andrews Clark Memorial Library, University of California, Los Angeles)

Gribelin's 1717 headpiece is both more artistically skillful and rhetorically appropriate than its 1714 model. The headpiece reflects Pope's continuing lightening of the poem's tone, most significantly in the *Works* by developing Clarissa, "A new character introduced in the subsequent [to 1714] Editions, to open more clearly the MORAL of the poem, in a parody of the speech of Sarpedon to Glaucus in Homer" (Pope's note to canto 5, line 7, 1736–51). Pope stresses that Belinda is foolish, not vicious. The synoptic headpiece puts the poem's subject of the triviality of women's vanities literally in perspective, as if we were looking through a reversed telescope, a fitting way of portraying a mock-epic. Unlike in the 1714 frontispiece, here our vision of Belinda depends solely on our imagination, undirected by pejorative iconography. Shifting the satyr-figure from within the oval to its borders downplays overt eroticism in favor of an emphasis on the satiric form that frames the undeniable sexually suggestive content. The visual emphasis on spatial perspective in the headpiece parallels the verbal emphasis on moral perspective in Clarissa's speech. The kind of Fame that Belinda earns is a comic Ill Fame.

To see a satiric rather than comic perspective we need only glance at the headpiece to the second of Pope's "Translations" in the *Works*, *The Wife of Bath Her Prologue, From Chaucer*. For Pope and his contemporaries, Chaucer was, as John Hughes calls him, "an excellent Satirist" and the first true English imitator of Juvenal.[32] In Pope's headpiece, the satyrs are again within the oval, along with Venus, Cupid, and Pan. The illustration is clearly synoptic, emphasizing the tone and theme of Chaucer and Pope's satire on feminine lust. Some possible sources for the headpiece are identifiable: the Wife of Bath twice associates herself with Venus (264, 266; 325, 370); Pope had earlier observed in the *Pastorals* that "And yet my numbers please the rural throng, / Rough *Satyrs* dance, and *Pan* applauds the song" ("Summer," 21; 49–50); Du Guernier's illustration for *Brittain's Ida* in Hughes's edition of Spenser shows a shepherd, Anchises, peering from behind bushes at Venus, nude and reclining, who looks into a mirror held before her by one of three Graces.[33] Pope and Gribelin have adapted their sources to emphasize *The Wife of Bath*'s form and content as a postnuptial satire to complement the prenuptial comedy of *The Rape of the Lock*. Lines on *The Rape of the Lock* in Parnell's commendatory poem suggest that the "Satyr-train" in *The Wife of Bath* headpiece originally may have been intended to illustrate the other poem and that the Graces in the *Brittain's Ida* print were later replaced by the more appropriate Cupid:

THE
WIFE of BATH.
FROM
CHAUCER.

Ehold the woes of matrimonial life,
And hear with rev'rence an expe-rienc'd wife!
To dear-bought wisdom give the credit due,
And think, for once, a woman tells you true.
In all these trials I have born a part;
I was my self the scourge that caus'd the smart;

For,

Headpiece and engraved initial "B" of *The Wife of Bath*
(courtesy of the William Andrews Clark Memorial Library,
University of California, Los Angeles)

> But know, ye fair, a point conceal'd with art,
> The Sylphs and Gnomes are but a woman's heart.
> The Graces stand in sight; a Satyr-train,
> Peeps o'er their head, and laughs behind the scene.

The link between the two poems is further strengthened by the engraved initial B shared by the two poems about the folly and vanity of women.[34] The engraved initial with its card table suitably opens canto 4 of *The Rape of the Lock* and is one of the poem's three initials that had not earlier appeared in the *Praelectiones* or the *Iliad*. The three that had are the N of canto 2, the C of canto 3, and the I of the "Dedication": the N with the caduceus, trumpet, and helmet of Mercury, reflects the theme of Fame in the poem and celebrates the poem's eloquence; the C, Apollo the sun, illustrates one of the dominant images of a poem in which the progress of the sun is pointedly paralleled by Belinda, "the rival of his beams" (130; 2: 3); the I taken from the "Observations on the First Book" of the *Iliad*, shows Fame blowing one of two trumpets.

Of the two other original engraved initials, the S of canto 5, with its crossed quivers of Cupid's flaming arrows and sword-knots, looks back to the iconography of the poem's headpiece as well as forward to the iconography in Pope's translation of *Sapho to Phaon*, a much more serious treatment of the theme of frustrated and unrequited love. The most interesting of all *The Rape of the Lock* initials is the synoptic W of canto 1 that was obviously designed for this particular poem and to complement the headpiece. We recognize in it a mask, fans, sword-knots, ribbons, gloves, a manteau, and at the lower center "the sparkling Cross she wore, / Which Jews might kiss, and Infidels adore" (130; 2: 7–8). If Pope indeed borrows initials from the *Iliad* translation to lend prestige to his own *Works*, he cleverly returns the favor with the initial W, which appeared on the same day for the first time in both Pope's *Works* and volume 3 of the *Iliad*. The W, especially the anachronistic cross, is strikingly inappropriate for the *Iliad*, and yet we know that Pope had control over its illustrations. There can be no doubt that the W went from the *Works* to the *Iliad* rather than vice versa, and because this is the only case of an anachronistic and blatantly inappropriate engraving in the *Iliad*, Pope presumably had a reason for his little joke. The explanation may be that Pope sought to call attention subtly to the appearance in volume 3 of the *Iliad* of Sarpedon's speech, the model for Clarissa's speech, both of which were published on 3 June 1717. Not until 1736 did Pope explicitly link the two speeches in a footnote to *The Rape of the Lock*.

SAPHO
TO
PHAON.

 AY, lovely youth, that doſt my heart command,
Can *Phaon*'s eyes forget his *Sapho*'s hand?
Muſt then her name the wretched writer prove,
To thy remembrance loſt, as to thy love?
Ask not the cauſe that I new numbers chuſe,
The Lute neglected, and the Lyric muſe;

Headpiece and engraved initial "S" of *Sapho to Phaon*
(courtesy of the William Andrews Clark Memorial Library,
University of California, Los Angeles)

The themes of Fame, of veneration of Classical models, and of prophecy we have traced through the poems of the first section of the *Works* culminate in the last poem in that section, *The Temple of Fame*, subtitled *A Vision* in the 1715 edition. In the temple, the poet discovers six columns, on which he identifies, respectively, Homer, Virgil, Pindar, Horace, Aristotle, and Cicero. In their midst is "proud Fame's imperial seat" (184; 248). Fame has both "The golden trumpet of eternal praise" (187; 307) and the "black trumpet" of slander (188; 338). "Beneath, in order rang'd, the tuneful Nine / (Her virgin handmaids) still attend the shrine" (185; 270–71). All of these details are illustrated in the headpiece, which seems to be a representation of a particular passage:

> From the black trumpet's rusty concave broke,
> Sulphurious flames, and clouds of rolling smoke:
> The pois'nous vapor blots the purple skies,
> And withers all before it as it flies.   (188–89; 338–41)[35]

The engraved initial I is a repetition of the initial to *The Rape of the Lock*, whose theme of foolish Fame reappears in the crowd of the Beau Monde who approach Fame's shrine (190–91; 378–93) and in the reference to "portents seen in air, / Of fires and plagues, and stars with blazing hair (194; 452–53).

As a poet publishing his first collected *Works*, Pope has risked earning Ill rather than Good Fame, and he has guaranteed himself the attention of Slander. His *Works* represent his own attempt in words and pictures to build a monument of Fame, "a work outlasting monumental brass" (183; 227).[36] Like the Temple of Fame described in the final poem of the most important section of his *Works*, Pope has offered the world a verbal and visual edifice with "a sumptuous frontispiece" (175; 75), a structure in which "images reflect from art to art" ("To Mr. Jervas, With Fresnoy's Art of Painting, Translated by Mr. Dryden," 391; 30). What the Twickenham Edition says of the ending of *The Temple of Fame* may be applied to the position Pope gives that passage at the conclusion of the first section of the 1717 *Works:* "Pope certainly chose his ending wisely. He knew that his particular kind of moral poetry was the best, the most original, poetry he could write. It is the same kind of moral poetry which towers in the conclusion of the various *Imitations of Horace*. Pope keeps his most resonant string for the end."[37]

Having seen in the *Works* the range of genius at Pope's command, his knowledge of the poetic kinds, and the skill with which he has constructed his own monument to Fame, the reader of the 1717 *Works* is prepared to judge the validity of Pope's claim to a place in the poetic tradition Homer started. The conclusion to *The Temple of Fame* is unfamiliar enough to merit full quotation:

> While thus I stood, intent to see and hear,
> One came, methought, and whisper'd in my ear:
> What could thus high thy rash ambition raise?
> Art thou, fond youth, a candidate for praise?
>   'Tis true, said I, not void of hopes I came,
> For who so fond as youthful bards of fame?
> But few, alas! the casual blessing boast,
> So hard to gain, so easy to be lost:
> How vain that second life in others breath,
> Th' estate which wits inherit after death!
> Ease, health, and life, for this we must resign,
> (Unsure the tenour, but how vast the fine!)
> The great man's curse, without the gains, endure,
> Be envy'd wretched, and be flatter'd, poor;
> All luckless wits our enemies profest,
> And all successful, jealous friends are [sic] best.
> Nor Fame I slight, nor for her favours call;
> She comes unlook'd for, if she comes at all.
> But if the purchase costs so dear a price,
> As soothing folly, or exalting vice:
> Oh! if the Muse must flatter lawless sway,
> And follow still where fortune leads the way;
> Or if no basis bear my rising name,
> But the fal'n ruins of another's fame:
> Then teach me heav'n! to scorn the guilty bays;
> Drive from my breast that wretched lust of praise;
> Unblemish'd let me live, or die unknown;
> Oh grant an honest fame, or grant me none!
>   (196–98; 497–524)

The final architectural metaphor of building on a "basis," or foundation, transfers the central image of the poem to the poet's own career and reminds us that we are to see Pope in the 1717 *Works* "as a man building a monument." The *ethos* Pope establishes in the conclusion of *The Temple of Fame* is that of the humble but ambitious aspirant we have seen before in the *Works*. The appropriate placement of *The Temple of Fame* at the end of the first section is anticipated and paralleled by the placement of Simon Harcourt's "To Mr. Pope, on the publishing his Works" as the last of the commendatory verses. Pope allows Harcourt to make explicit the prophecy prepared for by the conclusion of section one:

> The Chariot now the painful steep ascends
> The *Paeans* cease; thy glorious labour ends
> Here fix'd, the bright eternal Temple stands,
> Its prospect an unbounded view commands:
> Say, wonderous youth, what Column wilt thou chuse,
> What laurell'd Arch for thy triumphant Muse?
> Tho' each great Ancient court thee to his shrine,
> Tho' ev'ry Laurel thro the dome be thine;
> (From the proud Epic, down to those that shade
> the gentler brow of the soft *Lesbian* maid)
> Go to the *Good* and *Just,* an awful train,
> Thy soul's delight, and glory of the Fane:
> While thro' the earth thy dear remembrance flies,
> "Sweet to the world, and grateful to the skies."

In the *Works, The Temple of Fame* is transitional as well as terminal, naturally leading into the second section, "Translations," while ending the first. From Chaucerian imitation we go to Chaucerian translation in *January and May*, whose headpiece is an illustration of the encounter between Damian and May in the tree. The "Translations" section is fairly strictly organized in reverse chronological order from Chaucer to Homer, and only *January and May, The Wife of Bath,* and *Sapho to Phaon* have headpieces. We need to keep in mind that a very high value was placed on the art of translation in Medieval and Renaissance literature, before the later over-emphasis on originality. The "Translations" section enables Pope to display his powers over the three degrees of translation John Dryden identified in his *Preface to the Translation of Ovid's Epistles* (1680): metaphrase, paraphrase, and imitation. And, as we have seen, the translations are often thematically and iconographically linked backward and forward to Pope's own more original poems in the 1717 *Works*.

One such example is *Sapho to Phaon*, which is linked visually back to a comic treatment of frustrated love in *The Rape of the Lock* and thematically forward to *Eloisa to Abelard,* another serious treatment.[38] *Sapho to Phaon* and *Eloisa to Abelard* stand in much the same relation to each other as the *Pastorals* do to *Messiah; Eloisa to Abelard* is the Ovidian Heroic Epistle Christianized. In some of the quartos these thematic and formal links are reinforced by the repetition of the tailpiece of *Sapho* as the illustration to the "Argument" of *Eloisa,* the only illustration accompanying any of the poems, except the "Ode for Musick on St. Cecilia's Day," in "Miscellanies," the last section of the 1717 *Works.*

Pope distinguished *Eloisa to Abelard* not only by having it illustrated but also by giving it, the most substantial of the seven original poems in the heterogeneous final section, pride of place as the last poem of the 1717 *Works.* The illustration, which had appeared earlier as the tailpiece to book 3 of the *Iliad,* once again links Pope to Homer, but more importantly serves as a guide to how we are to read the poem. In the *Iliad,* the illustration is described in Pope's note to verse 531: "This Interview of the two Lovers, plac'd opposite to each other and over-look'd by *Venus, Paris* gazing on *Helena,* she turning away her Eyes shining at once with Anger and Love, are particulars finely drawn, and painted up to all the Life of Nature." Eloisa and Abelard become Christian types of the pagan Helen and Paris. The repetition of the illustration, moreover, suggests that Pope hopes his readers will have the same ambivalent response to Eloisa that he directs them to have to Helen in his notes to book 3. In his note to verse 165, "where we have the first sight of *Helena,*" Pope seeks to keep us from condemning the fallen woman:

> . . . But her amiable Behaviour here, the secret Wishes that rise in favour of her rightful Lord, her tenderness for her Parents and Relations, the Relentings of her Soul for the Mischiefs her Beauty had been the Cause of, the Confusion she appears in, the veiling her Face and dropping a Tear, are particulars so beautifully natural, as to make every Reader no less than *Menelaus* himself, inclin'd to forgive her at least, if not to love her.

And the note to verse 479 calls on us to "look upon [Helen] with Compassion as constrain'd by a superior Power, and whose Speech tends to justify her in the Eye of the Reader." As I think the shared illustrations should remind us, Pope wants us to respond to Eloisa in the same way, to sympathize with rather than easily condemn or approve her character.

By placing *Eloisa to Abelard* at the end of the 1717 *Works,* Pope demonstrates that his reputation does not depend solely on his past performance

The ARGUMENT

*A*Belard *and* Eloisa *flourish'd in the twelfth Century; they were two of the most distinguish'd persons of their age in learning and beauty, but for nothing more famous than for their unfortunate passion. After a long course of Calamities, they retired each to a several Convent, and consecrated the remainder of their days to religion. It was many years after this separation, that a letter of* Abelard's *to a Friend which contain'd the history of his misfortunes, fell into the hands of* Eloisa. *This awakening all her tenderness, occasion'd those celebrated letters (out of which the following is partly extracted) which give so lively a picture of the struggles of grace and nature, virtue and passion.*

ELOISA

Illustration of "The Argument" of *Eloisa to Abelard*
(courtesy of the William Andrews Clark Memorial Library,
University of California, Los Angeles)

and that his talent can be displayed in a kind of poetry he had previously left untried. The appearance of *Eloisa to Abelard* in the same volume with *Sapho to Phaon*, like his earlier coupling of the *Pastorals* and *Messiah*, invites the reader to measure Pope against his Classical model. *Eloisa to Abelard* treats anew the "best of passions, Love and Fame" (419; 40), apparently in conflict in a poem whose very existence preserves them both, and in so doing fulfills Eloisa's prophecy of "some future Bard":

> Such if there be, who loves so long, so well;
> Let him our sad, our tender story tell;
> The well-sung woes shall sooth my pensive ghost;
> He best can paint 'em, who shall feel 'em most.
>
> (435, 363–66)

The poetic monument Pope constructs to "graft [Eloisa's] love immortal on [Abelard's] fame" (434; 344) becomes the last piece of his *Works* of 1717, his own Temple of Fame, "a work outlasting monumental brass."[39]

NOTES

1. Reprinted in 1935 as *Pope's Own Miscellany*, ed. Norman Ault (London: The Nonesuch Press).

2. For the various folio and quarto versions of the *Works*, see Reginald Harvey Griffith, *Alexander Pope: A Bibliography* (Austin: University of Texas Press, 1922), 1:65–70, items 79–86. The quarto I cite throughout is item 79, Huntington shelf number 143018.

3. *Lives of the English Poets By Samuel Johnson*, ed. George Birkbeck Hill (Oxford: Clarendon Press, 1905), 3:200.

4. *The Correspondence of Alexander Pope*, ed. George Sherburn (Oxford: Clarendon Press, 1956), 1:396. Hereafter cited parenthetically in the text.

5. Maynard Mack, "Pope's 1717 Preface with a Transcription of the Manuscript Text," in *Collected in Himself: Essays Critical, Biographical, and Bibliographical on Pope and Some of His Contemporaries* (Newark: University of Delaware Press, 1982), p. 166; Dustin Griffin, *Alexander Pope: The Poet in the Poems* (Princeton: Princeton University Press, 1978), p. 92.

6. Mack, "Pope's 1717 Preface," p. 161; Griffin, *Alexander Pope*, p. 92.

7. *Poems on Several Occasions* may have been intended as an indirect advertisement for the *Works*: many of the poems in the miscellany praise Pope and his poems.

8. David Foxon, *Pope and the Early Eighteenth-Century Book Trade* (forthcoming), p. 78 of typescript on deposit at the William Andrews Clark Memorial Library.

9. Foxon, *Pope*, p. 89. Pope and Gribelin had collaborated in 1716 in the second

edition of *The Art of Painting: By C. A. Du Fresney . . . Translated into English . . . By Mr. Dryden,* published by Bernard Lintot. Small details in the headpieces to *An Essay on Criticism* and *Windsor-Forest* are adapted from Gribelin's designs for the 1714 and subsequent editions of Shaftesbury's *Characteristicks,* I, A4 and III, title page. Gribelin may have been the anonymous engraver of the 1715 and 1716 volumes of the *Iliad* translation as well.

10. Quoted by Foxon, *Pope,* p. 80.

11. Foxon, *Pope,* pp. 81–82.

12. The Twickenham Edition of the Poems of Alexander Pope, *Minor Poems,* eds. Norman Ault and John Butt (London: Methuen, 1954), 6:202. Subsequent quotations from Pope are cited in the text by page number from *Works* and by line number from the Twickenham Edition, hereafter referred to as TE.

13. Samuel Johnson, *Rambler,* No. 106, in the Yale Edition of the Works of Samuel Johnson, *Samuel Johnson: The Rambler,* ed. W. J. Bate and Albrecht B. Strauss (New Haven: Yale University Press, 1969), 4:200; Johnson is translating Horace, *Odes,* III. 30.

14. The frontispiece is reproduced in Morris Brownell, *Alexander Pope and the Arts of Georgian England* (Oxford: Clarendon Press, 1978), plate 79, facing p. 344; see also pp. 346–47.

15. For a complementary discussion of Pope's attempts to create an image of himself as a lover, see James A. Winn, "Pope Plays the Rake: His Letters to Ladies and the Making of the *Eloisa,*" in *The Art of Alexander Pope,* eds. Howard Erskine-Hill and Anne Smith (London: Vision Press, 1979), pp. 89–118.

16. *The Critical Works of John Dennis,* ed. Edward Niles Hooker (Baltimore: The Johns Hopkins University Press, 1939), 1:416–17.

17. Johnson, *Lives of the English Poets,* 3:136.

18. I am reluctant to make much of the tailpieces in the *Works* because they are not consistent in the various quartos and folios. They apparently were chosen primarily to satisfy demands of space rather than meaning.

19. Mack, "Pope's 1717 Preface," p. 164.

20. Martin Battestin, "The Transforming Power: Nature and Art in Pope's Pastorals," *Eighteenth-Century Studies* 2 (1969): 183–204.

21. TE, 1:104.

22. Pope was certainly not unique in trying to improve on his model. Daniel Baker announces his own attempt in the "Preface" to "Virgilius Evangelizans. A Poem Upon Christmas-Day. In Imitation of the Fourth Eclogue of Virgil, Entitled, Pollio" (*Poems on Several Occasions,* 1697):

> I have here endeavoured to rectifie Virgil's Mistake, and restore this excellent Poem to its right owner: there being several things in it, which cannot, with any shew of Truth, be applied to an Person, but the Son of God. And herein I have taken the Liberty . . . to leave out some things, to add others, and by a Paraphrase to make the Sense more plain and easie.
>
> . . . Virgil was not so happy as to understand his own Verses. . . ." (pp. 117–18)

23. Joseph Guerinot, *Pamphlet Attacks on Alexander Pope 1711–1744: A Descriptive Bibliography* (London: Methuen, 1969), pp. 33–34, describes Harris's *A Treatise Upon the Modes* (1715).

24. See Robert Halsband, *The Rape of the Lock and Its Illustrations 1714–1896* (Oxford: Clarendon Press, 1980), pp. 9–23.

25. Halsband, *The Rape*, p. 18.

26. Halsband, *The Rape*, p. 19.

27. The headpiece in Trapp, *Praelectiones,* p. 123, is engraved by Michael van der Gucht after Joseph Goupy. For more on the association of masks and satire see Howard Weinbrot, "Masked Men and Satire and Pope: Toward a Historical Basis for the Eighteenth-Century Persona," *Eighteenth-Century Studies* 16 (1982–83): 265–89.

28. Halsband, *The Rape*, p. 22.

29. Halsband, *The Rape*, p. 18.

30. In, respectively, *Reflections Critical and Satyrical, A New Rehearsal,* and *The Catholick Poet* (1716).

31. Halsband, *The Rape*, p. 21.

32. See John Hughes, ed. *The Works of Mr. Edmund Spenser* (1715), 1:xxvii; *The Works of Monsieur Boileau* (1712), p. 104.

33. Hughes, ed., *The Works of Spenser*, 6: facing p. 1487; *Brittain's Ida,* mistakenly attributed to Spenser in the seventeenth century, is a pirated edition of Phineas Fletcher, *Venus and Anchises.*

34. Pope and Gribelin could have chosen the B from "Autumn," which had appeared in the *Iliad* and whose rural scene is appropriate to the *Pastorals.*

35. The headpiece is reproduced as plate 2 in TE, 2: facing 209.

36. The reprinting of the *Temple of Fame* in the *Works* serves as a denial of the assertion Thomas Burnet had made in *Numb. XIV. The Grumbler* (1715), quoted in Guerinot, *Pamphlet Attacks,* p. 33: "Let the unwary take warning from a Poet, who not long ago raised a *Temple of Fame* to himself, which was no sooner finished, than it fell to the Ground, and buried the Architect under its Ruins."

37. TE, 2:234.

38. "The Fable of Dryope," another poem of love lost, shares the S initial, too. The remaining "Translations" have the following engraved initials and no headpieces: "Vertumnus and Pomona," the I of "Winter" and *Windsor-Forest;* "The First Book of Statius His Thebias," The F of "Spring"; "Part of the Thirteenth Book of Homer's Odysseus," the I of *January and May;* "The Gardens of Alcinous," The C of *The Rape of the Lock,* canto 3.

39. I am very grateful to have received two grants that made completion of this study possible: a Henry E. Huntington Library Fellowship enabled me to research and write the first draft of this article; a National Humanities Center Fellowship allowed me to revise the essay into its final form and to have it prepared for publication.

Stuart Curran
Multum in Parvo
Wordsworth's *Poems, in Two Volumes* of 1807

It is a paradox of history, at least of literary history, that what is arguably Wordsworth's greatest collection of verse, the *Poems, in Two Volumes* of 1807, has not simply gained less attention than the original *Lyrical Ballads* but has, as a collection, been virtually ignored. Yet its contents form the staples for both anthologies and critical commentary on the poet. Many of the famous short lyrics on natural subjects were first collected in the *Poems, in Two Volumes,* as were "Resolution and Independence," the "Ode to Duty," "Elegiac Stanzas," and the "Ode: Intimations of Immortality." Moreover, in the first of these volumes appeared the most impressive group of sonnets to be published in England since those included in the *Poems of Mr. John Milton* of 1645: "Miscellaneous Sonnets" and "Sonnets Dedicated to Liberty." *Poems, in Two Volumes* was the mature Wordsworth's first true venture on his own, at the ripe age of thirty-seven, and, though it came forth without a statement of principles comparable to the preface rewritten for each edition of *Lyrical Ballads,* readers immediately discerned a "system" underlying the volumes. Most of them did not like it, but the hostility of the notices paradoxically established Wordsworth's preeminence among contemporary poets.[1]

The voices who rose to Wordsworth's defence recognized as well how systematically his *Poems, in Two Volumes* had mounted a radical assault on the received standards of poetry. In less than a decade, however, Wordsworth, stung by the hostile criticism, had rewritten a number of the poems, and in the collection of his poetry published in 1815 he wholly rearranged them. Only recently have the two volumes been restored in a responsible modern edition, allowing us to trace their evolution and to read them with the sense of dramatic development and of nuanced interconnection that Wordsworth clearly intended his original readers to experience.[2] What we can ascertain in this retrospect is the intricate nature of the system by which Wordsworth hoped to revolutionize not simply the language of poetry, but its subject matter and the way it was read as well.

The complex interior balancing that recent criticism has illuminated in the *Lyrical Ballads* is replicated and even extended in the elaborate formal symmetries of *Poems, in Two Volumes*.³ Even a brief survey will suggest the rich counterpoint of its harmonies. There are six sections, three in each volume: "The Orchard Pathway," "Poems Composed during a Tour, Chiefly on Foot," and "Sonnets" (themselves divided into twenty Miscellaneous Sonnets and twenty-six Sonnets Dedicated to Liberty) comprising volume 1; and "Poems Written during a Tour in Scotland," "Moods of my Own Mind," and "The Blind Highland Boy; with Other Poems" in volume 2. The Intimations Ode, separated by a short-title page as if to indicate a summary statement, concludes the second volume. Simply looking over the table of contents, we can discern the balance between types of sonnets extending also to that between different excursions. To begin reading in the volumes is to recognize as well the continuity between the spontaneities of "The Orchard Pathway" and of the "Moods" in the second volume. But within each of the sections there are further symmetries. The "Moods of my Own Mind" begins with a poem "To a Butterfly" and continues with verses celebrating twilight, ending after nine intervening poems with another "To a Butterfly" and another celebration of twilight. Similar in pattern, though darker in theme, is the development of the first group of tour poems from the poet's chance meeting with "Beggars" to his confrontation with the leech-gatherer in "Resolution and Independence." The clearest, and in its way the most startling, of doublings is between the first and last sections. In "The Orchard Pathway" Wordsworth begins by celebrating the solid and unprepossessing claims of the natural in "To the Daisy" and concludes with internalizing those virtues in the Horatian "Ode to Duty." "The Blind Highland Boy" is a fireside or bedtime story told in the language of children, its subject a venturing forth upon the unknown sea and a safe return home. The section ends with the "Elegiac Stanzas" in which the sea claims its adult victim, and we are left to "suffer and mourn" with only a dutiful hope to sustain us. But the Horatian ode ending the first section is then juxtaposed with the Pindaric sonorities of the "Intimations Ode" in which youth and age, desire and experience, success and failure—all the multiple contraries developed through both volumes—coalesce and confront each other in an attempt at reconciliation. The final great lines—"To me the meanest flower that blows can give / Thoughts that do often lie too deep for tears"—deliberately return us to the opening poem of volume 1, "To the Daisy," now reconceptualized in almost cosmic terms. The entire process is itself neatly encapsulated by Wordsworth's two epigraphs from Virgil: on the title page, "*Posterius graviore sono tibi Musa loquetur / Nostra: dabunt cum securos mihi tempora fructus*" (Our muse will speak to you in a darker tone when the times give me their produce with assurance); and as epigraph to the "Intimations Ode" the opening lines of the messianic *Fourth Eclogue: "Paolo majora canamus"* (Let us sing of somewhat larger themes).[4] The development of the two volumes is not, we realize at once from the linked epigraphs and upon reflection from the ebb and flow of symmetries in the poems, a simple linear ascent from youthful innocence to troubled self-consciousness but a continual readjustment of perspective between the simple and complex, the quotidian and cosmic. What is essential is the amplitude that comes from the mind's mediation among differing perspectives.

Wordsworth states his purpose with customarily understated clarity in the original introduction to "The Orchard Pathway," which Longman's inexplicably deleted from the final form of the 1807 *Poems:*[5]

> ORCHARD PATHWAY, to and fro,
> Ever with thee did I go,
> Weaving Verses, a huge store!
> These, and many hundreds more,
> And, in memory of the same,
> This little lot shall bear *Thy Name!*

Perhaps the firm of Longman's had a sense of what reviewers of Francis Jeffrey's mold would do to such lines and cancelled them out of embarrassment. And yet, their "namby-pamby" tones are deliberate, virtually ideological in import, recurring with systematic insistence again and again through both volumes as Wordsworth vaunts his unadorned simplicity. It is on this unpretentious orchard pathway that the meanest flower grows, and it is there that intimations of the immortal, of what survives the mutable everywhere attested to, will be discerned. In the dynamics of process, the to and fro of a pathway or the walking tours far from domestic security, will be found the saving continuities of human experience. It is these the poet "weaves" into patterns of mental response for readers to recreate and replicate.

Obviously those readers have the right, as they have the opportunity, to unthread the intricate texture of this cloth. But there is a clear danger in the process. To remove poems from the context in which Wordsworth intended them to be read at the very least leads to a narrowing of their meaning. In a few extreme cases it may wholly alter it. As an example of the first problem, let us take "Resolution and Independence" as it would typically appear in an anthology. Lacking its four companion poems, its meaning is likely to be construed as residing in the message Wordsworth extracts for himself from meeting the leech-gatherer, and the poem is thus reduced to something like a moralistic homily. But inasmuch as the poem has a troubled interpretative history, provoking wholly antithetical responses and at least the suspicion that Wordsworth extracted the wrong message from his meeting with the leech-gatherer, the context supplied by the larger grouping certainly has bearing. The group of "Poems Composed during a Tour, Chiefly on Foot" is anything but homiletic; its tones are multivalent, perhaps even ambivalent. In both "Beggars" and "Alice Fell," for instance, Wordsworth as poetic narrator sets himself, rather in the line of "We Are Seven" or "Anecdote for Fathers" in *Lyrical Ballads,* as a well-intentioned adult removed from the ways in which children think and therefore not quite fathoming their integral otherness. Irresolvable distance is similarly enforced by "To a Sky-Lark" and the redaction of the Sidney sonnet, "With how sad steps, O moon, thou climb'st the sky." In context the point of "Resolution and Independence" may well be not that we should adopt a nose-to-the-ground stoicism but that we should at once recognize the irreducibility of otherness and yet acknowledge that our experience is created out of the urge to find a bridge to what we can never be. If Wordsworth seems a little too comfortable in the rock-like stability of the leech-gatherer, the context of the other poems would suggest that stability is to be honored precisely because it so seldom occurs.

The "Poems Composed during a Tour, Chiefly on Foot," of which "Resolution and Independence" is the culminating piece, embody instability or, at least, unrootedness in their linking conception. However delicately the group adds resonance to any single poem within it, as a whole they powerfully counteract the supposed assurances of the poem that precedes them, the "Ode to Duty," which is a convenient example of the type of poem where separation from its context actually reshapes its meaning. Within the two-volume collection it is simply impossible to read the "Ode to Duty"—and the same should be said for the penultimate poem as well, "Elegiac Stanzas, Suggested by a Picture of PEELE CASTLE, in a Storm"—as representing a new, philosophical voice, the introduction of the late Wordsworth. "I long for a repose which ever is the same" ("Ode to Duty," line 40) suggests an underlying drive in Wordsworth as he chronicles multiple losses and the evanescence of all natural joys, but that desire for repose immediately gives way to the pointed unrootededness of his walking tour. Moreover, the "Ode to Duty" is itself placed so as to follow the celebration of the "exquisitely wild" in "To H. C., Six Years Old" (line 12) and the last two of the Lucy poems. The difficulty Wordsworth had in writing the ode might be construed as a sign of unease with its claims. Probably, it testifies more to the problems he experienced in endeavoring to forge a delicate balance between it and its surrounding context. The context demands that we look beyond the mere subordination of personal impulse to the "Stern Lawgiver," Duty, (line 49) and stress the internal dialectical pressure of the poem. Wordsworth was also once like H. C. and Lucy, "loving freedom and untried" (line 25), and if with maturity he has tired of "this uncharter'd freedom" (line 36), he honors the extent to which the child's spontaneity is an implicit critique of too self-binding a commitment to Duty. Within the context of the collection Duty is not Christian stoicism, but rather a responsible contemplation of the self, of experience, of others. A poet truly alive to experience can embrace what he is not, celebrating the thoughtless exuberance of H. C. or the unencumbered and unintellectual leech-gatherer, delighting in the natural spontaneities of butterflies and skylarks, even daffodils and rainbows, but the Duty to which Wordsworth binds himself is contemplative, self-testing, perhaps truly vocational. It is best exemplified as it is elaborated in the companion ode with which the *Poems, in Two Volumes* concludes, the "Intimations Ode," where Wordsworth enacts his reclamation and reconciliation of opposites and explicitly exerts his claims to the attention of a thinking posterity.

The dialectical patterning of the *Poems, in Two Volumes* is conspicuous: paradoxically, a "repose which ever is the same," which might simply be taken as the stance of the poetic voice, is in ceaseless motion among contraries; but in their composite unity there is the undoubted equipoise of a great artistic vision. That it was systematic, which is to say, deliberately programmatic, was the judgment of Wordsworth's contemporaries, both those like Jeffrey, who thought they had the taste to reeducate him, and the critical arbiters of *Blackwood's,* who hoped they could knock their Edinburgh competitor from his pedestal by raising Wordsworth onto another. The almost abstract nature of that program can best be discriminated by turning to the one section of the collection that was praised without demur, by friend and foe alike, the two sequences of sonnets. In them Wordsworth wrote a virtual history of the sonnet form and revolutionized its character in the process. In the midst of these two volumes, the rich testament to the poet's mature powers, they stand as an awesome achievement, however miniature its appearance in the history of English letters.

Wordsworth came to the sonnet comparatively late, well after his friends and associates, who helped perpetrate the sonnet rage of the 1790s, had given up on the form as indelibly tainted with a protracted adolescence.[6] Or, perhaps it is more appropriate to remark that while Coleridge,

Southey, Lamb, and Lloyd were fashioning sonnets of isolated sensibility, Wordsworth was experimenting with the same subjects in more extended narrative and lyrical forms: his female vagrants and forsaken wives, not to speak of the long-lived and increasingly long-winded Pedlar, as fortune would have it could not be confined to fourteen lines of sorrow-laden verse. Actually, Wordsworth's one adolescent venture in this direction, his "Sonnet on Seeing Miss Helen Maria Williams Weep at a Tale of Distress," is a model of the type, a pastiche of exquisite clichés that the poet was well to have vented and superseded early.[7] It took Coleridge, so truly was his original career under the sway of William Lisle Bowles, much longer to free himself from his addiction to sonnets; and, indeed, it could be persuasively argued that it was his meeting with Wordsworth and the dual venture they shortly embarked upon that was the cause of his abandoning the form for more ample expressions of his genius. His swan-song, the three "Sonnets Attempted in the Manner of Contemporary Writers" (1797), was a parody of the style he had employed and, worse, had encouraged in others, and it provoked the enmity of a betrayed Charles Lloyd.

If one friendship was destroyed by Coleridge's sonnets, another grew to poetic fruition in their absence. And yet, when Wordsworth returned to the form in 1802 to begin an involvement that is unparalleled in English literature, how was it possible for him not to have recalled Coleridge's ventures, whether for his excesses or his limited achievements? This supposition is materially strengthened when it is recognized that virtually all the sonnets printed in the *Poems, in Two Volumes,* already separated into two parts, were transcribed early in 1804 for the notebook that Coleridge was to take with him on his excursion to Malta. One of those sonnets, the thirteenth of the "Sonnets Dedicated to Liberty" ("O Friend! I know not which way I must look"), was originally addressed to Coleridge and would have extended the personal frame of reference already established by the partial manuscript of *The Prelude* that was also prepared for the notebook.[8]

Two aspects of Coleridge's career as a writer of sonnets are of particular interest for Wordsworth's later endeavors. The best of his sonnets are the twelve that he contributed as a series to the *Morning Chronicle* in December 1794 and January 1795, later known as "Sonnets on Eminent Characters." Their mixture of praise and vitriolic censure, distributed among public figures like Burke and Pitt, and their celebration of poets like Bowles and Southey who promise a rebirth of culture, are a premonition of the balance Wordsworth attempts to strike in his "Sonnets Dedicated to Liberty." Whatever their lapses in an ultimate scale of value, the "Sonnets on Eminent

Characters" stand out from the thousands of sonnets published in the closing decade of the eighteenth century for their creation of a sustained public posture and unified cultural vision. Wordsworth's address to Coleridge in the thirteenth of the "Sonnets Dedicated to Liberty" is more than a gesture of friendship, more even than an echo of Coleridge's addresses to Bowles and Southey; it is as well an implicit acknowledgement of obligation to his example.

The second point at which Coleridge's influence would have been felt by Wordsworth is less in the way of a debt than a revision. Whether Wordsworth ever saw the strange compilation of sonnets by contemporary writers gathered into a pamphlet by Coleridge in the autumn of 1796, he would have known its self-assured preface from its being reprinted in the second edition of Coleridge's poems in 1797.[9] There Coleridge essentially eliminates the history of the sonnet, instead "deducing its laws from [the] compositions" of Charlotte Smith and William Lisle Bowles. He confesses that he has "never yet been able to discover either sense, nature, or poetic fancy in Petrarch's poems," thereby dismissing their pretensions as models and freeing himself to define the form from the example of his contemporaries as a vehicle for self-contemplating sensibility: "a small poem, in which some lonely feeling is developed" (p. 71). Wordsworth was to reject so parochial a horizon as this, but even where his tones are most stentorian, the sonnets of the *Poems, in Two Volumes* uniformly attain to power out of a self-consciousness intensified by formal enclosure. As he began his tutelage with the sonnet, Wordsworth stressed the element of confinement, "crowding into narrow room more of the combined effect of rhyme and blank verse than can be done by any other form of verse I know of." Many years later, reflecting on his mastery of the form, he elaborated this figure, celebrating the "pervading sense of intense Unity in which the excellence of the Sonnet has always seemed to me mainly to consist. Instead of looking at this composition as a piece of architecture, making a whole out of three parts, I have been much in the habit of preferring the image of an orbicular body,—a sphere,—or a dew-drop."[10] It may be that "'twas pastime to be bound / Within the Sonnet's scanty plot of ground," as Wordsworth testifies in the "Prefatory Sonnet" of the 1807 *Poems* (lines 10–11), but the sense of isolation, of "some lonely feeling," however sophisticated the emotion or privileged the experience, underlies all the great sonnets of his maturity.[11]

Although Wordsworth put his indelible stamp on the form, his sonnets are deeply imbued with the mode of the prospect sonnet popularized by Bowles and frequently used by Coleridge and Southey. Indeed, aside from the closing tribute to Raisley Calvert (number 20) and the triplets "To Sleep" (numbers 5–7) and "From the Italian of Michelangelo" (numbers 10–12), all of the "Miscellaneous Sonnets" in some pointed way invoke this central type of the sonnet of sensibility. But, it is true as well of the "Sonnets Dedicated to Liberty," which, beginning with the very first—"Composed by the Sea-Side, near Calais, August, 1802"—continually surprise the reader either by enforcing immense distances that link nations and cultures or by a sudden reversion to saving particularities like "Those Boys that in yon meadow-ground / In white-sleev'd shirts are playing by the score" (lines 3–4), celebrated in the tenth, "Composed in the Valley, near Dover, on the Day of landing." The entire sequence of "Sonnets Dedicated to Liberty" suggests that to Wordsworth's mind prospect rightly viewed must become vision. Yet, both sequences subtly convey a sense of "some lonely feeling" being in constant definition, self-contemplating and self-creating on the axis of its visionary extension. In the "Miscellaneous Sonnets," if the two triplets, "To Sleep" and "From the Italian of Michelangelo," are momentarily exempted, a surprisingly coherent pattern emerges among the sonnets preceding the final poems of the sequence in which the tone deepens. The two sonnets in which ships are perceived at a distance (numbers 2 and 8) have an obvious corollary in the sonnets in which cloud shapes spur the imagination (numbers 3 and 4): these poems, as it were, surround and condition our response to the sonnets "To Sleep." Likewise, the translations from Michelangelo are surrounded by sonnets linked by their rusticity and their connections with the poet's past, "To the River Duddon" (number 9) and "Written in very early youth" (number 13). Further indication of this pattern is provided by the sonnet of nostalgic return, "'Beloved Vale!' I said, 'when I shall con'" (number 15) which stands between two poems in which life seems or is suspended, with the sleeping city of the Westminster Bridge sonnet (number 14) and the dead child glimpsed in a dream—sleep once more intruding upon the sequence in both—in number 16, "Methought I saw the footsteps of a throne." The interweaving of theme and subject is as apparent as the interconnections are at first obscure; Wordsworth goes out of his way to indicate that he is practicing upon the reader but forces our active intelligence to engage his in the process of discovery.

To turn after this process to the triplets is immediately to be struck by their conventional subject matter. The undisguised Catholicism of the Michelangelo translations is as unexpected as the humorous deflation of the conventions of the sonnet on sleep. At once Wordsworth defines a context and distances himself from it. However puzzled a contemporary might be by his aims, the context is as obvious as it is initially odd. Wordsworth's "Miscellaneous Sonnets" are a sequence in the Petrarchan mode as surely as the "Sonnets Dedicated to Liberty" derive from the Miltonic. Although the three translations were understandably not included in the manuscript intended for Coleridge's trip to Malta, they probably reflect his influence, at least negatively. His full statement justifying his preference for Bowles and Charlotte Smith as founders of an indigenous English school against the Italian model associated with Petrarch is this: "I have never yet been able to discover either sense, nature, or poetic fancy, in Petrarch's poems; they appear to me all one cold glitter of heavy conceits and metaphysical abstractions" (*Poems* [1797], p. 71). Such a sentiment would have struck a responsive chord among Coleridge's readers, who at this point were almost universal in their condemnation of Renaissance sonnets. Yet Wordsworth resurrects the Petrarchan tradition dismissed by Coleridge as irrelevant to a modern sensibility, demanding that we see its affinities with his own far more radical departure from the customary grounds of the sonnet. At the same time, in an intricate balancing act, he deflates both the hyperbole lodged in tradition, especially in the humorous central poem of the "Sleep" group ("A flock of sheep that leisurely pass by"), and the posturing of his own sensibility, at which he actually records himself laughing in the last of the lighter sonnets, number 15.

The first two of the Michelangelo sonnets reassure the poet that his love is not a mere capitulation to the things of this earth, but through them he aspires to an eternal ideal; the last testifies that God animates what is otherwise the "barren clay" of the poet's "unassisted heart" (12.3), thereby inspiring his verse. Together the three express conventional sentiments of the Renaissance sonnet and reinforce its focus as mediator between this world and an idealized conception of it in order to confirm that the intelligence that is properly schooled and disciplined "breathes on earth the air of paradise," as the final line of the first affirms. And yet, it is because of this "air of paradise"—or something very like it—that

> Nuns fret not in their Convent's narrow room;
> And Hermits are contented with their Cells;
> And students with their pensive Citadels.

Everywhere in the "Miscellaneous Sonnets" are recorded moments of wonder—distant ships, a distant city, shifting cloud formations, the sea as a "mighty Being [that] is awake" (19.7). Even as one laughs at how one's imagination recasts treasured memories, it recurs:

> To see the Trees, which I had thought so tall,
> Mere dwarfs; the Brooks so narrow, Fields so small.
> A Juggler's Balls old Time about him toss'd;
> I looked, I stared, I smiled, I laughed; and all
> The weight of sadness was in wonder lost.   (15.10–14)

The Michelangelo sonnets provide Wordsworth with a traditional focus for two pervasive modes of thought in the "Miscellaneous Sonnets": the moments of wonder all harbor a recognition of how the small and localized can intimate the grand and universal; and the connection of the two produces a motivating force, a movement out and back, that, almost abstract, seems truly unmotivated, spontaneous, essential. The "Miscellaneous Sonnets" are entirely free of the "cold glitter" Coleridge associated with Petrarch, but they retain in a remarkable transformation the "heavy conceits and metaphysical abstractions" of the Renaissance sonnet tradition. The modes of thought Wordsworth explores are not the ostensible subject of his sonnets, as they are in the strictly philosophical elaboration of those he translates from Michelangelo. They are instead implicit, universally felt impulses within the mind—indeed, the primary means by which we recognize the workings of the imagination in all its "miscellaneous" guises.

"How sweet it is, when mother Fancy rocks / The wayward brain, to saunter through a wood!" (1.1–2). Exclamation point to the side, the group of sonnets begins in such an offhand manner that the reader, unless shrewdly discerning the dynamics of "The Orchard Pathway" being reinvoked, scarcely realizes that Wordsworth has announced the unifying theme of the sequence. It becomes even clearer as the sestet opens out into its predictable complementarity:

> Verily I think,
> Such place to me is sometimes like a dream
> Or map of the whole world.   (1.9–11)

Thus the imagination stretches to escape what confines it; and yet, even here the second process, ebb succeeding upon flow, is simultaneously at work, as the continuing lines demonstrate:

> thoughts, link by link,
> Enter through ears and eyesight, with such gleam
> Of all things, that at last in fear I shrink,
> And leap at once from the delicious stream.   (1.11–14)

The imagination in transcending its confinement draws the mind beyond its capacity to hold the center stable, until finally the centering impulse must reassert its control and reinstate mundane reality.

This simple pattern is present everywhere, but often in oblique ways that surprise the reader with their extensions. It is implicit in the combined urge for identification and awareness of difference that create the tensions of the second sonnet. "Where lies the Land to which yon Ship must go? / . . . / Yet still I ask, what Haven is her mark? (2.1,9). But the ship eludes the poet's stationary perspective and is only truly at home without referents: "a beaten way / Ever before her, and a wind to blow" (2.7–8).[12] The same kind of relationship is juxtaposed in the succeeding dual sonnets, "Composed after a Journey across the Hamilton Hills, Yorkshire," and "Ere we had reach'd the wish'd for place, night fell" (3.1). Denied the prospect they had longed to see, the visitors create another one, sublime and with happily incompatible elements, in the cloud formations still suffused with light. The two sonnets balance the evanescent and substantial: even as the former are elevated almost to the terms of Michelangelo—the cloud formations representing "A contrast and reproach to gross delight, / And life's unspiritual pleasures" (4.3–4)—the poet's principle of reality reasserts itself, demanding his share of the flowers of paradise in the here-and-now: "The immortal Mind craves objects that endure" (4.12). And yet, no sooner is this principle laid down as an enduring premise than the poet yearns to break it, even if in an essentially comic way: the ensuing triplet of sonnets "To Sleep," deflated into the protestations of an insomniac, depict a mind whose source of irritation is its very inability to leave the realm of the sensible, even after imagining the clichéd prospect of "A flock of sheep that leisurely pass by" (6.1).

As usual with Wordsworth at this point in his career, there is nothing doctrinaire about his employment of a universal rhythm except his assertion of its universal applicability. Even the moral outcry of "The world is too much with us" (number 18) traces its lineage to this aesthetic rhythm whose perversion is everywhere evident: "late and soon, / Getting and spending, we lay waste our powers" (18.1–2)—powers of imaginative growth and renewal, connecting singular and universal, the palpable and ineffable, not to be reduced to materialistic contracts without being destroyed. The poem does not merely inveigh against such perversions; it enacts through its intrinsic structural rhythm the necessary antidote, moving from the chill moralism of its opening to a pagan remythologizing of the world with Proteus and Triton envisioned arising from the sea at its end. The effect is scarcely isolated but joins with the Westminster Bridge sonnet and its own surrounding poems—"Lady! the songs of Spring were in the grove" (number 17) and "It is a beauteous Evening, calm and free" (number 19)—in a reinforced sense of the sublimity attendant upon the internalization of the rhythm already subtly marked. Each begins in the local and mundane, yet discovers there a locus for the infinite, discovers beyond the fixed and known—like the ship embarking for an open ocean— an incarnate potentiality. The sonnets virtually explode from their access to power: a sleeping city is discovered to be animated by a "mighty heart" (14.14); a dormant winter garden is seized by "All the mighty ravishment of Spring" (17.14); the ocean beside which the poet and innocent child walk is both a "mighty being" and "awake" (19.6). The repeated adjective acknowledges dynamic force underlying all experience. These concluding sonnets of the sequence grandly expound the intrinsic value of even the slightest of the "Miscellaneous Sonnets," which is truly the same as Wordsworth's ringing assertion as he recalls crossing the Simplon Pass: "Our destiny, our being's heart and home, / Is with infinitude" (*Prelude,* 6.604– 605). However preoccupied with the things of this world, we are continually drawn forth to touch the infinite, reverting, as we must, to solid ground again. The Petrarchan system has been transfigured, its principles discovered to be those not of cosmology but of psychology. Of course, that had always been true, as Coleridge especially ought to have known.

Wordsworth not only reestablishes the underlying mode of Petrarchan thought within the sonnet but does so by eschewing the romantic and divine subjects by which that mode was conventionally expressed. If only by example, he suggests the innumerable ways in which the earthly and universal intersect, the infinite capacity of the mind to charge the mundane with spiritual import. The achievement is as brilliant on the one hand as it is, on the other, vernacularly conceived, the two poles of conception and execution in terms of their art wonderfully recreating the reach between the spiritually charged and the mundane. Yet, there is an even subtler aspect of this achievement, one directly related to the inner dynamics of the form Wordsworth employs. The Petrarchan sonnet, reduced to abstract principle, balances, as the Michelangelo sonnets so clearly demonstrate, here and there, finite and infinite, micro- and macrocosm. The tension existing between these poles empowers Wordsworth's series of "Miscellaneous Sonnets"; invariably, octave and sestet turn on some variation of this division. Whatever Coleridge in a momentary lapse of self-recognition may have thought improper about a sonnet's harboring "metaphysical abstractions," Wordsworth shows an extraordinary capacity to conceive the Petrarchan form with the eye of a geometrician, reducing it to its abstract relations before imagining it anew.

Recognizing the structural intricacies of the "Miscellaneous Sonnets," we should expect of the "Sonnets Dedicated to Liberty" a comparable richness of effect in the Miltonic mode. Unlike the variations on an abstract pattern that motivate the earlier series, these sonnets are organized in a narrative sequence, yet, if we try to pursue a simple line of plot through them, we immediately recognize their affinities with the *Lyrical Ballads* and *The Prelude*. For the true narrative is internalized, events serving as integers for the mental and imaginative growth discerned in the narrative voice.[13] As with the "Miscellaneous Sonnets," the prospect sonnet accentuates perspective. Wordsworth, whether deliberately or not, recapitulates the pattern that Bowles had popularized, extending his sonnet sequence as travelog into a public and political realm, so insistently forcing moral questions to the center of the observing consciousness that it becomes a conscience for its times. In the process, throughout the twenty-six-poem sequence that constituted the original "Sonnets Dedicated to Liberty," Wordsworth recaptures the tone and moral grandeur of Milton with an almost unerring touch, one inspired as much by past example as by present urgency.

With powerful effect Wordsworth incorporates the mixed emotions of his countrymen into the quandaries of the sequence. Written, except for the last poem, between May 1802 and October 1803 and insisting on this temporal framework through conspicuous dating, the poems reflect the general public ambivalence that accompanied the Peace of Amiens (25 March 1802 to 18 May 1803). After ten years of war England was financially strapped, physically exhausted, and morally dispirited; and yet, the Peace settled nothing. If anything, it threw into sharp relief the futility of the war abroad and the ignominy of an English state where financial speculation made fortunes for some while others were deprived of what had long been assumed to be constitutional rights. Relief over the cessation of war antithetically combined with disgust over the means of peace.

Wordsworth supplies no answers but rather confronts directly what in a rigorous analysis might be said to distinguish England from France. The evening star that shines over his homeland as he stands on the Calais beach in the first sonnet is greeted with patriotic emotion: "Fair Star of Evening, Splendour of the West, / Star of my Country!" (1.1–2). Yet, the subtle shift of syntax that follows presages the course of the ensuing sequence: "Thou, I think, / Shouldst be my Country's emblem" (1.5–6). By the middle of the sequence the star no longer represents his country, nor is it even perceived as participating in the times but is set apart in the distant memory of John Milton: "Thy soul was like a Star and dwelt apart" (14.9). As Lee Johnson has perceptively observed, the star of sonnet 1 is portrayed in nuptial terms, that of sonnet 14—"London, 1802"—is conceived elegiacally.[14] In the opening sonnet Wordsworth finds himself isolated in France

> with many a fear
> For my dear country, many heartfelt sighs,
> Among Men who do not love her.   (1.12–14)

The sense of separation intensifies as he looks upon Napoleon's election as First Consul with a disgust wholly opposite the jubilation felt a decade before when he witnessed the birth of the Republic. But rather than dissipating upon his return to England, his alienation only increases, as does his fear for his country, now reconceived as "a fen / Of stagnant waters" (14.2–3). "London, 1802," at the center of the sequence, records a nadir of despair. Paradoxically, this most famous of the "Sonnets Dedicated to Liberty" is not the independent statement about the nature of English society it is customarily perceived to be when isolated from the sequence, but a momentary and partial denunciation in the midst of a psychological progression. Indeed, it justifies its crucial point midway through the sequence by serving as a fulcrum from which the demoralized poet allows himself tentatively to assert a sober optimism about the future state of Europe.

The ostentation of riches, the cynical accumulation of wealth through the marketing of warfare, the moral indifference, appal the traveler who has returned from a corrupt state to celebrate Britain as the bastion of freedom, of "Plain living and high thinking" (13.11), as he expresses it in the sonnet preceding "London, 1802." Yet, in the succeeding sonnet Wordsworth recovers his voice through distinguishing the idea of England from its current degenerate state:

> Great Men have been among us; hands that penn'd
> And tongues that utter'd wisdom, better none:
> The later Sydney, Marvel, Harrington,
> Young Vane, and others who call'd Milton Friend.   (15.1–4)

Milton is a continuing presence in the culture of England: it is not just that he should be, but that he is, "living at this hour" (14.1), if only within the consciousness of the dispirited successor who calls upon his memory.

The sonnet that marks that despair remarks as well its antidote. The second half of the sonnet sequence recovers motive force through the incorporation of Milton as abiding genius within it. The sequence does not simply pay tribute to Milton; it regains its sense of purpose and integrity, both cultural perspective and inner assurance, through incorporating Milton's voice and vision. If it is true that "by the soul / Only the Nations shall be great and free" (11.13–14), Wordsworth discovers his country's soul not in venal speculators who look to momentary advantage but in a consciousness that presides over the past and prefigures the future. Moreover, exactly what the presence of Milton allows Wordsworth is the perspective by which to free himself from his own trap in the momentary. The early group of poems that look beyond the particular confrontation of the French and English—"On the Extinction of the Venetian Republic," "The King of Sweden," and "To Toussaint L'Ouverture" (numbers 6 through 8)—implicitly affirm that civilized, humane values are superior to the vicissitudes of time. Venice can be oppressed but can never lose its force as a model of civilization; and, if failure is evident in this instance, new successes can be observed at the opposite extreme of Europe: the Swedish king

>   stands *above*
>   All consequences: work he hath begun
>   Of fortitude, and piety, and love.   (7.10–12)

Thus, as the succeeding poem argues, it makes no ultimate difference what will be the precise fate of Toussaint L'Ouverture, revolutionary leader of the newly independent Haiti now ironically languishing in a French prison. He, too, is "*above* all consequences," elevated to the realm where Milton will also be found to exist, among "exultations, agonies, / And love, and Man's unconquerable mind" (8.13–14).

Though the last of the "Sonnets Dedicated to Liberty" appear to fall off from this grandeur, as fears of French invasion prompt from Wordsworth conventional tributes to the yeomanry of England, those tributes are themselves the testaments to a regained faith in his countrymen and bring the sequence, except for its 1806 postscript, back around to the patriotic fears with which it began in the first sonnet. The spherical sonnet emulated by Wordsworth is thus translated into the structure of the sequence. But not utterly; the shift of syntax discernible in the opening sonnet is recapitulated in the structure as a whole. The final sonnet not only brings the sequence into rough contemporaneity with the point of publication but, through its sense of England's isolation in the Napoleonic Wars, demands that the true mettle of his culture show itself. The sestet balances the alternatives on the fulcrum of a conditional clause, an enabling possibility, but only if Miltonic virtues can be incorporated by a resolute people:

> We shall exult, if They who rule the land
> Be Men who hold its many blessings dear,
> Wise, upright, valiant; not a venal Band,
> Who are to judge of danger which they fear,
> And honour which they do not understand. (26.10–14)

The final line, with its unresolved ambivalence poised on a razor-thin edge, exactly mirrors the moral and intellectual construction of the entire sequence of "Sonnets Dedicated to Liberty."

These are public statements, but they are also notably self-reflexive. Infused with the power of his mentor, Wordsworth discovers himself and his vision renewed in the process. The sonnets record the process of their own creation, a coming to vision by discovering the mental preconceptions necessary to utter the Miltonic voice, to write a Miltonic sonnet. No less than the "Miscellaneous Sonnets" are the Miltonic "Sonnets Dedicated to Liberty" psychological in their orientation. What begins as a simple, if extreme, polarization of France and England soon prompts an inner division—one between the temptation to despair and the duty to hope, between the issue of the moment and the liberty not subject to time, between the alienated poet and the mentor whom he projects from himself and who speaks for the highest ideals of his culture. Wordsworth creates the greatest of neo-Miltonic sonnet sequences through the profound imagining of what Milton would have required of the poet who would emulate him. And yet the same might be said of Wordsworth's sense of the more distant Petrarch. Once we distinguish the styles and characteristic conceptions of the two poets that Wordsworth inherits, we should recognize the remarkable extent to which, however distinct the two traditions are—the one emphasizing links between the mundane and supernal, the other between individual and cultural values—they share common features that themselves make the two sonnet sequences aspects of one great and revitalizing whole that subsumes them within its commanding mental structure. The imaginative rhythm of the "Miscellaneous Sonnets" is in its essential drive the same urge that motivates the "Sonnets Dedicated to Liberty."

To concentrate at such length on these sonnet sequences is to reveal them as microcosmic of how the *Poems, in Two Volumes* is ordered and the aims it serves. With few exceptions the poems are brief, "moods of the mind," an apparently random yoking of isolated moments of contemplation. But in placing them within sequences like the "Sonnets Dedicated to Liberty" or within sections unified by underlying patterns like the "Poems Composed during a Tour, Chiefly on Foot," Wordsworth emphasizes the mental impulse of patterning itself. The repeated principle of the "Miscellaneous Sonnets," imaginative projection and return, is the poetic impulse in the abstract, binding the poet to the world around him, constantly renewing his sense of wonder at that world and, through identification with it, at his own mind. "To and fro" the imagination ranges among experiences, each poem being at once a celebration of human ordering and a testament to mental renewal, each momentary order figuring forth large patterns that transcend the temporal even as they are thus dependent upon it for their existence. And what is so for the poet is, in a complementary way, true as well for the reader who is drawn by identification to discern the complex of patterning and to become mentally renewed in the process of a further self-projection and return.

Within such a perspective the dialectical patterning of the *Poems, in Two Volumes* seems remarkably similar to the dynamics of the great dialectical narrative that was composed largely at the same time, *The Prelude*, reinforcing the truth of Wordsworth's analogy of his work, in the Preface to *The Excursion*, to a Gothic cathedral. It was that analogy that led him to restructure all of his shorter poems in presenting the collected edition of 1815; and yet one may surely wonder whether the rubrics used then and from that point on by the poet represent a true advance over the patterns that empower these two volumes of 1807. The later divisions codify abstractions, truly divide, whereas the fluid movement among contraries of the *Poems, in Two Volumes* suggests a unifying rhythm in the poet's self-consciousness, natural, spontaneous, encompassing the ephemeral and the visionary, attaining to vision through the very process of honoring the transitory.

That, finally, is the stance of the "Intimations Ode," which in its recognition of the cost of experience has seemed to many readers to overwhelm its uneasy acceptance of the "philosophic mind" (line 189) at the end. And yet the "Ode," written almost last among these poems, seems, like "Tintern Abbey," to have been deliberately conceived as a summary statement, dependent for its full effect on the 113 poems preceding it. Its worries over diminishing powers are counterbalanced by the abundant powers everywhere manifest. Its sense of how easy it is for "Shades of the prison-house

[to] . . . close / Upon the growing Boy" (lines 67–68) is relieved by our recognition that the adult imaginative projection patterned throughout the volumes is in its very principle liberating. The spring jubilee Wordsworth celebrates at the inception of the poem is everywhere enacted along that orchard pathway he walked at the beginning of the first volume, and the freshness of response in the poems on natural creatures and phenomena testifies to the truth of his assertion, "My heart is at your festival" (line 39).

But the grave undertones of the "Intimations Ode" are also everywhere present in the earlier poems. Even in the simplest of these celebrations, in the retrospect of the "Ode," we glean a cautionary insight, as if the poems were evidence of a continual mental therapy designed to insure imaginative vitality, to forestall that moment when the poet must acknowledge that "The things which I have seen I now can see no more" (line 9). The earlier poems comprise by their self-conscious tribute to the momentary the very continuity of "obstinate questionings / Of sense and outward things, / Fallings from us, vanishings" (lines 144–46) that the "Ode" so powerfully confronts. Their dialectical rhythms are in the aggregate both broad and dynamic, exhilarating and dangerous, and Wordsworth refuses to narrow them or deny their full energy in encompassing them within his poem. The almost unendurable maturity of the "Intimations Ode," he implies, is already present in the most simple-minded moment of identification with a butterfly or a rainbow, for each such moment is a record of that "primal sympathy / Which having been must ever be" (lines 184–85). The *Poems, in Two Volumes* adheres with radical insistence to that perspective, documenting thus obliquely to *The Prelude* how such sympathy is responsible for, imperative to, "the Growth of a Poet's Mind." What is most to be prized in this collection, it might be said, is exactly what Jeffrey detested in it: no other poet has ever written the small so very large or been so true to the value of its inner, absolute life.

NOTES

1. Francis Jeffrey had his first opportunity to catch Wordsworth on his own and made use of the occasion for a broad attack in the *Edinburgh Review* 11 (October 1807). Interestingly, Lord Byron, who was also continually to decry Wordsworth's "system," also reviewed the two-volume collection in *Monthly Literary Recreations* 3 (July 1807). These notices are conveniently reprinted in Donald H. Reiman, ed. *The Romantics Reviewed* (New York: Garland Publishing, 1972), part A, vol. 2: 437–38; 661–62.

2. William Wordsworth, *Poems, in Two Volumes, and Other Poems, 1800–1807*, ed.

Jared Curtis (Ithaca: Cornell University Press, 1983). However daunting to the uninitiated is Curtis's elaborate apparatus, his edition for the first time allows one to determine the evolution of the contents, organization, and texts of these poems. Before it appeared, the student was forced to revert to the not readily available facsimile editions prepared by Thomas Hutchinson (London: David Nutt, 1897) and Helen Darbishire (Oxford: Clarendon, 1914) or to trace the original texts through the apparatus scattered through the five-volume de Selincourt-Darbishire edition (Oxford: Clarendon Press, 1940–49), a much more daunting task than is posed by the Curtis edition. This estimable text is cited here for all quotations from Wordsworth's *Poems, in Two Volumes.*

3. See James Averill, "The Shape of *Lyrical Ballads* (1798)," *Philological Quarterly* 60 (1981): 387–407, and Neil Fraistat, "The 'Field' of *Lyrical Ballads* (1798)," in *The Poem and the Book: Interpreting Collections of Romantic Poetry* (Chapel Hill and London: The University of North Carolina Press, 1985), pp. 47–94.

4. The initial epigraph is from *Culex,* ll. 8–9, now considered apocryphal. The tag from the *Fourth Eclogue* accentuates the continuity between the natural spontaneities of pastoral celebrated through the *Poems, in Two Volumes* and their cultural and psychological ramifications.

5. For this and all such questions concerning the development of the text, see Curtis's introduction, *Poems, in Two Volumes,* pp. 3–49.

6. For this background, which is distilled here, see my extended discussion of the history of the Romantic sonnet in *Poetic Form and British Romanticism* (New York: Oxford University Press, 1986).

7. Published in *The European Magazine* 40 (1787): 202, under the pseudonym "Axiologus," this sonnet constituted Wordsworth's debut in print and, though recalled with wry amusement later, was never reprinted by him. For the text, see *Poetical Works,* ed. Ernest de Selincourt (Oxford: Clarendon Press, 1940–49), 1:269.

8. This notebook, now known as DC MS.44, survives in an incomplete state, but its contents and order have been shrewdly resuscitated in the prefatory matter and appendix I of Curtis's edition of *Poems, in Two Volumes.*

9. Three copies of the pamphlet survive: in the Cornell University Library, the Huntington Library, and the Victoria and Albert Museum. Paul M. Zall has analyzed its contents in "Coleridge and 'Sonnets from Various Sources'," *Cornell Library Journal* (1967): 48–62, and has reprinted both this essay and the pamphlet in *Coleridge's "Sonnets from Various Authors"* (Glendale, Calif.: La Siesta Press, 1968). The preface, slightly revised and entitled "Introduction to the Sonnets," is to be found on pp. 71–74 of Coleridge's *Poems, to which are now added Poems by Charles Lamb and Charles Lloyd* (Bristol, 1797), a volume containing thirty-seven sonnets by the three authors. Quotations from the preface refer to this edition as being the most practically available.

10. *Letters of William and Dorothy Wordsworth: The Early Years, 1787–1805,* ed. Ernest de Selincourt, 2nd ed., rev. Chester L. Shaver (Oxford: Clarendon Press, 1967), p. 367; *Letters: The Later Years, 1821–1834,* ed. Ernest de Selincourt, 2nd ed., rev. Alan G. Hill (Oxford: Clarendon Press, 1978–79), 2:652–53.

11. The opening line of the "Prefatory Sonnet," which was written about the same time as the first passage quoted from the letters, clearly reflects the same notion. Compare "Nuns fret not at their Convent's narrow room" to the "narrow room" in which the poet crowds his effects.

12. In his remarkable analysis of these poems in a letter to Lady Beaumont of 21 May 1807, Wordsworth uses the second of these sonnets on ships (number 8) as exemplary text; but his explicit acknowledgment of the dynamics of identification and differentiation apply to number 2 as well: see *Letters: The Middle Years,* ed. Ernest de Selincourt, 2nd ed. rev. Mary Moorman (Oxford: Clarendon Press, 1969), 1:148–49.

13. Wordsworth emphasizes the "weight" of this sequence in the letter to Lady Beaumont of 21 May 1807: De Selincourt and Moorman, *Letters: The Middle Years,* 1:147.

14. Lee M. Johnson, *Wordsworth and the Sonnet,* Anglistica 19 (Copenhagen: Rosenkilde and Bagger, 1973), p. 49.

Jerome J. McGann
The Book of Byron and the Book of a World

Byron wrote about himself, we all know, just as we all know that his books, like God's human creatures, are all made in his image and likeness. This quality of his work is apparent from the very beginning. His first book, *Fugitive Pieces,* was privately printed in 1806 for an audience of friends and acquaintances who were privy to its local references and biographical connections—many of which were connections with themselves. *Hours of Idleness,* his first published work, appeared the following year, and it sought to extend the range of Byron's intimacies to a somewhat larger book purchasing audience. In *Hours of Idleness* Byron projected himself before his English audience as a recognizable figure whom, he trusted, they would be happy to take to their breasts. In *Hours of Idleness* the English world at large met, for the first time, not the Man but the Lord of Feeling, a carefully constructed self-image that was fashioned to launch him on his public career. This was not conceived, at the time, as a literary career.[1]

Byron succeeded in his effort, though not precisely as he had expected. Certain hostile reviews—most notoriously, Brougham's in the highly visible and influential *Edinburgh Review*—interrupted Byron's initial, unruffled expectations. Had he reflected more critically on the hostile reception that *Fugitive Pieces* had provoked in certain narrow quarters of its local (Southwell) society, he might have anticipated some trouble for his next book.[2] But he did not, apparently, and seems only to have realized later that he was destined to be both the darling and the demon of his age.

The attack on *Hours of Idleness* was another opportunity for Byron to produce yet a third Book of Himself: this time, *English Bards and Scotch Reviewers,* the fiery counter-attack on his persecutors and the culture that supported such beings.[3] If it is true that Byron was "born for opposition," this book revealed that fact, for the first time unmistakably.

And so it went on. In 1809 Byron left benighted England to chew over the high rhetoric of his last book, and he plunged into Europe and the Levant, where his next productions began to accumulate their materials in the much larger context of European affairs. He wrote a continuation, or sequel, to *English Bards and Scotch Reviewers* called *Hints from Horace,* which was not published in his lifetime, and he composed the first two cantos of that unsurpassed act of literary self-creation, *Childe Harold's Pilgrimage. A Romaunt.*[4]

This book is worth pausing over—not the poem, but the book.[5] It is a handsome and rather expensive (30s.) quarto volume beautifully printed on heavy paper. It comprises four distinct parts: (1) the title poem in two cantos (pp. iii–109); (2) the extensive notes to these cantos (pp. 111–61); (3) a section headed "Poems" that included fourteen short pieces (pp. 163–200); (4) an appendix containing bibliographical materials, translations, Romaic transcriptions, and one facsimile MS, all having to do with the current state of the literary culture of modern Greece (pp. 201–[27]). Its publisher conceived its audience to be a wealthy one, people interested in travel books and topographical poems, people with a classical education and with a taste for antiquarian lore and the philosophical musings of a young English lord. As it turned out, all of England and Europe were to be snared by this book's imaginations. It went through a dozen (cheaper) editions in three years and established all of the principal features of that imaginative (but not imaginary) world-historical figure known as Byron. Later circumstances would only provide the public with slightly different perspectives on this figure.

The book of *Childe Harold* published in 1812 picks up the autobiographical myth that Byron had left *in medias res* when he left England in 1809.[6] The notes specifically recall the controversy surrounding *English Bards and Scotch Reviewers,* the section of "Poems" is so arranged as to mirror the personal tale narrated through the title poem, and the latter presents a dramatic picture of a young lord who leaves his local home and friends, as well as his country, in a condition of psychic and cultural alienation. Simply, he is disgusted with himself and the world as he has thus far seen it. He finds, when he flees to other lands and in particular to the fabulous Levantine seat of western culture, that his own personal anomie, experienced in the tight little island of Britain, mirrors the condition of Europe (or, in Byron's startling and important variation on this ancient topos, that Europe and the entire world mirrors *his* personal condition). Thus does Byron force himself—and the individual person through himself—to the center of attention. What his book says is not simply that we should deplore the condition of western culture in this critical time, but that we should deplore it because its debasement has poisoned its chief, indeed, its only, value: the individual human life. In particular, Byron's life.

Byron inserts his personal history into the latest phase of the European crisis that began in 1789. The outbreak of the Peninsular War in 1809 initiated the last act in the drama of the Napoleonic Wars, which would end in the defeat of Napoleon and the restoration of the European monarchies under the hegemony of England. In *Childe Harold* (1812) Byron's itinerary takes him first to the very heart of the Peninsular events, where his initial mood of disgust at his English existence acquires its European dimensions. When he moves to the East and the dominions of the Turkish Empire, including Greece, his cynicism is confirmed: Greece, the very symbol of the west's highest ideals and self-conceptions, lies in thrall not merely to the military rule of the Porte but to the contest of self-serving political interests of the English, French, and Russians.

This is the context that explains Byron's peculiar appendix, with its heterogeneous body of Romaic materials. *Childe Harold* (1812) is obsessed with the idea of the renewal of human culture in the west at a moment of its deepest darkness. This means for Byron the renewal of the value of the individual person, and the renewal of Greece as an independent political entity becomes Byron's "objective correlative" for this idea. *Childe Harold* (1812) is thus, on the one hand, a critique of present European society and politics and, on the other, a pronouncement of the crucial need throughout Europe for the independence of Greece. As Byron would later say: "There is *no* freedom—even for *Masters*—in the midst of slaves."[7] The question of Greece thus becomes for Byron a way of focusing the central questions that bear upon the present European epoch. The Europeans normally date this epoch from 1789, and rightly so, but in this book (as well as in his next two books, *The Giaour* and *The Bride of Abydos*), Byron argues that the conflict of European self-interests can be best and most clearly understood in terms of the recent history of Greece, whose abortive efforts for independence in the late eighteenth century were either neglected by the European powers or actively betrayed.

Thus, in *Childe Harold* (1812) Byron enlarged his personal myth, which he had already begun to develop in his earlier books, by inserting it into the wider context of the European political theatre as it appeared to him in 1809–1812. The central ideological focus of the entire myth involves the question of personal and political freedom in the oppressive and contradictory circumstances that Byron observed in the world of his experience. More than anything else this book says that the most personal and intimate aspects of an individual's life are closely involved with, and affected by, the social and political context in which the individual is placed. Byron goes further to say that such a context is more complex and extensive than one ordinarily thinks, that each person is more deeply affected by (as it were) invisible people, places, and events than we customarily imagine. Ali Pacha and his Albanians may appear far removed from England and the Napoleonic Wars, but to the perspicacious European they will have more than a merely exotic interest. Similarly, Byron's rather ostentatious use of antiquarian and classical materials is not merely a clumsy display of learning and artistic pedantry. On the contrary, Byron invokes the classical world and the later history of Europe's investment in that world because this complex ideological and political network impinges directly upon current European affairs and hence on the experience of each single person living in Europe. A powerful and illuminating irony runs through Byron's flight from contemporary England and Europe and his pursuit of ancient Greek ideals:

> Of the ancient Greeks we know more than enough; at least the younger men of Europe devote much of their time to the study of Greek writers and history, which would be more usefully spent in mastering their own. Of the moderns, we are perhaps more neglectful than they deserve; and while every man of any pretensions to learning is tiring out his youth, and often his age, in the study of the language and of the harangues of the Athenian demogogues in favour of freedom, the real or supposed descendants of these sturdy republicans are left to the actual tyranny of their masters. . . . (p. 143)

Byron's proposal in his book is to look at England, Europe, and Greece, not as these political entities appear in their ideological self-representations, but "as they are" (p. 144) in fact. The reality reveals an Islam and a modern Greece very different from what they are commonly represented to be in English and European commentaries; it also reveals the hypocritical fault lines that run through the high-minded and Greek-derived ideologies of liberty to which the major European powers give lip-service. In Byron's book, the image of the young European gentleman acquiring a classical education is contradictory and deeply satiric. Such a person's mind is filled with self-congratulating and self-deluding ideas that permit him to identify with the dream of ancient Greece even as they also allow him to remain blind to certain important actualities: that the Russians "have twice . . . deceived and abandoned" the Greeks; that the French seek "the deliverance of continental Greece" as part of their policy for "the subjugation of the rest of Europe"; and that the English, in addition to the pursuit of their economic self-interests, profess to seek the freedom of Greece even as they subjugate the rights of "our Irish Helots" (p. 161) and "Catholic brethren" (p. 143).

In Byron's books—*Childe Harold* (1812) is merely prototypical in this respect—the variety of materials often conveys an image of heterogeneity, but in fact this image is no more than the sign of intrinsic connections that are not normally perceived, of connections between "opposite and discordant" matters that only *appear* to be separated but that are in fact fundamentally related. The soon-to-be-published Oriental Tales are not merely a set of exotic adventure stories. They constitute a series of symbolic historical and political meditations on current European ideology and politics in the context of the relations between East and West after the breakup of the Roman Empire and the emergence of Islam.[8] That later readers and critics have often taken Byron's Levantine materials as a sign of a (presumptively shallow) poetic interest in local color and oriental ornamentation merely testifies to a failure of critical intelligence and historical consciousness. Byron was deeply interested in these social and political questions and he used his poetry to probe their meaning and their roots. Later criticism has too often translated *its* disinterest into a myth of the intellectual poverty of Byron's verse.

Byron's skill at manipulating his publications produced some of the strangest and most interesting books of poetry ever printed in England. *The Giaour* may stand as one example out of many.[9] Like the other tales that were soon to follow, this poem is a political allegory told from the point of view of those "younger men of Europe" whom Byron described in the notes to *Childe Harold* (1812). The subject of the poem, at the plot level, is the state of modern Greece around 1780. At the narrative level, the poem is a contemporary (1809–13) meditation on the meaning of the European (and especially the English) understanding of Levantine politics between 1780 and 1813. The poem's story (its plot level) is a nihilistic tragedy in which all parties are involved and destroyed. The meditation on the story is carried most dramatically in the introductory 167 lines, which appear as the "original" work of the poem's redactor (Byron himself), as well as in the poem's "Advertisement" and its many prose notes, also represented in *The Giaour* as the "original" work of the editor/redactor Byron. The entire significance of this excellent work does not appear unless one responds to the interplay between the poem's two "levels." Briefly, the "original" work of the editor/redactor comprises a set of deeply contradictory materials: on the one hand, a complete romantic sympathy with the characters and events as well as an absorption in the heroic ideology that they exhibit; on the other, a mordant series of comical remarks on Eastern mores and commonplace European ideas about such matters. This radical split in the poem's attitude at its meditative level reflects back upon, and interprets, the European understanding of the Levant between 1780 and 1813. The interpretation that Byron produces is a critical one: the European understanding is self-deluded and helpless, and Byron's own exposure of this failed understanding is represented as the one-eyed man's vision in the kingdom of the blind. The comedy of the poem's notes, apparently so urbane, is in fact a flinching away, the laughter, spoken of in *Don Juan,* that serves to hold back weeping and bleaker realities.

All of Byron's works, and especially his published books, exhibit intersections of these kinds. Thus, his bibliography is more than a scholar's guide and resource, it is as well a graphic display of his life in books and of the extension of his life through books. The piracies, the huge number of translations, the numerous printings all attest and perpetuate the poetic explorations of reality that he initially set in motion. And it is the "books," rather than the "poems" (or least of all the "texts"), that draw attention to the central quality of Byron's poetical work; for when we study the works through their material existences we are helped to see and understand the social and historical ground that defines their human meanings.

Nowhere is this fact about Byron's work more clear than in the case of his masterwork, *Don Juan.* We respond to its name as if it were one thing, as indeed it is; but it is also, like the world it expresses and represents, incredibly various and polyglottal. Readers have of course always responded to that variety, but we must do so even as we also bear in mind that the variety is of a determinate and specifiable sort. *Don Juan* is, formally, a romantic fragment poem comprising six authorized and published volumes, along with a body of material that was not published until after Byron's death, at different times and with various justifications. The first two volumes were published by John Murray in a certain way, and the next four volumes were published by John Hunt in a very different way. Important aspects of the meaning of the poem are bound up with these interesting events in the work's publication history.[10]

Most important to see is that when Byron began publishing the poem with John Hunt he was released from certain constraints that he had to struggle against when he was publishing with the conservative house of Murray. *Don Juan*'s (rejected) preface and (suppressed) dedication emphasize the political and social critique that is finally so fundamental to the poem.[11] But Murray and his allies forced Byron to revise the published version of the first five cantos so as to *de*-emphasize this aspect of the epic. As a consequence, the original cantos 1–5 (the first two published volumes of the poem) preserve the poem's social and political critique as a peripheral and subsidiary matter, an incidental topic that seems to appear and disappear in the poem in a random way. The suppressed dedication was not published until 1832, and the rejected preface did not appear until 1901.

With the appearance of cantos 6–8, published by Hunt, the situation changes radically. These cantos are introduced with a prose preface where the social and political issues are finally raised to a great, even to a dominant, position; and the poetic materials as well undergo a shift in emphasis toward more explicitly social and political matters. This change in the poem has been recognized for some time and critics have described the differences between the earlier and the later cantos in various (often useful) ways. What has not been seen, however, is the structural change brought about in the poem as a whole when Byron began his epic "again" (as it were) with cantos 6–8 and John Hunt.

We can begin to see what is involved here by looking briefly at the original preface to cantos 1–2. Byron never completed this preface, which descends to us in his fragmentary draft MS. Nevertheless, what he did complete gives us some interesting information about Byron's initial conception of his work. In the course of satirizing Wordsworth, Byron tells his readers that "the following epic Narrative" is to be regarded as the work of a certain "Story-teller" who is living, and delivering his narrative, at a certain place and time: specifically, "in a village in the Sierra Morena on the road between Monasterio and Seville" sometime during the Peninsular War (the reference to the village in the Sierra Morena is autobiographical and specifies the date as 1809). As for the narrator himself, "The Reader is . . . requested to suppose him . . . either an Englishman settled in Spain—or a Spaniard who had travelled in England—perhaps one of the Liberals who have subsequently been so liberally rewarded by Ferdinand of grateful memory—for his restoration."[12] This passage establishes a second point of view on the events treated in the poem: that is, one subsequent to 1814 and the early years of the period of European restoration following the fall of Napoleon. As it turns out, the reader inevitably places this historical vantage point at that moment of contemporaneity that attaches to the poem's date of composition and/or publication (in this case, 1818–19).

Byron finally dropped his preface with its specific historical perspectives, and he did not fully exploit the structural advantages of his poem's double perspectivism until he began to reconceive the project of *Don Juan* in 1822–23. Before considering that act of reconception, however, we should reflect upon the double historical perspective in terms of which the work was initially conceived and set in motion. Like the later cantos, cantos 1–5 organize their materials in two dialectically functioning historical frames of reference: on the one hand, the frame of the poem's plot or "story," which contains the narrated events of Juan's life; and, on the other hand, the frame of the poem's narrating voice, which comprises Byron speaking to his world between 1818 and 1824 via the six published volumes of *Don Juan*. Byron's rejected and incomplete preface to cantos 1-2 reminds us that he initially had some idea of using the plot level and the narrative level to comment on each other and that he thought of Juan's life in specific historical terms. As it turned out, he rejected the idea of setting the poem's narrative frame in the complicated way suggested by the initial preface, where it is unclear whether the narrator speaks from the vantage of 1809 or 1818, or both. In cantos 1-5 Byron also neglected to specify clearly the historical frame in which Juan's career is placed. When he published cantos 6–8 with John Hunt, however, he finally let his contemporary readers see very clearly the exact relation between the history of Juan's career and the history of the poem's narrator, Byron *in propria persona*.

We can date Byron's reconception of his epic fairly exactly; in January and February 1822, which is the period when Byron resumed his composition of *Don Juan* (he left off his poem when he finished canto 5 at the end of 1820). Byron wrote to Murray on 16 February 1821 (*BLJ*, 8.78) and outlined a projected plot for Juan's adventures.[13] This outline, however, only corresponds in a loose and general way to the episodes of the poem that he was soon to write and hence shows that Byron had not yet fixed on a definite plan. Byron first articulated this plan to Medwin between December 1821 and March 1822:

> I left him [Juan] in the seraglio. There I shall make one of the favourites, a Sultana . . . fall in love with him, and carry him off from Constantinople. . . . Well, they make good their escape to Russia; where, if Juan's passion cools, and I don't know what to do with the lady, I shall make her die of the plague. . . . As our hero can't do without a mistress, he shall next become man-mistress to Catherine the Great. . . . I shall . . . send him, when he is *hors de combat,* to England as her ambassador. In his suite he shall have a girl whom he shall have rescued during one of his northern campaigns, who shall be in love with him, and he not with her. . . . I shall next draw a town and country life at home. . . . He shall get into all sorts of

scrapes, and at length end his career in France. Poor Juan shall be guillotined in the French Revolution! What do you think of my plot? It shall have twenty-four books too. . . .[14]

This scheme corresponds fairly closely to the poem as we now have it, and it holds to the general plan that Byron gave to Murray at the beginning of 1821 (though not to the particular details of the episodes). The most important episode missing from Byron's outline is the siege of Ismail, though it is clear from this and Byron's immediately preceding discussion that he planned to send Juan into war. But in the first few months of 1822 Byron seems not yet to have decided on the Ismail episode, as he had not yet worked out how to separate Juan and Gulbeyaz. These decisions would be made in the next few months. The idea of having Juan die on the guillotine in the French Revolution was certainly fundamental to the plot of the poem from the earliest stages of its conception as a plotted sequence.

The preface to cantos 6–8, written in September 1822, calls attention, on the one hand, to the historical immediacy of the poem as it is Byron's act of discourse with his world and, on the other, to the specific (past) historical nexus in which Byron's story of Juan's career is imbedded. The second part of the preface is a bitter diatribe against Castlereagh, who had recently taken his own life, against the present condition of Europe under the restored thrones and their allied policies, and against those like Southey who were at once supporters of these institutions and detractors of Byron's recent work. The opening sentences of the preface, on the other hand, tell us that the material in cantos 7 and 8 is based upon an actual event: the siege of Ismail by the Russians in November–December 1790. The latter was the chief episode in the (latest) Russo-Turkish War, which had been renewed in 1787. The preface tells the reader, in other words, that Juan's career in Byron's poem is unfolding within real historical time, and—specifically—that we are to map his career in terms of specific places, dates, and events. When Juan goes to Catherine's court after the siege of Ismail, the date is early 1791. Shortly afterwards he goes to England.

Clearly, then, Byron's projected scheme for the plot of Juan's career was actually being implemented when Byron renewed the poem's composition at the beginning of 1822. That he was preparing Juan for a trip to Paris and death on the guillotine in 1793 at the end of the poem is borne out by the fulfillment of the other details that he gave to Medwin, as well as by the chronology of Juan's exploits established in the siege of Ismail episode.[15] We should note that this precise dating of Juan's life in the poem accommodates itself to the events of cantos 1–6. Byron had not, before the preface to cantos 6–8, forced his audience to read the events of cantos 1–6 within a specific historical frame of reference. After the preface, however, those events are drawn into the poem's newly defined historical scheme. Juan's life in Byron's poem begins in Seville just as the French Revolution has broken out, or is about to break out. His life will end at the end of Byron's poem, and the date for him will be 1793.

Lacking the precise historical frame that Byron established for his poem in 1822, Juan's career would appear episodic, the verse equivalent of the fictional careers of characters in Smollett, Sterne, and Fielding.[16] The exact historical placement changes the situation dramatically. Juan at first appears to move through Byron's poem in a picaresque fashion, but as the poem develops and his life is brought into ever-closer relations with the great and epochal events shaking Europe in the early 1790s, the reader begins to glimpse an order, or perhaps a fate, that was not at first evident or even suspected. Having Juan die in the Reign of Terror at the end of Byron's poem is a daring conception: on the one hand, it seems a surprising, even an arbitrary, end for Byron's inoffensive hero, but, on the other, it calls attention to a hidden constellation of forces drawing together far-flung and apparently unrelated people and events. History proceeds "according to the mighty working" of forces that gather up the odd and the disparate, and historical explanation, in Byron, proceeds according to the mighty working of a poem that *reveals* these odd and unapparent connections.

Not least of all does it reveal the connections that hold between the pan-European world of 1787–93 and its counterpart in 1818–24. The revolutionary epoch in which Juan's career begins and ends is explicitly examined from the vantage of the period of Europe's restoration. Juxtaposing these two worlds allows each to comment on the other. More crucially for the poem, however, the juxtaposition gives Byron the opportunity to expose certain congruences between these periods and to suggest that the second period is a variant repetition of the first. These congruences are established via the third historical frame that gives a structure to *Don Juan*: the period in which the Book of Byron was initially composed, and more especially the central years of that period, 1809 to 1817/18.

The congruences appear most dramatically as a series of related and repeating sequences of gain and loss, rise and fall, triumph and disaster. Juan's career illustrates this pattern both in its particular episodes and in the larger scheme that Byron projected for his hero. Adversative forces of various kinds interrupt and thwart Juan's plans and hopes. Some of these are represented as his responsibility while others originate in external circumstances over which he can have no control. In both cases, the pattern of an early promise that later fails or is betrayed appears in Juan's life as well as in the course of the French Revolution. Juan's life follows the moral arc of the revolution even as his career follows its early chronological development. But what is most important, so far as Byron's poem is concerned, is that both of these sequences recur in the next generation. The second phase of the revolution is dominated by the rise and fall of Napoleon, whose professed aim (at any rate) was to establish the revolution on a secure European footing. The consequence of his career was, on the contrary, the final defeat of the revolution's historic agenda. This repetition, in Napoleon's life, of the historical course of the early years of the revolution appears in Byron's poem through its autobiographical analogue: the meteoric rise and subsequent fall of Lord Byron, a series of events that we—following Byron—associate with the years 1809–1817/18. In Byron's and Napoleon's careers the reader of *Don Juan* observes, once again, the pattern established in Juan's life and in the course of the early revolution.

Following his self-exile from England in 1816 Byron meditated on the meaning of this pattern in his life and on its relation to similar patterns in past and contemporary history. The most important of these meditations comes down to us as *Childe Harold's Pilgrimage,* canto 4, which Byron completed shortly before he began *Don Juan.* Here Byron decides that all history, when judged by meliorist or revolutionary standards, is a story of disaster and unsuccess. What he also decides, however, is that against this fatal and repeating story may be, and has been, placed the deed of the opposing mind and will, the individual voice which, while it recognizes the evil pattern, refuses to accept or assent to it.

> Yet, Freedom! yet thy banner, torn, but flying,
>   Streams like the thunder-storm *against* the wind;
> Thy trumpet voice, though broken now and dying,
>   The loudest still the tempest leaves behind.
>
>   (*CHP* 4, stanza 98)

> Yet let us ponder boldly—'tis a base
>   Abandonment of reason to resign
> Our right of thought—our last and only place
>   Of refuge. . . .
>
>   (*CHP* 4, stanza 127)

These attitudes establish the ground on which *Don Juan* comes to judge the patterns of historical repetition. Byron begins the poem from the vantage of 1818, a point in European history when time appears to have rolled back upon itself. Thirty years have passed, yet the enormous upheavals that marked those years seem to have returned the European world virtually to the same political position that it occupied in 1788. Furthermore, Byron observes in this period a series of repetitions that suggest that the cycle of revolutionary disappointment is a general pattern that is found in many historical periods and is replicated for the individual as well as for society. In terms of the narrator's historical frame (1818–24), *Don Juan* is yet another revolutionary undertaking begun in a period of darkness. As such, the bleak patterns of repetition over which the Byron of 1818–24 will brood—the pattern of Juan's career and the early phase of the revolution, the pattern of Byron's career and the Napoleonic wars—threaten the narrative project of 1818–24 with a fearful end.

Byron begins *Don Juan* already knowing that individual and social history, from a revolutionary point of view, always follows a curve of disappointment or disaster. In this sense (but only in this sense) the poem is "nihilistic." In every other respect the poem is a great work of hope, for it insists that projects of change and renewal must continue to be raised up despite the fact of absolute adversity. The Byron who set *Don Juan* in motion understands that the eye begins to see only in a dark time, and—more crucially—that there never is a time that is or was not dark. Those who seek not merely to understand the world, but to change it, strive toward an ideal of human life that will have to be "anywhere out of the world." This is the strife of *Don Juan*'s hope, the deed of its mind—the fact of its books. The poem begins its quest for renewal under its own prophecy of failure, and it seeks to persuade its readers that one begins in this way simply because there is no other place *to* begin, that the renewal arrives with the event, not in the end. For in the end you lose, always.

Thus Byron begins his poem in 1818 by calling for a new hero to take the place of all the failed heroes of the past and, in particular, of all the failed heroes of the preceding revolutionary epoch. Byron catalogues their names in canto 1 only to toss them aside in favor of "our friend, Don Juan," whose history he purposes to tell. As we have seen, however, and as every reader of the poem has always recognized, that fictive history recollects and alludes, at every point, to the actual history of Lord Byron, who is the poem's true "hero" and central figure. Juan's progress from Seville to the Levant, and thence via Russia to England and (prospectively) to Paris and his death, is shadowed by the actual career of Byron. In fact, Juan's career is no more than a displaced re-presentation of Byron's, a coded fiction through which the reader may glimpse the friends, enemies, and the incidents of Byron's life, as well as the patterns and epochs of that life. The English cantos, at the level of the poem's plot, should be located in the summer and early autumn of 1791; at the level of the poem's recollective autobiographical structure, as everyone knows, these cantos reflect Byron's life in England during his Years of Fame.

When Byron reinitiated his *Don Juan* project at the beginning of 1822, therefore, he did so with two objects clearly in his mind. The first of these involved structural matters: specifying a precise chronology for Juan's life in the poem. This move entailed, as a consequence, a dramatic refocusing of the poem's materials. Because of the move readers would be better able to see the tripartite organization of the poem's historical vision. *Don Juan* examines the period 1789–1824 in terms of its three dominant phases: the early years of the French Revolution (the poem's displaced fiction); the epoch of the Napoleonic Wars (viewed through Byron's analogous and contemporary experience of those years); and the epoch of the European restoration (dramatically fashioned and presented at the poem's immediate narrative level).

Byron's second object, which is related to the first, aimed to reassert in an unmistakable way the socio-political character of his work. When he began *Don Juan* he spoke of it as "bitter in politics,"[17] but as he struggled to get Murray to publish his cantos he was gradually led to de-emphasize both the bitterness and the politics. The de-emphasis appeared in the published work itself—the removal of the dedication, the decision not to print the Wellington stanzas in canto 3, and so forth—as well as in Byron's letters back to England in which he raised his defense of the poem against his publisher's and his friends' objections.[18] During 1819–21 these letters take a conciliating and mollifying line. Byron tried to get his poem accepted by assuring his friends that it was actually a harmless thing, an elaborate *jeu d'esprit* conceived more in a comic than a satiric mode, "to giggle and make giggle."[19] In 1822 the structural changes are accompanied by an uncompromising and candid political stance. In his resumed poem, he told Moore in July 1822, he meant to "throw away the scabbard" and make open ideological war with the new reactionary spirit of the age. By December he was equally clear on the subject in a letter to Murray: *Don Juan* "is intended [as] a *satire* on *abuses* of the present *states* of Society.[20] Cantos 6–8, issued by the liberal Hunt rather than the conservative Murray, are prefaced with Byron's prose declaration of mental war, and the next volume—cantos 9–11—begins with the diatribe against war and Wellington which Byron, in 1819, had withdrawn from canto 3.

Byron's purposes with his poem, then, are accompanied by important changes in his aesthetic and political consciousness. Not the least of these was his new and clearer understanding of the *wholeness* of the period 1789–1824, of the intimate relations that held between the three major phases of this period, and of the connections between people and events that might appear, at first, to have little to do with each other. No episode in the poem reveals more clearly Byron's increased understanding of these historical repetitions and relations than the Siege of Ismail, the episode in which Byron initially focused the historical and political restructuring of his epic.

The siege is, at least in part, what it appears to be: a satire on war and its violence. Byron was not a pacifist, however. He supported patriotic struggles and wars of liberation, and he eventually went to serve in the Greek effort to break free of the Turkish Empire. We have to specify, therefore, the ground of Byron's satire. This ground begins to emerge when we reflect upon Byron's chief source for his details. He used the account in Marquis Gabriel de Castelnau's *Essai sur l'Histoire ancienne et moderne de la nouvelle Russie* (3 vols., Paris, 1800).[21] The ideology of this book is reactionary and monarchist, and its narrative of the siege is largely based on the first-hand details supplied to Castelnau from the diary of Armand Emmanuel du Plessis, Duc de Richelieu (1767–1822). Byron mentions Castelnau's *Essai* in the preface to cantos 6–8, where he also speaks of the Duc de Richelieu as "a young volunteer in the Russian service, and afterwards the founder and benefactor of Odessa."[22] The irony and satire implicit in these remarks arises from Byron's negative approach to Castelnau's glorifying account of the siege, as well as from his ironic sense of the young Richelieu's benefactions.

Reading Castelnau, Byron saw that many of the officers in Catherine's army at the siege of Ismail were "distinguished strangers" (canto 7, line 254), a wickedly oblique phrase calling attention to the fact that these men, like the young Duc de Richelieu, were emigrés from France and the revolution. Richelieu and the other distinguished strangers are not patriots fighting for their country, they are military adventurers. That Byron intended this line of attack on the French emigrés at Ismail is perfectly plain from the letter to Moore in which he said that his new cantos (the siege cantos, that is) constitute an attack upon "those butchers in large business, your mercenary soldiery."[23] Lying behind the satire of this battle and the entire Russian episode in the poem is the idea, commonly found in liberal thought of the period, that monarchists like Richelieu have no other business in life except to fight in wars (any wars will do) and intrigue at court. The fact that Juan's rescue of Leila is based upon an actual incident in Richelieu's life only underscores Byron's mordant comments on the indiscriminate militarism of aristocratic ideology:

> If here and there some transient trait of pity
>   Was shown, and some more noble heart broke through
> Its bloody bond, and saved perhaps some pretty
>   Child, or an aged, helpless man or two—
> What's this in one annihilated city?   (8, stanza 124)

These lines, and the larger passage from which they are drawn, cut back against Castelnau's account of the war and the supposed "noble heart" of the young duke. The man celebrated by reactionaries like Castelnau as "the founder and benefactor of Odessa" is as well one of those who destroyed a city in which he had no personal or political interest whatsoever, who fled his own country at a moment of crisis, and who later—after the fall of Napoleon—returned to France to become minister for foreign affairs in the restored monarchy.[24]

Richelieu merely epitomizes what Byron wishes to attack in his narrative of the siege and in the Russian cantos generally: the character of monarchist regimes. He is even more important in Byron's poem, however, as a focus for the political filiations that connect, on the one hand, such apparently separated events as the siege of Ismail and the events in France in 1789–90 and, on the other, the strange twists and eventualities of European history between 1789 and 1818. Richelieu and the other distinguished strangers do not find their way into Catherine's army merely by chance, nor is it chance that brings him back, at the Bourbon restoration, to serve as an important functionary in the reactionary alliance. Neither is it chance that leads Byron in 1822 to expose this pattern of relations through his narrative of the siege. Byron was well aware, at least since 1809, of the imperialist stake that various European powers had in Balkan and Levantine affairs. The narrative of the siege of Ismail forces the reader to recall to mind that network of political and economic interests, as well as to see that the power and self-interests of the monarchies has not been broken by the revolutionary and Napoleonic years. When Byron looks at the siege from the vantage of the restoration, then, he integrates it into the pattern of pan-European affairs of 1789–93 (that is to say, the event is integrated into the order and fate of Juan's fictional-historical career), and he also uses it to comment upon current European conditions. In effect, Byron's employment of his sources involves him in a massive critical-revolutionary reinterpretation of the history of Europe from the outbreak of the French Revolution to the early years of the restoration.

Thus, in 1822 Byron transforms *Don Juan* into a book of the European world, a comprehensive survey and explanation of the principal phases of the epoch 1789–1824. The period is dominated by repetitions, by the violence that has accompanied them, and by the ignorance and indifferences that have abetted these repetitions and their violences. Against these things Byron sets the project of *Don Juan,* which is itself finally recognized to be involved in, to be a part of, the epoch and its repetitions. *Don Juan* becomes a book of the European world by becoming, finally, the Book of Byron, an integrated meditation and commentary upon his own life as it is and was and continues to be a revelation of the meaning of his age.

Don Juan is the Book of Byron because he is its hero, because the poem gives the reader a history of 1789–1824 that is set and framed, at all points, in terms of Byron's history. Juan's fictional movements retraverse actual places and scenes that Byron once passed through, and their details recollect persons and events in his past. In addition, the digressive narration often ruminates Byron's career to comment on and finally to judge it. In short, the poem repeatedly gives the reader views of Byron's past life in the coded sequence of its fictional level as well as in the memorial sequence of its narrative level. All this is widely recognized, as is the related fact that the history of an entire epoch is to be glimpsed in the reflective details of the poem.

Less apparent is the significance of the narrative as it is an *immediate* rather than a recollective event. Cantos 1–5 constitute the fictional level and the narrative level through two volumes of verse issued by John Murray in 1819 and 1821, and the remaining cantos constitute themselves through the four succeeding volumes issued by Hunt in 1823 and 1824. In addition, however, the last four volumes reconstitute what was originally printed in the first two volumes (a) by forcing the reader to place the whole of the fictional level in a specified historical frame of reference, and (b) by making this important interpretive shift a part of the poem's developing structure, a part of its own self-criticism. Byron begins the Hunt volumes of his poem, cantos 6–16, with a preface announcing his ideological purposes and describing the key elements in the historical restructuring of the poem. Cantos 6–16 then carry out these changes of direction and thereby force cantos 1–5 to accommodate the changes. The structural accommodations we have already discussed. The ideological changes appear as a more comprehensive understanding of the subjects taken up by the project of *Don Juan*. Most noticeable here is Byron's effort to present a totalized interpretation and critique of his age: to compel his readers to understand how the several phases of the period 1789–1824 hang together and to persuade them that his critical-revolutionary reading of the period is the correct one. Related to this polemic is the poem's vision of self-judgment, its critical-revolutionary reading of the limits and blindnesses of cantos 1–5. Byron's revisionary turn on the first five cantos is not, of course, a repudiation of them. Though an act of self-criticism, the change of direction in cantos 6–16 assumes—indeed, it demonstrates—a dialectical continuity with its objects of criticism. The advances and the retreats of cantos 1–5, their boldness and timidity, accumulate a set of dynamic contradictions that eventually generate cantos 6–16.

In this way *Don Juan* represents not merely a comprehensive interpretation of the period 1789–1824 but a comprehensive critical interpretation that incorporates its own acts of consciousness in its critique as part of a developing and changing act of interpretation. All readers have recognized this quality of the poem's digressive and shifting style, but it is important to see that this stylistic feature is grounded in the work's ideological structure. Even more important to see, however, is that the ground of this ideological structure is not in some definable form of critical interpretation that we may educe from the work. Rather, it lies in the act of the poem, the social and historical deeds of its consciousness that appear to us, most immediately, as a set of specific acts of publication. Of course, the fragmentary character of the work has heretofore obscured somewhat the comprehensiveness of its historical argument. Scholarship helps to bring that argument into sharper focus, to lift it from the sphere of a reader's intuition into a more explicit and defined frame of reference.

Late in the poem Byron says of himself that like his own work *Don Juan* he is "Changeable too—yet somehow '*Idem semper*'" (17, stanza 11). Readers have not found it easy to say what exactly in the poem is "changeable" and what exactly stands resistant to change. I think we can now make an attempt to isolate these factors. What changes in the poem are its ideas; these are continually subjected to qualification, revision, even repudiation. What remains the same is the perpetual dialectic of the individual mind in its social world, the active deed of its committed intelligence. Fichte called this ground of permanence "Tat," Schopenhauer "Wille." These are of course nothing more than conceptual markers for an act of social consciousness that can only be *carried out* in words but that cannot be defined in them. The act of the poem's mind, then, is an understanding that changes and brings about change. In *Don Juan*—to adapt a contemporary formulation of a fragment from Herakleitos—"What does not change / is the will to change."[25]

NOTES

1. For a discussion of these matters see my *Fiery Dust: Byron's Poetic Development* (Chicago: University of Chicago Press, 1968), chap. 1, and *Lord Byron: Complete Poetical Works*, ed. Jerome J. McGann (Oxford: Clarendon Press, 1980–) 1:360–63. The latter work is hereafter referred to as *CPW*.

2. See poems 24, 25, 28, in *CPW* 1.

3. *CPW*, 1:398–99.

4. *CPW*, 1:426–27 and 2:268–71.

5. For complete bibliographical details see *Byron's Works: Poetry*, ed. E. H. Coleridge (London: John Murray, 1901–1904) 7:180–84 and T. J. Wise, *Byron: A Bibliography* . . . (London: n.p., 1932–33) 1:50–54. The history of the book's publication is discussed in the *CPW*, 2:268–69. The prose quotations below from *Childe Harold's Pilgrimage. A Romaunt* are taken from the first edition, and page numbers are given in the text.

6. For a more detailed discussion of the context and meaning of the poem see *CPW*, 2, and *Fiery Dust*, part 2.

7. See *Byron's Letters and Journals,* ed. Leslie A. Marchand (Cambridge, Mass.: Harvard University Press, 1973–82) 9:41; hereafter referred to as *BLJ*.

8. See the commentaries to the Oriental Tales in *CPW*, 3.

9. *CPW*, 3:406–415. For an excellent discussion of the political aspects of two of the books of Byron's tales see Peter Manning, "Tales and Politics: *The Corsair, Lara,* and *The White Doe of Rylstone*," in *Byron. Poetry and Politics* . . . , ed. E. A. Stürzl and James Hogg (Salzburg: Institut für Englische Sprache und Literatur, 1981), pp. 204–30.

10. For a discussion of the history of the poem's publication see *Don Juan: A Variorum Edition*, ed. T. G. Steffan and W. W. Pratt (Austin, Tex.: University of Texas Press, 1958) 1:25–52 *passim* (hereafter cited as *DJV*).

11. See *DJV*, 2:3–20 and 4:4–15. The preface is placed at the beginning of the text of *Don Juan* in *DJV* as well as its sequel, the Penguin modernized edition. Leslie A. Marchand's school edition also places it at the poem's beginning. Such a placement is seriously misleading, however, for Byron not only left this preface in an uncompleted state, he discarded it.

12. *DJV*, 2:4–5.

13. *BLJ*, 8:78.

14. *Medwin's Conversations of Lord Byron*, ed. Ernest J. Lovell Jr. (Princeton, N.J.: Princeton University Press, 1966), pp. 164–5.

15. Some of Byron's marginal jottings in canto 14 schematize two of the poem's future episodes, including the death of Juan. These marginalia appear on a scrap of MS (not known to the *DJV* editors) now in the Murray archives. The notations occur on a MS carrying a variant version of lines 479–80.

16. Critics have frequently drawn attention to *Don Juan*'s parallels with eighteenth-century picaresque novels. See Elizabeth Boyd, *Byron's "Don Juan"* (1945; rpt. New York: Humanities Press, 1958), esp. chaps. 4–7; Andras Horn, *Byron's 'Don Juan' and the 18th Century Novel*, Swiss Studies in English, No. 51. (Bern: Frank Verlag, 1962), and A. B. England, *Byron's Don Juan and Eighteenth Century Literature* (Lewisburg, Pa.: Bucknell University Press, 1975), esp. chap. 3.

17. *BLJ*, 6:76–77.

18. See *DJV*, 1:13–24; Samuel C. Chew, *Byron in England* (London: John Murray, 1924), chap. 4; and J. J. McGann, *Don Juan in Context* (Chicago: University of Chicago Press, 1976), pp. 51–67.

19. See *BLJ*, 6:208; see also 6:67.

20. *BLJ*, 9:191 and 10:68.

21. See Boyd, *Byron's "Don Juan,"* pp. 148–50 and Nina Diakonova, "The Russian Episode in Byron's 'Don Juan'," *The Ariel* 3 (1972): 51–57.

22. *DJV*, 3:3.

23. *BLJ*, 9:191.

24. Byron's critique of the contemporary world of the restoration operates as well in his treatment of "Suwarrow" in the Russian cantos. For a good discussion see Philip W. Martin, *Byron: A Poet Before His Public* (Cambridge: Cambridge University Press, 1982), pp. 213–17.

25. This is Charles Olson's translation of Herakleitos, frag. 23, which appears as the first line of Olson's poem "The Kingfishers."

George Bornstein
The Arrangement of Browning's *Dramatic Lyrics* (1842)

"It is an honourable distinction of Mr. Browning that in whatever he writes, you discover an *idea* of some sort or other," wrote Browning's early champion John Forster in his favorable review of the original *Dramatic Lyrics* for *The Examiner* in 1842. "There is purpose in all he does."[1] The early *Dramatic Lyrics* contained some of Browning's most famous short poems. As reviewer, Forster had an advantage over subsequent critics who usually encounter the poem in one of the later rearrangements by Browning or his editors. Forster necessarily took the volume as unit of his attention. As a result, he saw that Browning had designed the book around contrasting pairs of poems. His brief sketch of the pairs anticipated modern Browning criticism by over a hundred years, for only recently have scholars begun to grasp the importance of pairing in Browning's patterning of his verse.[2] Browning's overall concern for arrangement is well known, particularly as displayed in the 1863 reordering of the poems that had comprised *Dramatic Lyrics* (1842), *Dramatic Romances and Lyrics* (1845), and *Men and Women* (1855), and in the design of a later volume like *Dramatis Personae* (1864).[3] His most complexly structured work, *The Ring and the Book* (1868–69), consists of an intricate interlocking of related monologues. I should like to argue here that Browning's earliest collection of mature verse, *Dramatic Lyrics,* displays considerable architectonic skill in its deployment of paired poems punctuated by individual, free-standing ones. The pairs emphasize individual emotion in their thematic contrasts of love and its relation to moral or social law, while the independent poems reinforce the implicit contention of the pairs for a vital rather than antiquarian use of history by tying the collection to political events affecting the England of 1842.

A look at the original titles in the 1842 collection provides the best survey of its plan.[4] The poems appeared in this order:

Cavalier Tunes
    I. Marching Along
    II. Give a Rouse
    III. My Wife Gertrude [later called Boot and Saddle]

Italy and France
    I. Italy [later called My Last Duchess]
    II. France [later called Count Gismond]
Camp and Cloister
    I. Camp (French) [later called Incident of the French Camp]
    II. Cloister (Spanish) [later called Soliloquy of the Spanish Cloister]

In a Gondola
Artemis Prologuizes
Waring
Queen-Worship
    I. Rudel and [later, to] the Lady of Tripoli
    II. Cristina
Madhouse Cells
    I. [untitled; later called Johannes Agricola in Meditation]
    II. [untitled; later called Porphyria's Lover]
Through the Metidja to Abd-el-Kadr.—1842
The Pied Piper of Hamelin

While not joined by title, "In a Gondola" and "Artemis Prologuizes" form an obvious thematic pair based on death in illicit love, one quasi-historical and the other mythological. The volume thus runs from its opening triad of "Cavalier Tunes" through three related pairs to reach the independent "Waring" near the middle, and then presents two more related pairs en route to its original ending, "Through the Metidja to Abd-El-Kadr.—1842." Faced with his publisher Moxon's report that the collection as constituted was too short to fill the projected sixteen double-columned pages, Browning hastily added "The Pied Piper of Hamelin" the month before publication.[5] *Dramatic Lyrics* thus has alternate endings. Far from marring the original design, Browning improvised brilliantly by placing at the end of the volume "The Pied Piper," with its comic focusing of the collection's increasing preoccupation with the role of the poet.

The arrangement of poems does not follow their chronology of composition. On the contrary, Browning wrote the opening "Cavalier Tunes" only a few months before publication, and he placed the earliest poems—"Madhouse Cells"—almost at the end.[6] The order instead follows a different principle, a thematic one, with formal considerations sometimes reinforcing the formation of the pairs. By consisting of three lyrics, the opening "Cavalier Tunes" stands apart from the pairs as much as the unpaired lyrics do. Far from merely antiquarian, "Cavalier Tunes" capitalizes on the intense interest in the English Civil Wars that swept the country in the bicentennial year 1842 and inaugurates the theme of loyalty and proper devotion on both the personal and political levels that dominates the ensuing volume. The first pair, "My Last Duchess" and "Count Gismond," contrasts the treatment of women in that regard within a frame which remains more personal than political and which calls attention to the acts of mind of the speakers. The second pair, "Camp and Cloister," suggests far more than the mere "pleasures of alliteration" to which one critic has limited it;[7] the self-sacrifice for love in "Incident of the French Camp" contrasts with the egocentric hatred of "Soliloquy of the Spanish Cloister," both set within the context of social institutions. Similarly, in the following implicit pair, "In a Gondola" presents the death of a lover in a true but illicit love, while "Artemis Prologuizes" presents the vengeful death of Hippolutos through the unrequited and illicit passion of his stepmother Phaedra. Standing by itself, "Waring" returns the volume to the social world of England in 1842, particularly the problem of emigration, and makes explicit the concern with poetry that will climax in the final poem. "Queen Worship" then contrasts amorous devotion in a courtly and a contemporary context in which the modern seems almost tawdry by comparison. "Madhouse Cells" treats egoistic delusions about God and the moral law, with "Johannes Agricola in Meditation" offering a theological equivalent to the corruption of personal relations in "Porphyria's Lover." The original ending, "Through the Metidja to Abd-El-Kadr.—1842" returns the volume to the contemporary world, with an Arab horseman's devotion to his prince in a colonial war of independence balancing the opening treatment of Cavalier devotion at the start of the volume. The alternate ending, "The Pied Piper of Hamelin," ponders in comic guise the role of the poet in society, and of history or legend in contemporary life, that has increasingly preoccupied *Dramatic Lyrics*. The remainder of this essay explores the pertinence to each poem of its place in the overall scheme. Such analysis illuminates not only the neglected poems of the collection but also even those that have attracted copious individual commentary.

The title "Cavalier Tunes," like that of *Dramatic Lyrics* itself, diverts attention to the form and speaker of the poems, and encourages us to separate persona from poet. Stung by criticism of the personal nature of his earlier verse, Browning described the new poems in his 1842 "advertisement" as "often Lyric in expression, always Dramatic in principle, and so many utterances of so many imaginary persons, not mine" (p. 347). No one was likely to confuse the young poet with the bluff Royalist speaker of the tunes, particularly since his sympathies with the Parliamentarians had crept into *Strafford* five years before (they would surface again as late as the song for Pym at the end of "Parleying with Charles Avison," 1887). To animate such a speaker required an act of historical imagination. Capitalizing on the interest surrounding the 1842 bicentenary of the start of the English Civil War may have been another way of bolstering Browning's continually disappointed hopes for early popularity, which had prompted issuance of the *Dramatic Lyrics* number of *Bells and Pomegranates* in the first place.[8] But more importantly, "Cavalier Tunes" suggests the imaginative recovery of living history that Browning preferred to mere antiquarian or factual narrative, and that he practiced in the remainder of the volume as he had previously in *Sordello*. The tunes provided an accessible paradigm to a contemporary English reader of the strategies that shape the ensuing succession of medieval and Renaissance courts, Spanish cloister, French camp, Greek myth, madhouse cells, or exotic contemporary locales like Venice, Trieste, and Algeria.

The sequence of Cavalier poems both establishes an internal order and introduces the volume thematically. They pertain to three different stages of the Civil War, from the road to Nottingham where the war began in 1642 (in "Marching Along") through the intermediate phase of struggle (in "Give a Rouse") to the rejection of surrender (in "Boot and Saddle"). The fierce political loyalty of the Cavalier anticipates that of the French boy and Arab horseman later in the volume, and it contrasts with the emotions driving the envious monk, the gentle Waring, the lascivious Queen Cristina, or the duplicitous burghers of Hamelin. Similarly, the Cavalier enjoys the full support of a united family, including his son George and wife Gertrude. This family harmony contrasts, of course, with the intrigues of Ferrara, Aix, and Spain, the extramarital passion of contemporary Venice or ancient Greece, and the perverse emotions of Porphyria's lover; it finds an echo in the devotion of Count Gismond and of Rudel. The original title of "Boot and Saddle" in 1842, "My Wife Gertrude," emphasized the familial solidarity in particular preparation for the following pair of poems.

While the original titles of that pair, "Italy" and "France," emphasize place, the revised ones by which we now know them, "My Last Duchess" and "Count Gismond," stress character, with setting (Ferrara and Aix in Provence) relegated to subtitles. Initially, Browning obviously meant to contrast the forms of aristocratic attitudes toward marriage in patriarchal Italy and chivalric Provence. But the revised titles point attention to an aspect of the two poems that illuminates the rationale of their original pairing and later dispersal. The later titles call attention not just to character but to particular characters, the Duchess and the Count, both of whom are innocents. More importantly, they function analogously in their respective poems as stimuli to the mental action of the more complicated character who delivers each dramatic monologue. For all the thematic links—innocence versus corruption, wife as chattel versus wife as chivalric Lady, Italian society versus French, and the like—the link in mental action of the speaker binds the two poems together most tightly.

As he utters his discourse, the acts of mind of the Duke recapitulate those in a Greater Romantic Lyric, which Browning would adapt more subtly in "Pictor Ignotus" three years later. Briefly, as M. H. Abrams has argued, Greater Romantic Lyrics exhibit a three-part structure based on mental action rather than formal verse divisions; they present a definite speaker in a determinate landscape with which mind interacts first in a detached, then involved, then again detached way in a series that may be described as out-in-out or, as I have argued elsewhere, description-vision-evaluation, with accompanying displacements in time or space.[9] Such poems always return to their opening scene at the end, and the middle section typically involves memory (as in Wordsworth) or imagination (as in Keats). Wordsworth's "Tintern Abbey" and "Elegiac Stanzas Suggested by a Picture of Peele Castle," Coleridge's "Eolian Harp" and other conversation poems, and Keats's "Ode on a Grecian Urn" and "Ode to a Nightingale" all exemplify the pattern. So, too, do "My Last Duchess" and "Pictor Ignotus," among other works of Browning, whose speaker—like Keats's contemplating the urn or Wordsworth's before Beaumont's painting—typically substitutes an art work (here, the portrait of the Duchess) for a natural landscape.

In "My Last Duchess" a tripartite structure re-enacts the Romantic paradigm even while parodying it by denying the imaginative insight that the Romantics represented there. The Duke begins with present description of the painting and of his guest's alleged reaction to it. In the middle of line 13 ("Sir, 'twas not . . .") he shifts to past tense, in which memory recounts the Duchess's behavior until her death. Memory continues until the middle of line 46, when he breaks off its flow to return to the present tense and original scene ("There she stands") for a new purpose. The monologue thus presents a three-part progression based on acts of mind (description-memory-description/evaluation) supported by displacements in time (now-then-now) and place (in front of the portrait—elsewhere in the palace and grounds—in front of the portrait again). But while earlier Greater Romantic Lyrics typically climax the intense second section at a moment of imaginative intensity, like Keats imagining a town not on the urn or the perilous seas of fairyland, the Duke builds toward an act of murder that represents the opposite of imaginative sympathy before his return to the present scene. Wrapped in his egotism, he remains wholly within himself even as his discourse follows a form originally designed to show annihilation of selfhood through imagination. Like the other villains of the volume, the alpha and omega of his discourse are "that's my" and "for me!" in contrast to the devotion to others shown by the positive figures. A perverse desire to possess the moment reduces a living person to a dead object both literally and figuratively, as Browning emphasizes later in the collection (most markedly in "Porphyria's Lover") and elsewhere.

Similar formal and thematic patterns underlie the superficially different companion poem, "Count Gismond," which displays both an overt contrast and a covert kinship to "My Last Duchess." The contrast, of course, concerns the treatment of women, while the kinship involves the revelation of egoistic manipulation of others through a particular form of discourse. Without joining the revisionist ranks intent on supporting the 1842 pairing by turning the Countess into a counterpart of the depraved Duke, I do think that the more solid arguments for that position compel a reading that at least holds open the possibility of her duplicity. Chief among them are the predatory emphasis of the falcon imagery, the preoccupation with details like the dripping sword, the distinction in appearance of the two boys, and the fact that the Countess does conclude with a lie intended to deceive Gismond, whether tactfully caring or symptomatically corrupt.[10]

The parallels between the Countess's discourse and the Duke's reinforce a subversive reading. Here Browning's revisions in the titles help, for each emphasizes a character, the Duchess and the Count, who resemble each other and play analogous roles in their respective poems. They are innocents, and they inspire the monologues of their more complicated spouses. Like the Duke, the Countess begins in the present with her prayer for the Count's salvation, moves into the past through memory for the bulk of her utterance, and returns to the present at the end ("Gismond here?"). The one break in the central section, a fleeting return to the present in lines 49–50, both follows Romantic precedent in poems like "Tintern Abbey" and calls attention to the content of that interruption, a concern that Gismond not hear her. Further, like the Duke, the Countess favors first-person pronouns at revealing times; at the beginning she wants God to save Gismond because he "saved me," and at the end she accepts his bringing "my" tercel back, while her whole middle account focuses on her changing status and situation. The Countess may or may not equal the Duke in depravity, but she does resemble him in an egotism that sees others only as means to her own ends and that forswears the potential for imaginative self-transcendence in the acts of mind that structure her account.

The ensuing 1842 pairing, "Camp and Cloister," extends the contrast between egoistic hatred and self-sacrifice for love from marriage to two other social institutions, the army and religion. The two poems thus contrast with each other thematically even as they continue the larger dichotomy between virtuous and vicious characters that the volume repeatedly presents. In form, too, the overt correspondence of their eight-line stanzas composed of alternately rhyming quatrains yields to a deeper contrast by which the straight-forward narrative of the boy's heroism serves as foil to the circuitous associations of the monk's rancor. When Browning retitled the poems for 1849, he again de-emphasized geography, this time stressing character in action rather than the action in character of "My Last Duchess" and "Count Gismond." As title, "Incident of the French Camp" highlights the event as much as the locale, while "Soliloquy of the Spanish Cloister" suggests an ensuing action to follow the self-revelation of soliloquy.

The poems themselves belie the stock expectations of their own titles, with the armed camp, associated with martial violence, here featuring loving devotion and the cloister, associated with contemplative quiet, here full of sound and fury. The characters both contrast with each other and establish a series of links to other figures in the collection. The French boy, like the Italian Duchess and the French Count Gismond, displays the virtue of innocence in his selfless devotion to the emperor. But Napoleon differs from the Duke in responding sympathetically to such traits. Similarly, the use of predatory bird imagery contrasts with the Countess's fondness for fighting falcons; at sight of the boy's wound, the emperor's eye softens "as sheathes / A film the mother-eagle's eye / When her bruised eaglet breathes." Just as the devoted boy's happiness in death anticipates that of the lover of "In a Gondola" and of Rudel, so has the exasperated reaction of vice to virtue in "My Last Duchess" prefigured that of the monk to Friar Lawrence in "Soliloquy of the Spanish Cloister." Lawrence obviously belongs with the boy and the Duchess, while the speaker belongs with the Duke and, later in the volume, Porphyria's lover. The interruptions, tags of conversation, and disturbed rhythms that give the poem its modernity all betoken the monk's derangement at the sight of a virtue that he remakes into a projection of his own vices. He is a powerless Duke, who would kill Lawrence if he could. Just as his empty formalism recalls the Duke's preoccupation with protocol, so does the monk's monologue begin and end with a keynote—in his case the animalistic "Gr-r-r" that reduces him from the human to the bestial level even as he brands his enemy a "swine." Both this poem and its companion play central roles in the evolving unity of the volume as a whole.

Unlike the previous groupings, "In a Gondola" and "Artemis Prologuizes" do not share a common title, but they do form an implicit pair in which a male lover meets his death through illicit passion. They thus continue the troubled relationships between men and women that preoccupy the volume. As a diptych they display a series of contrasts that rival those of Browning's other pairings of poems with related themes. The Venetian lover of "In a Gondola" dies of his own reciprocated passion for a married woman, whereas the Greek Hippolutos dies because of his refusal to share the adulterous love of his infatuated stepmother. Both poems present an intense moment with catastrophic aftereffects, in one a moment of love and the other of lust for revenge. The Venetian woman seems to rejoice in the death of her lover at the height of his passion (as he himself does), whereas Artemis strives to resuscitate her votary. Formally, the dialogue of the first poem allows it to contrast the attitudes of the two lovers themselves, while the second depends upon the retrospective omniscience of Artemis. Perhaps most important for overall design, "In a Gondola" presents actual human speakers placed in a contemporary if distant city, while "Artemis Prologuizes" avows frankly its mythological status. Although earlier in the volume "Cavalier Tunes" recalls the bicentenary of the Civil Wars, "Incident of the French Camp" may remember the impressive second burial of Napoleon in December of 1841, and even "Soliloquy of the Spanish Cloister" may glance at the debate over religious ritual stirred by the Oxford Movement, "Artemis Prologuizes" stands at the farthest remove from Victorian England of any poem in the volume. Browning has followed his recurrent themes into a mythic dimension, but he has also left the contemporary world behind.

He returns to that world abruptly and ambivalently in "Waring." Placed in the middle of the volume, immediately after the escape from history into Greek mythology, "Waring" redirects the reader's attention to contemporary England. The poem not only draws on the general interest of the increased emigration from England to the colonies that would continue to swell as the Hungry Forties progressed, but also has a particular model in Browning's friend Alfred Domett, who had just departed for New Zealand.[11] Further, the poem itself assumes a chatty topicality as it progresses through the conditions of early Victorian art, literature, and society. Its colloquial tone, by turns mock-heroic, bantering, and lyrical, reinforces the contrast to "Artemis Prologuizes," with its stately blank verse. Calling attention to itself by being unpaired in a volume of pairs, "Waring" arrests the historical and mythic movement of the volume.

Waring himself evokes an ambivalent response. On the one hand, the tone clearly is sympathetic toward him: the speaker misses Waring, believes in his promise, and implores him to return and "Bring the real times back, confessed / Still better than our very best!" On the other hand, the speaker gently mocks his friend "With no work done, / But great works undone," addresses him in a mock-heroic, Biblical lament ("Ichabod, Ichabod, / The glory is Departed!"), and betrays a recurrent scepticism about Waring's ability to translate his powers into achievement. For Waring himself has forsaken the England to which the poem calls so much attention, even in the fantasy of his possible, secret return. Like Arnold's scholar-gypsy, whom he resembles in cultivation, gentleness, and flight from Victorian England, Waring turns out to be an insufficient artist-figure to redeem modern malaise.[12] The glimpse of Waring on the Trieste boat at the end of the poem mirrors the glimpse of the scholar-gypsy in the English countryside. Both poems require a sterner figure as alternative to contemporary ills. "The Scholar Gypsy" ends with the alternate vision of the Tyrian trader; Browning's poem ends only with Waring, but the volume itself will conclude first with the fierce image of the Arab horseman and then with the Piper, still outside society but more effective in his art than the gentle exile of "Waring."

Between "Waring" and the concluding poems, Browning placed two more pairs, "Queen-Worship" and "Madhouse Cells." Comprising "Rudel and the Lady of Tripoli" and "Cristina," "Queen-Worship" presents a diptych of male devotion to contrasting female beloveds. The first poem contains two direct links to "Waring": first, like Waring, Rudel is a poet; and secondly, just as "Waring" urges us to "Look East" (line 261), so does Rudel in the last line look "to the East—the East!" Among the many revisions, the change of "and" to "to" in the title focuses attention all the more on Rudel, the Troubadour poet-lover. According to legend, he fell in love with the Princess of Tripoli by hearing pilgrims' accounts of her beauty, wrote several poems of chaste but hopeless love for her, eventually sailed to Tripoli, and died in her arms. The story presents a typical tale of a Troubadour's chivalrous devotion to the beauty of his married lady, who herself behaves with perfect circumspection. In contrast, Browning selected as the lady for the modern poem of the pair the licentious Maria Cristina of Spain. Cristina, the young fourth wife of Ferdinand VII, acted as Queen until his death in 1833 and then as regent for her daughter until 1840, when revelation of her secret marriage to the soldier Muñoz forced her to abdicate. Throughout her career she earned a reputation as a notorious coquette.[13] Her promiscuity thus opposes the Lady of Tripoli's virtue. Yet the male lover of "Cristina" expresses devotion to her in an avowal of a "moment" when their "souls rushed together" that accords with Browning's sympathy elsewhere for the doctrine of Elective Affinities.[14] Without the title, such doctrines could be taken at face value here, too. But the title ascribes the affinities to such a ludicrously inappropriate figure that it calls into question the stability of the speaker. He creates a fantasy world for himself that has little relation to the actual one surrounding him. In that way, he prepares us for the more exaggerated pathology of the next two speakers, Johannes Agricola and Porphyria's lover.

Browning chose for the final pair in the volume the two he had written and published first. The placement does not derive from an attempt to bury early works of poor quality; except for "My Last Duchess" and "Soliloquy of the Spanish Cloister," the poems now known as "Johannes Agricola in Meditation" and "Porphyria's Lover" can stand with any in the collection, as their frequent inclusion in anthologies suggests. Rather, the poems serve as thematic culmination to the collection. A clue to this lies in their joint title, "Madhouse Cells," which Browning devised for the 1842 volume (it was not part of their first appearance, in Fox's *Monthly Repository* for January 1836), kept for the 1849 *Dramatic Romances and Lyrics* when he reprinted the poems of 1842 and 1845 in their original order, and dropped when he broke the pairing as part of the general rearrangement of 1863. Through the title Browning controls our responses more obtrusively than he has heretofore done. "Madhouse Cells" brands the speakers as unreliable, even deranged, from the start. Yet it only makes explicit what other poems have left implicit. All of Browning's villainous speakers figuratively inhabit cells betokening isolation and social deviance, ringed round with self-delusion. The Duke, Countess Gismond (in the more negative interpretation of her), and the Spanish monk, for example, betray the same traits as Browning's madhouse speakers: they hold themselves exempt from laws that bind others, confuse empty formalism with moral legitimacy, and see others only as projections of their own psychic needs. In contrast, positive figures like the Cavalier, French boy, Rudel, and Arab horseman accept their social obligations, place spirit above letter, and serve others.

While the two poems overlap, "Johannes Agricola" stresses exemption from the laws that bind others, "Porphyria's Lover" the treatment of a lover as an object which corrupts the male-female relations of the volume.

Browning allots each view equal space: both poems contain exactly sixty lines of iambic tetrameter rhymed a b a b b in the most exact parallelism of any of the pairs. The historical Johannes Agricola (1494–1566) at first supported Luther but then broke with him to help found Antinomianism, a doctrine that Browning summarized in the 1836 printing by a headnote taken from Defoe's *Dictionary of All Religions:*

> Antinomians, so denominated for rejecting the Law as a thing of no use under the Gospel dispensation: they say, that good works do not further, nor evil works hinder salvation; that the child of God cannot sin, that God never chastiseth him, *that murder, drunkenness, &c. are sins in the wicked but not in him,* that the child of grace being once assured of salvation, afterwards never doubteth . . . that God doth not love any man for his holiness, that sanctification is no evidence of justification, &c. Pontanus, in his Catalogue of Heresies, says John Agricola was the author of this sect, A.D. 1535.[15] (italics mine)

The whole volume, as well as Browning's positions elsewhere, rejects such a view. The suppression of Johannes's name from the title for only the 1842 text reinforces the general applicability of the poem by removing the possibility of historical restriction. Like the villains of *Dramatic Lyrics,* Johannes combines his exemption from laws that bind others with excessive reliance on the first-person pronoun in inappropriate contexts: his first ten lines emphasize "I" and the next twenty "me," as though God had designed the cosmos expressly for Johannes Agricola or, as he says, "for me."

"Porphyria's Lover" extends Johannes's doctrines to the personal realm, with disastrous results. Like "My Last Duchess," "Count Gismond," and "Artemis Prologuizes," the poem presents a murder between the sexes as both the literal and figurative result of treating the beloved as an object. And like the Duke, Porphyria's lover seems unable to distinguish an inanimate object, whether portrait or corpse, from the living person. In place of the Duke's abortion of the Greater Romantic Lyric pattern in a failure of imaginative sympathy, the lover here lapses into a syntactic pattern of ands that seem to connect his narrative syntactically and yet rob it of true connection by placing all events, including the murder, on the same syntactic level. The result is a freezing of mental action, which imprisons the lover in his own mind as surely as he is imprisoned in his madhouse cell. Whatever the flirtatiousness of Porphyria herself, her lover is no lover at all. Neither are any of the other villains of the volume, whereas the heroes and heroines display the ability to love so central to Browning's later work.

Following the thematic climax of "Madhouse Cells," the volume reaches its original conclusion with "Through the Metidja to Abd-El-Kadr.— 1842." This poem gives the collection a circular shape by returning to the situation of the opening lyric and, like all the unpaired poems, tying it to the historical present. A popular hero of the day, the sultan and emir Abd-El-Kadr waged a war of resistance against the French after their conquest of Algeria in 1830. After initial successes, including occupation of the Metidja or great plain of Algiers, he encountered increased French pressure under Marshal Bugeaud from 1842 onwards and finally surrendered in 1847. The Algerian's attempt to rally the tribes behind him was reported in *The Times* throughout June of 1842, at about the time of the poem's composition.[16] Like the bicentenary of the Civil Wars and the emigration of which Domett was a part, then, the events of the poem return the reader to political news in contemporary England. The poem also would have concluded the volume fitly. Like "Cavalier Tunes," it presents a horseman riding to the support of his beleaguered prince. Like the portraits of positive figures and unlike those of the villains, it presents a character devoted to a cause or person outside of himself. The Arab horseman's "full heart" combines allegiance to Abd-el-Kadr with satisfaction and pride in that service. Equally importantly for Browning, the horseman is a figure of activity, striving to realize his ideals in the world rather than to rationalize them. He represents character in action.

When the publisher Edward Moxon informed Browning that the poems he originally submitted for *Dramatic Lyrics* did not fill the projected sixteen-page format, Browning responded by sending him the recently-completed "Pied Piper of Hamelin."[17] Far from spoiling the design of the volume, this improvisation preserved its integrity while refocusing its major preoccupations. Admittedly, Browning subtitled the poem "A Child's Story" written for William Macready the Younger, son of the great tragedian. Yet within its comic plot and occasionally doggerel verse, "The Pied Piper" offers a humorous meditation on the role of the artist in society that had begun in the volume with "Waring." Indeed, the two poems were written nearly at the same time, together with the essay on Chatterton.[18] All three works worried a great deal over the character of the unappreciated and perhaps ineffectual artist within a mercantile society. The poem itself presents the piper as an artist-figure. To begin with, he is a piper, a traditional image of the poet. His clothes and appearance distinguish him from others, in a manner familiar at least since Werther and Byron. His fingers are never far from his pipe. He possesses "a secret charm" for affecting others (line 72) and makes "wonderful music" (line 207). Most important of all, like much post-romantic poetry his music offers visions of paradise to its audience. This paradise assumes an appropriately mock-epic form in the apples, conserves, and butter-casks of the rats and a more lyrical and pastoral one in the "joyous land" (line 240) of fruit-trees, gushing water, and "strange and new" creatures that attract the children. When the burghers break their promise to reward the piper, his art turns from beneficent to demonic in its effects.[19]

Besides its stress on the role of the poet, "The Pied Piper" picks up three other themes from the volume. First, it professes a double status both as an historical account and as a legendary one. Browning carefully begins by fixing the location of the town of Hamelin and establishing the date of the ensuing events as "Almost five hundred years ago." As always, his treatment is neither antiquarian nor annalistic but rather concerned to revivify events for the present in a way that stresses their contemporary application. Secondly, the burghers of Hamelin belong with the company from the Duke onward who seek to use others only for their own ends and to exempt themselves from normal social obligations. They have promised him a thousand guilders for his performance, but renege upon their pledge as soon as he has provided his service. And thirdly, like the other unpaired poems this one has special relevance to England in 1842. For in that year a new Literary Copyright Act was passed after long advocacy by Macaulay and petitions to the House of Commons by Carlyle among others.[20] The issue of payment to the artist, and the implications of that payment as an index of his relation to bourgeois society, troubled not just fourteenth-century Hamelin but also nineteenth-century England. It troubled as well Robert Browning, whose works had never sold well and whose new effort at reaching a wider public in *Dramatic Lyrics* was to suffer the customary disappointment of those years. Yet in *Dramatic Lyrics* Browning had not only concluded major dramatic monologues of the sort that would eventually cement his reputation, but he had also artfully arranged them into an overall design that deepened the significance of each individual part. Just as inclusion of "The Pied Piper" in the volume increases the pertinence of its ironic presentation of the poet's role, so do the various pairs highlight contrasts and continuities within each diptych and among the groupings themselves. "Cavalier Tunes" and "Through the Metidja" enrich each other. So, too, does the Duke's manipulative egotism interact with the account of the Countess, or the chivalric devotion of Rudel rhyme with the skewed dedication of Porphyria's lover. His audience is still learning to read Robert Browning.

NOTES

1. John Forster's review appeared in *The Examiner* for 26 November 1842 and is conveniently reprinted in *Browning: The Critical Heritage*, ed. Boyd Litzinger and Donald Smalley (New York: Barnes and Noble, 1970), pp. 82–84. The remark cited is on page 83.

2. William E. Harrold's *The Variance and the Unity: A Study of the Complementary Poems of Robert Browning* (Athens, Ohio: Ohio University Press, 1973), the most detailed study to date, briefly discusses four of the groupings from *Dramatic Lyrics* but concentrates on later poems. Harrold's commitment to Gestalt and Jungian psychology, his focus on pairs rather than volumes, and some of his individual readings (e.g., of Porphyria's lover as a Neoplatonist) lead him to conclusions quite different from mine. Nancy B. Rich has some comments on "Madhouse Cells" in the course of her "New Perspective on the Companion Poems of Robert Browning," *Victorian Newsletter* 36 (1969): 5–9. Lawrence Poston III, in "Browning Rearranges Browning," *Studies in Browning and His Circle* 2 (1974): 39–54, studies the 1863 rearrangement as "a kind of backward look" over Browning's career. Like Harrold, Poston denies an overall significance to the early volumes but does include helpful remarks on two pairings and two more individual poems. More recently, Daniel Karlin in "Browning's Paired Poems," *Essays in Criticism* 31 (1981): 210–27, deals with a few poems from 1845 onwards.

3. On *Dramatis Personae* see Lawrence Poston III, *Loss and Gain: An Essay on Browning's Dramatis Personae*, University of Nebraska Studies No. 48 (Lincoln: University of Nebraska Press, 1974) and Thomas Wyly, "Unity and Design in Browning's *Dramatis Personae*," *Revue des Langues Vivantes* 43 (1977): 38–53.

4. The pamphlet itself lacks a table of contents; I have simply listed the titles in the order in which they appear. Browning kept the same ordering but removed most of the titular pairings for the 1849 collected edition *Dramatic Romances and Lyrics,* which combined the 1842 *Dramatic Lyrics* with the 1845 *Dramatic Romances and Lyrics*. In 1863, he redistributed the poems from the first two volumes and *Men and Women* but confusingly kept the old titles as categories. Basic accounts of the later versions can be found in William Clyde DeVane, *A Browning Handbook* (New York: Appleton-Century-Crofts, 1955), pp. 102–104, 150–53, and 205–208, in the text and notes to volumes 3 and 5 of *The Complete Works of Robert Browning,* ed. Roma A. King et al. (Athens, Ohio: Ohio University Press, 1969–), and in the notes to *Robert Browning: The Poems,* ed. John Pettigrew, supplemented and completed by Thomas J. Collins (New Haven: Yale University Press, 1981), vol. 1. Quotations in the present article come from the Pettigrew-Collins volume because of its accessibility and reliability; most of the poems are short enough for quotations to be located readily, but I have supplied line numbers within parentheses in my text for citations from the few lengthy poems of the volume. For those few cases dealing with the original wording I have followed the Ohio Browning, giving volume and page numbers.

5. See Mrs. Sutherland Orr, *Life and Letters of Robert Browning,* New Edition (London: Smith, Elder & Co., 1908), p. 122.

6. DeVane, *Browning Handbook,* p. 106, assigns composition of "Cavalier Tunes" to the summer of 1842. W. Hall Griffin and Harry Christopher Minchin in their standard *The Life of Robert Browning* (London: Methuen, 1910), p. 73, date composition of "Madhouse Cells" as April–May 1834, but later commentators have been sceptical; Collins, *Robert Browning: The Poems,* vol. 1, p. 1084, makes a case for 1835. The pair was first published in *The Monthly Repository* for January 1836.

7. Poston, "Browning Rearranges Browning," p. 41.

8. See Browning's letter to Alfred Domett, the model for Waring, on 22 May 1842, in which he announces his intention to "print a few songs and small poems which Moxon advised me to do for popularity's sake!" The letter is included in F. G. Kenyon, ed., *Robert Browning and Alfred Domett* (New York: E. P. Dutton & Co., 1906), pp. 33–39; the quotation is on p. 36.

9. M. H. Abrams, "Structure and Style in the Greater Romantic Lyric," in *From Sensibility to Romanticism,* ed. Frederick W. Hilles and Harold Bloom (New York: Oxford University Press, 1965), pp. 527–60. I have argued for adapting Abrams' schema to description-vision-evaluation in *Transformations of Romanticism in Yeats, Eliot, and Stevens* (Chicago: University of Chicago Press, 1976), pp. 9–10, 50–53, and passim, and have applied it to Browning's "Pictor Ignotus" in "The Structure of Browning's 'Pictor Ignotus,'" *Victorian Poetry* 19 (1981): 65–72.

10. John V. Hagopian in "The Mask of Browning's Countess Gismond," *Philological Quarterly* 40 (1961): 153–55, and John W. Tilton and R. Dale Tuttle in "A New Reading of 'Count Gismond'," *Studies in Philology* 59 (1962): 83–95 argue for a negative view of the Countess but go too far, as perhaps does Michael Timko in the other direction in his exasperated rejoinder, "Ah, Did You Once See Browning Plain?" *Studies in English Literature* 6 (1966): 731–42. Agreeing with some of Timko's reservations and with his rejection of the attempt to paint Count Gismond as tyrant in Sister Marcella M. Holloway's "A Further Reading of 'Count Gismond'," *Studies in Philology* 60 (1963): 549–53, I would take a middle ground and maintain that the evidence of the Countess's duplicity is neither definitive nor negligible, and that Browning exploits the resultant uncertainty in his subtle psychological probing. Harrold in *The Variance and the Unity* assumes the worst about the Countess; his passing remarks on the time sequence (p. 39) are suggestive.

11. In the often-quoted phrase of Browning's friend Joseph Arnould, "Waring" presents a "fancy portrait of a very dear friend"; see Kenyon, *Robert Browning and Alfred Domett,* p. 62. On the proof-sheets at Harvard, Browning wrote "Alfred Domett or" above the printed title. Browning borrowed the name Waring itself from a diplomatic messenger he met in Russia.

12. For a helpful discussion relating the poem to Browning's own artistic problems and biographical dilemmas, see John F. McCarthy, "Browning's 'Waring': The Real Subject of the 'Fancy Portrait'," *Victorian Poetry* 9 (1971): 371–82. McCarthy sees the poem as "an ironic treatment of the early Browning's favorite theme—the dilemma of the non-communicating artist-prophet"; I am unable, however, to share his view of Waring as "hard-boiled."

13. For example, Lord Malmesbury wrote in his *Memoirs of an Ex-Minister* (London: Longmans, Green, and Co., 1884) that she "was said at the time to be the cause of more than one inflammable victim languishing in prison for having too openly admired this royal coquette, whose manners with men foretold her future life after her marriage to old Ferdinand." (1:30)

14. Other passages pertaining to Elective Affinities in Browning include lines 25–30 of "The Statue and the Bust" and lines 1162–75 of "Caponsacchi" in *The Ring and the Book*. In his brief "Browning's 'Cristina'," *Explicator* 2 (1943–44), Item 16, Clyde S. Kilby helpfully corrects traditional commentary by suggesting that the speaker is "eccentric."

15. The headnote is conveniently reprinted in the Pettigrew-Collins edition, *Robert Browning: The Poems,* vol. 1, p. 1084.

16. See DeVane, *Browning Handbook,* pp. 126–27, and the Ohio Browning 3:384.

17. According to Mrs. Orr, *Life and Letters,* p. 122, the poem "was added to the *Dramatic Lyrics,* because some columns of that number of *Bells and Pomegranates* still required filling." Pettigrew and Collins, *Robert Browning: The Poems,* vol. 1, p. 1085, note that "The Pied Piper" appears in the second set of proofs but not in the first.

18. See Arthur N. Kincaid and Peter W. M. Blayney, "A Book of Browning's and His Essay on Chatterton'," *Browning Society Notes* 2 (1972): 11–25, esp. p. 23.

19. For more extended treatments of the artist theme in "The Pied Piper" see Milton Millhauser, "Poet and Burgher: A Comic Variation on a Serious Theme," *Victorian Poetry* 7 (1969): 163–68, and Wolfgang Francke, "Browning's 'Pied Piper of Hamelin': Two Levels of Meaning," *ARIEL: A Review of International English Literature* 2 (1971): 90–97. Francke confuses *Dramatic Lyrics* (1842) with the 1849 collection.

20. Francke, "Browning's 'Pied Piper'," pp. 96–97.

James E. Miller, Jr.
Whitman's *Leaves* and the American "Lyric-Epic"

"Certain writers belong not only to the history of literature but to history itself, and Whitman is one of them. . . . Psychically, his life stretched from the Revolution through the Civil War to the era of the robber barons. Truly an American poet of change . . . Whitman was several men in one: Brahmin, bohemian, spokesman for a new democratic society, dandy, creator of an original kind of American poetry—a self-educated and self-intoxicated peasant of the ecstatic."[1]

These words open Howard Moss's 1981 *New Yorker* review of Justin Kaplan's *Walt Whitman—A Life*. I have quoted this passage not only because it is a remarkable summary view of Whitman's achievement but also because the general nature of the review (a lengthy outpouring of praise for Whitman) together with its appearance in *The New Yorker* may be taken to symbolize the radical shift in Whitman's fortunes during the past thirty or forty years—a period of time during which his poetry was more frequently scorned than praised, especially by successive dominant critical movements, beginning with the New Criticism.

Indeed, Moss places Whitman in rarefied company in the concluding sentence of his review: "Whitman bears a relation to Lincoln not unlike Shakespeare's to Elizabeth I and Michelangelo's to the Medici. In each instance, as the years pass the more obvious it becomes that the representative figure of the age, like a negative gradually developing in time, is not the ruler, but the artist." If Whitman's placement in such company is to be justified, surely the justification would have to be based on his creation of what Moss described earlier as "an original kind of American poetry." I want to take that statement as my theme and inquire into the general nature of this "original kind of American poetry."

EVOLUTION OF THE "LYRIC-EPIC"

Whitman himself was not bashful about coupling his name with major poets of the past. In "A Backward Glance O'er Travel'd Roads," a prose piece written by Whitman near the end of his life as a review and assessment of his poetic career, Whitman set forth the "embryonic facts" of *Leaves of Grass*. One of these "embryonic facts" was, he tells us, his long-ago reading of the Bible, Homer, Shakespeare, the "old German Nibelungen," the "ancient Hindoo poems," and Dante.[2] Whitman clearly saw himself and *Leaves of Grass* as the heirs of such a lineage.

But Whitman also saw himself, surprisingly, as indebted to Edgar Allan Poe. Although he confessed his lack of admiration for Poe's poetry in "A Backward Glance," he magnanimously embraced him ("the poetic area is very spacious—has room for all—has so many mansions!"), and then described Poe's influence on him: "I was repaid in Poe's prose by the idea that (at any rate for our occasions, our day) there can be no such thing as a long poem. The same thought had been haunting my mind before, but Poe's argument, though short, work'd the sum and proved it to me" (p. 450).

Poe's argument, in "The Philosophy of Composition," had been a relatively simple and direct one: "What we term a long poem is, in fact, merely a succession of brief ones—that is to say, of brief poetical effects. It is needless to demonstrate that a poem is such, only inasmuch as it intensely excites, by elevating, the soul; and all intense excitements are, through a psychal necessity, brief. For this reason, at least one half of the 'Paradise Lost' is essentially prose—a succession of poetical excitements interspersed, *inevitably,* with corresponding depressions—the whole being deprived, through the extremeness of its length, of the vastly important artistic element, totality, or unity, of effect."[3] In "The Poetic Principle," Poe noted that separate readings of *Paradise Lost* could discover quite different sequences of passages of lyric intensity—the prose passages becoming lyric, and the lyric becoming prose.[4]

Whitman's confession that Poe convinced him there could be no such thing as a long poem may seem strange, coming as it does from the poet of "Song of Myself" as well as that greatest of all American long poems, *Leaves of Grass*. But in effect, what Poe did for Whitman (confirming a "thought [that] had been haunting [his] mind before") was to enable him to see how to write his long poem without violating "psychal necessity"—that is, by making the long poem out of a sequence of subtly related lyric moments. In the very next paragraph of "A Backward Glance," Whitman lists another "embryonic fact" about his *Leaves* that sets forth what was, with elaboration, to become the new American genre, the personal or lyric-epic. Notice in Whitman's opening language here his sense of discovery and innovation: "Another point had an early settlement, clearing the ground greatly, I saw, from the time my enterprise and questionings positively shaped themselves (how best can I express my own distinctive era and surroundings, America, Democracy?) that the trunk and centre whence the answer was to radiate, and to which all should return from straying however far a distance, must be an identical body and soul, a personality—which personality, after many considerations and ponderings I deliberately settled should be myself—indeed could not be any other" (p. 450).

It appears clear from the beginning, at least as he remembered that beginning in old age, that Whitman's ambition was epic, but that he had to invent a new epic form for the new era and the new country. Poe gave him the clue for his basic structure of a lyric-epic, and out of his deeply rooted sense of his American self-hood he concluded that his own personality must be the "trunk and centre" of an enterprise that was to express his time and his country, America and Democracy.

Throughout "A Backward Glance," Whitman emphasized the intimate connection of his book with his country, of his selfhood with America's "nationhood": "Behind all else that can be said, I consider 'Leaves of Grass' and its theory experimental—as, in the deepest sense, I consider our American republic itself to be, with its theory." By placing emphasis on theory—the theory of *Leaves of Grass,* the theory of the "American republic"—Whitman emphasizes form, form in its most comprehensive sense. In getting at the essence of that form, Whitman describes in embryo the lyric-epic. He would, he said, "articulate and faithfully" express his "physical, emotional, moral, intellectual, and aesthetic Personality," while at the same time "tallying . . . current America," and he would "exploit that Personality, identified with place and date, in a far more candid and comprehensive sense than any hitherto poem or book" (p. 444). Self and society, the one and the all, the individual and the nation—or, as set forth in the opening lines of *Leaves of Grass:* "One's-self I sing, a simple separate person, / Yet utter the word Democratic, the word En-Masse" (p. 5).

Can we, in any legitimate sense, say that this form, the lyric-epic, is genuinely new and genuinely American? There is no doubt that Whitman thought so; but he was at pains to make his claims with careful discrimination, emphasizing continuities as well as new beginnings. He wrote: "As America fully and fairly construed is the legitimate result and evolutionary outcome of the past, so I would dare to claim for my verse. Without stopping to qualify the averment, the Old World has had the poems of myths, fictions, feudalism, conquest, caste, dynastic wars, and splendid exceptional characters and affairs, which have been great; but the New World needs the poems of realities and science and of the democratic average and basic equality, which shall be greater. In the centre of all, and object of all, stands the Human Being, towards whose heroic and spiritual evolution poems and everything directly or indirectly tend, Old World or New" ("A Backward Glance," p. 449). The key phrase here, as applied to the lyric-epic form of *Leaves of Grass,* is "legitimate result and evolutionary outcome of the past."

An important tenet of Marxist literary criticism, deriving from Georg Lukács among others, is that literary form in itself is ideological. One recent Marxist handbook affirms: "The true bearers of ideology in art are the very forms, rather than abstractable content, of the work itself. We find the impress of history in the literary work precisely *as literary,* not as some superior form of social documentation."[5] One need not subscribe to the dogma of Marxism to believe that literary form itself may embody or express values. Indeed, Whitman seems intuitively to have understood that to embody the new values he perceived and experienced in himself and his time and country, he needed a new form. In describing the initiating impulse behind *Leaves of Grass,* he wrote: "it seem'd to me . . . the time had come to reflect all themes and things, old and new, in the lights thrown on them by the advent of America and democracy—to chant those themes through the utterance of one, not only the grateful and reverent legatee of the past, but the born child of the New World—to illustrate all through the genesis and ensemble of today; and that such illustration and ensemble are the chief demands of America's prospective imaginative literature" ("A Backward Glance," p. 447). It is significant that Whitman sees his new form in effect called into being by the new order—the "advent of America and democracy"—and as important not only for him but also for "America's prospective imaginative literature."

Whitman saw, then, his masterwork both as an "evolutionary outcome of the past" and as a natural creation in response to the New World's new order. Focus on the self was related to the New World's elevation in importance of the human being, and constituted the *lyric* part of the new form. Focus on the en-masse, the country, "America and democracy," was related to the new political reality of the "democratic average and basic equality," and constituted the *epic* part of the new form. The lyric-epic thus represented a split or paradoxically divided form that was itself, by its very nature, rooted in the paradoxical ideal of the New World—the ideal that celebrated the transcendence of the individual and of the society simultaneously. The danger in the New World democracy was that individualism would run rampant, as it sometimes did on the frontier, ending in chaos or nihilism, or that equality would induce stagnation (in Main Street America), suppressing individual genius and imposing universal mediocrity. Thus the very form of *Leaves of Grass,* the lyric-epic, holding in harmonious tension *individual* and *en-masse,* became a reflection of the political and social ideals of the new country and the new poet. The fact that the form does appear to bear this special relationship to the New World may explain its endurance into the twentieth century. Modern and contemporary poets have found the form a way of rescuing themselves from destructive nihilistic impulses on the one hand, or mere submergence in the massed mundane on the other. The American ideal, as opposed to the American reality (whatever that may be), continues to be the paradoxical and perhaps mystical goal of reconciling individuality and equality, freedom and fraternity.

Another apparently paradoxical element of Whitman's theory is his assumption that his ambition to write a work "tallying . . . current America" was perfectly compatible with his decision to "exploit" his "Personality" in a "far more candid and comprehensive sense than any hitherto poem and book." The question immediately arises as to how such comprehensive personal exploitation can possibly be made to relate to the "tallying" of America. For example, how can Whitman's celebrations, revelations, and confessions of the Self in "Song of Myself" and "Children of Adam" and "Calamus" have any relationship to America and the democratic ideal? This question becomes even more puzzling, perhaps, when it is recalled that in these parts of *Leaves of Grass,* Whitman's candid revelations about the Self are quite explicitly (though of course not entirely) related to sexuality. It might prove useful at this point to turn briefly to Sigmund Freud's *Civilization and Its Discontents,* a work that, like Whitman's, is deeply interested in the way individual psychology underlies or sheds light on the nature of civilization.

Freud's conception of the interrelationship of the individual and society is primarily sexual: "The love which founded the family continues to operate in civilization both in its original form, in which it does not renounce direct sexual satisfaction, and in its modified form as aim-inhibited affection. In each, it continues to carry on its function of binding together considerable numbers of people, and it does so in a more intensive fashion than can be effected through the interest of work in common." Freud turned to the "careless way in which language uses the word 'love'" for demonstration of his point: "People give the name 'love' to the relation between a man and a woman whose genital needs have led them to found a family; but they also give the name 'love' to the positive feeling between parents and children, and between brothers and sisters of a family, although *we* are obliged to describe this as 'aim-inhibited love' or 'affection.'"

Such "aim-inhibited love," Freud believed, was originally "fully sensual love, and it is so still in man's unconscious. Both—fully sensual love and aim-inhibited love—extend outside the family and create new bonds with people who before were strangers. Genital love leads to the formation of new families, and aim-inhibited love to 'friendships' which become valuable from a cultural standpoint because they escape some of the limitations of genital love, as, for instance, its exclusiveness."[6] There are many passages from *Leaves of Grass* called to mind by Freud's remarks here, but perhaps the most interesting are the concluding lines of a "Calamus" poem entitled "The Base of all Metaphysics":

> Having studied the new and antique, the Greek and Germanic systems,
> Kant having studied and stated, Fichte and Schelling and Hegel,
> Stated the lore of Plato, and Socrates greater than Plato,
> And greater than Socrates sought and stated, Christ divine having studied long,
> I see reminiscent to-day those Greek and Germanic systems,
> See the philosophies all, Christian churches and tenets see,
> Yet underneath Socrates clearly see, and underneath Christ the divine I see,
> The dear love of man for his comrade, the attraction of friend to friend,
> Of the well-married husband and wife, of children and parents,
> Of city for city and land for land.   (p. 89)

What Whitman finds the base of all metaphysics Freud asserts as the base for all civilization. Both writers see society as based on complex webs of love and friendship that in turn both see rooted in sexuality.

The point to be made here is not that Whitman and Freud exhibit identical conceptions of the origin and nature of social bonds (they don't), but rather that both see significant connections between the psycho-sexuality of individuals and the society made up by bonds among those individuals. As the self is found in society, so society is discovered in the self. It is clear, of course, that Freud is committed to a relatively narrow definition of selfhood as determined by psycho-sexuality, while Whitman assumes an expanded, certainly non-restrictive, definition—something perhaps as all-embracing as that idea of self he has sworn to "articulate and faithfully express" in his poem—his "physical, emotional, moral, intellectual, and aesthetic Personality" (ponder, for example, his beginning the list of attributes of the self with *physical* and *emotional,* and ending with *intellectual* and *aesthetic*). At the same time that Whitman will "articulate and faithfully express" this complex self, he also will *tally* "current America." Whitman links the two elements, the self and society, the lyric and epic dimensions, so closely that his articulation and expression of the one (the self) appears to be simultaneously the *tallying* of the other (current America). To know the self profoundly is to know society, in all its possibilities and deeper realities.

Just how the probing into self leads to insight into society is, perhaps, in part suggested by Whitman's statement in his 1855 preface about the necessary relationship between the poet and his time: "The direct trial of him who would be the greatest poet is today. If he does not flood himself with the immediate age as with vast oceanic tides . . . and if he does not attract his own land body and soul to himself and hang on its neck with incomparable love and plunge his semitic muscle into its merits and demerits . . . and if he be not himself the age transfigured . . . and if to him is not opened the eternity which gives similitude to all periods and locations and processes and animate and inanimate forms, and which is the bond of time . . . let him merge in the general run and wait his development" (pp. 424–25). This startling passage was included, with some changes and revisions, in "By Blue Ontario's Shore" in a description of the American bard:

> incarnating this land,
> Attracting its body and soul to himself, hanging on its neck with
>   incomparable love,
> Plunging his seminal muscle into its merits and demerits,
> Making its cities, beginnings, events, diversities, wars, vocal in him,
> Making its rivers, lakes, bays, embouchure in him.   (p. 243)

Whitman's image of the American bard embracing his country as lover and "plunging his seminal muscle into its merits and demerits" is astonishing, not to say shocking (*semitic* became *seminal* in the revision). The figure suggests Whitman's obscure awareness of sexual energy as source not only for the poet's lyric but also his epic-function, inspiring his probing of the nation's virtues as well as its faults.

If the poet has become the "age transfigured," has come to incarnate "this land," or if he can say with Whitman in "By Blue Ontario's Shore," "O I see flashing that this America is only you and me" (p. 250), then he has his justification for writing his lyric-epic in which he sets himself forth as his own hero; he is ready, as Pound said of Whitman, to go "bail for the nation."[7] The poets who have come after Whitman and have devoted their energies and talents to the construction of their own lyric-epics have not all appeared ready to "go bail for the nation," but they have appeared eager to plunge their seminal muscles into America's merits and demerits, sometimes as an act of love, sometimes in rapacious assault.

RECENT EXAMPLES OF THE "LYRIC-EPIC"

In 1976, Donald Davie, in a review of John Berryman's posthumously published essays, *The Freedom of the Poet,* noted that Berryman had shifted his "stance toward his art" in mid-career and attributed the change to the author of *Leaves of Grass:* "the shift seems to have to do, not surprisingly, with that inescapable figure in every American poet's heritage, Walt Whitman."[8] Davie could say "not surprisingly," perhaps because of his awareness of Whitman's impact on an American poet about whom Davie had written an important book—Ezra Pound. In a 1909 essay on Whitman, Pound had written:

> Mentally I am a Walt Whitman who has learned to wear a collar and a dress shirt (although at times inimical to both). Personally I might be very glad to conceal my relationship to my spiritual father and brag about my more congenial ancestry—Dante, Shakespeare, Theocritus, Villon, but the descent is a bit difficult to establish. And, to be frank, Whitman is to my fatherland (*Patriam quam odi et amo* [the fatherland I love and hate so much] for no uncertain reasons) what Dante is to Italy and I at my best can only be a strife for a renaissance in America of all the lost or temporarily mislaid beauty, truth, valor, glory of Greece, Italy, England and all the rest of it.[9]

It is difficult to think of any important America poet who has not felt, like Pound, the need to produce his own long poem—and who has not felt that Whitman was looking over his shoulder as he wrote. And the long poems that have been produced have had the characteristics that Whitman brought together for the first time in *Leaves of Grass:* the form of the lyric-epic, in which the smaller units are connected to the whole poem not through a continuing narrative within the poem but rather through a single sensibility—the poet's personality—that lies behind and filters through them all and through this sensibility's engagement with history, with focus on the constantly flowing and shifting present. Thus the poem's structure reflects the contours of the poet's mind; the poem takes on the shape of a life, the configuration of a time. Whitman's achievement was that he brought into being an American form eminently adaptable to the American situation, a situation different from that of the European mother countries. America was perceived as the promised land, the last, great hope, a country without a past, without an identity. American poets have always felt an uneasiness in relation to their Americanness that would be impossible for Italians or Frenchmen or Englishmen to feel in their national identity. The lyric-epic has provided them a form in which to explore themselves and their country simultaneously.

Thus by delving into themselves and their deepest identity, these lyric poets have tried to reach, in personal-communal depths, the epic dimension of their enterprise. It is interesting that most of these poets who have written long poems have spoken of their work, at some point or other, as epic in form. And a number of the most celebrated works in this genre form a tradition resonant with interrelated images and allusions and rich in intertextual assumptions and implications: Ezra Pound's *Cantos*, T. S. Eliot's *The Waste Land*, William Carlos Williams's *Paterson*, Hart Crane's *The Bridge*, Charles Olson's *Maximus Poems*, John Berryman's *Dream Songs*, and Allen Ginsberg's *The Fall of America*.[10] But there are innumerable other examples of the lyric-epic that come to mind, ranging from Louis Zukofsky's *A* to Edward Dorn's *Gunslinger*, from Carl Sandburg's *The People, Yes!* to Melvin B. Tolson's *Harlem Gallery*. Robert Lowell's several revisions of *Notebook* (1970) and his final abandonment of its structure for other arrangements under other titles (*History* [1973] and *For Lizzie and Harriet* [1973]) present a case history of a poet struggling in public to come to terms with the form and leaving it at last behind with the cryptic comment—"the composition was jumbled."

A. R. Ammons has written what might be called a model for a "disposable epic" in *Tape for the Turn of a Year*, published in 1965. The 205-page poem was composed entirely on an adding-machine tape, started through the typewriter in early December and continued daily until the tape ran out in mid-January. On the very first page—and periodically throughout—Ammons calls on the muse for help in writing his seemingly endless and necessarily narrow poem.

But more interesting for us here is Ammons's poem, *Sphere: The Form of a Motion,* published in 1974. It is interesting not only because it is remarkably effective as a long, multi-faceted poem but also because it invokes Whitman at a critical juncture to explain what the enterprise in hand is about:

> I can't understand my readers:
> they complain of my abstractions as if the United States of America
> were a form of vanity: they ask why I'm so big on the
>
> one: many problem, they never saw one: my readers: what do they
> expect from a man born and raised in a country whose motto is *E
> pluribus unum*: I'm just, like Whitman, trying to keep things
>
> half straight about my country: my readers say, what's all
> this change and continuity: when we have a two-party system,
> one party devoted to reform and the other to consolidation:

Like Whitman, Ammons sees the necessity in America to "reconcile opposites": the two parties of the U.S. are

> . . . both trying to grab a chunk out of the middle: either we
> reconcile opposites or we suspend half the country into
> disaffection and alienation: they want to know, what do I
>
> mean *quadrants,* when we have a Southeast, Northeast, Southwest,
> and Northwest and those cut into pairs by the splitting
> Mississippi and the Mason-Dixon line: I figure I'm the exact
>
> poet of the concrete *par excellence,* as Whitman might say:
> they ask me, my readers, when I'm going to go politicized or
> radicalized or public when I've sat here for years singing
>
> unattended the off-songs of the territories and the midland
> coordinates of Cleveland or Cincinnati: when I've prized
> multeity and difference down to the mold under the leaf
>
> on the one hand and swept up into the perfect composures of
> nothingness on the other: my readers are baffling and
> uncommunicative (if actual) and I don't know what to make of
>
> or for them: I prize them, in a sense, for that: recalcitrance:
> and for spreading out into a lot of canyons and high valleys
> inaccessible to the common course or superhighway: though I

> like superhighways, too, that tireless river system of streaming
> unity: my country: my country: can't cease from its
> sizzling rufflings to move into my "motions" and "stayings":
>
> when I identify my self, my work, and my country, you may
> think I've finally got the grandeurs. . . .

Here Ammons shows that he has learned Whitman's American epic formula well—identifying self, work, and country. And when he supposes that his readers will think that he has "finally got the grandeurs," he is slyly confessing that indeed he has got "the grandeurs"—in his epic intentions.

But like Whitman in *Democratic Vistas,* Ammons envisions America as a nation of poets who, in their poetry, lay the groundwork for the genuinely democratic spirit:

> I didn't mean to talk about my poem but
> to tell others how to be poets: I'm interested in you, and
> I want you to be a poet: I want, like Whitman, to found
>
> a federation of loveship, not of queers but of poets, where
> there's a difference: that is, come on and be a poet, queer
> or straight, adman or cowboy, librarian or dope fiend,
>
> housewife or hussy: (I see in one of the monthlies an astronaut
> is writing poems—that's what I mean, guys): now, first of
> all, the way to write poems is just to start: it's like
>
> learning to walk or swim or ride the bicycle, you just go
> after it: it is a matter of learning how to move with
> balance among forces greater than your own, gravity, water's
>
> buoyance, psychic tides: you lean in or with or against the
> ongoing so as not to be drowned but to be swept effortlessly
> up upon the universal possibilities: you can sit around
>
> and talk about it all day but you will never walk the tightwire
> till you start walking: once you walk, you'll find there's
> no explaining it: do be afraid of falling off because it is
>
> not falling off that's going to be splendid about you, making
> you seem marvelous and unafraid: but don't be much afraid:
> fall off a few times to see it won't kill you: O compatriotos,

sing your hangups and humiliations loose into song's
disengagements (which, by the way, connect, you know, when
they come back round the other way)....

Ammons's "compatriotos" seems to be a comic corruption of Whitman's "Camerados," but his advice to them to sing their "hangups and humiliations loose into song's / disengagements" reveals Ammons's clear understanding of Whitman's use of the personal as the path to the public and national. By their singing they may make a social difference. In a Whitmanian voice, Ammons calls out:

... O comrades! of the

seemly seeming—soon it will all be real! soon we will know
idle raptures (after work) leaning into love: soon all our
hearts will be quopping in concert: hate's fun, no doubt

about that, tearing things up and throwing them around and
ending some: but love is a deep troubling concern that rises
to the serenity of tears in the eyes: prefer that: hold

hands: help people: don't make a big fuss and embarrass
them, and if your empathy is right you won't, but help people
where the message is that it's called for: and when you're

tired out, write songs about hate's death and love's birth:
you'll get it straight, you'll see.....[11]

At first glance, phrases like "hearts . . . quopping in concert" may seem like parodies of Whitman's style. But if the style hints at the parodic, the tone is obviously affectionate and the message meant to be heard. Both Whitman and Ammons could celebrate "hate's death and love's birth" in a colloquial style simultaneously serious and humorous.

It serves Ammons's purposes to draw direct attention to the Whitman tradition with which he identifies himself and his poem. Two other contemporary poets have adapted the lyric-epic to their purposes without making direct reference to Whitman: John Ashbery in "Litany" (1979) and James Merrill in "The Book of Ephraim" (1976), *Mirabell* (1978), and *Scripts for the Pageant* (1980), published together with the coda ("The Higher Keys") under the title *The Changing Light at Sandover* in 1982. It would be impossible to do justice to these works in the restricted space available. But some of the responses they have elicited from reviewers reveal the current conceptions and misconceptions found in discussions of the lyric-epic form as it has evolved since Whitman.

The cluster of misconceptions expressed by one reviewer of the Merrill poem reveals, I think, the typical confusions that the lyric-epic form often arouses. The reviewer is upset because Merrill's long poem refuses to conform to his sense of an orderly narrative:

> To make a poem hold together when it is five hundred pages long, the poet must keep a large design in mind as he composes his verses and stanzas. But the shape of *Ephraim-Mirabell-Scripts* changes obstructively during the course of our passage through it. Characters who are introduced as important figures turn out to have little or no part in the story. Doctrines promulgated in one section are casually discarded in another. Spokesmen whom we are urged to trust confess themselves to be liars. Facts laid down in one place are contradicted in another.[12]

In search of a "grand design," in expectation of a conventional narrative structure, the critic can only find failure wherever he looks in Merrill's poem. And he goes on to condemn the cryptic outer shape that Merrill *has* given his trilogy:

> In *Ephraim-Mirabell-Scripts* not only does the element of narrative fail us, but the poet also relies on arbitrary schemes to give an impression of order. He divides *The Book of Ephraim* according to the letters of the alphabet on the Ouija board, beginning each section with the appropriate letter and sometimes finding themes that are appropriate. In *Mirabell* the digits from nine to zero inherit the same function, and in *Scripts for the Pageant* the three words "Yes," "&," "No." But these arrangements seem mechanical; they want inner meaning.[13]

Thus our critic rejects the poet's shaping of his poem after the symbols on the common Ouija board—alphabet, numbers, Yes, &, and No. This rejection might be likened to rejection of the outer form of the sonnet, with its arbitrary fourteen lines and arbitrary rhyme scheme, as wanting "inner meaning." There is playfulness, certainly, in Merrill's design of his poem as a poetic Ouija board that the reader must play for whatever messages might mystically come from the other side—the poet's locus. Thus the reader is put in the position of confronting a Ouija board whose common symbols may or may not yield the secrets the reader desires. And thus the reader comes to the poem as Ouija board and, in reading the poem, asks the poet to supply the missing messages of life, the elusive truths of existence. But this structure signals the reader that Merrill is not striving after a conventional narrative with a conventional narrative structure; he is striving after what our critic elsewhere finds in the trilogy, lyric moments of intensity and insight in a poem shaped to the poet's own sensibility and his own time—in the tradition of the lyric-epic as developed by Whitman.

The reviewer is moved so deeply by what he perceives as the failure of Merrill's long poem that he attempts at one point in a long digression to straighten out the history of American poetry and to define the delusion of American poets:

> Wallace Stevens once told Harriet Monroe that he wished to put everything else aside and amuse himself "on a large scale for a while." If he supposed the advice was good for American poets in general, I disagree. Our best poets came of age after extended narratives and lengthy works of exposition had deserted verse for prose. The so-called long poems of the last hundred twenty-five years (or since the first edition of *Leaves of Grass*) never represent a triumph of structure; the stronger the narrative, the weaker the verse.
>
> Too many learned critics have wasted too many specious demonstrations on the effort to fit fragments together and show us a marble temple. Lowell could not make *Notebook* into one grand poem by mere fiat. As for the "long poems" of Wallace Stevens, they exhibit so many redefinitions of the same images, so many reconsidertions of the same points of view, that we should do well to call them sequences—collections of poems on related topics. They may have key words and themes in common; but they have little necessary order, little consistency of doctrine, and much material whose omission would leave no obvious gap.[14]

The misconceptions multiply so quickly in these side remarks that one is at a loss as to how to begin to pursue them all.

The sweeping condemnation of 125 years of long poems is breathtaking and includes the major American poets of the twentieth century. Robert Lowell and his *Notebook* demonstrate not so much a failure of the form as a failure of nerve on the part of the poet to yield to and create the form of the lyric-epic. To see a Wallace Stevens long poem—say "Notes toward a Supreme Fiction," for example—as a "collection of poems on related topics" having "little necessary order" betrays a misunderstanding of Stevens's play of mind, play of language, and his subtle ordering principle that does indeed provide a beginning, middle, and end—but not the conventional narrative the reviewer seeks. Consistency of doctrine may have been a touchstone of eighteenth-century poems. But Whitman, when he exclaimed, "Do I contradict myself? Very well then, I contradict myself," provided the rationale for a consistency in poems higher than the consistency of doctrine—a consistency of sensibility or personality often in conflict with itself, beset by contradictory impulses and conceptions.

More might be said about this critical condemnation that would banish so much of twentieth-century poetry, but perhaps its central flaw is contained in that serene and static metaphor for a poetic structure—"Too many learned critics have wasted too many specious demonstrations on the effort to fit fragments together and show us a marble temple." It is difficult to think of a structural metaphor more incongruous than a marble temple for the lyric-epic form. The critics who have seriously analyzed the form have tended to find that what looked like fragments often fit together not in a temple, marble or other, but in a process, a movement of flow and flux, a tracing through or a working out in an open form that is following the contradictory contours of a mind, the rough and rocky terrain of a Personality in dynamic change, growth or contraction, encountering the present and playing out the drama of life. And amazingly often that growth, that life, takes on a shadow-shape of a narrative—as a poet, like every aware being, turns his life inevitably into story, into minor and major actions and plots.

I now turn to a reviewer with a critical approach fluid and flexible enough to engage a poem with the open form of the lyric-epic. In confronting John Ashbery's "Litany," this reviewer was faced with a poem running down the page in two columns, with Ashbery's prefatory note warning that "The two columns of 'Litany' are meant to be read as simultaneous but independent monologues." One can imagine the uneasiness this form would arouse in our Merrill critic. But listen to our reviewer:

> The best moments in Ashbery are those of "antithesis chirping / to antithesis" in an alternation of "elegy and toccata," all told in a style of "ductility, its swift / Garrulity, jumping from line to line, / From page to page." The endless beginnings and endings in Ashbery, the changes of scenery, the shifting of characters ally him to our most volatile poets—the Shakespeare of the sonnets, the Herbert of "The Temple," the Keats of the letters, the Shelley of "Epipsychidion." He is different from all but Keats in being often very funny; in "Litany," for example, he gives himself mock commands and injunctions: ". . . And so / I say unto you: beware the right margin / Which is un-

justified; the left / Is justified and can take care of itself / But what is in between expands and flaps. . . ."[15]

Unlike our Merrill critic, our Ashbery reviewer is inspired by the eccentricities of her poet's poem to imagine through analogy the nature of the poem's structure:

> . . . the small liturgical opera of "Litany" goes on through three parts, in a Protean masque of genres. Different readers will prefer different arias and, through the device of the double columns, different counterpoints. My current favorite is an ode to love:
>
> > . . . It is, then,
> > Gigantic, yet life-size, And
> > Once it has lived, one has lived with it. The astringent,
> > Clear timbre is, having belonged to one,
> > One's own, forever, and this
> > Despite the green ghetto that intrudes
> > Its blighted charm on each of the moments
> > We called on love for, to lead us
> > To farther tables and new, surprised,
> > Suffocated chants just beyond the range
> > Of simple perception.

The reviewer observes that this ode to love continues for about forty lines and then notes that the poem running in the paired column, in companion lines, offers a "reflection on solitude, perhaps preceding death":

> > . . . The river is waning
> > On. Now no one comes
> > To disturb the murk, and the profoundest
> > Tributaries are silent with the smell
> > Of being alone. How it
> > Dances alone, in winter shine
> > Or autumn filth.[16]

"As always in Ashbery," the critic says, "there is a new beginning, an upswelling."

Thus our commentator remains open to the possibilities presented by John Ashbery's long poem, "Litany." Her responses are remarkable in their flexibility and adaptability, with no demand for a beginning, middle, and end, but even a delight in many beginnings and many endings, and with no feeling of uneasiness or demand for consistency when an ode on love is paired with a reflection on solitude. She suggests that "different readers will prefer different arias" in "Litany"—and she is not bothered by this pluralism. She is, indeed, bold enough to quote her "current favorite," allowing for a change of mind on another reading. Thus our critic assumes the notion, proffered by Poe and endorsed by Whitman, that a long poem by its very nature breaks down into a series of lyrics—and this becomes often a different series at a different reading. Without evoking it, our critic intuitively attunes herself to the tradition I have attempted to sketch out here. The contemporary American long poem—the lyric-epic—yields most fully and richly to such a sensitively responsive approach.

Jorge Borges, who has become the hero of many self-styled post-modernists, has distilled the essence of Whitman's achievement in the new lyric-epic form in one of his many tributes to the New World Bard. His comment appears in his introduction to a little volume entitled *Homage to Walt Whitman: A Collection of Poems in Spanish, with English Translations*. Among the Latin American poets paying homage to Whitman in this volume are Borges himself, Rubén Dario, and Pablo Neruda (the latter an epic poet who deliberately attached himself to the Whitmanian epic tradition). Borges's comments provide an admirable concluding summary view, and the Whitman lines he quotes take on a new dimension and depth when brought into the focus of Borges's words:

> The task at hand [in Whitman's writing of *Leaves of Grass*] was, thus, epic; his solution, not less so. Poetry until then had required a hero, a man looming larger than his fellows: Achilles, Ulysses, Aeneas, Beowulf, Roland, the Cid, and Sigurd stand out for our admiration. Clearly this tradition would run counter to the very essence of democracy; the new society demanded a new kind of hero. Whitman's response was an amazing one: he himself would be the hero of the poem—first, as common circumstance had made him, as an American of his time; second, as magnified by hope, by joy, by exultation, and by the proud, full sail of his great verse. . . . Here [in the opening lines from "Starting from Paumanok"], both strands are interwoven; biography soars into mythology:
>
>> Starting from fish-shape Paumanok where I was born, well-
>>   begotten, and rais'd by a perfect mother,
>> After roaming many lands, lover of populous pavements,
>> Dweller in Mannahatta my city, or on southern savannas,

> Or a soldier camp'd or carrying my knapsack and gun, or a miner in California,
> Or rude in my home in Dakota's woods, my diet meat, my drink from the spring,
> Or withdrawn to muse and meditate in some deep recess,
> Far from the clank of crowds intervals passing rapt and happy,
> Aware of the fresh free giver, the flowing Missouri, aware of mighty Niagara,
> Aware of the buffalo herds grazing the plains, the hirsute and strong-breasted bull,
> Of earth, rocks, Fifth-month flowers experienced, stars, rain, snow, my amaze,
> Having studied the mocking-bird's tones and the flight of the mountain-hawk,
> And heard at dawn the unrivall'd one, the hermit thrush from the swamp-cedars,
> Solitary, singing in the West, I strike up for a New World.[17]

"Biography soars [indeed] into mythology" in these lines. And we might adopt Borges's descriptive phrase as a summary definition of that new American form, the lyric-epic, which was the legacy Whitman left for American "poets to come"—as they too "strike up for a New World."

NOTES

1. Howard Moss, "A Candidate for the Future," *The New Yorker*, 14 Sept. 1981, 184.

2. Walt Whitman, *Complete Poetry and Prose*, ed. James E. Miller, Jr. (Boston: Houghton Mifflin Co., 1959), p. 449. Further quotations from Whitman will be from this edition and cited parenthetically in the text.

3. Edgar Allan Poe, *Literary Criticism of Edgar Allan Poe*, ed. Robert L. Hough (Lincoln: University of Nebraska Press, 1965), pp. 22–23.

4. Ibid., p. 34.

5. Terry Eagleton, *Marxism and Literary Criticism* (Berkeley: University of California Press, 1976), p. 24.

6. Sigmund Freud, *Civilization and Its Discontents*, trans. James Strachey (New York: W. W. Norton & Co., Inc., 1961), pp. 49–50.

7. Ezra Pound, "Patria Mia," in *Selected Prose: 1909–1965*, ed. William Cookson (New York: New Directions, 1973), p. 124.

8. Donald Davie, Review of John Berryman, *The Freedom of the Poet*, The New York Times Book Review, 25 April 1976, p. 4.

9. Ezra Pound, "What I Feel about Walt Whitman," *Selected Prose,* pp. 145–46.

10. See my treatment of these poets in *The American Quest for a Supreme Fiction: Whitman's Legacy in the Personal Epic* (Chicago: University of Chicago Press, 1979).

11. A. R. Ammons, *Sphere: The Form of a Motion* (New York: W. W. Norton, 1974), pp. 65–67. The lines come from sections 122–127 of the poem, but the section numbers have not been included here.

12. Irvin Ehrenpreis, "Otherworldly Goods," *New York Review of Books,* 22 Jan. 1981, p. 49.

13. Ibid., p. 51.

14. Ibid., p. 47.

15. Helen Vendler, "Understanding Ashbery," *The New Yorker,* 16 March 1981, 127–28.

16. Ibid., pp. 128–30.

17. Jorge Luis Borges, "Foreword," in *Homage to Walt Whitman: A Collection of Poems in Spanish, with English Translations* (University: University of Alabama Press, 1969), pp. xiv–xv.

Marjorie Perloff
The Two *Ariels*
The (Re)Making of the
Sylvia Plath Canon

The reception of a slim book of poems called *Ariel* (published in London in 1965 and in New York in the early summer of 1966)[1] is by now legendary. The foreword was by none other than Robert Lowell and it was printed, not just inside the book as anyone might reasonably expect, but, tantalizingly, on the front cover, in italics:

From the introduction by ROBERT LOWELL

"In these poems, written in the last months of her life, and often rushed out at the rate of two or three a day, Sylvia Plath becomes herself, becomes something imaginary, newly, wildly and subtly created. . ."

And a purple arrow points us toward the inside where, after the title page and table of contents, we continue to read Lowell's characterization of Sylvia Plath as "hardly a person at all, or a woman, certainly not another 'poetess,' but one of those super-real hypnotic, great classical heroines." Referring to the title poem, Lowell observes that "Dangerous, more powerful than man, machinelike from hard training, she herself is a little like a racehorse, galloping relentlessly with risked, outstretched neck, death hurdle after death hurdle topped." And, in a sentence that was to be muchly cited, he concludes: "These poems are playing Russian roulette with six cartridges in the cylinder, a game of 'chicken,' the wheels of both cars locked and unable to swerve" (A, p. x).

So began the myth of the "literary dragon who . . . breathed a burning river of bale across the literary landscape" (*Time*, 10 June 1966), the "infirm prophet," whose poems exhibit "the madness within" as "the ultimate term of the objectivity and narrowness of the lyric poem" (Irving Feldman in *Book Week*, 19 June 1966), the "extremist poet" (A. Alvarez's term) par excellence.[2] Whether *Ariel* was to be read, in George Steiner's words, as "representative of our present tone of emotional life,"[3] or whether, as

Stephen Spender observed in a review called "Warnings from the Grave" (*The New Republic,* 18 June 1966), Plath's "landscape is an entirely interior, mental one, Keatsian in its intensity,"[4] the consensus of the late sixties was that this was a poetry of great "risk-taking," a poetry anguished, demonic, feverish, obsessed, violent, and tragic.[5]

In the seventies, revisionary readings began to appear, readings that tried to place Plath more firmly in the poetic mainstream; I myself gave one such early reading, making the case for Plath's poetry as a lyric of process in the Laurentian tradition, oscillating between the poles of *angst* and animism.[6] M. L. Rosenthal grouped Plath with the confessional poets (Lowell, Berryman, Sexton), and Judith Kroll submitted her poetry to an archetypal analysis based largely on Robert Graves's myth of the White Goddess, arguing that the poet's oeuvre exhibits a "vision which is complete, self-contained, and whole, a vision of a mythic totality."[7] Other critics began to make a case for the earlier poetry, suggesting that *The Colossus* (1960) was remarkable not so much for its "controlled hallucination" (Lowell's phrase for *Ariel*) as for its careful craftsmanship and brilliant imagery.[8] And feminist critics began to take a closer look at the repressed anger at patriarchy expressed in *The Bell Jar* as well as in the poetry.[9]

At the same time, no one doubted that *Ariel* was indeed *Ariel;* no one, that is, raised the issue of whether or not Plath's book, as published by Faber & Faber in London and Harper & Row in New York, reflected the poet's own stated wishes. It was generally assumed that Plath's estranged husband, Ted Hughes (whose name appears neither on the title page of *Ariel* nor in Lowell's foreword) had put together a collection of the poems written in Plath's final year.[10] The publication in 1971 of *Crossing the Water* (a volume of "transitional poems" written between *The Colossus* and *Ariel*) and in 1972 of *Winter Trees,* a slim volume of previously unpublished or uncollected poems from the *Ariel* period, did little to change the assumption that *Ariel* was all of a piece. A *Collected Poems* was, of course, projected but for reasons that the publishers never made clear, it did not appear until 1981, almost twenty years after Plath's death.

By this time, of course, the literary landscape had changed and interest in Plath's poetry had appreciably declined. She was, after all, only thirty-one when she died and so her oeuvre is, of necessity, limited in scope. More important, the question of mental illness, of consuming interest to a generation brought up on R. D. Laing's *The Divided Self,* is now regarded either as a disease to be controlled biochemically or as part of a larger cultural phenomenon; Lacanian criticism, for instance, is more interested in unmasking the verbal strategies of "sane" discourse than in dealing with individual psychosis. Again, the feminist movement, only in its infancy in Plath's lifetime, has put the "marriage plus career" problem, at the center of Plath's life and writing, in a rather different perspective; it is not that the problem has been solved, but Plath's stated desire to have "millions of babies" and her scorn for the "spinster bluestockings" of Cambridge and Smith is not likely to strike a sympathetic chord in young women today. Most important, Plath's rhetoric, at least the rhetoric of the earlier poems, now seems anything but revolutionary. Her controlled stanzas, heavy with assonance and consonance, her elaborate syntax with its inversions and subordinate clauses, her ingenious metaphors—all these now look, to a generation of younger poets, almost genteel, almost Victorian. In the famous debate over the "raw" versus the "cooked," a debate that has been with us since the forties, Plath's "Russian roulette," as Lowell called it, now seems more "cooked" than "raw." After all, doesn't Woody Allen's Annie Hall, hardly an avant-garde reader, have a copy of *Ariel* on her bookshelf?

Not surprisingly, then, the response to the *Collected Poems,* as to *The Journals of Sylvia Plath* (1982), for which Ted Hughes served as consulting editor, has been polite and dutiful rather than partisan or polemic. True, reviewers have expressed some dismay over Hughes's admission, in the foreword to the *Journals,* that he destroyed the notebook that covers the last months of Plath's life "because I did not want her children to have to read it (in those days I regarded forgetfulness as an essential part of survival)."[11] In an acute review, Nancy Milford points out that even the earlier journals have been, in Hughes's own words, "curtailed." "The question about these Journals," says Milford, "is always the same: who is doing the cutting? And why?"[12]

But the same question applies even more urgently to *Ariel,* and yet it has not been asked. In Hughes's introduction to the *Collected Poems,* we read:

> [For Plath] a poem was always "a book poem" or "not a book poem." . . . Some time around Christmas 1962, she gathered most of what was now known as the "Ariel" poems in a black spring binder, and arranged them in a careful sequence. (At the time, she pointed out that it began with the word "Love" and ended with the word "Spring." . . .)
>
> The *Ariel* eventually published in 1965 was a somewhat different volume from the one she had planned. It incorporated most of the dozen or so poems she had gone on to write in 1963, though she herself, recognizing the different inspiration of these new pieces, re-

garded them as the beginnings of a third book. It omitted some of the more personally aggressive poems from 1962, and might have omitted one or two more if she had not already published them herself in magazines—so that by 1965 they were widely known. The collection that appeared was my eventual compromise between publishing a large bulk of her work—including much of the post-*Colossus* and pre-*Ariel* verse—and introducing her late work more cautiously, printing perhaps only twenty poems to begin with. (Several advisers had felt that the violent contradictory feelings expressed in those pieces might prove hard for the reading public to take. In one sense, as it turned out, this apprehension showed some insight.) (CP, pp. 14–15)

On a first reading, this sounds reasonable enough: the addition of the 1963 poems, the exclusion of "the more personally aggressive" ones—presumably because they failed to formalize or distance Plath's experience—and the respect for the "reading public" which, so "several advisers had felt," was not ready for "the violent contradictory feelings" expressed in certain poems. The fact remains that Plath herself had arranged the future *Ariel* poems "in a careful sequence," plotting out every detail including the first and last words of the volume. In the notes to the *Collected Poems*, we find the list of poems to be included and their exact order. To compare what we may call Plath's *Ariel* to the book that actually appeared—which is to say, to Hughes's construction of *Ariel*—turns out to be something of a shock. For both *Ariel 1* and *Ariel 2*, as I shall call them, have a plot, but the two plots are so different that we cannot help but wonder what it means to reconstruct a poetic sequence after the fact.

The *Ariel* manuscript contains forty-one poems. In the following table, reprinted from the *Collected Poems* (p. 295), I have placed in parentheses the dates of composition, as Hughes gives them in the text. Unless otherwise noted, all the poems date from 1962.

Table 1
1. Morning Song (19 Feb. 1961)
2. The Couriers (4 Nov.)
3. The Rabbit Catcher (21 May)
4. Thalidomide (8 Nov.)
5. The Applicant (11 Oct.)
6. Barren Woman (21 Feb. 1961)
7. Lady Lazarus (23–29 Oct.)
8. Tulips (18 March 1961)
9. A Secret (10 Oct.)
10. The Jailer (17 Oct.)
11. Cut (29 Oct.)
12. Elm (19 April)
13. The Night Dances (6 Nov.)
14. The Detective (1 Oct.)

Table 1 (*continued*)
15. Ariel (27 Oct.)
16. Death & Co. (14 Nov.)
17. Magi (1960)
18. Lesbos (18 Oct.)
19. The Other (2 July)
20. Stopped Dead (19 Oct.)
21. Poppies in October (27 Oct.)
22. The Courage of Shutting-Up (2 Oct.)
23. Nick and the Candlestick (29 Oct.)
24. Berck-Plage (30 June)
25. Gulliver (6 Nov.)
26. Getting There (6 Nov.)
27. Medusa (16 Oct.)
28. Purdah (29 Oct.)
29. The Moon and the Yew Tree (22 Oct. 1961)
30. A Birthday Present (2 Oct.)
31. Letter in November (11 Nov.)
32. Amnesiac (21 Oct.)
33. The Rival (July 1961)
34. Daddy (12 Oct.)
35. You're (Jan./Feb. 1960)
36. Fever 103° (20 Oct.)
37. The Bee Meeting (3 Oct.)
38. The Arrival of the Bee Box (4 Oct.)
39. Stings (6 Oct.)
40. The Swarm (7 Oct.)
41. Wintering (9 Oct.)

Note that, with the exception of seven poems, all the *Ariel* poems were written between 19 April and 14 November 1962—a mere seven-month span. Even more remarkable, twenty-three, or more than half the poems were written in a single month—October—and there are six more for November but none at all for August or September. I shall come back to this curious gap later.

Table 2 lists the poems in *Ariel* (Harper & Row, 1966); the date of composition, as recorded by Ted Hughes in the *Collected Poems,* is again enclosed in parentheses:

Table 2
1. Morning Song (19 Feb. 1961)
2. The Couriers (4 Nov.)
3. Sheep in Fog (2 Dec./28 Jan. 1963)
4. The Applicant (11 Oct.)
5. Lady Lazarus (23–29 Oct.)
6. Tulips (18 March 1961)
7. Cut (29 Oct.)
8. Elm (19 April)
9. The Night Dances (6 Nov.)
10. Poppies in October (27 Oct.)
11. Berck-Plage (30 June)
12. Ariel (27 Oct.)
13. Death & Co. (14 Nov.)
14. Lesbos (18 Oct.)
15. Nick and the Candlestick (29 Oct.)
16. Gulliver (6 Nov.)
17. Getting There (6 Nov.)
18. Medusa (16 Oct.)

Table 2 (*continued*)
19. The Moon and the Yew Tree (22 Oct. 1961)
20. A Birthday Present (2 Oct.)
21. Mary's Song (19 Nov.)
22. Letter in November (11 Nov.)
23. The Rival (July 1961)
24. Daddy (12 Oct.)
25. You're (Jan./Feb. 1960)
26. Fever 103° (20 Oct.)
27. The Bee Meeting (3 Oct.)
28. The Arrival of the Bee Box (4 Oct.)
29. Stings (6 Oct.)
30. The Swarm (7 Oct.)
31. Wintering (9 Oct.)
32. The Hanging Man (27 June 1960)
33. Little Fugue (2 April)
34. Years (16 Nov.)
35. The Munich Mannequins (28 Jan. 1963)
36. Totem (28 Jan. 1963)
37. Paralytic (29 Jan. 1963)
38. Balloons (5 Feb. 1963)
39. Poppies in July (20 July)
40. Kindness (1 Feb. 1963)
41. Contusion (4 Feb. 1963)
42. Edge (5 Feb. 1963)
43. Words (1 Feb. 1963)

In putting together his version of *Ariel*, Hughes has eliminated eleven of the forty-one poems on Plath's own list, eight of them dating from the period October–November 1962. Further, he adds nine poems from the last six weeks of Plath's life in 1963. The result is that the volume is skewed in quite a different direction. What Hughes himself calls Plath's "careful sequence" has, I shall argue, a particular narrative structure; it begins with the birth of Frieda (hence the inclusion of the earlier poem "Morning Song") and moves through the despair Plath evidently experienced when she learned, in April 1962, that Hughes was having an affair with another woman, to the period of rage and mysogyny that followed upon his actual desertion in mid-September, a rage best expressed in "Purdah" (a poem missing in *Ariel 2*), and then to a ritual death and a move toward rebirth, as chronicled in what many critics consider to be Plath's finest poems, the Bee sequence. The last stanza of "Wintering" goes like this:

> Will the hive survive, will the gladiolas
> Succeed in banking their fires
> To enter another year?
> What will they taste of, the Christmas roses?
> The bees are flying. They taste the spring.

Ariel 1 thus ends on a note of hope. In *Ariel 2*, on the other hand, the poems that make only too clear that Hughes's desertion was the immediate cause of Plath's depression are expunged; instead, the volume now culminates in ten death poems, poems written, as it were, from beyond rage, by someone who no longer blames anyone for her condition and reconciles herself to death:

> The heart shuts,
> The sea slides back,
> The mirrors are sheeted. ("Contusion")
>
> The woman is perfected.
> Her dead
>
> Body wears the smile of accomplishment. . . . ("Edge")
>
> Words dry and riderless. . . . ("Words")

Indeed, the arrangement of *Ariel 2* implies that Plath's suicide was inevitable ("I have done it again"), that it was brought on, not by her actual circumstances, but by her essential and seemingly incurable schizophrenia. Or so the critics have interpreted it for the past two decades. The classic interpretation of Plath's "problem" is probably that of Murray M. Schwartz and Christopher Bollas in a psychoanalytic essay called "The Absence at the Center: Sylvia Plath and Suicide."[13] Schwartz and Bollas confirm what early critics like Alvarez and Steiner had surmised: that "When her father died [when she was only eight years old] the erotic component of Plath's identity, her sexuality as a woman, remained unconfirmed. The good libidinal attachment to the father could not realize itself and her subsequent fantasized relations with men confirm instead both her ambivalence toward her father's loss and her struggle against that loss" (p. 186). And again, "Plath's response to her father's death was to become like her father. The compulsive aspect of Plath's ritual of self-destruction mirrors the strongly obsessional nature of her personality. . . . Unable to find daddy in the outside world, she will get back to him by dying" (pp. 187, 189).

Aside from the fact that this account underplays the crucial—and very peculiar—role Sylvia Plath's mother played in this drama, a role I have discussed elsewhere,[14] it also ignores the reality of what actually happened to Plath in 1962. Schwartz and Bollas do suggest that "the precipitating factor in her final self-destructive journey was [Plath's] feeling of having been abandoned by Ted Hughes" (p. 198). The implication is that Plath *felt* abandoned, not that she really *had been* abandoned. Indeed, Schwartz and Bollas tell the story as follows:

[The] crisis of motherhood seems gradually to have overwhelmed Plath's resources. Her daughter was born in April 1960. By April 1961, she was in the midst of writing *The Bell Jar*. In 1961 she suffered a miscarriage, an appendectomy and became pregnant again. . . . In January 1962, her son was born, and like her own mother she now had a daughter and a son. The birth of her son seems to have provided her both with new confidence and new access to her own rage. In the summer of 1962 she suffered flu and high fevers, and in June she was involved in a driving accident that she described to A. Alvarez as a suicide attempt. In the fall of 1962 she moved herself and her children from Devon to London, where she rented a house once occupied by Yeats. The move was probably a response to a triangular situation in which she felt abandoned by Ted Hughes. Early in the mornings, before the children awakened, she wrote at amazing speed many of the poems in *Ariel*. (p. 198)

This account was written prior to the publication of *Letters Home* (1975) or Edward Butscher's biography (1976); it is based, moreover, only on a reading of *The Colossus* and *Ariel*, no reference being made to *Crossing the Water* (1971) or *Winter Trees* (1972), and certainly not to the poems of 1962 published for the first time in the *Collected Poems*.[15] Now that we have access to these materials as well as to the Plath papers in the Lilly Library (Indiana University), a very different story begins to emerge.

In April 1962, just three months after the birth of her second child, Nicholas, Plath found out that her husband was having an affair with Assia Gutman; the discovery is documented in her unpublished letters as well as in the poem "The Rabbit Catcher," which Plath put in *Ariel 1*, and in an even more explicit poem that she chose not to include called "Words Heard, by Accident, Over the Phone," with its pun on Assia's name, "Now the room is ahiss. The instrument / Withdraws its tentacle" (CP, pp. 202–203).[16]

The import of such an overheard telephone conversation can be understood only against the background of Plath's total devotion to and dependency upon her husband; indeed, it is not too much to say that she worshipped him. When, for example, Hughes's *The Hawk in the Rain* won the first Harper's publication contest (February 1957), Plath writes in her journal: "I am so glad Ted is first. All my pat theories against marrying a writer dissolve with Ted: his rejections more than double my sorrow & his acceptances rejoice me more than mine—it is as if he is the perfect male counterpart to my own self: each of us giving the other an extension of the life we believe in living" (J, p. 154). And a year later, when they were both teaching at Smith, we read in the journal:

> Woke as usual, feeling sick and half-dead, eyes stuck together, a taste of winding sheets on my tongue after a horrible dream involving, among other things, Warren [Sylvia's brother] being blown to death by a rocket. Ted, my saviour, emerging out of the *néant* with a tall mug of hot coffee which, sip by sip, rallied me to the day as he sat at the foot of the bed dressed for teaching. About to drive off—I blink every time I see him afresh . . . he is unbelievable and the more so because he is my husband and I somehow love cooking for him (made a lemon layer cake last night) and being secretary, and all. And, riffling through all the other men in the world who bore me with their partialness, the only one. (J, p. 221)

"Sylvia Plath," Hughes reminds us in the foreword to the *Journals,* "was a person of many masks, both in her personal life and in her writings. Some were camouflage cliché facades, defensive mechanisms involuntary. And some were deliberate poses, attempts to find the keys to one style or another" (J, p. xii). But even if we surmise that Plath is never quite "herself," even in her own private journals, it is clear that, at least with respect to the "selves" that functioned in the world, Ted Hughes was her idol. There is, accordingly, no reason to doubt Plath's plaintive statement, made in a letter to her patroness Olive Higgins Prouty (20 November 1962), that the novel she wanted to write after *The Bell Jar* was to be about "a wife whose husband turns out to be a deserter and philanderer although she had thought he was wonderful and perfect."[17]

The man held to be "wonderful and perfect," moreover, was having a secret affair with the wife of a mutual friend; the couple had been houseguests of the Hugheses in Devon just weeks before. When we bear in mind that Nick was only four months old at the time and demanded regular night feedings, that Frieda was just two, and that Plath, who had feverishly remodeled the old Devon farmhouse, had not yet regained her strength, we can sense how devastating her discovery must have been. Hence the "flu and high fevers" and the "driving accident" of the summer of 1962, mentioned so matter-of-factly by Schwartz and Bollas. Toward the end of that summer, there seems to have been some attempt at reconciliation; indeed, on 11 September, the Hugheses left the children with a nanny and set off on a trip to Ireland. It was here that Hughes told Plath he was leaving her. He departed the next day for London, where he took a flat and began divorce proceedings.[18]

August and September are thus the months of crisis and there are no extant poems from this period. The bitter and explicit poems of October that follow are omitted from *Ariel 2,* and so critics like Schwartz and Bollas misinterpret what happened. "In the fall of 1962," they write, "she moved herself and her children from Devon to London." It sounds tame enough; "the move was *probably* a response to a triangular situation in which she *felt* abandoned by Ted Hughes" (my italics). The fact that she *was* quite literally abandoned is never confronted. Indeed, more attention has been paid to the coldness of January 1963 in London, of the frozen pipes and the breakdown of central heating, than to the simple fact that Sylvia Plath, who had been "abandoned" by her father when she was eight, now found herself, at thirty, abandoned by the man who was supposed to take his place. She had two children under the age of three, very little money, and no close friends or relatives in England. Given these circumstances, a much more stable woman than Plath was might easily have become despondent. If Plath was, as *Ariel 2* presents her, an "Electra on the Azalea Path," she was also, and perhaps more notably, a Medea, the betrayed and vengeful wife. For a brief time, in the fall of 1962, vengeance and rage found their outlet in a set of remarkable poems.

Both versions of *Ariel* open with "Morning Song," a poem of acute ambivalence about motherhood. In Plath's later poetry, as I have suggested elsewhere,[19] childbirth is regarded as the greatest of gifts but it is also the source of severe anxiety. For if carrying a child gives the poet a sense of being, of having weight, of inhabiting her own body, the separation of the child's body from her own is regarded as a frightening state in which one feels weightless, empty, disembodied. The point is made more baldly in "Barren Woman," written two days after "Morning Song" and not included in *Ariel 2:* "Empty, I echo to the least footfall, / Museum without statues," a museum in which "Marble lilies / Exhale their pallor like scent" (CP, p. 157).

The imagery of disembodiment and petrifaction ("New statue. In a drafty museum, your nakedness / Shadows our safety") has been noted often enough, but in the framework of *Ariel 1,* "Morning Song" is juxtaposed to the last poem in the volume, "Wintering," where the potential for rebirth is conveyed by the image of the flower bulb:

> Will the hive survive, will the gladiolas
> Succeed in banking their fires
> To enter another year? (CP, p. 219)

But here what is in question is not the birth of one's child but the birth into selfhood, the forging of a separate identity. That identity is symbolized by the queen bee:

> The bees are all women,
> Maids and the long royal lady.
> They have got rid of the men,
>
> The blunt, clumsy stumblers, the boors.
> Winter is for women— (CP, pp. 218–19)

Read against this text, the earlier "Morning Song" (one of only six poems from the period prior to 1962 included in the volume) takes on an ironic edge. If it is "Love" that set Plath's baby going "like a fat gold watch," the six jars of honey she has produced with the help of "the midwife's extractor" belong only to her. "Love"—the sexual act—can, in other words, produce a "bald cry . . . among the elements," a "new statue" whose mother and father "stand round blankly like walls." But there is another love, so "Wintering" implies, that can produce a poem: note the assertive tone of "I have my honey, Six jars of it, / Six cat's eyes in the wine cellar."

Between these two poles—the pole of the "Love" for a man that produces babies and the pole of rebirth as an isolate self, a rebirth that produces the honey of poetry—the narrative of *Ariel 1* unfolds. The note of distrust of the male is introduced in what is the second poem in both versions of *Ariel*, "The Couriers":

> The word of a snail on the plate of a leaf?
> It is not mine. Do not accept it.

And, more explicitly in the third couplet:

> A ring of gold with the sun in it?
> Lies. Lies and a grief.

This "disturbance in mirrors," the failure in vision that characterized the poet's marriage, is made quite explicit in the next poem, "The Rabbit Catcher," which seems to be the first poem Plath wrote after she found out about Hughes's infidelity. Here the speaker identifies with the rabbits for whom her husband has set traps: "it was a place of force— / the wind gagging my mouth with my own blown hair, / Tearing off my voice" (CP, p. 193). The rabbit traps are insidious for they cannot be easily detected: "the snares almost effaced themselves— / Zeros, shutting on nothing, / Set close, like birth pangs." The reference is, of course, to Plath's recent labor and the birth of Nick, a birth that should never have occurred in this context. Here are the last two stanzas of "The Rabbit Catcher":

> I felt a still busyness, an intent.
> I felt hands round a tea mug, dull, blunt,
> Ringing the white china.
> How they awaited him, those little deaths!
> They waited like sweethearts. They excited him.
>
> And we, too, had a relationship—
> Tight wires between us,
> Pegs too deep to uproot, and a mind like a ring
> Sliding shut on some quick thing,
> The constriction killing me also.   (CP, p. 194)

In her fevered vision, the poet confutes the rabbit snare with the male hand, squeezing the white china tea mug and, by extension, the throat of the woman who serves him his tea. The parent text here is Lawrence's "Love on the Farm," but whereas in Lawrence, the caress of "his fingers that still smell grim / of the rabbit's fur" produces instant sexual arousal, in Plath, the same image spells only death: indeed, the man's hand can caress only an inanimate object, while his mind is like a steel ring "Sliding shut on some quick thing."

It can be argued that Hughes omitted this poem from *Ariel* because it is too "personally aggressive," but, with the possible exception of the bald line, "And we, too, had a relationship," it is no more Gothic, no more sensational than, say, "Lady Lazarus" or even the famous "Daddy." No, the "fault" of "The Rabbit Catcher" would seem to be its explicit reference to the broken marriage; not surprisingly, Hughes replaces it with "Sheep in Fog," a much less personal lyric that belongs to the cycle of death poems of January–February 1963. Notice that the poet's anger is now internalized and that she speaks of her fate as inevitable:

> The hills step off into whiteness.
> People or stars
> Regard me sadly, I disappoint them.   (p. 262)

The "dolorous bells" toll for the poet who partly longs, partly fears the "dark water" beyond the "heaven / Starless and fatherless." She is beyond anger, which is to say, beyond life.

Touching as such poems are, they are not the poems Plath intended to publish in *Ariel*. "Sheep in Fog" is not on her list; rather, "The Rabbit Catcher" is followed by "Thalidomide" (not in *Ariel 2*), and "The Applicant." The former, despite its ostensible subject, refers indirectly to Hughes in such phrases as "The lopped / Blood-caul of absences," and "White spit / Of indifference!"; in the last lines, the image of the broken mirror, regularly associated with the betraying male, recurs: "The glass cracks across, / The image / Flees and aborts like dropped mercury."

The latter poem, "The Applicant," extends this imagery, but in the context of *Ariel 2*, where it follows "Sheep in Fog," it has been read primarily as a blistering attack on modern advertising techniques. Thus Richard Allen Blessing talks of its "language that mocks itself while mocking the consumer and the product"; the "chauvinistic applicant," argues Blessing, must be seen, as he is by the poet, for the "abomination" he is.[20] Such interpretations are in accord with Plath's own explanation, prepared for a BBC broadcast, that "the speaker is an executive, a sort of exacting supersalesman. He wants to be sure the applicant for his marvelous product really needs it and will treat it right" (see CP, p. 293).

But who is this applicant anyway? He is told to open his hand and, when it is revealed to be empty, he is promised "a hand / To fill it and willing / To bring teacups and roll away headaches / And do whatever you tell it. / Will you marry it?" Marriage, in other words, demands of the woman that she turn herself into a mindless robot, administering to the comforts of the man in the "waterproof, shatterproof" suit. This man is promised a "sweetie," who is rolled out of the closet, "Naked as paper to start":

> But in twenty-five years she'll be silver,
> In fifty, gold.
> A living doll, everywhere you look.
> It can sew, it can cook,
> It can talk, talk, talk.
>
> It works, there is nothing wrong with it.
> You have a hole, it's a poultice.
> You have an eye, it's an image.
> My boy, it's your last resort.
> Will you marry it, marry it, marry it.   (CP, pp. 221–22)

In the context of *Ariel 1,* this is a sardonic indictment of the traditional marriage that had been Sylvia Plath's. If the husband is to blame for his demands, so is the wife for her acquiescence to them, for her willingness to be "A living doll," an "It" that can sew and cook, that acts as a "poultice" for his "hole," an image or mirror reflection of what is in his eye. The phrasal repetitions and harsh ballad rhythms of the poem also act to cast a spell on the Other Woman, the one who is going to be put in the doll's house and asked to "bring teacups and roll away headaches," to sew and to cook and to apply the "poultice." "My boy, it's your last resort" thus has the force of a veiled threat; in marrying this "it" (Ted marrying Assia), the "applicant" is contemptuously dismissed to the realm of the "Empty," a realm of "Rubber breasts or a rubber crotch," that can no longer threaten the poet in her splendid isolation and superiority. Reborn as "Lady Lazarus" in the next poem, she sheds "A cake of soap, / A wedding ring, / A gold filling," and, rising above "The peanut-crunching crowd," becomes a red-haired demon who can "eat men like air."

The voice of "Lady Lazarus" is still that of outrage; the poet cannot yet transcend the sense of personal loss and the need for vengeance expressed in such tercets as

> Dying
> is an art, like everything else
> I do it exceptionally well.
>
> I do it so it feels like hell.
> I do it so it feels real.
> I guess you could say I've a call.   (CP, p. 245)

These famous lines may now strike us as merely overwrought: "Naked negation," as Hugh Kenner put it, "spilling down the sides of improvised vessels."[21] More poignant, I think, is the tension between the death wish and the longing for life expressed in the poems that follow "Lady Lazarus" in *Ariel 1:* first in "Tulips," written in March 1961, when Plath was recovering in the hospital from an appendectomy,[22] and then in two poems that were to be omitted from Hughes's *Ariel:* "A Secret" and "The Jailer." Both date from the same week of October 1962 as "The Applicant."

"A Secret" avoids the Gothic trappings of "Lady Lazarus" by locating the betrayal of the husband-father within the familiar and seemingly cosy world of the baby's nursery, with its colorful wallpaper, quilts, and coverlets. The threatening "you" thus becomes "blue and huge, a traffic policeman, / Holding up one palm," a figure in a child's picture book, whose presence is almost obscured by "the African giraffe in its Edeny greenery" (notice the purposely foolish rhyme) and the "Moroccan hippopotamus," both of whom "stare from a square, stiff frill." Silhouettes on the baby's coverlet or the canopy of the crib, these friendly creatures turn threatening, for they cannot help but embody the "secret" of the husband-father, even if it is only a "Faint, undulant watermark," which the poet, who has "one eye" (blindness) as compared to his two, has failed to decipher. So terrible is "the secret" that the speaker now perceives her baby as "illegitimate," a rotten apple stuck in the bureau drawer under the lingerie. Illegitimate because its father has disowned it, because his secret wish is to "Do away with the bastard." In the hallucinatory vision of the last four stanzas, the unwanted baby is seen as emerging from its hiding place in a sudden and violent rush that recalls the stampede on the Place de la Concorde when the traffic light changes ("My god, there goes the stopper!"). The cars suddenly pour out even as a bottle of stout explodes, "Slack foam in the lap." The infant leaps out from its mother's lap, a "Dwarf baby, / The knife in your back." The father has "killed" the child even as the mother has given it birth. The poem concludes with this terrifying "delivery":

> 'I feel weak.'
> The secret is out.   (CP, p. 220)

"The Jailer" presents the next phase in this family drama. Once "the secret is out," man and wife become jailer and jailed:

> My night sweats grease his breakfast plate.
> The same placard of blue fog is wheeled into position
> With the same trees and headstones.
> Is that all he can come up with,
> The rattler of keys?   (CP, p. 226)

The nursery is now replaced by the graveyard, the sex act by the "rape" of the sleeping pill, the only escape being "the black sack" of oblivion, where the poet can ironically "relax" by fueling not her husband's real but only "his wet dreams." But the sleeping pill wears off:

> O little gimlets—
> What holes this papery day is already full of!

> He has been burning me with cigarettes,
> Pretending I am a negress with pink paws.
> I am myself. That is not enough.

The recognition of the last line is especially poignant in its irony; the poet has no stable self, and the "self" that she projects is therefore not enough. Accordingly, she can only get through the day by "gluing my church of burnt matchsticks," trying to exorcise the image of the powerful male who has put her in this position ("How did I get here?"). The victim is now beginning to question the victimizer:

> I imagine him
> Impotent as distant thunder
> In whose shadow I have eaten my ghost ration.

Here the "ghost ration" is, of course, Plath's own poetry, a poetry she had always regarded as taking second place to Hughes's own. The poem moves toward the recognition that the dependency has perhaps been mutual, that the jailer needs to have someone in his jail:

> What would the dark
> Do without fevers to eat?
> What would the light
> Do without eyes to knife, what would he
> Do, do, do without me?   (CP, p. 227)

Once the context set up by poems like "The Rabbit Catcher," "The Secret," and "The Jailer" has been established, images in Plath's best-known *Ariel* poems take on a somewhat different edge. In "Cut" (which originally followed "The Jailer"), the strange detachment whereby the speaker can watch her own blood gushing forth from her cut thumb, gives way, in the seventh quatrain, to the bitter recollection of the "Saboteur" or "Kamikaze man" who has brought her to this pass, who has turned her into a "Trepanned veteran," even though the actual kitchen accident has nothing to do with the absent husband.[23] In "Elm":

> Love is a shadow.
> How you lie and cry after it.
> Listen: these are its hooves: it has gone off, like a horse.

In "The Night Dances," she must convince herself that "Their [the father and son's] flesh bears no relation," that the father's "Cold folds of ego" cannot touch the "small breath" of the baby. In the famous title poem, the "Dead hands, dead stringencies" which the "White Godiva" "unpeel[s]," are identical to "the smell of years burning, here in the kitchen" which the speaker of "The Detective" (see *Ariel 1* where this poem comes between "The Night Dances" and "Ariel") must destroy. And in "Lesbos," the "widow's frizz" applies not only to the "Coy paper strips for doors" but to her own condition.

In *Ariel 1,* "Lesbos" is followed by "The Other" and "Stopped Dead." In all three, the poet's rage is now directed not at her husband but at other women and their children. "Lesbos" was the fruit of a visit, in late October 1962, to a couple in Cornwall whom the Hugheses had befriended; the visit, far from comforting Plath, evidently fueled her sense of isolation and separate destiny. No longer is the infant seen as a "new statue in a drafty museum"; rather "there's a stink of fat and baby crap," and the poet's own little girl is seen as a "Little unstrung puppet, kicking to disappear."[24] "The Other" (written in July) is more explicitly addressed to Assia:

> You come in late, wiping your lips.
> What did I leave untouched in the doorstep—
>
> White Nike,
> Streaming between my walls? (CP, p. 201)

In the nightmare vision of the speaker, the victorious woman destroys everything: the very air motes become "corpuscles"; the handbag opens to give off a bad smell, the "knitting [is] busily hooking itself to itself" like "sticky candies." Yet the once subdued, despairing poet can now triumph over her adversary; "The Other," ironically, is sterile: "the fornications/ Circle a womb of marble." She is no more than "a cold glass," and so her attempt to "insert" herself "Between myself and myself" fails.

Indeed, the poet's triumph over the sterile "Other"—a Victory who is, after all, only a "white Nike"—is fueled by her fierce devotion to her infant. In "Nick and the Candlestick" and "Gulliver," the baby, no longer associated in her mind with his father ("O love, how did you get here?"), becomes her sole love object:

> Love, love,
> I have hung our cave with roses,
> With soft rugs— (CP, p. 241)

And finally the Christ child:

> You are the one
> Solid the spaces lean on, envious.
> You are the baby in the barn.

"Nick and the Candlestick," whose concluding lines these are, was written on 29 October. On the same day, Plath wrote what is generally considered to be one of her finest poems, "Purdah," not in *Ariel 2* but published in *Poetry* in August 1963 (Plath herself had submitted it before her death) and then in *Winter Trees*. Written in condensed, elliptical tercets with elaborate sound patterning (for example, "Jade"/"side"/"agonized" modulating into "Side"/"Adam"/"Smile"), "Purdah" presents the transformation of a prelapsarian Eve into Clytemnestra. At the outset the "I" is no more than a piece of jade, a "Stone of the / Side of green Adam." If she "gleam[s] like a mirror," the "bridegroom" is "Lord of the mirrors"; she knows that "I am his. / Even in his / Absence." "Purdah" is associated, in this fierce poem, not with the eroticism of the harem but with the "cancerous pallors" of the moon, the same "cold and planetary" blue moon that we meet in the next poem, "The Moon and the Yew Tree." But whereas the latter poem posits only "blackness and silence," "Purdah" posits the possibility of escape from the bridegroom: first the unloosing of "One feather," then "One note / Shattering / The chandelier / of air," and finally:

> And at his next step
> I shall unloose
>
> I shall unloose—
> From the small jeweled
> Doll he guards like a heart—
>
> The lioness,
> The shriek in the bath,
> The cloak of holes. (CP, pp. 243–44)

Here is the move toward rebirth that finds its culmination in the Bee poems. The reference, as Margaret Dickie Uroff points out, is to the two lioness-goddesses of Egyptian mythology: "One is Sekhmet, the terrible goddess of war and battle, whose name means 'the Powerful.' Claiming that her heart rejoiced in killing, she attacked men with such fury that the sungod, fearing the extinction of the human race, appeased her with a magic potion. The other is Bast, whose origin as a lioness-goddess personified the fertilizing warmth of the sun. Goddess of pleasure, she loved music and dance. Plath's conception embraces both goddesses."[25]

"Purdah" is thus one of Plath's most forceful statements about power—the power to assume a new identity, to shed the "veil" of harem wife and destroy her former persona as "small jeweled / Doll." But in *Ariel 2*, Plath as Sekhmet-Bast or as Clytemnestra ("The shriek in the bath") is replaced by Plath as the Mother of God: "Mary's Song" (19 November), a poem Plath chose not to include in *Ariel*, emphasizes the role of the poet as war victim, a Mary whose Jewish son finds his fate in the glowing ovens of Poland. Indeed, in foregrounding what have always struck me as rather empty and hence histrionic references to the Nazis, the gas chambers, and the holocaust (see CP, p. 257), Hughes presents us with a Sylvia Plath who is victimized by her time and place rather than by a specific personal betrayal.

My own guess is that Plath omitted "Mary's Song" from *Ariel* because she was less than satisfied with the bathos of lines like "O golden child the world will kill and eat." In reinstating it, Hughes, so to speak, gives Lady Lazarus a motive and disguises the fact that Lady Lazarus is really the destructive-creative lioness of "Purdah." Again, he uses the poem to set the stage for "Daddy," a poem that is read quite differently in the context of "The Jailer" and "Purdah" than it is in the war-holocaust context of "Getting There" and "Mary's Song."

As in the case of "The Applicant," Sylvia Plath's explanation of "Daddy" in her BBC script is purposely evasive. "The poem," she says, "is spoken by a girl with an Electra complex. Her father died while she thought he was God. Her case is complicated by the fact that her father was also a Nazi and her mother very possibly part Jewish. In the daughter the two strains marry and paralyze each other—she has to act out the awful little allegory once before she is free of it."[26] As such, "Daddy" has been praised for its ability "to elevate private facts into public myth," for dramatizing the "schizophrenic situation that gives the poem its terrifying but balanced polarity"—polarity, that is to say between the hatred and love the "I" feels for the image of the father/lover.[27]

More recently, critics have begun to ask whether the Satanic imagery in "Daddy" is coherent,[28] whether, for example, lines like "With your Luftwaffe, your gobbledygoo" or "Not God but a swastika / So black no sky could squeak through" are more than fairly cheap shots, demanding a stock response from the reader. Indeed, both the Nazi allegory and the Freudian drama of trying to die so as to "get back, back, back to you" can now be seen as devices designed to camouflage the real thrust of the poem which is, like "Purdah," a call for revenge against the deceiving husband. For the real enemy is less Daddy ("I was ten when they buried you")—a Daddy who, in real life, had not the slightest Nazi connection—than the model made by the poet herself in her father's image:

> I made a model of you,
> A man in black with a Meinkampf look
>
> And a love of the rack and the screw.
> And I said I do, I do.
> So daddy, I'm finally through.
> The black telephone's off at the root,
> The voices just can't worm through. (CP, p. 224)

The image of the telephone is one that Plath's early admirers like George Steiner or Stephen Spender simply ignored but, with the hindsight a reading of the *Collected Poems* gives us, we recognize it, of course, as the dreaded "many-holed earpiece," the "muck funnel" of "Words heard, by accident, over the phone." And indeed, the next stanza refers to the "vampire" who "drank my blood for a year, / Seven years if you want to know." This is a precise reference to the length of time Sylvia Plath had known Ted Hughes when she wrote "Daddy"—precise in the opposite sense from the imaginary references to Plath's father as "panzer-man" and "Fascist."

A curiously autobiographical poem, then, whose topical trappings ("Luftwaffe," "swastika," "Dachau, Auschwitz, Belsen") have distracted the attention of a generation of readers from the poem's real theme. Ironically, "Daddy" is a "safe" poem—and hence Hughes publishes it—because no one can chide Plath for her Electra complex, her longing to get back to the father who died so prematurely, whereas the hatred of Hughes ("There's a stake in your fat black heart") is much more problematic. The age demanded a universal theme—the rejection not only of the "real" father but also of the Nazi Father Of Us All—hence the label "The *Guernica* of modern poetry" applied to "Daddy" by George Steiner. But the image of a black telephone that must be torn from the wall—this, so the critics of the sixties would have held, is not a sufficient objective correlative for the poet's despairing vision. The planting of the stake in the "fat black heart" is, in any case, a final farewell to the ceremony of marriage ("And I said I do, I do"). What follows is "Fever 103°" and the metamorphosis of self that occurs in the Bee poems.

The first of these, "The Bee Meeting," is a dream sequence in which the poet finds herself a victim, unprotected in her "sleeveless summery dress" from the "gloved," "covered," and veiled presences of the villagers. In the initiation ritual that now takes place, there are two dreaded male figures: the "man in black" (compare the "fat black heart" of "Daddy") and the

> surgeon my neighbors are waiting for,
> This apparition in a green helmet,
> Shining gloves and white suit.

Neither the black man nor his white counterpart is named; indeed, the poet asks: "Is it the butcher, the grocer, the postman, someone I know?" She cannot, in any case, run away:

> I could not run without having to run forever.
> The white hive is snug as a virgin,
> Sealing off her brood cells, her honey, and quietly humming.

The virginal white hive now becomes the source of new life for the poet, identifying, as she does, with the queen bee: "Is she hiding, is she eating honey? She is very clever. / She is old, old, old, she must live another year, and she knows it." "Exhausted," she can finally contemplate the "long white box in the grove" which is both coffin and hive. She is "the magician's girl who does not flinch."

In the next poem, "The Arrival of the Bee Box," the "dangerous" box of bees becomes a challenge that is desired: "I have to live with it overnight / And I can't keep away from it." The poet is now tapping her own subconscious powers; at the end of "Stings" we read:

> They thought death was worth it, but I
> Have a self to recover, a queen.
> Is she dead, is she sleeping?
> Where has she been,
> With her lion-red body, her wings of glass?
>
> Now she is flying
> More terrible than she ever was, red
> Scar in the sky, red comet
> Over the engine that killed her—
> The mausoleum, the wax house.   (CP, p. 215)

"I have a self to recover, a queen"; here is the lioness of "Purdah," the avenging goddess, triumphing "over the engine that killed her," just as the "swarm" in the next poem must evade "The smile of a man of business, intensely practical," a man "with grey hands" that "would have killed *me*." In the final poem, "Wintering," this male figure is no longer present. "Daddy," the man in black, the rector, the surgeon—all have disappeared:

> The bees are all women,
> Maids and the long royal lady.
> They have got rid of the men,
>
> The blunt, clumsy stumblers, the boors.
> Winter is for women—
> The woman, still at her knitting,
> At the cradle of Spanish walnut,
> Her body a bulb in the cold and too dumb to think.
>
> Will the hive survive, will the gladiolas
> Succeed in banking their fires
> To enter another year?
> What will they taste of, the Christmas roses?
> The bees are flying. They taste the spring.   (CP, pp. 218–19)

With this parable of hibernation, a hibernation that makes way for rebirth and continuity ("The bees are flying"), *Ariel* was to have concluded. But Hughes, not content to leave it at that, added eleven poems, all of which concern, not the possibilities of renewal, but, on the contrary, death. Thus "Wintering" is immediately and oddly followed by a poem of 1960 called "The Hanging Man," which presents the poet as possessed by "some god," a kind of "desert prophet," and ends ominously with the line, "If he were I, he would do what I did" (CP, p. 142). "The Hanging Man" serves as a kind of prelude for the January 1963 poems that follow, poems in which the inevitability of death is everywhere foregrounded. No longer does the poet look forward to the "Years"; her thoughts turn on "greenness, darkness so pure / They freeze and are" (A, p. 72). In "Paralytic," "all/ Wants, desire [are] Falling from me like rings / Hugging their lights" (A, p. 78); in "Contusion," "The heart shuts, / The sea slides back, / The mirrors are sheeted" (A, p. 83). Finally, in "Edge," (dated 5 February 1963, six days before her suicide), Plath imagines herself in death:

> The woman is perfected.
> Her dead

> Body wears the smile of accomplishment,
> The illusion of a Greek necessity
>
> Flows in the scrolls of her toga
> Her bare
>
> Feet seem to be saying:
> We have come so far, it is over. (A, p. 84)

And the final poem, "Words" (1 February 1963), is despairing in its sense that the poet's "words" become "dry and riderless," that they are no longer connected to the poet who gave them birth. The connection between self and language has been severed; there is only fate in the form of the "fixed stars" that "From the bottom of the pool . . . Govern a life."

One can argue, of course, that Hughes is simply completing Plath's own story, carrying it to its final conclusion where "Each dead child coiled, a white serpent" has been folded back into the woman's body, where the "Words" are entirely cut off from the poet who created them. But it is also possible that, in taking advantage of a brief spell of depression and despair, when death seemed the only solution, Hughes makes the motif of inevitability larger than it really is. "The woman is perfected" in more ways than one.

In any collection of poems, ordering is significant, but surely *Ariel* presents us with an especially problematic case. For two decades we have been reading it as a text in which, as Charles Newman puts it, "expression and extinction [are] indivisible,"[29] a text that culminates in the almost peaceful resignation of "Years" or "Edge." The poems of *Ariel* culminate in a sense of finality, all passion spent.

Ariel 1 establishes quite different perimeters. Plath's arrangement emphasizes not death but struggle and revenge, the outrage that follows the recognition that the beloved is also the betrayer, that the shrine at which one worships is also the tomb. Indeed, one could argue that the very poems Hughes dismissed as being too "personally aggressive," are, in an odd way, more "mainstream," that is to say more broadly based, than such "headline" poems as "The Munich Mannequins" or "Totem," with its "butcher's guillotine that whispers: 'How's this, how's this?'" (A, p. 75). For, as long as the poet can struggle, as long as she still tries to defy her fate, as she does in "The Jailer" or "The Other" or "Purdah," the reader identifies with her situation; the "Cut thumb" is not only Plath's but ours.

Perhaps Sylvia Plath's publishers will eventually give us the original

Ariel. But it is not likely, given the publication of the *Collected Poems*, which now becomes our definitive text. How ironic, in any case, that the publication of Plath's poems has depended, and continues to depend, on the very man who is, in one guise or another, their subject. In a poem not included in *Ariel* called "Burning the Letters" (CP, pp. 204–5), the poet decides to do away with the hated love letters, with "the eyes and times of the postmarks":

> here is an end to the writing,
> The spry hooks that bend and cringe, and the smiles, the smiles.
> And at least it will be a good place now, the attic.

But the attic was soon invaded, the dangerous notebooks were destroyed, and the poems that were permitted to enter the literary world had to get past the censor. The words of the dead woman, to paraphrase Auden, were modified in the guts of the living. Only now, more than twenty years after her death, can we begin to assess her oeuvre. But then, as Plath herself put it in a poem written during the last week of her life:

> The blood jet is poetry,
> There is no stopping it.

NOTES

1. Sylvia Plath, *Ariel* (London: Faber and Faber, 1965); *Ariel* (New York: Harper & Row, 1966). The New York edition includes one poem, "The Swarm," not in the London edition. All further references to *Ariel* will be to the Harper & Row edition, subsequently noted as A.

2. These early reviews are cited in Mary Kinzie, "An Informal Check List of Criticism," in *The Art of Sylvia Plath, A Symposium,* ed. Charles Newman (London: Faber and Faber, 1970), pp. 293–303. This collection is subsequently cited as Newman. See also A. Alvarez, "Sylvia Plath," in Newman, pp. 56–68, and his *The Savage God: A Study in Suicide* (New York: Random House, 1972), pp. 5–34.

3. George Steiner, "Dying is an Art," *The Reporter* 33 (7 October 1965); rpt. in Newman, pp. 211–18. Plath, says Steiner, was "one of a number of young contemporary poets, novelists, themselves in no way implicated in the actual holocaust, who have done most to counter the general inclination to forget the death camps," and he calls "Daddy" "the 'Guernica' of modern poetry" (p. 218).

4. Stephen Spender, "Warnings from the Grave," rpt. in Newman, pp. 199–203.

5. Mary Kinzie writes, "Whether they are pedantic, musing, miffed, or so obviously confused that they can't find cover, most reviewers become 'adjectival' to a fault," and she provides us with a revealing catalogue; see Newman, p. 289.

6. Marjorie Perloff, "*Angst* and Animism in the Poetry of Sylvia Plath," *Journal of Modern Literature* 1 (1970): 57–74.

7. See M. L. Rosenthal, "Sylvia Plath and Confessional Poetry," in Newman, pp. 69–76, and *The New Poets: American and British Poetry Since World War II* (New York: Oxford University Press, 1967), pp. 79–89; Judith Kroll, *Chapters in a Mythology: The Poetry of Sylvia Plath* (New York: Harper & Row, 1976).

8. See, for example, John Frederick Nims, "The Poetry of Sylvia Plath—A Technical Analysis," in Newman, pp. 136–52; Hugh Kenner, "Sincerity Kills," in *Sylvia Plath: New Views on the Poetry*, ed. Gary Lane (Baltimore and London: The Johns Hopkins University Press, 1979), pp. 33–44. This collection of essays is subsequently noted as Lane.

9. See especially Sandra M. Gilbert, "'A Fine White Flying Myth': The Life/Work of Sylvia Plath," in *Shakespeare's Sisters: Feminist Essays on Women Poets*, ed. Sandra M. Gilbert and Susan Gubar (Bloomington: Indiana University Press, 1979), pp. 245–60; Lynda K. Bundtzen, *Plath's Incarnations: Woman and the Creative Process* (Ann Arbor: University of Michigan Press, 1983).

10. I have not found a single book or article that questions the principle of selection that governs *Ariel*. Even Lynda K. Bundtzen, in what is the most recent book on Plath, writes: ". . . there is a strong continuity between the early and late work in terms of content, and the new choices she makes in *Ariel* are primarily those of style and presentation" (*Plath's Incarnations*, p. 163). The implication is that the *Ariel* we read is composed and arranged by Plath.

11. *The Journals of Sylvia Plath, 1950–1962,* ed. Frances McCullough; Ted Hughes, consulting editor, foreword by Ted Hughes (New York: The Dial Press, 1982), p. xiii. Subsequently cited as J. *The Collected Poems,* ed. Ted Hughes (New York: Harper & Row, 1981) is subsequently cited as CP.

12. Nancy Milford, "From Gladness to Madness," *The New York Times Book Review,* 2 May 1982, p. 31.

13. Murray M. Schwartz and Christopher Bollas, *Criticism* 18 (Spring 1976): 147–72; rpt. in Lane, pp. 179–202.

14. Marjorie Perloff, "Sylvia Plath's 'Sivvy' Poems: A Portrait of the Poet as Daughter," in Lane, pp. 155–78.

15. *Crossing the Water* was published in London by Faber and Faber and in New York by Harper & Row in 1971; *Winter Trees,* in London by Faber and Faber in 1971 and in New York by Harper & Row in 1972. I discuss the contents of these two volumes and the editing problems involved in "On the Road to *Ariel*: The 'Transitional' Poetry of Sylvia Plath," *Iowa Review* 4 (Spring 1973): 94–110; rpt. in *Sylvia Plath: The Woman and the Work,* ed. Edward Butscher (New York: Dodd, Mead and Co., 1975), pp. 125–42.

Letters Home: Correspondence 1950–63, selected and edited with commentary by Aurelia Schober Plath, was published in 1975 in New York by Harper & Row; Edward

Butscher's biography, *Sylvia Plath, Method and Madness* was published in 1976 in New York by The Seabury Press. Both of these volumes, although somewhat unreliable due to crucial lacunae in the texts, provide essential clues for the reading of the poems.

16. The discovery clearly comes some time between the writing of "Elm" (19 April 1962) and "The Rabbit Catcher" (21 May 1962): see CP, pp. 192–94. In *Plath's Incarnations*, Lynda K. Bundtzen cites some unpublished letters, written a few months later; these are in the Plath Manuscript Collection, Lilly Library, Indiana University, and are labelled Box 6, MSS II. On 9 October 1962, for example, Plath complains to her mother of "The foulness I have lived, his wanting to kill all I have lived for six years by saying he was just waiting for a chance to get out, that he was bored & stifled by me, a hag in a world of beautiful women just waiting for him." And on October 21: "It is as if, out of revenge, for my brain and creative power, he wanted to stick me where I would have no chance to use it. I think now my creating babies and a novel frightened him— for he wants barren women like his sister and this woman." See Bundtzen, *Plath's Incarnations*, pp. 26–27.

17. Cited by Bundtzen, *Plath's Incarnations*, p. 11.

18. See Butscher, *Sylvia Plath, Method and Madness* pp. 320–22; Plath, *Letters Home*, pp. 459–61.

19. See Marjorie Perloff, "On the Road to Ariel," in *Sylvia Plath: The Woman and The Work*, pp. 127–29.

20. Blessing, "The Shape of the Psyche: Vision and Technique in the Late Poems of Sylvia Plath," in Lane, p. 68.

21. Kenner, "Sincerity Kills," in Lane, p. 42.

22. I discuss this poem in some detail in "On Sylvia Plath's 'Tulips'," *Paunch* 42–43 (December 1975): 105–109; see also my "Sylvia Plath's 'Sivvy' Poems," in Lane, pp. 170–73.

23. See my "*Angst* and Animism in the Poetry of Sylvia Plath," pp. 70–72.

24. For the background of these poems, see Butscher, *Sylvia Plath, Method and Madness*, pp. 322–24; Plath, *Letters Home*, p. 469.

25. Margaret Dickie Uroff, *Sylvia Plath and Ted Hughes* (Urbana: University of Illinois Press, 1979), pp. 164–65.

26. See Ted Hughes, Notes to the *Collected Poems*, p. 293.

27. A. R. Jones, "On 'Daddy'," in Newman, p. 234.

28. See Irving Howe, "Sylvia Plath: A Partial Disagreement," *Harper's Magazine*, January 1972, p. 90; Hugh Kenner, "Sincerity Kills," in Lane, p. 43.

29. Charles Newman, "Candor is the Only Wile: The Art of Sylvia Plath," in Newman, p. 24.

Index

Abrams, M. H., 277, 287 (n. 9)
Agricola, Johannes, 283
Alvarez, A., 308
Ambrose (bishop of Milan), 44
Ammons, A. R.: *Sphere: The Form of a Motion*, 297–300; *Tape for the Turn of a Year*, 297
Andrewes, Lancelot, 172, 182
Anne (queen of England), 211
Aristotle, 79–80; *Poetics*, 69
Arnold, Matthew: "The Scholar Gypsy," 281
Arnould, Joseph, 287 (n. 11)
Ashbery, John: "Litany," 303–5
Auden, W. H., 13
Audra, E., 209
Augustine, Saint, 44, 68–70, 73, 79
Austen, Jane: *Pride and Prejudice*, 34–35

Bacon, Francis, 101
Baker, Daniel, 232 (n. 22)
Bannatyne, George, 14 (n. 4)
Barker, Arthur, 168
Battestin, Martin, 209
Beal, Peter, 132, 158 (n. 9)
Beckett, Samuel: *Malone Dies*, 31
Berryman, John: *The Freedom of a Poet*, 296
Bible
—Epistles, 169–70
—Genesis, 69
—Gospels, 165, 169–70
—Judges, 165, 178, 182, 185, 186–87
—Revelation, 170, 187–88, 189
Blake, William, 190; *Poetical Sketches*, 10, 11; *Songs of Innocence and of Experience*, 190
Blessing, Richard Allen, 320
Boccaccio, Giovanni, 20, 68
Boileau, Nicolas, 215

Bollas, Christopher, 314–15, 316, 317
Borges, Jorge: *Homage to Walt Whitman: A Collection of Poems in Spanish, with English Translations*, 305–6
Boulter, Robert, 108
Bowles, William Lisle, 239, 240, 242, 246
Breval, John Durant: *The Confederates*, 202
Brower, Robert H., 41 (n. 10)
Browne, Thomas, 138
Browning, Robert
—"Artemis Prologuizes," 280
—"Camp and Cloister," 279
—"Cavalier Tunes," 274–77
—"Count Gismond," 276, 278–79
—*Dramatic Lyrics*, 273–88
—*Dramatic Romances and Lyrics*, 286 (n. 4)
—"In a Gondola," 280
—"Johannes Agricola in Meditation," 282–83
—"Madhouse Cells," 282
—"My Last Duchess," 276, 277–78, 279
—"Pied Piper of Hamelin," 274, 284–85
—"Porphyria's Lover," 282, 283
—"Queen Worship," 281–82
—*The Ring and the Book*, 288 (n. 14)
—*Sordello*, 276
—"Through the Metidja to Abd-El-Kadr.—1842," 284
—"Waring," 280–81
Buckingham, Duke of (John Sheffield): *Works*, 100
Bundtzen, Lynda K., 332 (n. 10), 333 (n. 16)
Burke, Edmund, 239
Burnet, Thomas, 233 (n. 36)
Byron, George Gordon, Lord, 11, 190, 251 (n. 1)

Byron, George Gordon, Lord (*continued*)
—*The Bride of Abydos,* 256
—*Childe Harold's Pilgrimage,* 255–56, 258, 264
—*Don Juan,* 13, 259–71
—*English Bards and Scotch Reviewers,* 254–55
—*Fugitive Pieces,* 254
—*The Giaour,* 256, 258–59
—*Hints from Horace,* 255
—*Hours of Idleness,* 254
—*Oriental Tales,* 258–59

Caesar, Augustus, 44, 47, 54, 63
Caesar, Sir Julius, 132
Callimachus: *Aetia,* 5; *Iambs,* 5, 15 (n. 8)
Cameron, Allen Barry, 160 (n. 31)
Castelnau, Gabriel de, Marquis, 267–68
Castlereagh, Robert, 262
Catullus, 5, 15 (n. 12)
Charles, Amy, 115 (n. 2)
Charles II (king of England), 97, 104–5, 107
Chaucer, Geoffrey, 205, 222; *Knight's Tale,* 31
Cicero, 108; *De Oratore,* 102; "Speech on Behalf of Archias the Poet," 202
Coiro, Ann Baynes, 116 (n. 8)
Cole, John, 200
Coleridge, Samuel Taylor, 238–40, 242, 245; "Sonnets Attempted in the Manner of Contemporary Writers," 239; "Sonnets on Eminent Characters," 239
Colie, Rosalie, 10, 11
Cooke, Thomas, 106
Cowper, William, 171
Crane, Hart: *The Bridge,* 6
Cristina, Maria (queen of Spain), 281–82
Cromwell, Oliver, 113–14
Crum, Margaret, 158 (n. 9)
Culler, Jonathan, 165
Curtis, Jared, 252 (n. 2)

Dante Alighieri, 67, 69, 83, 84, 88; *Divina commedia,* 69, 93 (n. 16); *La vita nuova,* 5–6, 15 (n. 13), 68, 69, 72–73, 89, 93 (n. 16), 93 (n. 18)
Darío, Rubén, 305
Davie, Donald, 296
Davies, Sir John, 137
Davison, Peter, 16 (n. 24)
Defoe, Daniel, 25; *Dictionary of All Religions,* 283
Delattre, Floris, 116 (n. 6)
Dennis, John, 197, 205, 215, 219; *Reflections Critical and Satyrical,* 197, 200–202
Dickinson, Emily, 13, 16 (n. 17)
Digby, Kenelm, 98
Donne, John, 73
—*The Anniversaries,* 129, 138, 139, 140
—*Divine Poems,* 130–35, 146
—*Epicedes,* 129–30
—*Epigrams,* 123
—"Epitaph on Himself," 130
—"Epithalamion Made at Lincoln's Inn," 121–22
—"The Feaver," 149–50
—*Holy Sonnets,* 120, 134–35, 162–63 (n. 50)
—"I am a little world made cunningly," 146–47
—"Image of her" ("The Dream"), 149
—"The Legacy," 149–50
—*Love Elegies,* 123–28
—"Metempsychosis," 128–29
—"O might those sighs," 147–48
—*Poems* (1633), 98
—*Poems* (1635), 120
—"Sapho to Philaenis," 163 (n. 51)
—"Song" ("Sweetest love, I do not go"), 149–50
—*Songs and Sonnets,* 88–90, 136
—"To C. B.," 143–44
—*Verse Letters,* 135–36
—"You that are she," 130
Drayton, Michael: *Idea,* 17 (n. 31)
Drummond, William, 99, 137–38
Dryden, John, 20, 24, 27, 30, 42 (n. 16), 156 (n. 1)
—*Absalom and Achitophel,* 20

—"Alexander's Feast," 20
—*Examen Poeticum*, 20
—*Fables*, 20–21, 23, 29, 31, 35
—*Miscellany Poems*, 20
—"A Monument to a Fair Maiden Lady," 20
—Preface to the Translation of Ovid's *Epistles*, 228
—*Sylvae: or, Second Part of Poetical Miscellanies*, 20–21
—*Works* (1701), 200
Du Bosc, Claude, 217
Du Guernier, Louis, 217, 218, 222
Duncan-Jones, Katherine, 93–94 (n. 31)
Dunster, Charles, 193 (n. 31)
Durling, Robert, 12, 15 (n. 11)

Eagleton, Terry, 174
Edelinck, Nicholas, 200
Eikon Basilike, 173
Eliot, T. S., 16 (n. 17)
Elizabeth I (queen of England), 102–3
Ellul, Jacques, 188
Evans, John, 170

Fairfax, Thomas, 116 (n. 14)
Fane, Mildmay, 116 (n. 12), 116 (n. 15); *Otia Sacra*, 97, 116 (n. 13)
Fanshawe, Richard (trans.): *Il Pastor Fido*, 97
Feldman, Irving, 308
Fenton, Elijah, 206, 208
Fichte, Johann Gottlieb, 270
Fish, Stanley, 7, 8, 11
Fitzgerald, James (earl of Desmond), 101, 102–3
Fletcher, Phineas: *Venus and Anchises*, 233 (n. 33)
Flynn, Dennis, 133
Forster, John, 273
Foucault, Michel, 42 (n. 17)
Fowler, Alastair, 162 (n. 42)
Foxon, David, 198, 199
Fraenkel, Eduard, 65 (n. 19)
Fraunce, Abraham, 66
Freud, Sigmund: *Civilization and Its Discontents*, 293–94
Frösch, Hermann H., 65 (n. 23)
Frye, Northrop, 176, 186, 190–91
Fujiwara Ariie, 32
Fujiwara Teika, 31, 32, 41 (n. 10)

Gall, Sally M., 16 (n. 17)
Gardner, Helen, 88, 126, 130, 131, 134–35, 138, 140, 147, 148, 158 (n. 9), 160 (n. 22)
Gascoigne, George, 91 (n. 4); *The Adventures of Master F.J.*, 16 (n. 13)
Gay, John, 206
Gifford, George, 93 (n. 31)
Gildon, Charles, 205, 219; *A New Rehearsal, Or Bays the Younger*, 197
Gleckner, Robert, 10–11
Googe, Barnabe, 136; *Eglogs, Epytaphes and Sonettes*, 119, 120
Gosse, Edmund, 134
Gotoba, 35
Graves, Robert, 309
Gribelin, Simon, 198, 215, 217, 219, 222, 231–32 (n. 9)
Grierson, H. J. C., 141, 149, 159 (n. 15)
Griffin, Dustin, 196
Griffin, W. Hall, 287 (n. 6)
Groupy, Joseph, 233 (n. 27)
Guild, William, 194 (n. 36)

Hagopian, John V., 287 (n. 10)
Halsband, Robert, 217, 219
Harcourt, Simon, 228
Harington, Sir John, 66–67
Harrington, James: *Aphorisms Political*, 188
Harris, John, 215
Harrold, William E., 286 (n. 2), 287 (n. 10)
Hawkins, Henry: *Partheneia Sacra*, 110, 118 (n. 36)
Heninger, S. K., 13, 15 (n. 13)
Herakleitos, 271
Herbert, George, 13, 21
—"The Altar," 19, 23, 34
—"The Church," 19, 20

Herbert, George (*continued*)
—"The Church Militant," 19
—"The Church Porch," 19, 23, 34
—"L'Envoy," 19
—"Love," 19
—"Love" (III), 23
—"The Sacrifice," 34
—"Super Liminare," 23, 34
—*The Temple*, 10, 11, 19, 20–21, 23, 25, 29, 30, 34, 35, 67, 95, 115 (n. 2)
Herford, C. H., 98
Herodas, 15 (n. 9)
Herrick, Robert
—*Hesperides*, 96, 97–98
—*Noble Numbers*, 97
—"To the King, Upon his welcome to Hampton-Court," 116 (n. 15)
Hieatt, A. Kent, 41 (n. 7)
Hill, Christopher, 167
Hobbes, Thomas, 27, 42 (n. 19)
Hollander, John, 174, 175
Holloway, Sister Marcella M., 287 (n. 10)
Homer, 28
Horace, 20, 27, 56, 205
—*Epodes*, 48
—*Odes*, 5, 48–49
—*Satires*, 48, 57–61, 62, 63
Hughes, John, 222
Hughes, Ted, 11, 309, 310–31 passim; *The Hawk in the Rain*, 315
Hulsbergh, Hendrik, 215
Hundred Stanzas by Three Poets at Minase, A, 37–39
Hunt, John, 259–60, 261, 266, 269
Hutchinson, F. E., 95

Iser, Wolfgang, 10, 16 (n. 18)

Jakobson, Roman, 71
Jakuren (priest), 31
James I (king of England), 102
James II (king of England), 107
Jeffrey, Francis, 238, 251 (n. 1)
Jervas, Charles, 199, 200
Johnson, Lee, 247
Johnson, Samuel, 195
Johnson, W. R., 162 (n. 42)

Jonson, Ben, 20, 111
—"A Celebration of Charis in Ten Lyrick Peeces," 100
—"An Epigram to K. Charles for 100. pounds he sent me in my sicknesse," 101, 104
—*Epigrams* (*Epigrammes*), 41, 41 (n. 7), 119, 137
—"An Epistle answering to one that asked to be Sealed of the Tribe of Ben," 105
—"Epistle Mendicant," 105
—"Eupheme," 100, 101
—*The Forrest*, 21, 41 (n. 7), 99, 120
—"Lord Bacons Birth-day," 101
—"The Mind of the Frontispice to a Booke," 101
—"Ode: To himselfe," 105
—*Timber, or Discoveries*, 99
—"To the immortall Memorie, and friendship of that noble paire, Sir Lucius Cary, and Sir H. Morison," 105–6
—*Under-wood*, 21, 98–106, 114, 117 (n. 22), 117 (n. 23)
Juvenal, 27

Kaplan, Justin, 289
Keats, John, 277
Kenner, Hugh, 321
Kilby, Clyde S., 288 (n. 14)
Kinzie, Mary, 332 (n. 5)
Kneller, Sir Godfrey, 200
Knight, G. Wilson, 185
Kokinshū, 18, 23
Konishi Jin'ichi, 43 (n. 26)
Kroll, Judith, 309

Laing, R. D.: *The Divided Self*, 309
Lawes, Henry, 115 (n. 4)
Legouis, Pierre, 109
Lintot, Bernard, 195, 196, 198, 199
Lloyd, Charles, 239
L'Ouverture, Toussaint, 248
Lovelace, Richard: *Lucasta*, 97, 108–9, 116 (nn. 14, 15)
Lowell, Robert, 16 (n. 17), 308; *Lizzie*

and Harriet, 297; *Notebook,* 297, 302
Lucan: *De Bello Civile,* 118 (n. 37)
Lucilius, 48, 57–59, 61
Lucretius, 20; *De Rerum Natura,* 20, 21, 27
Lukács, Georg, 292
Lyly, John: *Euphues,* 80

McCanles, Michael, 16 (n. 13)
McGann, Jerome J., 13
Mack, Maynard, 196–97, 208
Maecenas, 58, 59, 60
Malmesbury, Lord (James Howard Harris), 288 (n. 13)
Margoliouth, H. M., 98, 106–7, 111, 113, 115
Márquez, Gabriel Garcia: *A Hundred Years of Solitude,* 25
Marriott, John, 124
Marshall, William, 116 (n. 12)
Martin, L. C., 116 (n. 6)
Martz, Louis L., 19, 94 (n. 39), 95–96
Marvell, Andrew, 20
—*Account of the Growth of Popery and Arbitrary Government,* 107, 114
—"Ametas and Thestylis Making Hay-Ropes," 110
—"Bermudas," 110, 112
—"The Character of Holland," 113
—"Clorinda and Damon," 110
—Cromwell poems, 109, 113–14
—"A Dialogue between the Soul and Body," 110
—"A Dialogue between Thyrsis and Dorinda," 110, 118 (n. 40)
—"Epigrammata in Duos montes," 113
—"Eyes and Tears," 110
—"The First Anniversary of the Government under O.C.," 107
—"The Garden," 110
—"An Horatian Ode upon Cromwel's Return from Ireland," 107, 111
—*Last Instructions to a Painter,* 114
—"Letter to Dr. Ingelo . . . ," 114
—*Miscellaneous Poems,* 98, 106–15
—Mower poems, 20
—"Musicks Empire," 20
—"The Nymph complaining for the death of her Faun," 110
—"On a Drop of Dew," 110
—"On the Victory obtained by Blake . . .," 113
—"The Picture of little T. C. in a Prospect of Flowers," 111
—"A Poem upon the Death of O. C.," 107, 113
—*The Rehearsal Transpros'd,* 112
—"Tom May's Death," 110
—"Two Songs at the Marriage of the Lord Fauconberg and the Lady Mary Cromwell," 114
—"Upon Appleton House," 113
—"Upon the Hill and Grove at Bill-Borow," 113
Meleager: *The Garland,* 5
Merrill, James: *Ephraim-Mirabell-Scripts,* 301–2
Michelangelo: *Sonnets,* 241, 242–43
Milford, Nancy, 310
Milgate, W., 160 (n. 26), 162 (n. 48)
Miller, James E., Jr., 12
Milton, John, 11–12, 246–49
—*L'Allegro,* 167
—*Areopagitica,* 96
—*De Doctrina Christiana,* 181
—*An Epitaph on the Admirable Dramatic Poet W. Shakespeare,* 200
—*Justa Edovardo King Naufrago,* 167
—*Lycidas,* 167, 169
—*Maske (Comus),* 96, 115 (n. 4), 116 (n. 5), 169
—*Ode on the Morning of Christ's Nativity,* 96, 211
—*Paradise Lost,* 6, 25, 169, 170–72, 184, 190
—*Paradise Regained,* 164–91
—*Il Penseroso,* 167
—*The Poems of Mr. John Milton,* 12, 96–97, 167, 168, 190, 234
—*Samson Agonistes,* 42 (n. 13), 164–91
—*A Treatise of Civil Power,* 164, 174, 175
Minchin, Harry Christopher, 287 (n. 6)
Miner, Earl, 7, 13

Moseley, Humphrey, 115 (n. 4)
Moss, Howard, 289
Moxon, Edward, 274, 284
Murray, John, 259–60, 261, 262, 266, 269
Musa, Mark, 93 (n. 16)

Neruda, Pablo, 305
Newman, Barclay, 187
Newman, Charles, 330
Newman, Thomas, 66, 92 (n. 6)
Newton, Richard C., 120

Oldmixon, John, 219
Orr, Mrs. Sutherland, 288 (n. 17)
Otis, Brooks, 47–48, 52–53
Ovid, 5, 45–47, 55–56
—*Amores*, 61–63
—*Letters from the Black Sea*, 61, 63
—*Metamorphoses*, 31
—*Sad Poems (Tristia)*, 61

Paillet, Antoine, 215
Palmer, George Herbert: *English Works of George Herbert*, 95
Palmer, Mary ("Mary Marvell"), 106–7, 108
Parker, William Riley, 11–12, 164
Parnell, Thomas, 205, 215, 222
Patterson, Annabel, 7, 9, 167–68
Pembroke, Countess of, 66
Perloff, Marjorie, 11
Persius, 27
Petrarch, Francesco, 240, 242, 243, 249; *Canzoniere*, 5–6, 12, 15 (n. 11), 68, 72–75, 76, 83, 84, 88, 89, 93 (n. 20)
Pitt, William, 239
Plath, Sylvia
—"The Applicant," 320–21
—*Ariel*, 11, 308–33
—"The Arrival of the Bee Box," 328
—"Barren Woman," 317
—"The Bee Meeting," 328
—*The Bell Jar*, 309
—"Burning the Letters," 331
—*Collected Poems*, 309, 310–11, 315, 327
—*The Colossus*, 309
—"Contusion," 329
—"The Couriers," 318
—*Crossing the Water*, 309, 315, 332 (n. 15)
—"Cut," 323
—"Daddy," 319, 326–27, 329
—"Edge," 329–30
—"Elm," 323
—"Getting There," 326
—"The Hanging Man," 329
—"The Jailer," 321, 322–23, 326, 330
—*The Journals of Sylvia Plath*, 310
—"Lady Lazarus," 319, 321
—"Lesbos," 324
—"Mary's Song," 326
—"Morning Song," 313, 317, 318
—"The Munich Mannequins," 330
—"Nick and the Candlestick," 324–25
—"The Night Dances," 324
—"The Other," 324, 330
—"Paralytic," 329
—"Purdah," 313, 325–26, 330
—"The Rabbit Catcher," 315, 318–19
—"A Secret," 321–22
—"Sheep in Fog," 319–20
—"Stings," 328–29
—"The Swarm," 331 (n. 1)
—"Thalidomide," 320
—"Totem," 330
—*Winter Trees*, 309, 315, 332 (n. 15)
—"Wintering," 313, 317–20, 329
—"Words Heard, by Accident, Over the Phone," 315, 330
Plato: *Timaeus*, 69
Poe, Edgar Allan, 6, 290, 291, 305; "The Philosophy of Composition," 290; "The Poetic Principle," 290
Ponsonby, William, 66
Pope, Alexander, 11
—*Eloisa to Abelard*, 229–31
—*An Essay on Criticism*, 27, 213–15, 217
—*An Essay on Man*, 27
—*Iliad*, 195, 198, 199, 205, 208, 215, 224, 229, 233 (n. 34)
—*Messiah. A Sacred Ecologue, In Imitation*

of *Virgil's Pollio*, 205, 209–11
—*Pastorals*, 205, 208–11, 222, 233 (n. 34)
—*Poems on Several Occasions*, 195
—*The Rape of the Lock*, 205, 211, 217–24, 226, 229
—*Sapho to Phaon*, 224, 228–31
—*The Temple of Fame*, 205, 206, 226–28
—*The Wife of Bath Her Prologue, From Chaucer*, 222
—*Windsor-Forest*, 205, 211–13
—*The Works of Mr. Alexander Pope*, 195–233
Popple, William, 111
Poston, Lawrence, III, 286 (n. 2)
Pound, Ezra, 16 (n. 17), 296
Propertius, 56; *Elegies*, 49, 52–53, 54
Prynne, William: *Histriomastix*, 116 (n. 5)
Puttenham, George, 92 (n. 12)

Quintilian, 24–25

Racine, 186
Radzinowicz, Mary Ann, 189
Rajan, Balachandra, 164, 172
Raleigh, Sir Walter, 102, 103; *History of the World*, 101–2, 106
Rich, Nancy B., 286 (n. 2)
Richelieu, Armand Emmanuel du Plessis, Duc de, 267–68
Ringler, William A., 78
Ripa, Caesar: *Iconologia*, 219
Roberts, John R., 115 (n. 2)
Ronsard, Pierre de: *Bocage Royal*, 99–100
Rosenthal, M. L., 16 (n. 17), 309

Saigyō (priest), 31
Santirocco, Matthew, 15 (n. 8)
Scaliger, Julius Caesar, 99
Schopenhauer, Arthur, 270
Schulman, Grace: *Burn Down the Icons*, 141
Schwartz, Murray M., 314–15, 316, 317
Scott-Craig, T. S. K., 183

Serafino, 68
Shaftesbury, Earl of (Anthony Ashley Cooper), 107, 108; *Characteristicks*, 232 (n. 9)
Shakespeare, William, 90; *Sonnets*, 86–88
Shawcross, John, 13
Shelley, Percy Bysshe: *The Cenci*, 190; *Prometheus Unbound*, 190
Shih Ching, 18
Shinkokinshū, 22, 31–33, 35
Shohakū, 37
Sidney, Sir Philip, 66–69, 71, 72, 75–84, 88, 90
—*Arcadia*, 68, 79
—*Astrophel and Stella*, 66–68, 72, 76–84, 86, 88, 89, 92 (n. 6), 94 (n. 40), 120
—*The defence of poesie*, 72, 76, 79, 83, 84
Simpson, Percy, 98
Singleton, Charles S., 93 (n. 21)
Skutsch, Otto, 52
Sloman, Judith, 40 (n. 4)
Smith, A. J., 141
Smith, Barbara Herrnstein, 8
Smith, Charlotte, 240, 242
Sōchō, 38
Sōgi, 38
Soros, 5
Southey, Robert, 239, 240
Spender, Stephen, 309
Spenser, Edmund, 83, 88, 90, 208–9
—*Amoretti*, 83–86
—"Epithalamion," 122
—*Fowre Hymnes*, 80–81
—*The Shepheardes Calender*, 6
Statius, 99; *Silvae*, 21
Steiner, George, 308, 327, 331 (n. 3)
Stevens, Wallace, 302–3
Sturm-Maddox, Sarah, 15 (n. 13)
Swift, Jonathan, 25, 217–18

Tennyson, Alfred: *In Memoriam*, 35
Theocritus, 15 (n. 9), 20
Thibaudet, Albert, 1
Thomson, James: *The Seasons*, 6

Tibellus, 5, 48
Tilton, John W., 287 (n. 10)
Timko, Michael, 287 (n. 10)
Todd, Henry John, 193 (n. 31)
Tonson, Jacob, 20–21
Tottel's Miscellany (*Songes and Sonetes*), 66, 69, 119, 121, 136
Trapp, Joseph: *Praelectiones Poeticae*, 198, 205, 208, 219, 224
Trott, Sir John, 112–13
Tupper, F. S., 106, 108, 117 (n. 30)
Turbervile, George: *Epitaphes, Epigrams, Songs and Sonets*, 91 (n. 6)
Tuttle, R. Dale, 287 (n. 10)

Uroff, Margaret Dickie, 325

Vallet, Guillaume, 215
van der Gucht, Michael, 233 (n. 27)
Van Sickle, John, 5, 51
Vergil (Virgil), 55, 56, 205–6, 211, 232 (n. 22), 235
—*Aeneid*, 20, 26
—*Bucolics*, 56
—*Eclogues*, 47–48, 49–52, 54, 57
—*Fourth Eclogue*, 252 (n. 4)
Vertue, George, 200, 202

Waldron, F. G.: *Shakespearean Miscellany*, 124
Waller, Edmund, 115 (n. 4)
Walton, Izaak, 149; *The Life of George Herbert*, 160 (n. 28); *The Life of John Donne*, 132, 161 (n. 33)
Warkentin, Germaine, 67–68
Watson, George: *Of Dramatic Poesy and Other Critical Essays*, 24
Watson, Thomas: *The Hekatompathia or Passionate Centurie of Love*, 15 (n. 13)
Whitman, Walt, 11, 305–6
—"A Backward Glance O'er Travel'd Roads," 290, 291
—"Calamus," 293
—"Children of Adam," 293
—*Democratic Vistas*, 299
—*Leaves of Grass*, 12, 290, 291–93, 294, 296, 305
—"Song of Myself," 293
—"Starting from Paumanok," 305–6
Williams, Aubrey, 209
Williams, John (bishop of Lincoln), 104–5
Wood, Anthony à, 108
Woodhouse, A. S. P., 164
Wordsworth, William, 10, 260, 277
—"Alice Fell," 237
—"Beggars," 237
—"Elegaic Stanzas, Suggested by a Picture of PEELE CASTLE, in a Storm," 235, 237
—*The Excursion*, Preface to, 250
—"Intimations Ode," 235, 236, 238, 250–51
—"London, 1802," 247
—*Lyrical Ballads*, 9, 190, 234–37, 246
—"Miscellaneous Sonnets," 234, 241–46, 249–50
—"Ode to Duty," 237–38
—"The Orchard Pathway," 236, 243
—*Poems* (1815), 7
—"Poems Composed during a Tour, Chiefly on Foot," 237
—*Poems, in Two Volumes*, 234–51
—"Prefatory Sonnet" of *Poems* (1807), 240
—*The Prelude*, 246, 250
—"Resolution and Independence," 236–37
—"Sonnet on Seeing Miss Helen Maria Williams Weep at a Tale of Distress," 239
—"Sonnets Dedicated to Liberty," 234, 239, 241, 246–49

Yeats, William Butler, 11, 13, 17 (n. 32)

Notes on the Contributors

William S. Anderson is Professor of Latin and Comparative Literature at the University of California, Berkeley. He has published a book on the art of Vergil's *Aeneid*, a commentary on books 6–10 of Ovid's *Metamorphoses*—as well as the Teubner critical text of that poem—and *Essays on Roman Satire*, a collection of his own articles.

George Bornstein is Professor of English at the University of Michigan, Ann Arbor. Among his books on 19th and 20th century poetry are *Yeats and Shelley; Transformations of Romanticism in Yeats, Eliot, and Stevens;* and *Ezra Pound Among the Poets*. He has recently edited *W. B. Yeats: The Early Poetic Manuscripts, Volume 1* for the Cornell Yeats series.

Vincent Carretta is Associate Professor of English at the University of Maryland. He is the author of *"The Snarling Muse": Verbal and Visual Political Satire from Pope to Churchill* and has recently completed *George III and the Satirists from Hogarth to Byron*.

Stuart Curran is Professor of English at the University of Pennsylvania and Editor of *The Keats-Shelley Journal*.

Neil Fraistat is Associate Professor of English at the University of Maryland. He is the author of *The Poem and the Book: Interpreting Collections of Romantic Poetry*.

S. K. Heninger, Jr., is University Distinguished Professor of English at the University of North Carolina, Chapel Hill. He is the author of *Touches of Sweet Harmony: Pythagorean Cosmology and Renaissance Poetics* (1974) and *The Cosmological Glass* (1977).

Jerome J. McGann is The Doris and Henry Dreyfuss Professor of the Humanities at the California Institute of Technology.

James E. Miller, Jr., is the Helen A. Regenstein Professor of Literature at the University of Chicago. He is the author of books on Melville, Whitman, James, Fitzgerald, Eliot, and Salinger. His latest book is *The American Quest for a Supreme Fiction: Whitman's Legacy in the Personal Epic* (1979).

Earl Miner is Townsend Martin Class, 1917, Professor of English and Comparative Literature at Princeton University.

Annabel Patterson teaches at the University of Maryland. She is the author of *Hermogenes and the Renaissance* (1970), *Marvell and the Civic Crown* (1978), and *Censorship and Interpretation* (1984).

Marjorie Perloff's most recent books are *The Dance of the Intellect: Studies in the Poetry of the Pound Tradition* (1985), and *The Futurist Moment: Avant-Garde, Avant-Guerre, and the Language of Rupture* (1986). She is Florence R. Scott Professor of English and Comparative Literature at the University of Southern California.

John T. Shawcross, Professor of English at the University of Kentucky, is editor of *The Complete Poetry of John Donne* and an editor of the forthcoming variorum edition of Donne's poetry.

Joseph Anthony Wittreich, Jr. is Professor of English at the University of Maryland and the author of *Angel of Apocalypse* (1975), *Visionary Poetics* (1979), *Image of That Horror* (1984), and *Interpreting "Samson Agonistes"* (1985).